ENCYCLOPAEDIC DICTIONARY OF INTERNATIONAL BUSINESS MANAGEMENT

ENCYCLOPAEDIC DICTIONARY OF INTERNATIONAL BUSINESS MANAGEMENT

Vol. 2

by

A.S. SUDAN

ANMOL PUBLICATIONS PVT. LTD.
NEW DELHI-110 002 (INDIA)

ANMOL PUBLICATIONS PVT. LTD.
4374/4B, Ansari Road, Daryaganj
New Delhi-110 002
Phones: 23261597, 23278000, 23255577
Email: anmolpublications@vsnl.com

Encyclopaedic Dictionary of
International Business Management

First Edition 2003
ISBN 81-261-1508-4 (Set)

PRINTED IN INDIA

Published by J.L. Kumar for Anmol Publications Pvt. Ltd., New Delhi-110 002 and Printed at Mehra Offset Press, Delhi.

PREFACE

Conventionally, 'Business' is understood as a trade or profession; an industrial, commercial, or professional operation; purchase and sale of goods and services; a commercial or industrial establishment; commercial activity; volume or quantity of commercial activity; commercial policy or procedure etc. Business operations are mainly divided into—technical, commercial, financial, security, accounting and managerial activities. Till recently managerial skills had been most neglected aspect of business operations. The term 'managing' consists of various functions, main among which are—planning, organising, commanding, coordinating and controlling.

Amidst the various schools of management thought Business Management can rightly considered as an art, a science and a profession.

As is obvious from the name of the title, the present work contains judiciously selected and well explained terms covering the International Business Management in entirety. This encyclopaedic dictionary will prove a reliable asset to one and all in the field.

—A.S. Sudan

d

D

Fifth letter of a NASDAQ stock symbol specifying that it is a new issue, such as the result of a reverse split.

D/A

See: Documents Against Acceptance.

DA

See Development Assistance.

DACON

See Data on Consulting Firms.

Daily price limit

The level at which many commodity, futures, and options markets are allowed to rise or fall in a day. Exchanges usually impose a daily price limit on each contract.

Dairy Export Incentive Program

DEIP, one of four export subsidy programs operated by the Department of Agriculture, helps U.S. exporters meet prevailing world prices for targeted dairy products and destinations. USDA pays cash to U.S.

exporters as bonuses, allowing them to sell certain U.S. dairy products in targeted countries at prices below the exporter's costs of acquiring them. DEIP is used to help products produced by U.S. farmers meet competition from subsidizing countries.

Daisy chain

Manipulation of the market by traders to create the illusion of active volume to attract investors.

Data on Consulting Firms

DACON is a computerized roster of consulting firms interested in doing business on World Bank-financed projects. The Bank uses DACON registrations to select firms to be considered for short lists (that is, a select list of firms to be invited to submit proposals) as well as to review the qualifications of firms proposed by the borrower. Registration eligibility includes minimum size and experience requirements. Consulting firms are not required to register; registration does not constitute the Bank's endorsement of the firm's qualifications or the Bank's approval of the firm's appointment for any specific project. The use of the acronym DACON is not limited to the World Bank; for example, the Inter-American Development Bank also maintains data on consultants in its separately administered DACON.

Date Draft

A draft that matures in a specified number of days after the date it is issued, without regard to the date of acceptance. See Draft, Sight draft, and Time draft.

Date of issue

Used in the context of bonds to refer to the date on which a bond is issued and when interest accrues to the bondholder. Used in the context of stocks to refer to the date trading begins on a new stock issued to the public.

Date of payment

Date dividend checks are mailed.

Date of record

Date on which holders of record in a firm's stock ledger are designated as the recipients of either dividends or stock rights.

Dated date

The date one uses to calculate accrued interest on various debt instruments, specifically bonds.

Dates convention

Treating cash flows as being received on exact dates-date 0, date 1, and so forth-as opposed to the end-of-year convention.

Dating

Credit extension beyond normal terms of a credit supplier.

Dawn raid

A term of British origin used to describe the purchase of all available shares of a target company at the market's open by a raider. A dawn raid is a surprise technique that allows the raider to gain a substantial share of the target company before the target company knows what is happening

Day around order

A day order that supersedes (cancels and replaces) the previous order by altering its size or price limit.

Day of deposit to day of withdrawal account

A bank account that pays interest according to the number of days that the money is actually on deposit.

Day loan

A loan from a bank to a broker prior to the delivery of securities. Upon the delivery of the securities, a day loan becomes a regular broker call loan for which securities serve as collateral.

Day order

In the context of general equities, request from a customer to either buy or sell stock, that, if not canceled or executed the day it is placed, expires automatically. All orders are day orders unless otherwise specified. Traders often make calls before the opening to check for renewals.

Day trade

Also known as a "daylight trade." The purchase and sale or the short sale and cover of the same security in a margin account on the same day.

Day trading

Establishing and liquidating the same position or positions within one day's trading.

Days in receivables

Average collection period.

Days' sales in inventory ratio

The average number of days' worth of sales that is held in inventory.

Days' sales outstanding

Average collection period.

DCF

See: Discounted Cash Flows.

DDM

(1) The ISO 4217 currency code for East Germany Ostmark. (2) See: Discounted Dividend Model

DE

The two-character ISO 3166 country code for GERMANY.

Dead cat bounce

A small upmove in a bear market.

Deadweight Loss

The net loss in economic welfare that is caused by a tariff or other source of distortion, defined as the total losses to those who lose, minus the total gains to those who gain. Usually identified in a supply-and-demand diagram in terms of change in consumer and producer surplus together with government revenue. The net of these appears as one or two welfare triangles.

Deal flow

In investment banking, the rate at which new deals are referred to a brokerage firm.

Deal stock

Stock subject to merger or acquisition, either publicly announced or rumored.

Dealing desk (Trading desk)

Personnel at an international bank who trade spot and forward foreign exchange.

Dealer

An entity that stands ready and willing to buy a security for its own account (at its bid price) or sell from its own account (at its ask price). Individual or firm acting as a principal in a securities transaction. Principals are market makers in securities, and thus trade for their own account and risk. Antithesis of broker. See: Agency.

Dealer loan

Overnight, collateralized loan from a money market bank made to a dealer financing his position by borrowing.

Dealer market

Where trader's specializing in particular commodities buy and sell assets for their own accounts.

Dealer options

Over-the-counter options, such as those offered by government and mortgage-backed securities dealers.

Dealer's spread

See: markdown; underwriting spread.

Dear money

British term for tight money.

Death-backed bonds

Bonds backed by loans of a policyholder against a life insurance policy. The policyholder will repay the loans while alive or with the benefits from the insurance policy upon death.

Death play

A stock strategy that buys stock on the belief that a key executive will die, the company will be dissolved, and shares will command a higher price at their private market value.

Death Valley Curve

In venture capital, refers to the period before a new company starts generating revenues, when it is difficult for the company to raise money.

Debenture

1. A debt that is not backed by collateral, but only by the credit and good faith of the borrower.

2. A certificate issued by customs authorities entitling an exporter of imported goods to be paid back duties that have been paid when they were imported. Such a refund is called a drawback.

Debenture bond

An unsecured bond whose holder has the claim of a general creditor on all assets of the issuer not pledged specifically to secure other debt. Compare subordinated debenture bond and collateral trust bonds.

Debenture stock

A type of stock that makes fixed payments at scheduled intervals of time. Debenture stock differs from a debenture in that it has the status of equity, not debt, in liquidation.

Debit

Recorded as negative (-) in the balance of payments, any transaction that gives rise to a payment *out of* the country, such as an import, the purchase of an asset (including official reserves), or lending to foreigners. Opposite of credit.

Debit balance

The amount that is owed to a broker by a margin customer for loans the customer uses to buy securities.

Debit card

A card that resembles a credit card but which debits a transaction account (checking account) with the transfers occurring contemporaneously with the customer's purchases. A debit card may be machine reable, allowing for the activation of an automated teller machine or other automated payments equipment.

Debit spread

Applies to derivative products. Difference in the value of two options, when the value of the option bought exceeds the value of the one sold. One buys a "debit spread." Antithesis of a credit spread.

Debt

Money borrowed.

Debt bomb

A default on debt and obligations by a major financial institution that disrupts the stability of the economic system.

Debt capacity

Ability to borrow. The amount a firm can borrow up to the point where the firm value no longer increases.

Debt capital

Money raised by selling bonds, the principal and interest on which must be repaid.

Debt ceiling

See: Debt limit

Debt crisis

A situation in which a country, usually an LDC, finds itself unable to service its debts.

Debt default

When a debtor fails or refuses to pay a debt.

Debt displacement

The amount of borrowing that leasing displaces. Firms that do a lot of leasing are curtailed in their debt capacity.

Debt/equity ratio

Indicator of financial leverage. Compares assets provided by creditors to assets provided by shareholders. Determined by dividing long-term debt by common stockholder equity.

Debt/equity swap

An exchange of debt for equity, in which a lender is given a share of ownership to replace a loan. Used as a method of resolving debt crises.

Debt instrument

An asset requiring fixed dollar payments, such as a government or corporate bond.

Debt leverage

Amplification of the return earned on equity when an investment or firm is financed partially with borrowed money.

Debt limit

The maximum amount that a municipality can borrow.

Debt limitation

A bond covenant that restricts the firm's ability to incur additional indebtedness in some way.

Debt market

The market for trading debt instruments.

Debt outstanding subject to limitation

Obligations incurred by the Treasury subject to the statutory limit set by Congress. Until World War 1, a specific amount of debt was authorized for each separate security issue. Beginning with the Second Liberty Loan Act of 1917, the nature of the limitation was modified until, in 1941, it developed into an overall limit on the outstanding Federal debt. As of March 1999, the debt limit was $5,950,000 million; the limit may change from year to year.

The debt subject to limitation includes most of the Treasury's public debt except securities issued to the

Federal Financing Bank, upon which there is a limitation of $15 billion, and certain categories of older debt (totaling approximately $595 million as of February 1991).

Debt ratio

Total debt divided by total assets.

Debt relief

Reducing the principal and/or interest payments on Less developed country loans.

Debt rescheduling

Defaulted debt is renegotiated, giving the debtor a longer time to pay, a lower interest rate, or both.

Debt retirement

The complete repayment of debt. See: Sinking fund.

Debt securities

IOUs created through loan-type transactions-commercial paper, bank CDs, bills, bonds, and other instruments.

Debt service

Interest payment plus repayments of principal to creditors (retirement of debt).

Debt service coverage

The ratio of cash flow available to the borrower to the annual interest and principal payments on a loan or other debt.

Debt-service coverage ratio

Earnings before interest and income taxes, divided by interest expense plus the quantity of principal repayments divided by one minus the tax rate.

Debt service parity approach

Payment alternatives that provide the firm with the exact same schedule of after-tax debt payments (including both interest and principal).

Debt swap

A set of transactions in which a firm buys a country's dollar bank debt at a discount and swaps this debt with the central bank for local currency that it can use to acquire local equity. Also called a debt-equity swap.

Debtholder

See: Bondholder.

Debtor

Borrower of money.

Debtor in possession

A firm that continues to operate under the Chapter 11 bankruptcy process.

Debtor-in-possession financing

New debt obtained by a firm during the Chapter 11 bankruptcy process, Federal Bankruptcy Rule 4001 (c)(1). This financing is unique because it is secured, that is, it has priority over existing debt, equity and other claims.

DEC

See District Export Councils.

Decile rank

Performance over time, rated on a scale of 1-10. 1 indicates that a mutual fund's return is in the top 10% of funds being compared; while 3 means the return is in the top 30%.

Decimal trading

The quotation and trading of stock or bond prices in decimals, as opposed to the quotation of in fractions.

Decimalization

The quotation and trading of stock or bond prices in decimals, as opposed to fractions such as eighths.

Decision Break-Point Analysis

A type of sensitivity analysis that indicates the value at which a key variable will result in a negative NPV for an investment project.

Decision tree

Schematic way of representing alternative sequential decisions and the possible outcomes from these decisions.

Declaration date

The date on which a firm's directors meet and announce the date and amount of the next dividend.

Declare

The Board of Directors motion to authorize dividend payments.

Declaration by Foreign Shipper

The U.S. Customs Service defines this term as a statement by the shipper in the foreign country attesting to certain facts. For example, articles shipped from the United States to an insular possession and then returned must be accompanied by a declaration by the shipper in the insular possession, indicating that, to the best of his or her knowledge, the articles were exported directly from the United States to the insular possession and remained there until the moment of their return to the United States.

Decreasing Returns to Scale

A property of a production function such that changing all inputs by the same proportion changes output less than in proportion. Example: a function homogeneous of degree less than one. Also called simply *decreasing returns*. Not to be confused with diminishing returns, which refers to increasing some inputs while holding other inputs fixed.

DCS

See Defense Conversion Subcommittee.

Dedicated capital

Total par value (number of shares issued, multiplied by the par value of each share). Also called dedicated value.

Dedicating a portfolio

Related: Cash flow matching.

Dedication strategy

Refers to multiperiod cash-flow matching.

Deductible contribution

Amount paid into an IRA, an employer-sponsored retirement plan, or other type of retirement plan for a particular tax year that is a deduction from income for tax purposes.

Deduction

An expense that is allowable as a reduction of gross taxable income by the IRS e.g., charity donations.

Deductive reasoning

Using known fact to draw a conclusion about a specific situation.

Deed of Assignment

A banking arrangement between the beneficiary of a letter of credit and a third party - usually the supplier of the goods - who requires an assurance of payment. The beneficiary of the credit is the assignor part of the proceeds of the credit are irrevocably assigned to the assignee.

Deed of Protest

Document evidencing that a protest has been carried out. In a collection, a bank may be asked to do this if a bill of exchange is not paid, accepted or honored at maturity.

Deed of trust

See: Indenture.

Deep-discount bond

A bond issued with a very low coupon or no coupon that sell at a price far below par value. A bond that has no coupon is called a zero-coupon bond.

Deep in/out of the money

A call option with an exercise price substantially below the underlying stock's market price (deep in the money) or substantially above the market price (deep out of the money). Also put option with an exercise price substantially above the underlying stock's market price (deep in the money) or substantially below the underlying stock's market price (deep out of the money). Often substantially below is defined as more than one strike price below (for calls)/above (for puts) the current value of the underlying security.

Deep Integration

Refers to economic integration that goes well beyond removal of formal barriers to trade and includes various ways of reducing the international burden of differing national regulations, such as mutual recognition and harmonization. Contrasts with shallow integration.

De facto

Existing in actual fact although not by cfficial recognition.

Default

Failure to repay a loan. International loans by governments and private agents lack mechanisms to deal with default, comparable to the legal mechanisms that exist within countries.

Default premium

A differential in promised yield that compensates the investor for the risk inherent in purchasing a corporate bond that entails some risk of default.

Default risk

The risk that an issuer of a bond may be unable to make timely principal and interest payments. Also referred to as credit risk (as gauged by commercial rating companies).

Defeasance

The setting aside by a borrower of cash or bonds sufficient to service the borrower's debt. Both the borrower's debt and the offsetting cash or bonds are removed from the balance sheet. In securities trading, where a clearing house becomes counterparty to each side of a trade, after the trade has been agreed. This is necessary to facilitate netting, and reduce counterparty risk exposure. The term has become popular recently, because of the the growth of central counterparty clearing services in European cash equities markets.

Defense Conversion

"Defense conversion," as applicable to conversion of U.S. defense activity, is the transfer of defense production capabilities to non-defense production, either non-defense industrial products (e.g., pumps and valves) or consumer goods. The Russians, according to their Defense Conversion Law, have a broader definition, which includes the possibility of a plant maintaining its defense production while expanding its non-defense production for other purposes, including the generation of hard-currency exports.

Defense Conversion Subcommittee

The DCS promotes trade between U.S. industry and the Russian defense sector by identifying investment opportunities, supporting changes in U.S. government export control and other policies which limit opportunities for U.S. industry to participate in Russian defense conversion activities, and identifying prospective business contacts for U.S. industry. Subcommittee membership includes the Departments of Commerce, Defense, Energy, Labor, and State, the Agency for International Development, the Export-Import Bank, and the Overseas Private Investment Corporation. DCS is a subcommittee of the Intergovernmental U.S.-Russia Business Development Committee which was established in June 1992.

Defense Memoranda of Understanding

Defense MOUs are defense cooperation agreements. The MOUs are signed by DOD with allied nations and are related to research, development, or production of defense equipment or reciprocal procurement of defense items. See also: Coproduction.

Defense Priorities and Allocation System

The goals of the DPAS are to: (a) assure the timely availability of industrial resources to meet current national defense requirements and (b) provide a framework for rapid industrial expansion in case of a national emergency. The authority for DPAS, which is administered by the Commerce Department's Bureau of Export Administration, extends from Title I of the Defense Production Act of 1950, as amended (DPA). While the DPAS is designed to be largely self-executing, Special Priorities Assistance (SPA) may be provided, including:

(a) timely delivery of items needed to fill priority rated defense contracts,
(b) granting priority rating authority, and
(c) resolving production and delivery conflicts between rated defense contracts.

See also: Defense Production Act.

Defense Production Act

Under authority of the Defense Production Act (DPA) of 1950 and related executive Order 12656, the Commerce Department is charged with identifying critical defense-related industries, assessing their capability to meet peacetime and national security needs, identifying current and potential production constraints, and proposing remedial actions as appropriate. Title I of the DPA requires that:

(a) contracts or orders relating to certain approved defense and energy programs be accepted and performed on a preferential basis over all other contracts and orders and
(b) materials, facilities, and services be allocated in such a manner as to promote approved programs.

See also: Defense Priorities and Allocation System.

Defense Technology Security Administration

DTSA is the DOD organization that reviews applications for the export of items that are subject to the dual-use license controls of the Commerce Department and the munitions controls of the Department of State. DTSA has about 130-to-140 staff, is located in the Office of the Secretary, and administers DOD technology security policy so that the U.S. is not technologically surprised on the battlefield. DTSA reviews applications involving dual-use items for reasons of national security, proliferation cases and munitions controls. See also: Foreign Disclosure and Technical Information System.

Defense Trade Advisory Group

In March 1992, the Department of State established the Defense Trade Advisory Group to provide consultation and coordination with U.S. defense exporters. DTAG members are drawn from the U.S. defense industry, associations, academia, and foundations, and include technical and military experts, and the State Department and observers from other government agencies. Members of the Committee are appointed by the Assistant Secretary of State for Politico-Military Affairs. DTAG has three main working groups: - Policy Working Group (PWG): which provides advice on broad issues of defense trade, technology transfer and commercial arms sales in an effort to aid State in regulating commercial munitions exports. - Regulatory Working Group (RWG): which provides advice on possible changes and improvements to regulations and procedures related to defense exports of munitions articles, technical data and software related to defense articles. - Technical Working Group (TWG): which provides on technical issues related to the U.S. Munitions List.

Defense Trade Controls

DTC (formerly: the Office of Munitions Control, OMC) at State administers licenses for the export of defense articles and services including arms, ammunition, and implements of war. These items are listed in the International Traffic in Arms Regulations (ITAR) and the U.S. Munitions List. DTC is involved in the commodity jurisdiction (CJ) process. The CJ process is used to determine whether a particular item should be transferred to another control list (primarily, whether an item may be subject to the ITAR or considered either dual-use and subject to the Commodity Control List). See: International Traffic in Arms Regulations.

Defense Trade Regulations

The Defense Trade Regulations (formerly known as the International Traffic in Arms Regulations, ITAR) are administered by the State Department to control the export of weapons and munitions.

Defense Trade Working Group

The Defense Trade Working Group (DTWG), consisting of officials from Commerce, Defense, State and USTR, was established in FY 1990 to coordinate agency policies and resources in areas concerned with defense expenditures. The group works with industry to identify ways to target industry needs and increase the success of industry export efforts by minimizing government impediments, streamlining procedures, and improve the availability of market information. The DTWG includes three subgroups: - The Defense Exports Working Group, chaired by Commerce, which helps implement Administration defense export policy and enhances U.S. government support for U.S. defense exporters; - The European Defense Cooperation Group, chaired by State, which coordinates inter agency input to U.S.-NATO International Staff for the

NATO Council on National Armaments Directors (CNAD) study on defense trade; and - The Technology Transfer and Third Party Reexport Group, chaired by Defense, which works with industry to define a more proactive technology transfer regime that could be implemented within the limits of U.S. national security and industrial competitiveness interests.

Defensive securities

Low-risk stocks or bonds that will provide a predictable and safe return on an investor's money.

Deferred account

A type of account that delays taxes on that account until some later date.

Deferred annuities

Tax-advantaged life insurance products. Deferred annuities offer deferral of taxes with the option of withdrawing one's funds in the form of life annuity.

Deferred call

A provision that prohibits the company from calling the bond before a certain date. During this period the bond is said to be call protected.

Deferred charge

An expenditure treated as an asset that carries forward until it becomes pertinent to the business at hand, e.g., advance rent payment.

Deferred compensation

An amount that has been earned but is not actually paid until a later date, typically through a payment plan, pension, or stock option plan.

Deferred equity

A common term for convertible bonds, which recognizes their equity component and the expectation that the bond will ultimately be converted into shares of common stock.

Deferred futures

The most distant months of a futures contract.

Deferred interest bond

A bond that pays interest at a later date, usually in one lump sum, effectively reinvesting interest earned over the life of the bond. See: Zero coupon bond.

Deferred nominal life Annuity

A monthly fixed-dollar payment beginning at retirement age. It is nominal because the payment is fixed in a dollar amount at any particular time, up to and including retirement.

Deferred payment annuity

An annuity that stipulates payments be made to the annuitant at a later date, such as when the annuitant reaches a certain age.

Deferred Payment Credit

Type of letter of credit providing for payment some time after presentation of shipping documents by exporter.

Deferred taxes

A non-cash expense that provides a source of free cash flow. Amount allocated during the period to cover tax liabilities that have not yet been paid.

Deficiency letter

Notification from the SEC to a prospective issuer of securities that revisions or additions need to be made to the preliminary prospectus.

Deficit

In the balance of payments, or in any category of international transactions within it, the deficit is the sum of debits minus the sum of credits, or the negative of the surplus.

Deficit spending

When government spending overwhelms government revenue resulting in government borrowing.

Defined asset fund

A unit investment trust consisting of a fixed portfolio of securities, including blue chips, REITs, or high-yielding stocks on a major exchange such as the NYSE or FTSE.

Defined benefit plan

A pension plan obliging the sponsor to make specified dollar payments to qualifying employees. The pension obligations are effectively the debt obligation of the plan sponsor. Related: Defined contribution plan

Defined contribution plan

A pension plan whose sponsor is responsible only for making specified contributions into the plan on behalf of qualifying participants. Related: Defined benefit plan

Deflation

Decline in the prices of goods and services. Antithesis of inflation.

Deflator

A statistical factor used to convert current dollar purchasing power into inflation-adjusted purchasing power. Enabling the comparison of prices while accounting for inflation in two different time periods.

Delayed issuance pool

Refers to mortgage backed securities (MBS) that at the time of issuance were collateralized by seasoned loans originated prior to the MBS pool issue date.

Delayed opening

Postponement of the start of trading in a stock until correction of a gross imbalance in buy and sell orders. Such an imbalance is likely to follow on the heels of a significant event such as a takeover offer. See: Suspended trading.

Delayed settlement/delivery

In the context of general equities, transaction in which a contract is settled in excess of five full business days. Seller's option. See: Dividend play, settlement.

Delayering

Removing levels of middle management.

Delinquency

Failure to make a payment on a debt or obligation by the specified due date.

Delisting

Removal of a company's security from listing on an exchange because the firm has not abided by specific regulations.

Deliver

The sale of a futures or forward contract may require the seller to deliver the commodity.

Deliverable bills

The Treasury bills that fulfill a set of guidelines set forth by the exchange on which the bills are traded.

Deliverable instrument

The asset in a forward contract that will be delivered in the future at an agreed-upon price.

Delivered at Frontier (DAF)

Seller must supply the goods at his or her own risk and expense delivered to a named place (usually a border location) by a specified time. The buyer is responsible for the importation. This is normally is used with rail, truck, or multi-modal shipments.

Delivered Duty Paid (DDP)

While the term "Ex Works" signifies the seller's minimum obligation, the term "Delivered Duty Paid", when followed by words naming the buyer's premises, denotes the other extreme — the seller's maximum obligation. The term "Delivered Duty Paid" may be used irrespective of the mode of transport. If the parties wish that the seller should clear the goods for import but that some of the cost payable upon the import of the goods should be excluded — such as value added tax (VAT) and/or other similar taxes — this should be made clear by adding words to this effect (e.g., "exclusive of VAT and/or taxes").

Delivered Duty Unpaid (DDU)

Seller fulfills the contract obligations when the goods have arrived at a named place in the importing country. The seller bears all the costs and risk except for import duties and other customs clearance costs.

Delivered Ex Ship (DES)

Seller fulfills the contract obligations when the goods have been made available to the buyer on board a ship at the named port of destination. The seller must bear all costs and risks associated in bringing the goods to the named port of destination. The buyer is responsible for all costs necessary to unload the goods and clear them through customs. Since unloading costs are included the ocean freight charged by most ship lines. The DES is most often used for charter shipments.

Delivered Ex Quay (DEQ)

seller fulfills the contract obligations to deliver when the goods are made available to the buyer at the wharf of the destination port. A DEQ can further specify "Duty Paid" or "Duty Unpaid." If "Duty Paid" is specified, the seller is responsible for all risks and costs, including duty, to the wharf of the destination port. If "Duty Unpaid" is specified, the buyer is to clear the goods and pay duty. Since unloading costs are included in the ocean freight charged by most ship lines. This is most often used for charter shipments.

Delivery

The tender and receipt of an actual commodity or financial instrument in settlement of a futures contract.

Delivery date

Date by which a seller must fulfill the obligations of a forward or futures contract.

Delivery Instructions

Provides specific information to the inland carrier concerning the arrangement made by the forwarder to deliver the merchandise to the particular pier or steamship line. Not to be confused with Delivery Order which is used for import cargo.

Delivery notice

The written notice given by the seller of its intention to make delivery against an open, short futures position on a particular date. Related: Notice day.

Delivery options

The options available to the seller of an interest rate futures contract, including the quality option, the timing option, and the wild card option. Delivery options mean that the buyer is uncertain of which Treasury bond will be delivered or when it will be delivered.

Delivery points

Locations designated by futures exchanges at which the financial instrument or commodity covered by a futures contract may be delivered in fulfillment of such a contract.

Delivery price

The price fixed by the clearinghouse at which deliveries on futures are invoiced; also the price at which the futures contract is settled when deliveries are made.

Delivery Verification Certificate

The U.S. Customs Service defines a DVC as a form used to track imported merchandise from the custody of the importer to the custody of a manufacturer and is used to substantiate a manufacturing drawback claim. The DVC is also known as a Certificate of Delivery (Customs Form 331). An export license may be issued with a requirement for delivery verification by Customs in the receiving country. When delivery verification is required by a foreign government for goods imported into the U.S., the U.S. Customs Service will certify a delivery verification certificate (Form ITA-647). A U.S. export license may require submission of a similar form from an importing country.

Delivery versus payment

A transaction in which the buyer's payment for securities is due at the time of delivery (usually to a bank acting as agent for the buyer) upon receipt of the securities. The payment may be made by bank wire, check, or direct credit to an account.

Delphi technique

Collection of independent opinions without group discussion by the analysts providing the opinions; used for various sorts of evaluations (such as country risk assessment).

Delta

The ratio of the change in price of a call option to the change in price of the underlying stock. Also called the hedge ratio. Applies to derivative products. Measure of the relationship between an option price and the underlying futures contract or stock price. For a call option, a delta of 0.50 means a half-point rise in premium for every dollar that the stock goes up. As options near expiration, in-the-money call option contracts approach a delta of 1.0, while in the money put options approach a delta of -1. See: hedge ratio, neutral hedge.

Delta cross-hedge

A futures hedge that has both maturity and currency mismatches with an underlying exposure.

Delta hedge

A dynamic hedging strategy using options that calls for constant adjustment of the number of options used, as a function of the delta of the option.

Delta neutral

Describes value of a portfolio not affected by changes in the value of the asset on which the options are written.

Delta Spread

A ratio spread that is established as a neutral position by utilizing the deltas of the options involved. The neutral ratio is determined by dividing the delta of the purchased option by the delta of the written option. See also Ratio Spread and Delta.

DEM

The ISO 4217 currency code for Deutschemark.

Demand Curve

The graph of quantity demanded as a function of price, normally downward sloping, straight or curved, and drawn with quantity on the horizontal axis and price on the vertical axis. Demand curves for imports and for foreign exchange usually have the same qualitative properties as demand curves for goods, but for somewhat different reasons.

Demand Deposit

A bank deposit that can be withdrawn "on demand." The term usually refers only to checking accounts, even though depositors in many other kinds of accounts may be able to write checks and view their deposits as readily available.

Demand Draft

See Sight Draft.

Demand Elasticity

Normally the price elasticity of demand. References to other elasticities of demand, such as the income elasticity are normally explicit.

Demand line of credit

A bank line of credit that enables a customer to borrow on a daily or on-demand basis.

Demand loan

A loan which can be called by the lender at any time and carries no set maturity date.

Demand master notes

Short-term securities that are repayable immediately upon the holder's demand.

Demand Price

The price at which a given quantity is demanded; the demand curve viewed from the perspective of price as a function of quantity.

Demand-pull inflation

A theory of inflation or price increases resulting from so-called excess demand. Related: Cost-push inflation.

Demand shock

An event that affects the demand for goods and services in an economy.

Demarche

Official discussion with another government carried out on instructions.

Demurrage

Excess time taken for loading or unloading a vessel, thus causing delay of scheduled departure. Demurrage refers only to situations in which the charter or shipper, rather than the vessel's operator, is at fault.

Denomination

Corresponds to the face value of currency units, coins, and securities.

Dependent

Acceptance of a capital budgeting project contingent on the acceptance of another project.

Dependent variable

Term used in regression analysis to represent the element or condition that is dependent on values of one or more other variables.

Deposit of Estimated Duties

This refers to antidumping duties which must be deposited upon entry of merchandise which is the subject of an antidumping duty order for each manufacturer, producer or exporter equal to the amount by which the foreign market value exceeds the United States price of the merchandise.

Deposit insurance

See: FDIC: Federal Deposit Insurance Corporation.

Depositary

An agent appointed for a Tender or Exchange Offer who accepts certificates from shareholders, processes them and assures that the appropriate cash or new securities are properly remitted to the tendering party.

Depository institution

A financial institution that obtains its funds mainly through deposits from the public. This includes commercial banks, savings and loan associations, savings banks and credit unions. Although historically they have broadened their powers in recent years. For example, NOW accounts, credit union share drafts and other services similar to checking accounts may be offered by thrift institutions.

Depository Institutions Deregulation and Monetary Control Act

The 1980 federal legislation that ended the regulation of the banking industry.

Depository preferred

Device enabling an issuer to circumvent an arbitrary corporate limit on the number of preferred shares issuable. Applies mainly to convertible securities.

Depository receipt

See: ADR American Depository Receipt.

Depository transfer check (DTC)

Check made out directly by a local bank to a particular firm or person.

Depository Trust Company (DTC)

DTC is the world's largest central securities depository. It accepts deposits of over 2 million equity and debt securities issues (valued at $23 trillion) from over 65 countries for custody, executes book-entry deliveries (valued at over $116 trillion in 2000) records book-entry pledges of those securities, and processes related income distributions. DTC is a member of the Federal Reserve System and is owned by The Depository Trust and Clearing Corporation (DTCC), which is in turn owned primarily by most of the major banks, broker-dealers, and exchanges on Wall Street.

Depository Trust and Clearing Corporation (DTCC)

The Depository Trust and Clearing Corporation (DTCC), through its subsidiaries, provides post-trade clearance, settlement, custody and information services for equities, corporate and municipal debt, money market instruments, American depositary receipts, exchange-traded funds, unit investment trusts, mutual funds, insurance products and other securities The National Securities Clearing Corporation (NSCC) subsidiary, which acts as a central counterparty (CCP), provides trade guarantee, netting and risk management services for equity and debt ransactions from all U.S. stock exchanges and markets, valued at $105 trillion in 2000. The Depository Trust Company(DTC) subsidiary has custody of and provides asset servicing for 2 million securities issues of issuers from the U.S. and 65 other countries, valued at $23 trillion. DTC serves as a major clearinghouse for institutional post-trade settlement, and in 2000, processed book-entry deliveries valued at more than $116 trillion. DTCC's two subsidiary businesses have Standard and Poors' highest rating: AAA.

Depreciate

To allocate the purchase cost of an asset over its life.

Depreciated cost

In terms of economics: The measure of cost of capital consumption during production, e.g., machine and equipment wear. In terms of finance: The process of amortization of fixed assets (equipment) to spread the cost over the depreciable life of the assets.

Depreciation

A non-cash expense (also known as non-cash charge) that provides a source of free cash flow. Amount allocated during the period to amortize the cost of acquiring long-term assets over the useful life of the assets. To be clear, this is an accounting expense not a real expense that demands cash.

Depreciation tax shield

The value of the tax write-off on depreciation of plant and equipment.

Depressed market

Market in which supply overwhelms demand, leading to weak and lower prices.

Depressed price

In the context of stocks, stock whose market price is low in comparison to stocks in its sector.

Depression

Period when excess aggregate supply overwhelms aggregate demand, resulting in falling prices, unemployment problems, and economic contraction.

DEQ

Abbreviation for the Incoterm "Delivered Ex Quay."

Deregulation

The reduction of government's role in controlling markets, which lead to freer markets, and presumably a more efficient marketplace.

Derivative

A financial contract whose value is based on, or "derived" from, a traditional security (such as a stock or bond), an asset (such as a commodity), or a market index.

Derivative instruments

Contracts such as options and futures whose price is derived from the price of an underlying financial asset.

Derivative markets

Markets for derivative instruments.

Derivatives

Derivatives are leveraged instruments that are linked to either specific financial instruments or indicators (such as foreign currencies, government bonds, share price indices, or interest rates) or to particular commodities (such as gold, sugar, or coffee) that may be purchased or sold at a future date. Derivatives may also be linked to a future exchange, according to contractual arrangement, of one asset for another. The instrument, which is a contract, may be tradable and have a market value. Among derivative instruments are options (on currencies, interest rates, commodities, or indices), traded financial futures, warranties, and arrangements such as currency and interest rate swaps.

Derivative security

A financial security such as an option or future whose value is derived in part from the value and characteristics of another security, the underlying asset.

DES

Abbreviation for the Incoterm "Delivered Ex Ship."

Descending tops

A chart pattern which in which each successive peak in a security's price is lower than the preceding peak over a period of time. Antithesis of ascending tops.

Descriptor

A variable describing assets, used as an element of a risk index. For example, a volatility risk index, distinguishing high volatility assets from low volatility assets, could consist of several descriptors based on short term volatility, long term volatility, systematic and residual volatility, etc.

Designated order turnaround system (DOT)

Computerized order entry system that allows orders to buy or sell large baskets of stock to be transmitted immediately to the specialist on the exchange, where execution will occur quickly, depending on the basket size. Also used for odd-lot transactions to occur at the prices and quantities available. See: AOS.

Desk

The New York Federal Reserve Bank's trading desk (or securities department) where all transactions of the Federal Reserve System are executed in the money market or the government securities market.

Destabilizing Speculation

Speculation that increases the movements of the price in the market where the speculation occurs. Movement may be defined by amplitude, frequency, or some other measure.

Destination Control Statement

Exporters are required to place destination control statements on commercial invoices and bills of lading for most export sales. These statements alert foreign recipients of goods and documents that diversion contrary to U.S. law is prohibited. Destination control statements are discussed in the Code of Federal Regulations.

Detachable warrant

A warrant entitles the holder to buy a given number of shares of stock at a stipulated price. A detachable warrant is one that may be sold separately from the package it may have originally been issued with (usually a bond).

Determinism

Fully ordained in advance. A deterministic chaos system is one that gives random looking results, even though the results are generated from a system of equations.

Deterministic models

Liability-matching models that assume that the liability payments and the asset cash flows are known with certainty. Related: Stochastic models.

Detrend

To remove the general drift, tendency, or bent of a set of statistical data as related to time. Often accomplished by regressing a variable or a time index and perhaps time-squared and capturing the residuals.

Deutsche Börse

Gremany's major securities market, including the Frankfurt Stock Exchange.

Deutsche Börse AG (DBAG)

Deutsche Börse AG (DBAG) is the operating company for the German cash and derivatives markets. It has four subsidiaries: Deutsche Börse Clearing AG, Deutsche Börse Systems AG, Frankfurter Wertpapierbörse (FWB), and the derivatives market, EUREX Deutschland (formerly the Deutsche Terminbörse).

Deutsche Finanzierungsgesellschaft fur Beteilgungen in Entwicklungslndern GmbH

DEG (English: German Financing Company for Investments in Developing Countries) promotes direct private-sector investment in developing countries and provides advisory services in planning and implementing jointly financed and managed companies. DEG operations emphasize matching small and medium sized German companies with similar third world counterparts.

Deutsche Gesellschaft fur Technische Zusammenarbeit

The GTZ (English: German Agency for Technical Cooperation) plans, executes, and monitors technical cooperation projects and programs in conjunction with partner organizations in developing countries. The agency provides advisory services to German and other national organizations, selects and trains experts, and releases project funds.

Deutsche Terminbörse (DTB)

Formerly the German financial futures and options market. Merged with the Swiss Options and Financial Futures Exchange (SOFFEX) in 1998 to form EUREX, the European derivatives exchange.

Devaluation

1. Depreciation.
2. A fall in the value of a currency that has been pegged, either because of an announced reduction in the par value of the currency with the peg continuing, or because the pegged rate is abandoned and the floating rate declines.
3. A fall in the value of a currency in terms of gold or silver, meaningful only under some form of gold standard or silver standard.

Developed Countries (DCs)

Industrialized countries.

Developing Country

A country whose per capita income is low by world standards. Same as LDC. As usually used, it does not necessarily connote that the country's income is rising.

Development Assistance

DA refers to specific economic assistance provided by the Agency for International Development. DA includes "functional" accounts that emphasize long-term development objectives for Agriculture, Rural Development and Nutrition; Population Planning; Health; Child Survival Fund; AIDS Prevention and Control; Education and Human Resources Development; Private Sector; Energy and Environment, and Science and Technology Corporation, as well as the Development Fund for Africa, and other assistance — the Special Assistance Initiatives and Humanitarian and Technical Assistance for the former Soviet republics.

Development Assistance Committee

The DAC, which consists of most members of the Organization of Economic Cooperation and Development (OECD), coordinates member country aid policies and programs to Lesser Developed Countries.

Development Banks

Banks that aid developing countries in economic development. They may lend or invest money and encourage local ownership. They may be worldwide, regional, or national.

Diagonal spread

An options strategy requiring a long and a short position in the same class of option at different strike prices and different expiration dates. For example, two puts or two calls in the same stock. See: Calendar spread; vertical spread.

Dialing and smiling

See: Cold calling.

Dialing for dollars

A term used to describe the practice of cold calling, but which has negative implications as it is frequently applied to salespeople selling speculative or fraudulent investments.

Diamonds

Units of interest in the diamonds trust, a unit investment trust that serves as an index to the Dow Jones Industrial Average in that its holdings consist of the 30 component stocks of the Dow.

Diff

Short version of Euro rate differential, which is a Chicago Mercantile Exchange Futures contract that is founded on the interest rate spread between the U.S.

dollar and the British pound, the German mark, or the Japanese yen.

Difference check

The difference in interest payments that is paid to a swap counterparty to close out a deal.

Difference from S&P

A mutual fund's return minus the change in the Standard & Poor's 500 index for the same time period. A notation of -5.00 means the fund return is 5 percentage points less than the gain in the S&P, while 0.00 means that the fund and the S&P have the same return.

Differential

A small charge, typically 1/8 point, added to the purchase price and subtracted from the selling price by the dealer for odd-lot quantities.

Differential disclosure

The practice of reporting conflicting or markedly different information in official corporate statements including annual and quarterly reports and 10-Ks and 10-Qs.

Differential swap

Swap between two LIBOR rates of interest, e.g., yen LIBOR for dollar LIBOR Payments are in one currency.

Differentiated product

1. A firm's product that is not identical to products of other firms in the same industry. Contrasts with homogeneous product.
2. Sometimes applied to products produced by a country, even though there are many firms within the country whose products are the same, if buyers

distinguish products based on country of origin. This is called the Armington assumption.

Diffusion process

A conception of the way a stock's price changes that assumes that the price takes on all intermediate values.

Digits deleted

Designation on securities exchange tape meaning that because the tape has been delayed, some digits have been dropped (e.g., 26 1/2 becomes 6 1/2).

Dilution

Diminution in the proportion of income to which each share is entitled.

Dilution protection

Standard provision that changes the conversion ratio in the case of a stock dividend or extraordinary distribution to avoid dilution of a convertible bondholder's potential equity position. Adjustment usually requires a split or stock dividend in excess of 5% or issuance of stock below book value.

Dilutive effect

Result of a transaction that decreases earnings per common share (EPS).

Diminishing returns

The fall in the marginal product of a factor or factors that eventually occurs as input of that factor rises, holding the input of at least one other factor fixed, according to the Law of Diminishing Returns.

Dip

Slight drop in securities prices after a sustained uptrend. Analysts often advise investors to buy on dips, meaning to buy when a price is momentarily weak. See: Correction, break, crash.

Direct Claim

A financial claim issued by a deficit unit to acquire funds for investment in real assets.

Direct costs of financial distress

Costs such as fees or penalties incurred as a result of bankruptcy or liquidation proceedings.

Direct deposit

A method of payment which electronically credits your checking or savings account.

Direct deposit service

A service that electronically transfers all or part of any recurring payment—including dividends, paychecks, pensions, and Social Security payments—directly to a shareholder's account.

Direct estimate method

A method of cash budgeting based on detailed estimates of cash receipts and cash disbursements category by category.

Direct Exchange Rate

The home currency price of one unit of a foreign currency.

Direct exporting

The exporting of goods and services by the firm that produces them.

Direct Export Councils

Groups of volunteer businesspeople in every state that are appointed by the U.S. Department of Commerce to assist exporters.

Direct Factor Content

A measure of factor content that includes only the factors used in the last stage of production, ignoring factors used in producing intermediate inputs. Contrasts with direct-plus-indirect factor content.

Direct Financing Lease(Direct Lease)

A non-leveraged lease by a lessor (not a manufacturer or dealer) in which the lease meets any of the definitional criteria of a capital lease, plus certain additional criteria.

Direct investment

The purchase of a controlling interest in a company or at least enough interest to have enough influence to direct the course of the company.

Direct lease

Contract in which a lessor purchases new equipment from the manufacturer and leases it to the lessee.

Directly Unproductive Profit-Seeking Activities

Activities that have no direct productive purpose (neither increasing consumer utility nor contributing to production of a good or service that would increase utility) and are motivated by the desire to make profit, typically from market distortions created by government policies. Examples are rent seeking and revenue seeking. Term coined by Bhagwati (1982).

Direct overhead

A fraction of overhead costs devoted to the manufacturing sector of a firm to cover expenses such as rent and utilities.

Direct paper

Commercial paper sold directly by the issuer to investors.

Direct participation program

An investment program enabling investors to directly participate in the cash_flow and tax benefits of the partnership invested in by the investor, typically a form of passive investment.

Direct placement

Selling a new issue not by offering it for sale publicly, but by placing it with one of several institutional investors.

Direct-plus-indirect Factor Content

A measure of factor content that includes factors used in producing intermediate inputs, factors used in producing intermediate inputs *to* the intermediate inputs, and so forth. That is, it includes all primary factors that contributed however indirectly to production of the good. Contrasts with direct factor content.

Direct Purchase Plan

A plan that enables interested first-time individual investors to purchase a company's stock directly from the company or without the direct intervention of a broker. The administrator also ensures the safekeeping of the shares by registering them directly on the books of the company. No need for shareholders to hold on to physical certificates.

Direct quote

For foreign exchange, the number of US dollars needed to buy one unit of a foreign currency.

Direct Registration System

A system that allows shareholders to hold stock in book-entry form registered in their name on the books of the company. At any time, the shareholder may request a certificate which will be provided free of charge. Shareholders have the option to sell shares either through the company (or its transfer agent) or through a broker. The advantage to the shareholders is that they can directly participate in company or transfer agentsponsored plans that are usually only available to registered shareholders, while still maintaining the a to their brokers.

Direct rollover

Movement of tax-deferred retirement plan money from one qualified plan or custodian to another. No immediate tax liabilities or penalties are incurred, but there is an IRS reporting requirement.

Direct search market

Buyers and sellers seek each other directly and transact directly.

Direct stock-purchase programs

Investors purchase securities directly from the issuer.

Direct terms

The price of a unit of foreign currency in domestic currency terms, such as $.9850/Euro for a US resident. See: Indirect terms.

Director

See: Board of directors.

Director Exception

A proxy or ballot that withholds its votes from one or more, but not all, individuals on the slate of nominated directors.

Directors' Duties

In the context of corporate governance, Directors' Duties refers to stated responsibilities of the companys Board of Directors. These provisions allow directors to consider constituencies other than shareholders when considering a merger. These constituencies may include, for example, employees, host communities, or suppliers. This provision provides boards of directors with legal basis for rejecting a takeover that would have been beneficial to shareholders. A majority of states have Directors Duties Laws.

Directorship

Used in the context of general equities. Stock status whereby a trader may not maintain positions in the security, due to an investment bank employee serving as a director on the corporation's board of directors done to avoid conflicts of interest; signified by a flashing "D" on Quotron. Contrast to restricted.

Dirty Float

A currency that floats in value in terms of other currencies but is not free of government intervention. Governments intervene to "smooth" or "manage" fluctuations or to maintain desired exchange rates.

Dirty price

Bond price including accrued interest, i.e., the price paid by the bond buyer.

Dirty stock

A stock that fails to fulfill prerequisites to attain good delivery status.

Disability income insurance

An insurance policy that insures a worker in the event of an occupational mishap resulting in disability. Insurance benefits compensate the injured worker for lost pay.

Disbursement float

A decrease in book cash but no immediate change in bank cash, generated by checks written by the firm.

DISC

Domestic international sales corporation. Discrepancy - Letter of credit - When documents presented do not conform to the letter of credit it is referred to as a discrepancy.

Discharge of bankruptcy

The termination of bankruptcy proceedings, resulting in cancellation of the debtor's obligations.

Discharge of lien

An order terminating a lien on property.

Disclaimer of opinion

An auditor's statement that does not express any opinion regarding the company's financial condition.

Disclosure

A company's release of all information pertaining to the company's business activity, regardless of how that information may influence investors.

Disclosure Meeting

An informal meeting at which ITA discloses to parties to the proceeding the methodology used in determining the results of an antidumping investigation or administrative review. A disclosure meeting is generally held promptly after the preliminary or final determinations of an investigation or promptly after the preliminary or final results of a review.

Discontinued operations

Divisions of a business that have been sold or written off and that no longer are maintained by the business.

Discount

Convertible: Difference between gross parity and a given convertible price. Most often invoked when a redemption is expected before the next coupon payment, making it liable for accrued interest. Antithesis of premium. General: Information that has already been taken into account and is built into a stock or market. Straight equity: Price lower than that of the last sale or inside market.

Discount Arbitrage

A riskless arbitrage in which a discount option is purchased and an opposite position is taken in the underlying security. The arbitrageur may either buy a call at a discount and simultaneously sell the underlying security (basic call arbitrage) or maybuy a put at a discount and simultaneously buy the underlying security (basic put arbitrage). See also Discount.

Discount bond

Debt sold for less than its principal value. If a discount bond pays no coupon, it is called a zero coupon bond.

Discount broker

A brokerage house featuring relatively low commission rates in comparison to a full-service broker.

Discount factor

Present value of $1 received at a stated future date.

Discounting of Bills

Where the payoo of a term bill requires payment immediately, a bank may discount the bill, i.e. make immediate payment, deducting an amount for interest over the term of the bill.

Discount Interest

Interest at a beginning of the loan. For example if you take out a one-year loan of $100 at a discount interest rate of 10%, you would receive $90 at the outset.

Discount payment

The difference between the face value and the price paid for a security.

Discount period

The period during which a customer can deduct the discount from the net amount of the bill when making payment.

Discount Rate

1. The rate, per year, at which future values are diminished to make them comparable to values in the present. Can be either subjective (reflecting personal time preference) or objective (a market interest rate).
2. The interest rate that the Fed charges commercial banks for very short-term loans of reserves. One of the tools of monetary policy.

Discount securities

Non-interest-bearing money market instruments that are issued at a discount and redeemed at maturity for full face value, e.g., US Treasury bills.

Discount window

Facility provided by the Fed enabling member banks to borrow reserves against collateral in the form of governments or other acceptable paper.

Discount yield

The yield or annual interest rate on a security sold to an investor at a discount. A bond that is sold at $4875 that matures to $5000 has a discount of $125. To calculate the discount yield: (discount divided by the face value of the security) multiplied by the (number of days in the year divided by the number of days to maturity).

Discounted basis

To sell below maturity value, so that the difference makes up all or part of the interest.

Discounted cash flow (DCF)

Future cash flows multiplied by discount factors to obtain present values.

Discounted dividend model (DDM)

A formula to estimate the intrinsic value of a firm by figuring the present value of all expected future dividends.

Discounted payback

The length of time needed to recoup the present value of an investment.

Discounted payback period rule

An investment decision rule in which cash flows are discounted at an interest rate and one determines how long it takes for the sum of the discounted cash flows to equal the initial investment.

Discounted in/by market

Unannounced information that is widely accepted or anticipated, and hence is already taken into account in the pricing of the security/ market (e.g., poor earnings).

Discounting

Calculating the present value of a future amount. Discounting is opposite to compounding.

Discounting the news

An adjustment of a stock's price as speculators bid the price up or down in anticipation of news about the company, whether good or bad.

Discrepancy

Any deviation from the conditions stipulated in a letter of credit. Discrepancies void letter of credit protection.

Discrete compounding

Compounding the time value of money for separate time intervals.

Discrete random variable

A random variable that can take only a certain specified set of individual possible values-for example, the positive integers 1, 2, 3, . . .

Discrete Time

The division of time into indivisible units. In economic models, these units represent periods, such as days, quarters, or years.

Discrete variable

Variable like 1, 2, 3. Bond ratings are examples of discrete classifications.

Discretion

Freedom given to the floor broker by an investor to use his judgment regarding the execution of an order. Discretion can be limited, as in the case of a limit order that gives the floor broker 1/8 or 1/4 point from the stated limit price to use his judgement in executing the order. Discretion can also be unlimited, as in the case of a market-not-held order. See also: Market Not Held Order.

Discretionary account

Accounts over which an individual or organization, other than the person in whose name the account is carried, exercises trading authority or control.

Discretionary cash flow

Cash flow that is available after the funding of all positive net present value (NPV) capital investment projects; it is available for paying cash dividends, re-purchasing common stock, retiring debt, and so on.

Discretionary income

The amount of income a consumer has available after purchasing essentials such as food and shelter.

Discretionary order

A type of buy order that gives the broker the freedom and power to make the execution at any time and price that is seen fit and reasonable, given the investor's goals.

Discretionary Proposition

A proposal on a proxy card that brokers can cast in favor of management if they have not yet heard from the beneficial holder ten days before the annual meeting. See: Ten-Day Rule

Discretionary reserves

Balance sheet accounts representing temporary accumulations of earnings from the current year or the recent past.

Discretionary trust

In the context of mutual funds, refers to a mutual fund or unit trust whose management decides on the best way to use the assets without restriction to a specific type of security. In the context of trusts, refers to a personal trust in which a trustee has the power of decision as to how much income or principal each beneficiary receives.

Discriminate analysis

A statistical process that links the probability of default to a specified set of financial ratios.

Disequilibrium

1. Inequality of supply and demand.
2. A untenable state of an economic system, from which it may be expected to change.

Dishonor

A refusal to pay.

Disinflation

A decrease in the rate of inflation.

Disintermediation

Withdrawal of funds from a financial institution in order to invest them directly.

Disinvestment

A reduction in capital investment reflected by a decrease in capital goods and a company's decision not to replace depleted capital goods.

Dismissal of Petition

A determination made by the Commerce Department's International Trade Administration that the petition does not properly allege the basis on which antidumping duties may be imposed, does not contain information deemed reasonably available to the petitioner supporting the allegations, or is not filed by an appropriate interested party. This dismissal causes termination of the proceeding.

Disparity

Inequality, usually income disparity.

Dispatch

An amount paid by a vessel's operator to a charterer if loading or unloading is completed in less time than stipulated in the charter party.

Disposable Income

Income minus taxes. More accurately, income minus direct taxes plus transfer payments; that is, the income available to be spent (including on imports) and saved.

Dispute Settlement

In the GATT, the adjudication of disputes among parties. In the WTO this is done by the dispute settlement mechanism.

Dispute Settlement Mechanism

The procedure by which the WTO settles disputes among members, primarily by means of a three-person panel that hears the case and issues a report, subject to review by the Appellate Body.

Distortion

Any departure from the ideal of perfect competition that interferes with economic agents maximizing social welfare when they maximize their own. Includes taxes and subsidies, tariffs and NTBs, externalities, incomplete information, and imperfect competition.

Distress sale

The selling of assets under adverse conditions, e.g., an investor may have to sell securities to cover a margin call.

Distressed securities

A security of a firm that has declared or is about to declare bankruptcy. In the context of hedge funds, a style of management that focuses on securities of companies that have declared bankruptcy and may be undergoing reorganization. Investment holdings can include bonds as well as stock in these firms.

Distributed

As new Treasury issues in dealers' hands are said to be distributed.

Distributing syndicate

A syndicate consisting of a number of brokerage firms or investment bankers that work together to sell and disperse a large lot of securities.

Distribution

Selling a large lot of a security in such a way that the security price is not heavily influenced.

Distribution area

An established price range in which a stock has been trading in for a significant amount of time. See: Accumulation area.

Distribution Cost Advantage

A source of competitive advantage that depends on the efficient delivery of a product or service to customers.

Distribution by coupon

Classification of a portfolio's securities according to coupon rate—the interest rate that an issuer promises to pay, expressed as an annual percentage of face value.

Distribution by credit quality

Classification of a portfolio's securities according to credit rating.

Distribution by issuer

Classification of a portfolio's holdings by type of issuer or type of instrument.

Distribution License

The DL is a Special License that allows the holder to make multiple exports of authorized commodities to foreign consignees who are approved in advance by the Bureau of Export Administration. The procedure also authorizes approved foreign consignees to reexport among themselves and to other approved countries. Applicants and consignees must establish Internal Control Programs to ensure the proper distribution of items under the DL. Each program must include comprehensive procedures for ensuring that the items exported will be used only for legitimate end-uses.

Distribution by maturity

An indicator of interest rate risk. In general, the higher the concentration of longer-maturity issues, the more a portfolio's share price will fluctuate in response to changes in interest rates.

Distribution period

The few days between the board of directors' declaration of a stock dividend (declaration date) and the date of record, or the date an individual must own shares to be entitled to a dividend.

Distribution plan

A mutual fund's plan to charge distribution costs such as advertising to the investors of the fund.

Distribution schedule

The frequency (monthly, quarterly, semiannually, or annually) of a mutual fund's scheduled distributions of dividends or capital gains.

Distribution stock

A small amount of a specific stock that forms part of a larger block of stock that is sold small amount by small amount so as not to disrupt the stock's market price.

Distributions

Payments from fund or corporate cash flow. May include dividends from earnings, capital gains from sale of portfolio holdings and return of capital. Fund distributions can be made by check or by investing in additional shares. Funds are required to distribute capital gains (if any) to shareholders at least once per year. Some corporations offer Dividend Reinvestment Plans (DRP).

Distributor

A foreign agent who sells for a supplier directly and maintains an inventory of the supplier's products.

District Export Councils

DECs serve as a voluntary auxiliary of US&FCS district offices to support export expansion activities. There are 51 DECs with 1500 members which help with workshops and also provide counseling to less experienced exporters.

DITM

See: Deep in the money.

Divergence

When two or more averages or indexes fail to show confirming trends.

Diversification

Dividing investment funds among a variety of securities with different risk, reward, and correlation statistics so as to minimize unsystematic risk.

Diversified investment company

An investment vehicle such as a mutual fund that invests in an assortment of securities.

Diversionary Dumping

This occurs when foreign producers sell to a third country market at less than fair value and the product is then further processed and shipped to another country.

Divestiture

A complete asset or investment disposal such as outright sale or liquidation.

Dividend

A portion of a company's profit paid to common and preferred shareholders. A stock selling for $20 a share with an annual dividend of $1 a share yields the investor 5%.

Dividend Discount Return

The rate of return which equates the present value of future expected dividends with the current market price of a security.

Dividend in arrears

Accumulated dividends on cumulative preferred stock that are deemed payable to the current holder.

Dividend capture

See: Dividend rollover plan.

Dividend clawback

An arrangement under which sponsors of a project agree to contribute as equity any prior dividends received from the project to the extent necessary to cover any cash deficiencies.

Dividend clientele

A group of shareholders who prefer that the firm follow a particular dividend policy. Such a preference may be based on comparable tax situations.

Dividend Disbursing Agent

A commercial bank or financial institution that disburses dividend to the securityholders. Usually a Transfer Agent is also the Dividend Disbursing Agent.

Dividend Discount Model (DDM)

A method to value the common stock of a company that is based on the present value of the expected future dividends.

Dividend distribution

See: Dividend income.

Dividend growth model

An approach that assumes dividends grow at a constant rate in perpetuity. The value of the stock equals next year's dividends divided by the difference between the required rate of return and the assumed constant growth rate in dividends.

Dividend income

Distribution of earnings to shareholders that may be in the form of cash, stock, or property. Mutual fund dividends are paid out of income, usually on a quarterly basis, from interest generated by a fund's investments. Also known as a dividend distribution.

Dividend limitation

A bond covenant that restricts in some way the firm's ability to pay cash dividends.

Dividend Order

A letter or form signed by the shareholder instructing a corporation to issue and forward dividend and/or interest payments to a specific person or entity other than the registered owner, such as a bank or broker.

Dividend payout ratio

Percentage of earnings paid out as dividends.

Dividend policy

Standards by which a firm determines the amount of money it will pay as dividends.

Dividend rate

The fixed or floating rate paid on preferred stock based on par value.

Dividend record

S&P publication stating companies' payment histories and corporate policies.

Dividend Reinvestment Plan (DRP)

Automatic reinvestment of shareholder dividends in more shares of a company's stock, often without commissions. Some plans provide for the purchase of additional shares at a discount to market price. Dividend reinvestment plans allow shareholders to accumulate stock over the long term using dollar cost averaging. The DRP is usually administered by the company without charges to the holder.

Dividend requirement

The annual earnings minimum required for payment of dividends on a preferred stock.

Dividend rights

A shareholder's rights to receive per-share dividends identical to those other shareholders receive.

Dividend rollover plan

An investment strategy that entails the purchase and selling of a stock right before its ex-dividend date in order to collect the dividends paid out by the stock and capture a trade profit.

Dividend trade roll/play

Used for listed equity securities. Method of buying and selling stocks around their ex-dividend dates so as to collect the dividend (which is 80% tax-exempt) offset by a fully-taxable capital loss. Predicated on the 80% current exemption that some corporations receive on dividend income.

Dividend yield (Funds)

Indicated yield represents return on a share of a mutual fund held over the past 12 months. Assumes fund was purchased a year ago. Reflects effect of sales charges (at current rates), but not redemption charges.

Dividend yield (Stocks)

Indicated yield represents annual dividends divided by current stock price.

Dividends payable

The declared dividend dollar amount that a company is obligated to pay.

Dividends per share

Dividend paid for the past 12 months divided by the number of common shares outstanding, as reported by a company. The number of shares often is determined by a weighted average of shares outstanding over the reporting term.

Dividends-received deduction

A corporate tax deduction on income allowed by company A that is in ownership of shares of company B and receives dividends on the shares of company B.

Divisor

Used in construction of stock indices. Suppose you have 10 stocks in an index, each worth $10 and the index is at 100. Now suppose you want to replace one of the stocks with another stock (reshuffling happens). Suppose that the new stock to be included is worth $20. So the total value of the index is 110 after the swapping. But we really shouldn't have an increase in value because nothing has happened - other than switching two constituents. So, what people do is to change the divisor. In this case, the divisor goes from 1 to 1.10. Notice that the value of the index, 110/1.1 is now exactly 100 - which is where we began from.

Direct foreign investment (DFI)

Investment in real assets (such as land, buildings, or plants) outside one's own country.

Direct Loan Program

Fixed-rate loans offered by the Ex-Im Bank directly to the foreign buyer to purchase US capital equipment and services.

Divisor

Denominator in price-weighted indexes to adjust for security changes such as stock splits.

DJ

The two-character ISO 3166 country code for DJIBOUTI.

DJF

The ISO 4217 currency code for Djibouti Franc.

DK

The two character ISO 3166 country code for DENMARK.

DKK

The ISO 4217 currency code for Danish Krone.

DL

See Distribution License.

DM

Deutsche (German) marks.

DM

The two-character ISO 3166 country code for DOMINICA.

DNR Order

See: Do Not Reduce Order.

DO

The two-character ISO 3166 country code for DOMINICAN REPUBLIC.

Dock Receipt

A dock receipt is used to transfer accountability when the export item is moved by the domestic carrier to the port of embarkation and left with the international carrier for export.

Dock Statement

A receipt issued by an ocean carrier to acknowledge the receipt of a shipment at the carrier's dock or warehouse facilities.

Doctrine of sovereign immunity

Principle that a nation may not be tried in another country without its consent.

Documentary Collection

Documents Against Payment Stipulate that the exporter ships goods to the importer without a letter of credit or another form of guaranteed payment. The importer must sign a sight draft before receiving the necessary documents to pick up the goods. Documents Against Acceptance (D/A) are instructions given by a shipper to a bank stating that the documents transferring title to goods should be delivered to the buyer only upon the signing of a time draft. In this manner an exporter extends credit to the importer and agrees to accept payment at a readily determined future date. See: Draft Bill of Exchange.

Documentary Credit

Sometimes used as another name for a letter of credit.

Documented discount notes

Commercial paper backed by normal bank lines of credit plus a letter of credit from a bank stating that it will pay off the paper at maturity if the borrower defaults. Such paper is also referred to as L.O.C. paper.

Documentary Draft

A draft to which documents are attached.

Document of Title

A transport document (usually a bill of lading) which (when appropriately made out) entitles the bearer to claim the goods from the carrier.

Documents Against Acceptance

Instructions given by a shipper to a bank indicating that documents transferring title to goods should be delivered to the buyer (or drawee) only upon the buyer's acceptance (signature on) of the attached draft.

Documents against payment

Shipping documents that are released to the buyer once the buyer has paid for the draft.

Dogs of the Dow

T 10 stocks of the 30 on the Dow Jones Industrial Average with the most depressed prices and consequently the highest yields. The investor buying these stocks speculates that they will bounce back over a one-year period.

Dollar bears

Traders who capitalize on a falling dollar by buying other foreign currencies directly.

Dollar bonds

Municipal revenue bonds for which quotes are given in dollar prices. Not to be confused with "US Dollar" bonds, a common term of reference in the Eurobond market.

Dollar cost averaging

See: Constant dollar plan.

Dollar drain

The impact of importing from foreign countries more than exporting to them. The money required to finance the import purchases removes dollars from the importing nation.

Dollar duration

The product of modified duration and the initial price.

Dollar price of a bond

Percentage of face value at which a bond is quoted.

Dollar return

The return realized on a portfolio for any evaluation period, including (1) the change in market value of tho portfolio and (2) any distributions made from the portfolio during that period.

Dollar roll

Similar to the reverse repurchase agreement-a simultaneous agreement to sell a security held in a portfolio with purchase of a similar security at a future date at an agreed-upon price.

Dollar safety margin

The dollar equivalent of the safety cushion for a portfolio in a contingent immunization strategy.

Dollar shortage

Results when a nation importing US goods cannot pay for them without the aid of the United States.

Dollar-weighted rate of return

Also called the internal rate of return; the interest rate that makes the present value of the cash flows from all the subperiods in an evaluation period plus the terminal market value of the portfolio equal to the initial market value of the portfolio.

Domestic

From or in one's own country. A domestic producer is one that produces inside the home country. A domestic price is the price inside the home country. Opposite of "foreign" or "world."

Domestic bonds

Bonds issued and traded within the internal market of a country and denominated in the currency of that country.

Domestication

Term used to indicate process in which a host government brings pressure to force a foreign owner to turn over partial ownership to the host country government or host country citizens.

Domestic Content Requirement

A requirement that goods sold in a country contain a certain minimum of domestic value added.

Domestic corporation

A corporation that is conducting business and is based in the country in which it is established, as opposed to a foreign corporation.

Domestic Credit

Credit extended by a country's central bank to domestic borrowers, including the government and commercial banks. In the United States, the largest component by far is the Fed's holdings of U.S. government bonds, but it also makes some short-term loans to banks to use as their reserves.

Domestic Exports

Exports of domestic merchandise include commodities which are grown, produced, or manufactured in the United States, and commodities of foreign origin which have been substantially changed in the United States, including U.S. Foreign Trade Zones, from the form in which they were imported, or which have been enhanced in value by further manufacture in the United States.

Domestic International Sales Corporation

A type of U.S. corporation, authorized in 1971, with income primarily from exports. Usually wholly owned U.S. subsidiaries, DISCs had special treatment in borrowing or taxation. A 1976 GATT case found against the U.S., which reached a compromise settlement with the EC in 1981. DISC was replaced in 1984 by foreign sales corporations.

Domestic market

A nation's internal market representing the mechanisms for issuing and trading securities of entities domiciled within that nation. Compare external market and foreign market.

Domestic series

Nonmarketable, interest and noninterest-bearing securities issued periodically by the Treasury to the Resolution Funding Corporation (RFC) for investment of funds authorized under section 21B of the Federal Home Loan Bank Act.

Domicile

The place where a draft or acceptance is made payable.

Donor

One who gives property or assets to someone else through the vehicle of a trust.

Do Not Increase (DNI)

A restriction that an investor places on a good til' canceled order to prevent an order increase in the case of a stock dividend or stock split.

Do Not Reduce Order (DNR Order)

Limit order to buy or to sell, or a stop limit order to sell that is not to be reduced by the amount of an ordinary cash dividend on the ex-dividend date. A "do not reduce order" applies only to ordinary cash dividends, and not stock dividends or rights.

Don't fight the tape

Phrase advising not to trade against the market trend. If stock prices are rising, do not sell.

Don't know (DK, DKed)

"Don't know the trade." A Street expression used whenever one party lacks knowledge of a trade or receives conflicting instructions from the other party.

DOP

The ISO 4217 currency code for Dominican Republic Peso.

DOT

See: Designated Order Turnaround System.

DOTM

See: Deep out of the money.

Double auction market

Systems by which listed securities are bought and sold through brokers on the securities exchanges, as distinguished from the OTC market, where trades are negotiated. Unlike the conventional auction with one auctioneer and many buyers, double auction markets consist of many sellers and many buyers.

Double auction system

A market consisting of many sellers and many buyers, as opposed to a conventional auction with one market maker and many buyers.

Double-barreled

Describes backing of the principal and interest of a smaller municipal revenue bond the large municipal entity.

Double bottom

A term used in technical analysis to refer to the drop of a stock's price, a rebound, and then a drop back to the same level as the original drop.

Double-declining-balance depreciation method (DDB)

An accounting methodology in which depreciation is accelerated to twice the rate of annual depreciation by the straight-line method.

Double-declining-balance depreciation

Method of accelerated depreciation.

Double dip

Used for listed equity securities. Dividend roll in which the "dividend capturer" already owns the stock cum dividend .

Double-dip lease

A cross-border lease in which the different rules of the lessor's and lessee's countries let both parties be treated as the owner of the leased equipment for tax purposes.

Double-entry bookkeeping

Accounting method that records each transaction as both a credit and a debit in different accounts.

Double-tax agreement

Agreement between two countries that taxes paid abroad can be offset against domestic taxes levied on foreign dividends.

Double taxation

Government taxation of the same money twice; specifically, taxation of earnings at the corporate level and dividends at the stockholder level.

Double top

A term used in technical analysis to refer to the rise of a stock's price, a drop, and then a rise back to the same level as the original rise.

Double up

A stock buying strategy that doubles the risk when the price moves in the opposite direction from the direction the investor hoped for. For example, an investor with confidence in ABC buys 1000 shares at $100 and another 1000 shares when the price declines to $90.

Double witching day

A trading day when of two related classes of options and futures expire, resulting in a variety of arbitrage strategies to close out positions.

Doubling option

A sinking fund provision that may allow repurchase of twice the required number of bonds at the sinking fund call price.

Dow dividend theory

See: Dogs of the Dow.

Dow Jones Industrial Average

The best known US index of stocks. A price-weighted average of 30 actively traded blue-chip stocks, primarily industrials including, stocks that trade on the New York Stock Exchange. The Dow, as it is called, is a barometer of how shares of the largest US companies are performing. There are hundreds of investment indexes around the world for stocks, bonds, currencies, and commodities.

Dow Theory

Used in the context of general equities. Technical theory that a major trend in the stock market must be confirmed by simultaneous movement of the Dow Jones Industrial Average and the Dow Jones Transportation Average to new highs or lows.

Down round

Refers to a round of venture capital financing that is raised at a lower firm valuation than the previous round.

Down-and-in option

Barrier option that comes into existence if asset price hits a predetermined price level.

Down-and-out option

Barrier option that expires if asset price hits a predetermined price level.

Downgrade

A negative change in ratings for a stock, or other rated security.

Downside Protection

Generally used in connection with covered call writing, this is the cushion against loss, in case of a price decline by the underlying security, that is afforded by the written call option. Alternatively, it may be expressed in terms of the distance the stock could fall before the total position becomes a loss (an amount equal to the option premium), or it can be expressed as percentage of the current stock price.

Downside risk

The risk that a security will decline in value including the implications of risk.

Downsizing

A company's reduction in the number of employees, number of bureaucratic levels, and overall size in an attempt to increase efficiency and profitability.

Downstream

The transfer of corporate activity from the larger parent to the smaller subsidiary.

Downstream Dumping

This occurs when foreign producers sell at below cost to a producer in its domestic market, and the product is then further processed and shipped to another country.

Downtick

Move down in a particular stock. On U.S. stock exchanges, you cannot sell a stock short on a downtick.

Downturn

The transition point between a rising, expanding economy to a falling, contracting one.

D/P

Abbreviation for Documents Against Payment.

DPAS

See Defense Priorities and Allocation System.

Draft

An unconventional order in writing-signed by a person, usually the exporter, and addressed to the importer-ordering the importer or the importer's agent to pay, on demand (sight draft) or at a fixed future date (time draft) the amount specified on the face of the draft.

Draft Bill of Exchange

A written, unconditional order for payment from one person (the drawer) to another (the drawee). It directs the drawee to pay a specified sum of money, in a given currency, at a specific date to the drawer. A Sight Draft calls for immediate payment (on sight) while a Time Draft calls for payments at a readily determined future date.

Draining reserves

Federal Reserve System's course of action to tighten the money supply by (1) raising a bank's minimum reserve requirements, (2) selling bonds in the open market, (3) raising the rate at which banks borrow from the Fed.

Draw a call

In the context of general equities, provoking a customer indication/inquiry/order by up or doing large amount of the volume in a stock.

Drawback

Drawback is a rebate by a government, in whole or in part, of customs duties assessed on imported merchandise that is subsequently exported. Drawback regulations and procedures vary among countries.

Drawback System

The Drawback System, a part of Customs' Automated Commercial System, provides the means for processing and tracking of drawback claims.

Drawee

The individual or firm on whom a draft is drawn and who owes the stated amount. Compare Drawer. Also see Draft.

Drawer

The individual or firm that issues or signs a draft and thus stands to receive payment of the stated amount from the drawee. Compare Drawee. Also see Draft.

Drayage

A trucking company freight charge for the pick up or delivery of an ocean container.

Dressing up a portfolio

Money managers' strategy to make transactions for the sole purpose of making a portfolio look good to the investor near the end of a reporting period. See: Window dressing

Drip feed

The continual investment of capital in a small and growing company as the company needs it, rather than investing a lump sum at the company's inception.

Drive-by VC

A type of venture capitalist. In the usual model, the venture capitalist (VC) is involved in management and monitoring of the startup. A drive-by VC invests in a portfolio of startups and is often quick to exit.

Drop

Refers to over-the-counter trading. Remove from OTC trading list; hence, no longer making a market in a security.

Drop, The

In a dollar roll transaction, the difference between the sale price of a mortgage-backed pass-through, and its repurchase price on a future date at a predetermined price.

Drop-dead day

The date on which a deadline is final, with no exceptions.

Drop-dead fee

A term of British origin referring to fee that must be paid if a deal falls through because of financing issues.

Drop lock

The fixing of the interest rate on a floating-rate note or preferred stock if it falls to a specified level.

DRP

See: Dividend Reinvestment Plan.

DSM

Dispute settlement mechanism.

DTC

See: Depository Transfer Check.

DTCC

See: Depository Trust and Clearing Corporation.

DTSA

See Defense Technology Security Administration.

DTWG

See Defense Trade Working Group.

Dual banking

Describes United States custom in which a bank is chartered by the state or federal government.

Dual-currency issues

Eurobonds that pay coupon interest in one currency but pay the principal in a different currency.

Dual listing

Listing of a security on more than one exchange, thus increasing the competition for bid and offer prices, the liquidity of the securities, and the length time the stock can be traded daily (if listed on both the east and west coasts.) See: Listed security.

Dual Pricing

The selling of identical products in different markets for different prices. This often reflects dumping practices.

Dual-purpose fund

A closed-end fund consisting of two classes of shares. The two classes are preferred shares, on which shareholders receive all the dividends and interest from the portfolio, and common shares, on which shareholders receive all the capital gains.

Dual syndicate equity offering

An international equity placement that splits the offering is split into two branches - domestic and foreign - and each grantee is handled by a separate lead manager.

Dual trading

The custom of a trader on the commodities market to deal for its own account and the investor's account at the same time.

Due bill

An instrument evidencing the obligation of a seller to deliver securities sold to the buyer. Occasionally used in the bill market.

Due date

Date on which a debt must be paid.

Due diligence

An internal audit of a target firm by an acquiring firm. Offers are often made contingent upon resolution of the due diligence process.

Due diligence meeting

Meeting legally required to be held by an underwriter to enable brokers to question a new issuer about an upcoming issue.

Due-on-sale clause

A mortgage contract clause stipulating that the borrower to pay off the full remaining principal on a mortgage if the mortgaged property is sold before the mortgage is paid off.

Dumping

The sale of a commodity in a foreign market at less than fair value. Dumping is generally recognized as unfair because the practice can disrupt markets and injure producers of competitive products in an importing country. Article VI of the GATT permits imposition of antidumping duties equal to the difference between the price sought in the importing country and the normal value of the product in the exporting country. With price-to-price dumping, the foreign producer can use its sales in the high-priced market (usually the home market) to subsidize its sales in the low-priced export market. The price difference is often due to protection in the high-priced market. Price-cost dumping indicates that the foreign supplier has a special advantage. Sustained sales below cost are normally possible only if the sales are somehow subsidized.

Dumping Margin

The amount by which the imported merchandise is sold in the United States below the home market or third country price or the constructed value (that is, at less than its "fair value"). For example, if the U.S. "purchase price" is $200 and the fair value is $220, the dumping margin is $20. This margin is expressed as a percentage of the United States price. In this example, the margin is 10 percent.

Duopoly

An oligopoly with two firms.

Duplicate Proxy

A second proxy received on an account. If the second proxy bears a more recent date than the first proxy, and has a different voting pattern, the second proxy will override the first.

Duplicative portfolio

Mainly applies to derivative products. Basket of stocks that imitates the price movement of another set of securities (e.g., S&P 500 index).

Dupont system of financial control

Highlights the fact that return on assets (ROA) can be expressed in terms of the profit margin and asset turnover.

Durable merchandise

Goods that have a relatively lengthy life (television sets, radios, etc.).

Duration drift

Change in duration attributable to the passage of time.

Duration

A common gauge of the price sensitivity of a fixed income asset or portfolio to a change in interest rates.

Duration matching strategy

An immunization technique that matches asset duration with the duration of the liabilities.

Dutch auction

Auction in which the lowest price necessary to sell the entire offering becomes the price at which all securities offered are sold. This technique has been used in Treasury auctions. Often used in risk arbitrage. Auction system in which the price of an item (stock) is gradually lowered until it meets a responsive bid (government T-bills) or offer (corporate repurchase) and is sold. In a corporate repurchase, a range of prices is set by the company within which shareholders are invited to tender their shares. The tender offer is open for a specific period of time (i.e., 20 days), and the quantity of stock to be purchased is stated as well, subject to proration if more shares are tendered than can be legally purchased under the stated terms (often an additional amount equal to 20% of outstanding shares can be purchased). The price paid is that at which the amount stated to be purchased can be sold. Compare to double auction system.

Dutch Auction Preferred Stock

A form of adjustable-rate preferred stock in which the dividend is ascertained in a Dutch Auction process by corporate bidders every seven weeks.

Dutch Disease

The adverse effect on a country's other industries that occurs when one industry substantially expands its exports, causing a real appreciation of the country's currency. Named after the effects of natural gas discoveries in the Netherlands, and most commonly applied to effects of exports in natural resource extractive industries on manufacturing.

Dutiable Imports

Imports on which a positive duty, or tariff, is levied. (The term seems like it ought to include imports on which the duty is zero but which a government is somehow free, or able, to levy a positive duty. That does *not* seem to be the way the term is used, however.)

Duty

A tax imposed on imports by the customs authority of a country. Duties are generally based on the value of the goods (ad valorem duties), some other factors such as weight or quantity (specific duties), or a combination of value and other factors (compound duties).

Duty-free

Without tariff, usually applied to imports on which normally a tariff would be charged, but that for some reason are exempt. Travelers, for example, may be permitted to import a certain amount duty-free.

Dwarfs

Fannie mae issued mortgage-backed securities pool that have an original maturity of 15 years.

Dynamic

For option strategies, describing analyses made during the course of changing security prices and during the passage of time. This is as opposed to an analysis made at expiration of the options used in the strategy. A dynamic break-even point is one that changes as time passes. A dynamic follow-up action is one that will change as either the security price changes or the option price changes or time passes.

Dynamical Noise

When the output of a dynamical system becomes corrupted with noise, and the noisy value is used as input during the next iteration. Also called System Noise. See: Observational Noise.

Dynamical Systems

A system of equations where the output of one equation is part of the input for another. A simple version of a dynamical system is linear simultaneous equations. Non-linear simultaneous equations are nonlinear dynamical systems.

Dynamic Asian Economies

The DAEs is a collective reference, currently comprising six Asian countries: Hong Kong, Korea, Malaysia, Singapore, Taiwan, and Thailand.

Dynamic asset allocation

An asset allocation strategy in which the asset mix is quantitatively shifted in response to -changing market conditions, as in a portfolio insurance strategy, for example.

Dynamic Gains from Trade

The hoped-for benefits from trade that accrue over time, in addition to the conventional static gains from trade of trade theory. Sources of these gains are not well understood or documented, although there exist a variety of possible theoretical reasons for them and some empirical evidence that countries have benefited more than the static gains alone would suggest.

Dynamic hedging

A strategy that involves rebalancing hedge positions as market conditions change; a strategy that seeks to insure the value of a portfolio using a synthetic put option.

DZ

The two-character ISO 3166 country code for ALGERIA.

DZD

The ISO 4217 currency code for Algerian Dinar.

e

E

Fifth letter of a Nasdaq stock symbol specifying that an issue has not met the reporting date for the company's SEC regulatory filing requirements.

Each way

A broker's commission from his or her involvement on both the purchase and the sale side of a security.

EAFE index

See: European Australian and Far East index.

Early distribution

See: Premature distribution.

Early Exercise (assignment)

The exercise or assignment of an option contract before its expiration date.

Early withdrawal penalty

Penalty paid by the holder of a fixed-term investment penalizing an investor who withdraws money before the agreed-upon maturity date.

Earn-out

Refers to an additional payment in a merger or acquisition that is not part of the original acquisition cost, which is based on the acquired company's future earnings relative to a level determined by the merger agreement.

Earned income

Compensation earned from employment, which includes wages, salary, tips, and compensation.

Earned income credit

A tax credit for taxpayers with children.

Earned surplus

See: Retained earnings.

Earnest money

Money given to a seller by a buyer to demonstrate the buyer's good faith. If the deal falls through, the deposit is usually forfeited.

Earning asset

An asset that generates income, e.g., income from rental property.

Earning power

Earnings before interest and taxes (EBIT) divided by total assets.

Earnings

Net income for the company during a period.

Earnings before interest after taxes (EBIAT)

A financial measure defined as revenues less cost of goods sold and selling, general, and administrative expenses. In other words, operating and nonoperating profit before the deduction of interest plus cash income taxes. Equivalent to EBIT minus cash taxes.

Earnings before interest and, taxes (EBIT)

A financial measure defined as revenues less cost of goods sold and selling, general, and administrative expenses. In other words, operating and nonoperating profit before the deduction of interest and income taxes.

Earnings before interest, taxes, and depreciation (EBITD)

A financial measure defined as revenues less cost of goods sold and selling, general, and administrative expenses. In other words, operating and nonoperating profit before the deduction of interest and income taxes. Depreciation expenses are not included in the costs.

Earnings before interest, taxes, depreciation, and amortization (EBITDA)

A financial measure defined as revenues less cost of goods sold and selling, general, and administrative expenses. In other words, operating and nonoperating profit before the deduction of interest and income taxes. Depreciation and amortization expenses are not included in the costs.

Earnings before taxes (EBT)

A financial measure defined as revenues less cost of goods sold and selling, general, and administrative expenses. In other words, operating and nonoperating profit before the deduction of income taxes.

Earnings momentum

An increase in the earnings per share growth rate from one reporting period to the next.

Earnings per share (EPS)

A company's profit divided by its number of outstanding shares. If a company earning $2 million in one year had 2 million shares of stock outstanding, its EPS would be $1 per share. In calculating EPS, the company often uses a weighted average of shares outstanding over the reporting term. The one-year (historical or trailing) EPS growth rate is calculated as the percentage change in earnings per share. The prospective EPS growth rate is calculated as the percentage change in this year's earnings and the consensus forecast earnings for next year.

Earnings-price ratio

See: Earnings yield.

Earnings response coefficient

A measure of relation of stock returns to earnings surprises around the time of corporate earnings announcements.

Earnings retention ratio

Plowback rate.

Earnings surprises

Positive or negative differences from the consensus forecast of earnings by institutions such as First Call or IBES Negative earnings surprises generally have a greater adverse effect on stock prices than a reciprocal positive earnings surprise.

Earnings yield

The ratio of earnings per share, after allowing for tax and interest payments on fixed interest debt, to the current share price. The inverse of the price-earnings ratio. It is the total twelve months, earnings divided by number of outstanding shares, divided by the recent price, multiplied by 100. The end result is shown in percentage terms. We often look at earnings yield because this avoids the problem of zero earnings in the denominator of the price-earning ratio.

EASD

See: European Association of Securities Dealers.

East African Development Bank

The EADB was created in 1967 to promote economic development among Kenya, Tanzania, and Uganda. Bank headquarters are in Kampala, Uganda. East Asian Economic Caucus The EAEC is a regional consultative forum proposed by Malaysia in late 1990 under the name of East Asian Economic Grouping. Participation would be limited to Asian nations.

Eastern Caribbean Central Bank

ECCB, established in October 1983, promotes economic development, monetary stability and credit and exchange among eight member nations. Bank headquarters is in Basseterre, St. Kitts.

Eastern Europe Business Information Center

EEBIC provides information on trade and investment opportunities, trade regulations and legislation, sources of financing, and government and industry contacts in the former Eastern Bloc. The Center is a Department of Commerce service which was initiated in January 1990. EEBIC is a Department of Commerce service which was established in January 1990. The Center maintains a 24-hour automated flashfax system which is reached on 202-482-5745; voice telephone is 202-482-2645.

Easy money

See: Tight money.

Eating stock

When an underwriter can't find buyers for a stock and therefore has to buy them for his own account.

EBIAT

See: Earnings Before Interest after Taxes.

EBIT

See: Earnings Before Interest and Taxes.

EBITD

See: Earnings Before Interest, Taxes and Depreciation.

EBITDA

See: Earnings Before Interest, Taxes, Depreciation, and Amortization.

EBT

See: Earnings Before Taxes.

EC

The two-character ISO 3166 country code for ECUADOR.

ECN

(1) Electronic Communications Network. Defined under Rule 11Ac1- 1(a)(8) under the U.S. Securities Exchange Act of 1933. (2) See: Emerging company marketplace.

Eclectic paradigm

A theory that posits three types of advantages benefiting a multinational corporation: ownership-specific, location-specific, and market internalization advantages.

Eco-Label

An eco-label is a voluntary mark awarded by the European Community (EC) to producers who can show that their product is significantly less harmful to the environment than similar products. The EC environment ministers agreed to the concept of an eco-label in March of 1992. The EC Commission and member states are drafting proposals for eco-labelling criteria with the intention of providing a clear commercial benefit for developing less polluting products and processes.

Econometrics

The quantitative science of predicting the economy.

Economic and Social Commission for Asia and the Pacific

See: United Nations Regional Commissions.

Economic and Social Commission for Western Asia

See: United Nations Regional Commissions.

Economic and Social Council

ECOSOC was created in 1945 to coordinate the economic and social work of the United Nations. The Council undertakes studies and makes recommendations on development, world trade, industrialization, natural resources, human rights, the status of women, population, narcotics, social welfare, science and technology, crime prevention, and other issues. The Council structure includes five regional commissions and six functional commissions. The functional commissions include:

— Commission on Human Rights
— Commission on Narcotic Drugs
— Commission for Social Development

— Commission on the Status of Women
— Population Commission
— Statistical Commission.

See also United Nations Regional Commissions.

Economic assumptions

General market environment a firm expects to operate in over the life of a financial plan.

Economic Bulletin Board

The EBB is a personal computer-based economic bulletin board operated by the U.S. Department of Commerce in Washington, D.C. The EBB is an online source for trade leads and statistical releases from the Bureau of Economic Analysis, the Census Bureau, the International Trade Administration, the Bureau of Labor Statistics, the Federal Reserve Board, Department of the Treasury, and other Federal agencies. The EBB may be reached 24 hours each day, 7 days each week at 202-482-3870 (300/1200/2400 bps) with PC communication switches set to no parity, 8 bit words and 1 stop bit. The 9600 bps service uses US Robotics Dual Standard HST/V.32 modems and can be reached by dialing 202-482-2584. Information may be obtained by calling 202-482-1986 (M-F, 8:30 am - 4:30 pm, EST)

Economic Community of Central African States

The Economic Community of Central African States was created by the Customs and Economic Union of Central Africa to promote regional economic cooperation, eliminate trade restrictions, and establish a Central African Common Market. Members include: Burundi, the Cameroon, Central African Republic, Chad, Congo, Equatorial Guinea, Gabon, Rwanda, Sao Tom, and Principe, and Zaire. The Community was established in 1983 (became operational in 1985); headquarters are in Libreville, Gabon.

Economic Community of the Great Lakes Countries

The Economic Community of the Great Lakes Countries (French: Communaut, Economique des Pays des Grands Lacs, CEPGL) was created in September 1976 to promote regional economic cooperation and integration. The Community is associated with the Great Lakes States Development Bank. Community members include: Burundi, Rwanda, and Zaire. Headquarters are in Gisengi, Rwanda. See: Development Bank of the Great Lakes States.

Economic Community of West African States

ECOWAS, established in May 1975 by the Treaty of Lagos (first operating in November 1976), is an economic association of 16 West African nations aimed at creating a full customs union (not yet achieved) as well as social and cultural fellowship. Members include: Benin, Burkina Faso, Cape Verde, Cote d'Ivoire, Gambia, Ghana, Guinea, Guinea-Bissau, Liberia, Mali, Mauritania, Niger, Nigeria, Senegal, Sierra Leone, and Togo. Community headquarters are in Abuja, Nigeria.

Economic Cooperation Organization

The ECO strengthens cooperation to improve socioeconomic conditions among the populations of members. The Organization was founded in 1964; headquarters are in Tehran, Iran. Members include: Afghanistan, Azerbaijan, Iran, Kazakhstan, Kyrgyzstan, Pakistan, Tajikistan, Turkmenistan, Turkey, and Uzbekistan.

Economic defeasance

See: In-substance defeasance.

Economic dependence

When the costs and/or revenues of one project depend on those of another.

Economic earnings

The real flow of cash that a firm could pay out forever in the absence of any change in the firm's productive capacity.

Economic exposure

The extent to which the value of a firm will change because of an exchange rate change.

Economic growth

An increase in the nation's capacity to produce goods and services. Usually refers to real GDP growth.

Economic growth rate

The annual percentage rate of change in the Gross National Product.

Economic income

Cash flow plus change in present value.

Economic indicators

The key statistics of the economy that reveal the direction the economy is heading in; for example, the unemployment rate and the inflation rate.

Economic Life

The time period over which an asset's NPV is maximized. Economic life can be less than absolute physical life for reasons of technological obsolescence, physical deterioration, or product life cycle.

Economic Officers

Embassy officials who analyze and report on macroeconomic trends and trade policies and their implications for U.S. policies and programs. Economic Officers represent U.S. interests and arrange and participate in economic and commercial negotiations. See: Commercial Officers Foreign Service.

Economic order quantity (EOQ)

The order quantity that minimizes total inventory costs.

Economic Policy Council

The EPC was established by Executive Order in 1985 to address major trade policy issues in a single forum as a means of reducing tensions between different groups, such as the Trade Policy Committee and the Senior Interagency Group. The Council was modified in the Omnibus Trade and Competitiveness Act of 1988. Membership includes Treasury (chair pro tem), State, Agriculture, Commerce, Labor, Transportation, the OMB, the U.S. Trade Representative, the Council of Economic Advisers, and the Assistant to the President for Science and Technology.

Economic rents

Profits in excess of the competitive level.

Economic Research Service

The Agriculture Department's ERS provides expertise, data, models and research information about the agricultural economies and policies of foreign countries, the agricultural trade and development relationships between foreign countries and the United States, and U.S. agricultural policies. Topics include: (a) agricultural trade and trade policies and their relationship to the economic, technical, and political factors affecting agricultural trade among countries; (b) economic and agricultural market structure, efficiency, and performance of foreign countries; (c) technical production systems of foreign countries; and (d) foreign governments' production, consumption, monetary, and trade policies.

Economic risk

In project financing, the risk that the project's output will not be salable at a price that will cover the project's operating and maintenance costs and its debt service requirements.

Economics

The study of the economy. See also: Macroeconomics; microeconomics; Keynesian economics, monetarism, and supply-side economics.

Economic Sanctions

Economic sanctions used for foreign policy purposes are economic penalties, such as prohibiting trade, stopping financial transactions, or barring economic and military assistance, used to achieve the goal of influencing the target nation. Sanctions can be imposed selectively, stopping only certain trade and financial transactions or aid programs, or comprehensively, halting all economic relations with the target nation. While sanctions can be imposed to serve multiple goals, the measures are more successful in achieving the less ambitious and often unarticulated goals of: (a) upholding international norms by punishing the target nation for unacceptable behavior and (b) deterring future objectionable actions. Sanctions are usually less successful in achieving the most prominently stated goal of making the target country comply with the sanctioning nation's stated wishes.

Economic shock

Events that impact the economy, come from outside it, and are unexpected and upredictable (e.g., Hurricane Andrew in 1991, the rise in oil prices by OPEC).

Economic Stabilization Fund

The ESF is a fund used to stabilize the U.S. dollar in times of foreign exchange volatility. The fund is administered jointly by the Treasury Department and the Federal Reserve Board, through its New York offices. Fund resources, appropriated by Congress, are usually provided fifty percent by Treasury and the Fed. Although not a major role, the fund has also been used in swap agreements with other countries to support their currencies. The fund was established by the Gold Reserve Act of 1934.

Economic Support Fund

ESF is an Agency for International Development appropriation account for funding economic assistance to countries based on considerations of economic and foreign policy interests of the United States, often in conjunction with military base rights or access rights agreements. Country allocations are determined by the State Department consistent with Congressional earmarks. To the extent possible, the use of ESF conforms to the basic policy directions underlying development assistance. Funds can be used for commodity imports, balance of payments support or as cash grants for budget support. See: Development Assistance.

Economic surplus

For any entity, the difference between the market value of all its assets and the market value of its liabilities.

Economic union

An agreement between two or more countries that allows the free movement of capital, labor, and all goods and services, and involves the harmonization and unification of social, fiscal, and monetary policies.

Economic value added (EVA)

A method of performance evaluation that adjusts accounting performance for investors' required return on investment. Suppose a division produces a 12%

return on capital invested. Given the risk of the division's business line would have. If investors would usually require 14% on capital invested, the division destroyed shareholder value by the EVA metric. This description is trade marketed by Stern-Stewart.

Economic Zones

Economic zones are designated regions in a country which operate under rules that provide special investment incentives, including duty free treatment for imports, for manufacturing plants which reexport their products. The term "economic zone" is currently used in the People's Republic of China and the former Soviet Union. See also Free Trade Zones.

Economies of scale

Achievement of lower average cost per unit through increased production.

Economies of scale

The decrease in the marginal cost of production as a firm's extent of operations expands.

Economies of scope

Scope economies exist whenever the same investment can support multiple profitable activities less expensively in combination than separately.

Economies of vertical integration

Produced by achieving lower operating costs by owning all components of production and sometimes sales outlets rather than contracting for companies in the outside marketplace.

Ecotourism

Ecotourism is a broad term which encompasses nature tourism, adventure tourism, ethnic tourism, responsible or wilderness-sensitive tourism, soft-path or small-scale tourism, low-impact tourism, responsible or wilderness tourism, and sustainable tourism. Scientific, educational, or academic tourism (such as biotourism, archetourism, and geotourism) are also forms of ecotourism. The definition of the term stresses the destinations and objectives of ecotourism from the traveler's point of view.

ECS

The ISO 4217 currency code for the Ecuadorian Sucre.

ECU

See: European Currency Unit.

EDGAR (Electronic Data Gathering, Analysis and Retrieval System)

The system through which companies electronically file reports and registration statements with the SEC. This requires converting the paper or word-processing document to be filed into a universal ASCII format, a process known as EDGAR-izing the document. The filings can then be accessed by the public through the SEC's Web site on the Internet.

Edge Act corporation

Corporation chartered by the Federal Reserve to engage in international banking. The Board of Governors acts on applications to establish Edge Act corporations and also examines the corporations and their subsidiaries. Named after Senator Walter Edge of New Jersey, who sponsored the original legislation to permit formation of such organizations. See also: agreement corporation.

Edge corporations

Specialized banking institutions, authorized and chartered by the Federal Reserve Board of Governors in the U.S., that are allowed to engage in transactions of a foreign or international character. They are not subject to restrictions on interstate banking. Foreign banks operating in the US are permitted to organize and own an edge corporation.

EDI

See: Electronic Data Interchange.

Education IRA

A type of individual retirement account enabling the contribution of up to $500 per year for each child up to the age of 18 by the parents in the family.

EE

The two-character ISO 3166 country code for ESTONIA.

EEK

The ISO 4217 currency code for the Estonian Kroon.

Effective annual interest rate

An annual measure of the time value of money that fully reflects the effects of compounding.

Effective annual yield

Annualized interest rate on a security computed using compound interest techniques.

Effective call price

The strike price in a market redemption provision plus the accrued interest to the redemption date.

Effective convexity

The convexity of a bond calculated using cash flows that change with yields.

Effective date

In an interest rate swap, the date the swap begins accruing interest.

Effective debt

The total debt owed by a firm to its creditors.

Effective duration

The duration calculated using the approximate duration formula for a bond with an embedded option, reflecting the expected change in the cash flow caused by the option. Measures the responsiveness of a bond's price-taking into account that expected cash flows will change as interest rates change due to the embedded option.

Effective Interest Rate

The annual rate at which an investment grows in value when interest is credited more often than once a year.

Effective margin (EM)

Used with SAT performance measures, the amount equal to the net earned spread, or margin of income, on assets in excess of financing costs for a given interest rate and prepayment rate scenario.

Effective net worth

Net worth plus subordinated debt.

Effective rate

A measure of the time value of money that fully reflects the effects of compounding.

Effective sale

A sale based on the most recent round-lot price, which determines the price of the next odd lot. The difference created between the last round-lot price and the odd-lot price is referred to as the odd-lot differential.

Effective spread

The gross underwriting spread adjusted for the impact that a common stock offering's announcement has on the firm's share price.

Effective tax rate

The net rate a taxpayer pays on income that includes all forms of taxes. It is calculated by dividing the total tax paid by taxable income.

Effective yield

Yield or return on a short-term investment after adjustment for the change in exchange rates over the period of concern.

Efficiency

The degree and speed with which a market accurately incorporates information into prices.

Efficient capital market

A market in which new information is very quickly reflected accurately in share prices.

Efficient diversification

The organizing principle of modern portfolio theory, which maintains that any risk-averse investor will search for the highest expected return for any particular level of portfolio risk.

Efficient frontier

The combinations of securities portfolios that maximize expected return for any level of expected risk, or that minimizes expected risk for any level of expected return. Pioneered by Harry Markowitz.

Efficient market

Economy in which prices correctly reflect all relevant information.

Efficient Market Hypothesis

States that all relevant information is fully and immediately reflected in a security's market price, thereby assuming that an investor will obtain an equi librium rate of return. In other words, an investor should not expect to earn an abnormal return (above the market return) through either technical analysis or fundamental analysis. Three forms of efficient market hypothesis exist: weak form (stock prices reflect all information on past prices), semistrong form (stock prices reflect all publicly available information), and strong form (stock prices reflect all relevant information including insider information).

Efficient markets theory (EMT)

Principle that all assets are correctly priced by the market, and that there are no bargains.

Efficient portfolio

A portfolio that provides the greatest expected return for a given level of risk (i.e., standard deviation), or, equivalently, the lowest risk for a given expected return.

Efficient set

Graph representing a set of portfolios that maximize expected return at each level of portfolio risk.

Efficient surface

In mean variance skewness analysis, the set of portfolios that result from investors' preference for higher means, lower variance and higher (positive) skewness. The efficient surface is analogous (in three dimensions, mean, variance and skewness) to the effficient frontier (in two dimensions, mean and variance).

EG

The two-character ISO 3166 country code for EGYPT.

EGP

The ISO 4217 currency code for the Egyptian Pound.

EH

The two-character ISO 3166 country code for WESTERN SAHARA.

Eighth[-ed]

Used in the context of general equities. A specialist or another broker is bidding higher or offering lower than we are, often topping or undercutting us by an eighth.

Either/or facility

An agreement permitting a bank customer to borrow either domestic dollars from the bank's head office or Eurodollars from one of its foreign branches.

Either-or order

Used in the context of general equities. See: Alternative order.

Either-way market

In the interbank Eurodollar deposit market, an either-way market is one in which the bid and offered rates are identical.

Elasticity of demand and supply

The degree of buyers' responsiveness to price changes. Elasticity is measured as the percent change in quantity divided by the percent change in price. A large value (greater than 1) of elasticity indicates sensitivity of demand to price, e.g., luxury goods. Goods with a small value of elasticity (less than 1) have a demand that is insensitive to price, e.g., food.

Elasticity of an option

Percentage change in the value of an option given a 1% change in the value of the option's underlying stock.

Elect

The conversion of a conditional order into a market order.

Electronic data interchange (EDI)

The direct exchange of information electronically, from one firm's computer to another firm's computer in a structured format.

Electronic Data Interchange for Administration, Commerce, and Transportation

EDIFACT is an international syntax used in the interchange of electronic data. Customs uses EDIFACT to interchange data with the importing trade community.

Electronic depository transfers

The transfer of funds between bank accounts through the Automated Clearing House (ACH) system.

Electronic funds transfer (EFT)

Transfer of funds electronically rather than by check or cash. The Federal Reserve's Fedwire and automated clearninghouse services are EFT systems.

Electronic Funds Transfer Systems

A variety of systems and technologies for transferring funds (money) electronically rather than by check. Includes Fedwire, automated clearringhouses (ACHs) and other automated systems.

Electronic License Application and Information Network

ELAIN is a BXA 24-hour on-line service which allows exporters to submit license applications electronically through value-added network vendors.

Electronic Queriable Carrier

A transporter of goods which allows tracking of goods in transit electronically using a waybill number such as United Parcel, Federal Express, etc.

Elephants

A term used to refer to large institutional investors.

Eleven bond index

An index based on the average yield of 11 municipal bonds that mature in 20 years and carry an average AA rating. The eleven bonds used to calculate the index are also found in the 20 bond index, which serves as a benchmark in tracking municipal bond yields.

Eligible bankers' acceptances

In the BA market, an acceptance may be referred to as eligible because it is acceptable by the Fed as collateral at the discount window and/or because the accepting bank can sell it without incurring a reserve requirement.

Elliott Wave Theory

Technical market timing strategy that predicts price movements on the basis of historical price wave patterns and their underlying psychological motives. Robert Prechter is a famous Elliott Wave theorist.

Elves

A term the host uses to refer to guests on the PBS television show, "Wall Street Week", who are technical analysts attempting to predict the direction of stock prices over the next six months.

EM

See: Effective margin.

Embedded option

An option that is part of the structure of a bond that gives either the bondholder or the issuer the right to take some action against the other party, as opposed to a bare option, which trades separately from any underlying security.

EMC

See Export Management Company.

Emergency fund

A reserve of cash kept available to meet the costs of any unexpected financial emergencies.

Emergency Home Finance Act of 1970

The federal legislation creating the Federal Home Loan Mortgage Corporation, a partially government-run program initiated to stimulate the development of a secondary mortgage market and expand mortgages available to veterans and other groups.

Emerging Company Marketplace (ECM)

A service once offered by the American Stock Exchange to help small growth companies fulfill special listing requirements. The service is no longer available.

Emerging Markets

Financial markets in nations that are developing market-based economies and have become popular with U.S. investors.

Emerging Markets Free index (EMF)

A Morgan Stanley Capital International index created to track stock markets in selected emerging markets that are open to foreign investment like Argentina, Chile, Jordan, Malaysia, Mexico, Philippines, and Thailand.

Emerging markets fund

A mutual fund that invests primarily in countries with developing economies (that is, those that are becoming industrialized). Emerging markets funds tend to be more volatile than domestic stock funds due to currency fluctuation and political instability. Consequently, fund prices can fluctuate dramatically.

Employee contribution

An employee's own deposit to a company retirement plan.

Employee Retirement Income Security Act (ERISA)

The law that regulates the operation of private pensions and benefit plans.

Employee stock fund

A firm-sponsored program that enables employees to purchase shares of the firm's common stock on a preferential basis.

Employee stock ownership plan (ESOP)

A company contributes to a trust fund that buys stock on behalf of employees.

Employee Stock Purchase Plan (ESPP)

A plan usually linked to a Corporation's payroll deduction system allowing employees to purchase shares at a discount from current market value.

Employer matching contribution

The amount, if any, a company contributes on an employee's behalf to the employee's retirement account, usually tied to the employee's own contribution.

Employment rate

The percentage of the labor force that is employed. The employment rate is one of the economic indicators that economists examine to help understand the state of the economy. See also: Unemployment rate.

Empty head and pure heart test

Securities and Exchange Commission rule that allows only the bidder of a tender offer to trade in the stock while possessing inside information.

EMS

See: European Monetary System.

Enabling Clause

Part I of the General Agreement on Tariffs and Trade (GATT) framework which permits developed country members to give more favorable treatment to developing countries and special treatment to the least developed countries, notwithstanding the most-favored-nation provisions of the GATT.

Encumbered

A property owned by one party on which a second party reserves the right to make a valid claim, e.g., a bank's holding of a home mortgage encumbers property.

End-of-year convention

Treating cash flows as if they occur at the end of a year as opposed to the date convention. Under the end-of-year convention, the present is time 0, the end of year 1 occurs one year hence; and so on.

Endogenous uncertainty

Describes factors within the control of the firm, such as a decision to reveal information about price or input costs. Converse of exogenous.

Endogenous variable

A value determined within the context of a model. Related: Exogenous variable.

Endorse

Transferring asset ownership by signing the back of the asset's certificate.

Endowment

Gift of money or property to a specified institution for a specified purpose.

Endowment funds

Investment funds established for the support of institutions such as colleges, private schools, museums, hospitals, and foundations. The investment income may be used for the operation of the institution and for capital expenditures.

Energy mutual fund

Mutual fund investing in energy stocks only, e.g., oil and gas companies.

Enhanced indexing

Also called indexing-plus, an indexing strategy whose objective is to exceed or replicate the total return performance of some predetermined index.

Enhanced Proliferation Control Initiative

In December 1990, the United States announced a series of measures — collectively referred to as the Enhanced Proliferation Control Initiative (EPCI) — to reduce certain proliferation risks. Under the initiative, the U.S. requires licenses for exports of:

(a) precursor chemicals that can be used in making chemical weapons and whole chemical plants to make such precursors;
(b) potential chemical and biological weapon-related industrial facilities, related designs, technologies, and equipment; and
(c) any items to destinations that raise proliferation concerns when the exporter knows, or is informed by the Commerce Department, of such concerns. The initiative also calls for:
(d) penalties on U.S. firms and individuals that promote the spread of chemical weapons and missile technology;

(e) control lists of (i) dual-use equipment and technologies related to chemical and biological weapons and missiles, and (ii) countries to which exports of such items should be controlled; and

(f) multilateral adoption of the initiative's measures.

Enhanced Structural Adjustment Facility

The ESAF is a system by which the International Monetary Fund loans concessional resources to assist poor countries. These countries have extended balance of payments deficits and pursue an orderly plans for correcting the deficits and promoting medium-term economic structural adjustment and macroeconomic programs. While similar to the Structural Adjustment Facility (SAF), ESAF has triple the resources available for supporting structural adjustment and monitors performance more closely. Both facilities use the Policy Framework Paper as a means for attracting additional support structural adjustment. SAF was established in March 1986, ESAF in December 1987; both facilities require repayments to be made in 5« to 10 years. More than 60 countries are eligible for assistance under these facilities. See also International Monetary Fund Policy Framework Paper.

Enhancement

An innovation that has a positive impact on one or more of a firm's existing products.

Enterprise

A business firm.

Enterprise for the Americas Initiative

The EAI, launched in June 1990, supports development of a new economic relationship between the United States and Latin America. The EAI has trade investment, debt, and environment aspects. Trade aspects include efforts to advance free trade agreements with markets in Latin America and the Caribbean, particularly with groups of countries that have associated for purposes of trade liberalization. As part of this process, the U.S. seeks to enter into "framework" agreements on trade and investment with interested countries or groups of countries. These agreements set up intergovernmental councils to discuss and, where appropriate, to negotiate the removal of trade and investment barriers. Investment aspects include the establishment of an Investment Sector Loan program and the Multilateral Investment Fund to support investment reforms. See: Investment Sector Loan Program Multilateral Investment Program.

Enterprise Unipersonnelle ... Responsabilite Limitee

EURL (French: "sole ownership limited liability company") combines features of both a corporation and a partnership. This form of organization can be established with only one shareholder.

Enterprise Value

The market capitalization of a firm's equity plus the market value of the firm's debt. Often the value of assets that are non-core are excluded the final calculation.

Entrepot

An intermediary storage facility where goods are kept temporarily for distribution within a country or for reexport.

Entrepreneur

A person starting a new company who takes on the risks associated with starting the enterprise, which may require venture capital to cover start-up costs.

Entropy

The level of disorder in a system.

Entry Summary System

An entry is the minimum amount of documentation needed to secure the release of imported merchandise. The Entry Summary System, a part of Customs' Automated Commercial System, contains data on release, summary, rejection, collection, liquidation, and extension or suspension.

Entry Summary Selectivity System

The Entry Summary Selectivity System, a part of Customs' Automated Commercial System, provides an automated review of entry data to determine whether team or routine review is required. Selectivity criteria include an assessment of risk by importer, tariff number, country of origin, manufacturer, and value. Summaries with Census warnings, as well as quota, antidumping and countervailing duty entry summaries are selected for team review. A random sample of routine review summaries is also automatically selected for team review.

Entry Value

The U.S. Customs Service defines entry value (or entered value) as the value reflected on the entry documentation submitted by the importer.

Environmental fund

A mutual fund that invests strictly in stocks of companies that are environmentally friendly and/or have the goal of environmental betterment. The investors are trying to support and profit from opportunities related to the environmental movement.

EOE

See: European Options Exchange.

EOQ

See: Economic Order Quantity.

EPS

See: Earnings per share.

Equal dollar swap

Selling common stock/convertibles in one company and reinvesting the proceeds in as many shares of (1) another type of security issued by the company, or (2) another security of the same type but of another company — as can be bought with the proceeds of the sale. See: Equal shares swap.

Equal percentage contribution rule (EPCoR)

Principle that each asset contributes the same proportion to the equilibrium portfolio rate premium and risk.

Equal shares swap

Applies mainly to convertible securities. Selling the underlying common and reinvesting the proceeds in as much of the convertible as can be converted into the number of shares of common just sold. See equal dollar swap.

Equalizing dividend

Special dividends received by investors of a firm for income the investor lost because the firm altered the dividends payment schedule.

Equilibrium

The stable state of the system. See: Attractor.

Equilibrium exchange rate

Exchange rate at which demand for a currency is equal to the supply of the currency in the economy.

Equilibrium market price of risk

The slope of the capital market line (CML). Since the CML represents the expected return offered to compensate for a perceived level of risk, each point on the line is a balanced market condition, or equilibrium. The slope of the line determines the additional expected return needed to compensate for a unit change in risk. The equation of the CML is defined by the capital asset pricing model.

Equilibrium price

The price when the supply of goods matches demand.

Equilibrium rate of interest

The interest rate that clears the market. Also called the trade-clearing interest rate.

Equipment

Any item having a life expectancy of one year or more.

Equipment leasing partnership

A limited partnership that receives income and tax benefits such as depreciation costs by purchasing equipment and leasing it to other parties.

Equipment trust certificates

Certificates issued by a trust that is formed to purchase an asset and lease it to a lessee. When the last of the certificates has been repaid, title and ownership of the asset transfers to the lessee.

Equitable owner

The beneficiary of a property held in a trust.

Equity

Ownership interest in a firm. Also, the residual dollar value of a futures trading account, assuming its liquidation is at the going trade price. In real estate, dollar difference between what a property could be sold for and debts claimed against it. In a brokerage account, equity equals the value of the account's securities minus any debit balance in a margin account. Equity is also shorthand for stock market investments.

Equity cap

An agreement in which one party, for an up-front premium, agrees to pay the other at specific time periods if a designated stock market benchmark tops a predetermined level.

Equity claim

Also called a residual claim; a claim to a share of earnings after debt obligations have been satisfied.

Equity collar

The simultaneous purchase of an equity floor and sale of an equity cap.

Equity contribution agreement

An agreement to contribute equity to a project under certain specified conditions.

Equity floor

An agreement in which one party agrees to pay the other at specific time periods if a specific stock market benchmark falls below a predetermined level.

Equity funding

An investment consisting of a life insurance policy and a mutual fund. The insurance policy is paid by the collateral value of fund shares, give the investor the advantages of insurance protection with the growth potential of a mutual fund.

Equity kicker

Stock warrants issued attached to privately placed bonds.

Equity-linked Eurobonds

A Eurobond including a convertibility option or warrant.

Equity-linked policies

Related: Variable life.

Equity market

Related: stock market.

Equity multiplier

Total assets divided by total common stockholders' equity; the total assets per dollar of stockholders' equity.

Equity options

Securities that give the holder the right (but not the obligation) to buy or sell a specified number of shares of stock, at a specified price for a certain (limited) time period. Typically one option equals 100 shares of stock.

Equity REIT

A Real Estate Investment Trust that assumes ownership status in the property it invests in enabling investors of the REIT to earn dividends on rental income from the property and appreciation in property resale. Antithesis of a Mortgage REIT.

Equity swap

A swap in which the cash flows exchanged are based on the total return on some stock market index and an interest rate (either a fixed rate or floating rate). Related: Interest rate swap.

Equityholders

Stockholders; those holding shares of the firm's equity.

Equivalent annual annuity

The amount per year for some number of years that has a present value equal to a given amount.

Equivalent annual benefit

The annual annuity with the same value as the net present value of an investment project.

Equivalent annual cash flow

Annuity with the same net present value as the company's proposed investment.

Equivalent annual cost

The cost per year of owning an asset over its entire life.

Equivalent bond yield

Annual yield on a short-term, noninterest-bearing security calculated for comparison to yields quoted on coupon securities.

Equivalent loan

Given the after-tax stream associated with a lease, the maximum amount of conventional debt that the same period-by-period after-tax debt service stream is capable of supporting.

Equivalent taxable yield

The yield that must be offered on a taxable bond issue to give the same after-tax yield as a tax-exempt issue.

ER

The two-character ISO 3166 country code for ERITREA.

ERM

See: Exchange Rate Mechanism.

Erosion

A negative impact on one or more of a firm's existing assets.

ES

The two-character ISO 3166 country code for SPAIN.

Escalator clause

Provision in a contract allowing cost increases to be passed on. In an employment contract, for example an escalator clause may call for wage increases in line with inflation.

Escape Clause

The escape clause, which can be invoked under GATT Article XIX, allows countries to temporarily violate their GATT obligations to the degree and time necessary to protect a domestic industry from serious injury. Countries taking such actions, however, must consult with affected contracting parties to determine appropriate compensation for the violation of GATT rights, or be subject to retaliatory trade actions. Section 201 of the Trade Act of 1974 requires the U.S. International Trade Commission to investigate complaints filed by domestic industries or workers claiming that they are injured or threatened by rapidly rising imports. Section 203 of the Act provides that if the ensuing investigation establishes that the complaint is valid, relief may be granted in the form of adjustment assistance, which may be training, technical, and financial assistance, or temporary import restrictions in the form of tariffs, quotas, tariff rate quotas, and/or orderly marketing agreements. Import restrictions imposed under the escape clause authority are limited in duration. They may last no longer than five years but can be extended by the President for a three-year period.

Escheat

Reversion of monies or securities to the state in which the securityholder was last known to reside, when no claim by the securityholder has been made after a certain period of time fixed by state law. This known as the holding period or cut-off date.

Escheat Period

The period of elapsed time required by applicable state law for property to be presumed abandoned.

Escheatment

The process of turning over unclaimed or abandoned property to a state authority. Escheatment laws require mutual funds to turn over uncashed or returned check dollars and/or client account fund shares if the owner cannot be located within a length of time determined by each state.

Escrow

Property or money held by a third party until the agreed upon obligations of a contract are met.

Escrow Account

An escrow account is a special bank account into which earnings from sales (e.g., convertible currency proceeds from exports) are accumulated. These revenues are set aside for subsequent acquisition of goods and services from a foreign supplier. The escrowed money, usually interest-bearing, is disbursed by the bank to the foreign supplier under payment terms and against documents specified in the supplier's sale contract..

Escrow receipt

A document provided by a bank in options trading to guarantee that the underlying security is on deposit and available for potential delivery.

Escrowed to Maturity (ETM)

Holding of the proceeds from a new bond issue to pay off an existing bond issue at its maturation date.

ESOP

See: Employee Stock Ownership Plan.

ESP

The ISO 4217 currency code for the Spanish Peseta.

Essential purpose (or function) bond

See: Public purpose bond

Estate planning

The preparation of a plan to carry out an individual's wishes as to the administration and disposition of his/her property before or after his/her death.

Estate tax

A federal or state tax imposed on an individual's assets inherited by heirs.

Estimated tax

Tax to be paid quarterly on income that is not subject to withholding tax, including self-employed income, investment income, alimony, rent, and capital gains.

ET

The two-character ISO 3166 country code for ETHIOPIA.

ETB

The ISO 4217 currency code for the Ethiopian Birr.

ETC

See Export trading company.

Ethical fund

See: Social conscious mutual fund.

Ethics

Standards of conduct or moral judgment.

EU

See: European Union.

Euclidean Geometry

The Plane geometry we learn in high school, based upon a few ideal, smooth, symmetric shapes.

EUR

The ISO 4217 currency code for Euro.

EUREX

The European derivatives exchange formed in 1998 by a merger of the Deutsche Terminbörse (DTB) and the Swiss Options and Financial Futures Exchange (SOFFEX).

Euro

Originally for a deposit outside one's home country but in the home country currency. This terminology is confusing now since the new European currency unit, also called the Euro, was introduced on January 1, 1999.

Eurobank

A bank that regularly accepts foreign currency-denominated deposits and makes foreign currency loans.

Eurobond

A bond that is (1) underwritten by an international syndicate, (2) issued simultaneously to investors in a number of countries, and (3) issued outside the jurisdiction of any single country.

Euro CDs

CDs issued by a US bank branch or foreign bank located outside the US Almost all Euro CDs are issued in London.

Euroclear

The Euroclear group is the world's largest settlement system for domestic and international securities transactions, covering both bonds and equities for financial institutions located in over 80 countries.

Euro-commercial paper

Short-term notes with maturities up to 360 days that are issued by companies in international money markets.

Eurocredit market

Comprises banks that accept deposits and provide loans in large denominations and in a variety of currencies. The banks that constitute this market are the same banks that constitute the Eurocurrency market; the difference is that Eurocredit loans are longer-term than so-called Eurocurrency loans.

Eurocredits

Intermediate-term loans of Eurocurrencies made by banking syndicates to corporate and government borrowers.

Eurocurrency

Instrument issued outside your country, but denominated in your currency. A Eurodollar is a Certificate of Deposit in US dollars in some other country (though mainly traded in London). A Euroyen is a CD in yen outside Japan.

Eurocurrency deposit

A short-term fixed-rate time deposit denominated in

a currency other than the local currency (i.e., US dollars deposited in a London bank).

Eurocurrency market

The money market for borrowing and lending currencies that are held in the form of deposits in banks located outside the countries where the currencies are issued as legal tender.

Eurodollars

Eurodollars are deposits of U.S. dollars in banks or other financial institutions which are located outside the borders of the United States. In every other way, Eurodollars are identical to any other U.S. dollars. These same dollars are also called offshore dollars, or depending where the money is on deposit, Asian dollars. The use of "Euro" in connection with dollars reflects the beginnings of holding deposits offshore. Likewise, a Eurocurrency (or external currency) is the deposit of one nation's currency in another country. A Eurobond is a bond which is denominated in a currency and traded in a market outside of the issuing country.

Eurodollar bonds

Eurobonds denominated in U.S.dollars.

Eurodollar certificate of deposit

A certificate of deposit paying interest and principal in dollars, but issued by a bank outside the United States, usually in Europe.

Eurodollar obligations

Certificates of deposit issued in US dollars by foreign banks and foreign branches of US banks.

Euroequity issues

Securities sold in the Euromarket. That is, securities initially sold to investors simultaneously in several national markets by an international syndicate. Related: External market.

Euro lines

Lines of credit granted by banks (foreign or foreign branches of US banks) for Eurocurrencies.

Euroloans

Loans of dollar-denominated deposits in banks outside the U.S. and of other deposits in banks outside the depositor's country of origin.

Euromarkets

A general term for the Eurobond and Euroloans markets.

Euro straight

A fixed-rate coupon Eurobond.

Euro-medium term note (Euro-MTN)

A nonunderwritten Euronote issued directly to the market. Euro-MTNs are offered continuously rather than all at once as a bond issue is. Most Euro-MTN maturities are under five years.

Euro.NM

Created on March 1, 1996, Euro.NM is a pan- network of regulated markets dedicated to growth companies, regardless of their sector of activity or country of origin. Euro.NM member exchanges and their respective new markets consist of the Paris Stock Exchange (Le Nouveau Marché), the Deutsche Börse AG (Neuer Markt), the Amsterdam Exchanges (NMAX), and the Brussels Stock Exchange (Euro.NM Belgium).

Euro-note

Short- to medium term debt instrument sold in the Eurocurrency market.

European, Australia, and Far East index (EAFE index)

Stock index, computed by Morgan Stanley Capital International.

European Association of Securities Dealers Automated Quotation (EASDAQ)

European equivalent of Nasdaq.

European Bank for Reconstruction and Development

The EBRD provides assistance through direct loans. The loans are designed to facilitate the development of market-oriented economies and to promote private and entrepreneurial initiatives. The EBRD's charter mandates that at least 60 percent of EBRD lending contribute to privatization of state-owned enterprises. The remaining 40 percent may fund public infrastructure or environmental projects that promote private sector development, as well as state-owned enterprises that operate in a competitive fashion. EBRD was established in May 1990 and began financing operations in June 1991. EBRD headquarters are in London, England.

European Central Bank

The ECB, as envisioned by the Treaty of Maastricht, would be created to oversee performance of economic policy and exchange rate policy tasks conferred on the European System of Central Banks. The ECB would have the exclusive right to issue bank-notes within the European Community. The national central banks would be the sole subscribers to and holders of the capital of the ECB. The funding formula for the ECB would be based both on a Member State's population and on its gross domestic product. The ECB will form, together with the national central banks, the European System of Central Banks. See: Maastricht Treaty.

European Commission

One of the five major institutions of the European Community, the Commission is responsible for ensuring the implementation of the Treaty of Rome and Community rules and obligations; submission of proposals to the Council of Ministers; execution of the Council's decisions; reconciliation of disagreements among Council members; administration of EC policies, such as the Common Agricultural Policy and coal and steel policies; taking necessary legal action against firms or member governments; and representing the Community in trade negotiations with non-member countries.

European Committee for Electrotechnical Standardization

The European Committee for Electrotechnical Standardization, CENELEC, is a non-profit-making international organization under Belgian law. CENELEC seeks to harmonize electrotechnical standards published by the national organizations and to remove technical barriers to trade that may be caused by differences in standards. CENELEC members include: Austria, Belgium, Denmark, Finland, France, Germany, Greece, Iceland, Ireland, Italy, Luxembourg, Netherlands, Norway, Portugal, Spain, Sweden, Switzerland, and the United Kingdom.

European Committee for Standardization

The European Committee for Standardization, or CEN (from Comit, Europeen de Normalisation), is an association of the national standards organizations of 18 countries of the European Economic Communities (EEC) and of the European Free Trade Association (EFTA). CEN membership is open to the national standards organization of any European country which is, or is capable of becoming, a member of the EEC or

EFTA. CEN develops voluntary standards in building, machine tools, information technology, and in all sectors excluding the electrical ones covered by CENELEC. CEN is involved in accreditation of laboratories and certification bodies as well as quality assurance.

European Community

A regional organization created in 1958 providing for gradual elimination of intraregional customs duties and other trade barriers, applying a common external tariff against other countries, and providing for gradual adoption of other integrating measures, including a Common Agricultural Policy (CAP) and guarantees of free movement of labor and capital. The original 6 members were Belgium, France, West Germany, Italy, Luxembourg, and the Netherlands. Denmark, Ireland, and the United Kingdom became members in 1973; Greece acceded in 1981; Spain and Portugal in 1986. The term European Community (EC) refers to three separate regional organizations which operate under separate treaties:

— European Coal and Steel Community (ECSC), established in 1952

— European Atomic Energy Community (EURATOM), established in 1958, and

— European Economic Community (EEC), established in 1958.

Since 1967, the European Community have been served by four common institutions — the EC Commission, the EC Council, the European Parliament, and the Court of Justice of the European Community. The present 12 member states of the EC are also members of the ECSC and Euratom. While the expression "European Community" (or "EC") was meant to refer to the three Communities, frequent use of the expression "European Community" (or "EC") has become common as a reference to the European Economic Community (EEC). Prior to November 1, 1993 (the date on which the Maastricht Treaty on European Union entered into force), the acronym "EC" was used as a reference to "European Community" and "European Communities." Part I, Article I of the Maastricht Treaty on European Union formalized "EC" as a reference to "European Community." The Treaty also introduced the term "European Union" as a broader legal entity than the European Community.

European Cooperation for the Long-term in Defense

EUCLID is a coordinated defense R&D initiative which was approved in a June 1989 meeting of the Independent European Program Group (IEPG). EUCLID was designed to overcome deficiencies in European defense R&D spending, minimize individual nation's duplicative efforts, improve planning, and overcome legal and administrative obstacles. EUCLID is divided into 11 technological categories: (a) modern radar technology, (b) microelectronics, (c) composite structures, (d) modular avionics, (e) electric gun, (f) artificial intelligence, (g) signature manipulation, (h) opto-electronic devices, (i) satellite surveillance technologies (including verification), (j) underwater acoustics, and (k) "human factors," including technology for training and simulation. Each of the 11 categories is assigned a lead coordinating nation.

European Court of Justice

The ECJ, located in Luxembourg, was established in 1958 to support interpretation and application of European Community law. The Court has jurisdiction to settle actions brought by: (a) the Commission against member states for failing to implement EC legislation, (b) the member states against EC institutions, referrals for interpretations from national courts where a question of EC law is at issue, and individuals under a provision of EC law.

European Currency Unit (ECU).

The ECU is a "basket" of specified amounts of each E.C. currency. Amounts were determined according to the economic size of EC members, all of whose currencies participate in the ECU basket. In the European Monetary System (EMS), the ECU is used as a basis for setting central rates in the exchange rate mechanism, as an accounting unit, and as a reserve instrument and means of settlement among EMS central banks. Under provisions of the Maastricht Treaty, the ECU is scheduled to be adopted as the single European currency in Stage III of European Monetary Union (by 1999 at the latest). The composition of the basket comprising the ECU was frozen on November 1, 1993 in accordance with a provision of the Maastricht Treaty which entered into force also on November 1. See: Maastricht Treaty.

European Development Fund

The EDF is the principal means by which the European Economic Community provides aid, concessionary finance, and technical assistance to developing countries. The Fund was originally established in 1958 to grant financial aid to dependencies of the six nations which founded the EEC.

European Economic Area

The EEA, which became effective in January 1994, consists of Austria, Finland, Iceland, Norway, Sweden and the 12 member nations of the European Union. The EEA, encompassing an area inhabited by 370 million people, allows for the free movement of goods, persons, services and capital throughout all 17 countries. It also opens cooperation possibilities in many areas, including research and development, environment, promotion of tourism, social, and consumer policy.

Following the negative result of the Swiss referendum in December 1992, the remaining six countries of the European Free Trade Association (Austria, Finland, Iceland, Liechtenstein, Norway, and Sweden) signed an Adjusting Protocol in March 1993 with the intent to proceed without Switzerland. The Adjusting Protocol contains provisions which allow Switzerland to participate in the EEA at a later stage if it so wishes. Liechtenstein will remain a Contracting Party to the European Economic Area Agreement, but it will not be part of the EEA until the EEA Council decides that the accord's good functioning will not be impaired. Liechtenstein's status in the EEA accord was reviewed following Switzerland's negative vote on the EEA in a December 1992 referendum. In particular, Liechtenstein's customs union with Switzerland requires renegotiation.

Significant differences exist between the EEA and full membership in the European Economic Community (EEC). The EEA is a free trade area, not a customs union. Border controls between the EEC and EFTA, while relaxed, are expected to continue. EFTA will not adopt the EEC's Common Customs Tariff nor participate in the Common Commercial Policy or Common Agricultural Policy. EFTA nations will continue to set their own tariffs for third countries subject to GATT and OECD agreements. Further change is anticipated with Austria, Finland, Norway, and Sweden expected to join the European Economic Community by January 1995 or shortly afterwards. See: European Economic Community European Free Trade Association European Union

European exchange rate mechanism (ERM)

The system that countries in the European Union once used to pay exchange rates within bands around an ERM central value.

European Exercise

A feature of an option that stipulates that the option may only be exercised at its expiration. Therefore, there can be no early assignment with this type of option.

European Free Trade Association

EFTA is a regional organization established in December 1959 by the Stockholm Convention as an alternative to the Common Market. EFTA was designed to provide a free trade area for industrial products among member countries. In contrast with the EC, EFTA does not have a common external tariff and nor a common agricultural trade policy. Original EFTA members included the United Kingdom, Austria, Denmark, Norway, Portugal, Sweden, and Switzerland. The UK, Denmark, and Portugal left the Association when they joined the EC. EFTA currently has seven members: Austria, Finland, Iceland, Liechtenstein, Norway, Sweden, and Switzerland — Austria and Sweden have applied for EC membership. Association headquarters are in Geneva, Switzerland.

European Investment Bank

The Luxembourg-based EIB, established in 1957, is an independent public institution set up the Treaty of Rome to contribute to balanced and steady development in the European Community. The EIB provides loans and guarantees to companies and public institutions to finance regional development, structural development, and achieve cross-border objectives. The EIB has emphasized regional development and energy, with Italy, Greece, and Ireland receiving major support.

European Monetary and Cooperation Fund

The EMCF, originally created in 1973, was revised and linked with the European Monetary System in 1979. While intended to support the European Currency Unit and support a reserve system of central banks, the Fund has been used to keep account of short-term borrowings and support currencies through intervention in foreign exchange markets at the request of member states. The Fund uses the Bank for International Settlements as its agent.

European Monetary Institute

Under provisions of the Maastricht Treaty, the EMI will manage the national currency reserves of EC central banks and encourage international acceptance of the European Currency Unit (ECU). The EMI is also intended to strengthen coordination of monetary policies among European Community member states and to study and develop the infrastructure and procedures required for the conduct of single monetary policy. The EMI will be established on January 1, 1994. See: Maastricht Treaty.

European Monetary System (EMS)

A system adopted by European Community members with the aim of promoting stability by limiting exchange-rate fluctuations. The system was originated in 1979 by the nine members of the European Community (EC). The EMS comprised three principal elements: the European Currency Unit (ECU), the monetary unit used in EC transactions; the Exchange Rate Mechanism, ERM, whereby those member states taking part agreed to maintain currency fluctuations within certain agreed limits; and the European Monetary Cooperation Fund, which issues the ECU and oversees the ERM. The 1992 Maastricht Treaty provided for the move to Economic and Monetary Union (EMU) , including a European Monetary Institute to coordinate the economic and monetary policy of the EU, a European Central Bank (ECB) to govern these policies, and the presentation of a single European currency.

European Norm

The “EN” mark is a designation of a standards directive issued by CEN (Comit, Europien de Normalisation) or CENELEC (Comit, Europien de Normalisation Electrotechnique). Notations regarding En generally don’t appear on the product.

European option

Option that may be exercised only at the expiration date. Related: American option.

European Options Exchange (EOE)

Now AEX-Optiebeurs. See: Amsterdam Exchanges (AEX).

European Organization for Testing and Certification

The EOTC promotes mutual recognition of tests, test and certification procedures, and quality systems within the European private sector for product areas or characteristics not covered by EC legislative requirements. The Organization was created in April 1990 by the European Community Commission under a memorandum of agreement with CEN/CENELEC and the European Free Trade Association countries. EOTC headquarters are in Brussels, Belgium.

European Patent Convention

The European Patent Convention, EPC, is an agreement between European nations to centralize and standardize patent law and procedure. The EPC, which took effect in 1977, established a single "European patent" through application to the European Patent Office in Munich. Once granted, the patent matures into a bundle of individual patents — one in each member country designated by the patent applicant. Patent applicants must indicate the countries to which they wish to have patent protection.

European Patent Office

The EPO (German: Europieisches Patentamt; French: Office Europien de Brevets) promotes easier, cheaper, and more reliable patent protection by establishing a single procedure for granting patents on the basis of a single European patent law. Standards are available in English from the World Intellectual Property Organization. The Office was established in October, 1973; its headquarters are in Munich, Germany. EPO membership is not open to the U.S., but close relations are maintained through the Commerce Department's Patent and Trademark Office.

European Research Coordination Agency

The European Research Coordination Agency, EUREKA, coordinates advanced technology projects being carried out by European industry. The Agency was created in 1985; headquarters are in Brussels, Belgium; membership includes the European Community countries, plus Norway, Sweden, Finland, Switzerland, Austria, Iceland, and Turkey.

European Space Agency

The ESA designs and coordinates construction of satellite and launching systems. Members include: Austria, Belgium, Denmark, France, Germany, Ireland, Italy, the Netherlands, Norway, Spain, Sweden, Switzerland, and the United Kingdom

European-style exercise

A method of exercising options contracts in which the buyer can exercise the contract on the last day before expiration.

European-style option

An option contract that can be exercised only on the expiration date.

European System of Central Banks

The ESCB, as envisioned by the Treaty of Maastricht, would be created for the primary purpose of maintaining price stability within the European Community. The ESCB would be composed of the European Central Bank and of the central banks of the Members States. It would be independent of national governments and Community authorities.

European Technical Approval

An ETA is a favorable technical assessment of the fitness for use of a product for an intended use, based on the fulfillment of the essential requirements for building works for which the product is used, as provided for under the EC Construction Products Directive (89/106/EEC). A European technical approval may be granted to products for which there is neither a harmonized European standard, nor a recognized national standard, nor a mandate for a harmonized standard; and to product which differ significantly from harmonized or recognized national standards. Such approval permits free circulation of the products within the member countries of the European Community and the European Free Trade Association.

European Telecommunications Standards Institute

ETSI was established in March 1988 in response to the inability of the European Conference of Postal and Telecommunications Administrations (CEPT) to keep up with the schedule of work on common European standards and specifications agreed to in the 1984 Memorandum of Understanding between CEPT and the EC. ETSI has a contractual relationship with the EC to pursue standards development for telecommunications equipment and services, and it cooperates with other European standards bodies such as CEN/CENELEC. ETSI membership includes the telecommunications administrations that constitute the CEPT as well as manufacturers, service providers, and users.

European terms

A foreign exchange quotation that states the foreign currency price of one US dollar.

European Trade Union Confederation

ETUC, founded in 1973, is the primary organization which speaks for European trade unions. ETUC consists of more than 30 organizations in 20 Western European countries and has over 40 million members. The Confederation's principal goal is to influence European policies affecting workers; it is active with the European Community, the Council of Europe, the European Free Trade Association, and the OECD Trade Union Advisory Committee. ETUC headquarters are in Brussels, Belgium.

European Union (EU)

The EU is an umbrella reference to the European Community (EC) and to two European integration efforts introduce by the Maastricht Treaty: Common Foreign and Security Policy (including defense) and Justice and Home Affairs (principally cooperation between police and other authorities on crime, terrorism, and immigration issues). The term "European Union" was introduced in November 1993 (when the Maastricht Treaty on European Union entered into force). The term "European Community" (EC) continues to exist as a legal entity within the broader framework of the EU.

Euroyen bonds

Eurobonds denominated in Japanese yen.

Evaluation period

The time interval over which funds assess a money manager's performance.

Even lot

See: Round lot.

Evening up

Buying or selling to offset an existing market position.

Event anomalies

Occurrences such as earnings surprises or stock splits that seem to present opportunity to generate abnormal returns for those trading on the news.

Event driven

In the context of hedge funds, a style of management that combines many different types of hedge fund investing such as merger arbitrage, distressed securities and high yield investing, in conjunction with an important "event" that is supposed to unlock firm value (like a merger announcement, earnings announcement, or a regulator decision).

Event risk

The risk that the ability of an issuer to make interest and principal payments will change because of rare, discontinuous, and very large, unanticipated changes in the market environment such as (1) a natural or industrial accident or some regulatory change or (2) a takeover, or corporate restructuring.

Event study

A statistical study that examines how the release of information affects prices at a particular time.

Events of default

Contractually specified events that allow lenders to demand immediate repayment of a debt.

Evergreen credit

Revolving credit without maturity.

Evergreen funding

A British term referring to the gradual injection of capital into a new or existing enterprise.

Evidence Account

Umbrella agreement contracted between a Western supplier and a government agency in a developing country (e.g., an industrial ministry, or a provincial or state authority), which is designed to facilitate reciprocal trade flows. The agreement stipulates trade conditions between the Western firm, other independent firms designated by it, and commercial organizations under the jurisdiction of the developing country signatory. It also requires that the cumulative payment turnovers for the traded goods, not payments of individual transactions, be balanced in an agreed-upon proportion within a specified period of time (typically 1 to 3 years). Trade flows are monitored and financial settlements occur through banks designated by the agreement's signatories.

Evidence of Origin

Information presented in the Exporter's Certificate of Origin (or Customs Form 353) that certifies that the goods described are eligible for a preferential rate of duty under a trade program.

EX (Point of Origin)

When used in pricing terms such as "ex factory" or "ex dock," it signifies that the price quoted applies only at the point of origin (in the two examples, at the seller's factory or a dock at the import point). In practice, this kind of quotation indicates that the seller agrees to place the goods at the disposal of the buyer at the specified place within a fixed period of time. From the point where the shipment begins movement, e.g., "Ex Factory" "Ex Mine" or "Ex Warehouse." See "Terms of Sale."

Exact interest

Interest paid based on the basis of a 365-day/year schedule by a bank or other financial institution as opposed to a 360-day basis (ordinary interest). Difference can be material when large principal sums of money are involved.

Exact matching

A bond portfolio management strategy that involves finding the lowest cost portfolio generating cash inflows exactly equal to cash outflows that are being financed by investment.

Ex-all

The sale of a security without the privileges associated with the security such as dividends, voting rights, or warrants.

Ex ante return

The expected return or anticipated return of an asset or portfolio.

Ex ante value

The forecasted rate of return.

Except for opinion

An auditor's opinion reflecting the fact that the auditor is unable to audit certain areas of the company's operations because of restrictions imposed by management or other conditions beyond the auditor's control.

Excepted rate of inflation

The public's exceptations for inflation. These expectations determine how large an effect a given policy action by the Fed will have on economic activity.

Exception

A proxy which does not authorize the proxy committee to act on its behalf concerning any other business, adjournments or substitutions.

Exceptional Return

Residual return plus benchmark timing return. For a given asset with beta equal to one, if its residual return is 2%, and the benchmark portfolio exceeds its consensus expected returns by 1%, then the asset's exceptional return is 3%.

Excess accumulation

The amount of a required minimum distribution that an IRA holder fails to remove from an IRA in a timely manner. Excess accumulations are subject to a 50% IRS penalty tax.

Excess contribution

The amount by which an IRA contribution exceeds the allowable limits. If an excess contribution is not properly corrected, a 6% IRS penalty applies.

Excess-Currency Country

A country where the local currency supply available to the U.S. Government for conducting official business exceeds U.S. requirements for the 2 years following the year for which the designation is made.

Excess kurtosis

Kurtosis measures the "fatness" of the tails of a distribution. Excess kurtosis means that distribution has fatter tails than a normal distribution. Fat tails means there is a higher than normal probability of big positive and negative returns realizations.

Excess margin

Equity present in an individual's account above the legal minimum required for a margin account or the maintenance requirement at a brokerage firm.

Excess profits tax

Additional federal taxes placed on the earnings of a business, used only in time of national emergency such as war.

Excess reserves

Amount of reserves held by an institution in excess of its reserve requirement and required clearing balance. Also see reserves.

Excess return on the market portfolio

Difference between the return on the market portfolio and the riskless rate.

Excess returns

Difference between asset return and riskless rate. Sometimes confused with abnormal returns, returns in excess of those required by some asset pricing model.

Exchange

A marketplace in which shares, options and futures on stocks, bonds, commodities, and indexes are traded. Principal US stock exchanges are: New York Stock Exchange (NYSE), American Stock Exchange (AMEX), and National Association of Securities Dealers Automatic Quotation System (Nasdaq).

Exchange, The

A nickname for the New York Stock Exchange. Also known as the Big Board, where more than 2000 common and preferred stocks are traded. The exchange is the oldest in the United States, founded in 1792, and the largest. It is located on Wall Street in New York City.

Exchangeable

Applies mainly to convertible securities. Means the issuer, if so stated, may substitute a convertible debenture for an existing convertible preferred with identical terms. Most often used when a corporation has an immediate need for equity capital and a low tax rate, and expects either or both conditions to change. This would make the debenture less attractive if the interest tax-deductibility is lost.

Exchangeable instrument

Applies mainly to convertible securities. Bond or preferred stock that may be exchangeable into the common stock of a different public corporation.

Exchangeable Security

Investment instrument that grants its holder the right to exchange it for the common stock of a firm other than the issuer of the instrument.

Exchange of assets

Acquisition of another company by purchase of its assets in exchange for cash or stock.

Exchange controls

Government restrictions on the purchase of foreign currencies by domestic citizens or on the purchase of the local domestic currency by foreigners.

Exchange distribution

A sale on an exchange floor of a large block of stock in a single transaction. A broker bunches a large number of buy orders and sells the block all at once. The broker receives a special commission from the seller.

Exchange fund (also known as swap fund)

Investment vehicle introduced in 1999 that appeals to wealthy investors with large holdings in a single stock who want to diversify without paying capital gains taxes. These funds allow investors to exchange their stock for shares in the diversified portfolio of stocks in a tax-free transaction.

Exchange members

See: Member firm; seat

Exchange offer

An offer by a firm to give one security, such as a bond or preferred stock, in exchange for another security, such as shares of common stock.

Exchange Permit

A government permit sometimes required by the importer's government to enable the import firm to convert its own country's currency into foreign currency with which to pay a seller in another country.

Exchange privilege

A mutual fund shareholder's right to switch from one fund to another within one fund family, usually at no additional charge.

Exchange Rate

The price of one currency expressed in terms of another, i.e., the number of units of one currency that may be exchanged for one unit of another currency. Influences on exchange rates include differences between interest rates and other asset yields between countries; investor expectations about future changes in a currency's value; investors' views on the overall quantity of dollar-denominated assets in circulation; arbitrage; and central bank exchange rate support.

Exchange Rate Classifications

Following are the different types of possible exchange rate regimes and how they work:

— Single Currency Peg: the country pegs to a major currency — usually the U.S. dollar or the French franc — with infrequent adjustment of the parity;

— Composite Currency Peg: the country pegs to a basket of currencies of major trading partners to make the pegged currency more stable than if a single currency peg were used. The weights assigned to the currencies in the basket may reflect the geographical distribution of trade, services, or capital flows. They may also be standardized, as in the Special Drawing Right (SDR) and the European Currency Unit (ECU);

— Limited Flexibility vis-a-vis a Single Currency: the value of the currency is maintained within certain margins of the peg;

— Limited Flexibility Through Cooperative Agreements: this applies to countries in the exchange rate mechanism of the European Monetary System and is a cross between a peg of individual EMS currencies to each other and a float of all these currencies jointly vis-a-vis non-EMS currencies;

— Greater Flexibility Through Adjustment to an Indicator: the currency is adjusted more or less automatically to changes in selected indicators. A common indicator is the real effective exchange rate, which reflects inflation-adjusted changes in the currency vis-a-vis major trading partners;

— Greater Flexibility Through Managed Float: the central bank sets the rate but varies it frequently. Indicators for adjusting the rate include, for example, the balance of payments position, reserves, and parallel market developments. Adjustments are not automatic;

— Full Flexibility Through an Independent Float: rates are determined by market forces. Some industrial countries have floats — except for the EMS countries — but the number of developing countries in this category has been increasing.

Exchange Rate Mechanism

The ERM is a program through which member countries of the European Economic Community agree to maintain parity in exchange rates among their currencies. Limits are set on the amounts by which exchange rates may vary between any two currencies. If an exchange rate reaches the limit, the central banks of the two countries intervene in the market to ensure that the limit is not exceeded. The ERM was established in 1979 with agreement by Belgium, France, West Germany, Luxembourg, the Netherlands, and Denmark to limit fluctuation in the bilateral exchange rates between their currencies to ñ2.25%. Italy, which was also a member, did not limit fluctuation to ñ25% until 1990. Spain joined in 1989, the UK in 1990, and Portugal in 1992, each agreeing to a wider band of 6% fluctuation in the bilateral exchange rates in the value of their currencies against other ERM members. Disruptions in September 1992 led to the withdrawal of Italy and the UK and to some parity realignments. The ERM has since resumed, with provisions allowing currency fluctuations of 15 percent.

Exchange rate risk

Also called currency risk; the risk that an investment's value will change because of currency exchange rates.

Exchange Ratio

The number of new shares in an acquiring firm that are timed for each outstanding share of an acquired firm.

Exchange risk

The variability of a firm's value that results from unexpected exchange rate changes, or the extent to which the present value of a firm is expected to change as a result of a given currency's appreciation or depreciation.

Exchange of stock

Acquisition of another company by purchase of its stock in exchange for cash or shares.

Exchange Traded Funds

Also known as ETF. A basket of stocks similar to an index mutual fund. However, there are a number of important differences between ETFs and mutual funds. The ETF can be traded within the day, they can be shorted, purchased on margin and there even exists options on some ETFs.

Excise Tax

A domestic tax assessed on the manufacture, sale, or use of a commodity within a country. Usually refundable if the product is exported.

Exclusionary self-tender

A firm's offer to buy a given amount of its own stock while excluding targeted stockholders.

Exclusive

In the context of general equities, having sole possession of the customer order/indication; not in competition with other dealers.

Exclusive Economic Zone

The EEZ refers to the rights of coastal states to control the living and nonliving resources of the sea for 200 miles off their coasts while allowing freedom of navigation to other states beyond 12 miles, as agreed at the sixth session of the Third U.N. Conference on the Law of the Sea (UNCLOS). The EEZ also gives the coastal states the responsibility for managing the conservation of all natural resources within the 200-mile limit.

EXDEC

See: Shipper's Export Declaration.

Ex-dividend

This literally means "without dividend." The buyer of shares when they are quoted ex-dividend is not entitled to receive a declared dividend. It is the interval between the record date and the payment date during which the stock trades without its dividend-the buyer of a stock selling ex-dividend does not receive the recently declared dividend. Antithesis of cum dividend (with dividend).

Ex-dividend date

The first day of trading when the seller, rather than the buyer, of a stock will be entitled to the most recently announced dividend payment. The date set by the NYSE (and generally followed on other US exchanges) is currently two business days before the record date. A stock that has gone ex-dividend is denoted by an x in newspaper listings on that date.

EX-DOCK

From dock. Seller owns goods until they are unloaded on dock at port of discharge; selling price includes all costs so far plus cost of unloading from vessel.

Execution

The process of completing an order to buy or sell securities. Once a trade is executed, it is reported by a Confirmation Report; settlement (payment and transfer of ownership) occurs in the US between one (mutual funds) and five (stocks) days after an order is executed. Settlement times for exchange-listed stocks are in the process of being reduced to three days in the U. S. The time varies greatly across countries. In France, for example settlements are only once per month.

Execution costs

The difference between the execution price of a security and the price that would have existed in the absence of a trade, which can be further divided into market impact costs and market timing costs.

Executor

An individual or trust institution nominated in a will and appointed by a court to settle the estate of a deceased person.

Exemption

Direct reductions from gross income allowed by the IRS.

Exempt securities

Instruments exempt from the registration requirements of the Securities Act of 1933 or the margin requirements of the SEC Act of 1934. Such securities include government bonds, agencies, munis, commercial paper, and private placements

Exercise

To implement the right of the holder of an option to buy (in the case of a call) or sell (in the case of a put) the underlying security.

Exercise limit

Cap on the number of option contracts of any one class of contract that can be exercised within a five-day period contract. Stock option's exercise limit is typically 2000 contracts.

Exercise notice

A broker's notification a client want to exercise a right to buy or sell (depending on the type of contract) the underlying security of the option contract.

Exercise price

The price at which the security underlying a future or options contract may be bought or sold.

Exercise settlement amount

The difference between the exercise price fo the option and the exercise settlement value of the index on the day an exercise notice is tendered, multiplied by the index multiplier.

Exercise value

The amount of advantage over a current market transaction provided by an in-the-money option.

Exercising the option

The act of buying or selling the underlying asset via the option contract.

EX-FACTORY

Seller owns goods until they are picked up at his factory; selling price is the cost of the goods.

Exhaust price

The low price at which a broker must liquidate a client's holding in a stock purchased in a margin account in order to meet a margin call when the client cannot meet the call.

Exim bank

See: Export-Import Bank.

Exit fee

See: Back-end load.

Ex-legal

A municipal bond offered without a law firm's legal opinion. As the majority of bonds are issued with legal opinions.

Exogenous

Describes facts outside the control of the firm. Converse of endogenous.

Exogenous variable

A variable whose value is determined outside the model in which it is used. Related: Endogenous variable.

Exon-Florio

The "Exon-Florio" provision (section 721 of the Defense Production Act) provides the President with authority to investigate proposed or pending mergers, acquisitions, and takeovers by or with foreign persons to determine their effects on national security. The provision also grants the President authority to suspend or block those transactions that lead to control of a domestic firm by a foreign person if the President determines that the foreign purchaser might take actions that would threaten the national security. See:

Committee on Foreign Investment in the United States Foreign Direct Investment in the United States.

Exotic option

Refers to options that are more complex than simple puts or call options. For example, a Caput is a call option on a put option.

Expansion

Phase of the business cycle as it climbs from a trough toward a peak.

Expatriate

An employee who is a U.S. citizen living and working in a foreign country.

Expectations hypothesis theories

Theories of the term structure of interest rates, which include the pure expectations theory; the liquidity theory of the term structure, and the preferred habitat theory. These theories hold that each forward rate equals the expected future interest rate for the relevant period. These three theories differ, however, on whether other factors also affect forward rates, and how.

Expectations theory of forward exchange rates

A theory of foreign exchange rates that states that the expected future spot foreign exchange rate *t* periods from now equals the current *t*-period forward exchange rate.

Expected dividend yield

Total amount of dividends received during the life of a futures contract or total dividends received for holding a particular stock one year. See: Current yield.

Expected future cash flows

Projected future cash flows associated with an asset.

Expected future return

The return that is expected to be earned on an asset in the future. Also called the expected return.

Expedite

To accelerate delivery of goods.

Expected return

The expected return on a risky asset, given a probability distribution for the possible rates of return. Expected return equals some risk-free rate (generally the prevailing U.S. Treasury note or bond rate) plus a risk premium (the difference between the historic market return, based upon a well diversified index such as the S&P 500 and the historic US Treasury bond) multiplied by the assets beta. The conditional expected return varies through time as a function of current market information.

Expected return-beta relationship

Implication of the CAPM that security risk premiums will be proportional to beta.

Expected return on investment

The return one can expect to earn on an investment. See: Capital asset pricing model.

Expected Spot Rate

The exchange rate between two currencies that is anticipated to prevail in the spot market on a given future date. It differs from the current spot rate primarily by the extent to which inflation expectations in the two currencies differ.

Expected value

The weighted average of a probability distribution. Also known as the mean value.

Expected value of perfect information

The expected value if the future uncertain outcomes could be known minus the expected value with no additional information.

Expense ratio

The percentage of the assets that are spent to run a mutual fund (as of the last annual statement). This includes expenses such as management and advisory fees, overhead costs, and 12b-1 (distribution and advertising) fees. The expense ratio does not include brokerage costs for trading the portfolio, although these are reported as a percentage of assets to the SEC by the funds in a Statement of Additional Information (SAI). The SAI is available to shareholders on request. Neither the expense ratio nor the SAI includes the transactions costs of spreads, normally incurred in unlisted securities and foreign stocks. These two costs can add significantly to the reported expenses of a fund. The expense ratio is often termed an Operating Expense Ratio (OER).

Expensed

Charged to an expense account, fully reducing reported profit of that year, as is appropriate for expenditures for items with useful lives under one year.

Experience rating

A technique insurance companies use to determine the correct price of a policy premium.

Expiration

The time an option contract lapses.

Expiration cycle

Dates on which options on a particular security expire. A given option will be placed in one of three cycles;

the January cycle, the February cycle, or the March cycle. At any time, an option has contracts with four expiration dates outstanding: two in near-term months and two in far-term months. Last day on which an option may be exercised.

Expiration date

The last day (in the case of American-style) or the only day (in the case of European-style) on which an option may be exercised. For stock options, this date is the Saturday immediately following the third Friday of the expiration month; brokerage firms may set an earlier deadline for notification of an option holder's intention to exercise. If Friday is a holiday, the last trading day will be the preceding Thursday.

Expiration time

The time of day by which all exercise notices must be received on the expiration date. Technically, the expiration time is currently 5:00PM on the expiration date, but public holders of option contracts must indicate their desire to exercise no later than 5:30PM on the business day preceding the expiration date. The times are Eastern Time. See also Expiration Date.

Ex-pit transaction

The purchase of commodities off the exchange's floor.

Explicit Bankruptcy Costs

Specific costs incurred during the bankruptcy process such as legal fees, court costs, consultants' fees, and document preparation expenses.

Explicit tax

A tax specifically collected by a government; includes income, withholding, property, sales, and value-added taxes and tariffs.

Exploding term sheet

Venture capital jargon. Often a proposed term sheet, might explode or be null and void in a fixed period set to negotiate the final contract.

Export Administration Act

The EAA of 1979, as amended, authorizes the President to control exports of U.S. goods and technology to all foreign destinations, as necessary for the purpose of national security, foreign policy, and short supply. As the basic export administration statute, the EAA is the first big revision of export control law since enactment of the Export Control Act of 1949. The EAA is not a permanent legislation; it must be reauthorized — usually every three years. There have been reauthorizations of the EAA in 1982, 1985 (the Export Administration Amendments Act), and 1988 (Omnibus Amendments of 1988) which have changed provisions of the basic Act. The Act was extended in 1993 until June 30, 1994.

Export Administration Regulations

The Export Administration Regulations provide specific instructions on the use and types of licenses required and the types of commodities and technical data under control.

Export Administration Review Board

The EARB is a cabinet-level export licensing dispute resolution group. The EARB was originally established in June 1970 under Executive Order 11533. Under Executive Order 12755 of March 1991, EARB membership includes Commerce (as chair), State, Defense, and Energy, and Arms Control and Disarmament Agency and, as non-voting members, the Joint Chiefs of Staff and the Central Intelligence Agency. The EARB is final review body to resolve differences among agency views on the granting of an export license. [Preceding EARB review are: (a) an interagency committee <known generally as the "Operating Committee"> and (b) the Advisory Committee on Export Policy.] National Security Directive 53 requires escalation of disputes regarding an export license to the Advisory Committee on Export Policy (ACEP) not later than 100 days from the filing date of the applicant's application. Any cases not resolved at the ACEP level must be escalated to the EARB within a specified number of days of the date of the ACEP meeting. Cases not resolved by the EARB must be escalated to the President for resolution.

Export Assistance Center

An Export Assistance Center (EAC) system was established by the state of Texas to link agencies, associations, and local governments in efforts to increase exports by assisting current and prospective exporters. The US&FCS has been considering using the Texas model to develop similar export assistance networks.

Export Broker

An individual or firm that brings together buyers and sellers for a fee but does not take part in actual sales transactions.

Export Commission House

An organization which, for a commission, acts as a purchasing agent for a foreign buyer.

Export Commodity Control List

A listing administered by the U.S. Department of Commerce of items requiring validated export licenses for shipment to some or all countries.

Export Contact List Service

The ECLS is an ITA service that provides mailing lists of prospective overseas customers from ITA's file of foreign firms (the Foreign Traders Index). The ECLS identifies manufacturers, distributors, retailers, service firms, and government agencies. A summary of the information on the company includes contact information, product and service interests, and other data.

Export Control Automated Support System

ECASS was implemented by the Commerce Department in 1985 to automate a paper-based system. The system currently provides: - electronic submission of application forms directly with the use of value-added network vendors; - optical character recognition of applications submitted on paper; - paperless workstations for all licensing officers to review the application, route it to other officers, branches, or external agencies, and to enter their final action along with most riders and conditions; - automated audit of all licenses issued; and - real time management reporting on Licensing Officer workloads, average processing times, counts and times by license type, destination country, commodity code, and other data.

Export Control Classification Number

Every product has an export control classification number (formerly: Export Control Commodity Number) within the Commerce Control List. Each ECCN consists of five characters that identify the category, product group, type of control, and country group level of control.

Export Credit Agency

Public or semipublic agency that provides export credits and guarantees. Examples are the Export-Import

Bank of the United States, the Export Development Corporation (EDC) of Canada, the Export-Import Bank of Japan (JEXIM), and the Export Credits Guarantee Department (ECGD) of the United Kingdom.

Export Credit Enhanced Leverage

The export credit enhanced leverage, EXCEL, program was developed in 1990 by the World Bank in conjunction with a working group of the International Union of Credit and Investment Insurers (the Berne Union). The objective of EXCEL is to provide export credits at consensus rates for private sector borrowers in highly indebted countries, which would previously have been too great a risk for most agencies to cover.

Export Credit Guarantee Department

The ECGD of the Department of Industry and Trade is the primary source of official British export credit. The ECGD helps exporters by providing: (a) insurance against the risk of not being paid for exports and (b) guarantees to banks for exporters of capital goods, under which finance can be obtained for export business, often at a favorable rate of interest. Subject to Parliamentary approval, ECDG's short-term underwriting division, the Insurance Service Group, is to be privatized. The medium and long-term underwriting group is introducing a new system for assessing premiums which will more realistically reflect the risk involved. The Department was originally established in 1919; headquarters are in London, England.

Export Declaration

See Shipper's export declaration.

Export Development Corporation

EDC is Canada's official export credit agency, responsible for providing export credit insurance, loans, guarantees, and other financial services to promote Canadian export trade.

Export Development Office

Export Development Offices (EDOs) in seven cities (Tokyo, Sydney, Seoul, Milan, London, Mexico City, and Sao Paulo) provide services to U.S. exporters, including market research to identify specific marketing opportunities and products with the greatest sales potential; and to organize export promotion events. EDOs are staffed by U.S. and Foreign Commercial Service officers. When not in use for trade exhibitions, EDOs with exhibit and conference facilities are made available to individual firms or associations.

Export Disincentives

Export disincentives are policies which may serve to deter U.S. exports, such as sanctions, export controls, and domestic and regulatory policies with a coincidental impact of handicapping U.S. competitiveness.

Export Enhancement Act of 1992

The Export Enhancement Act of 1992 required the Trade Promotion Coordinating Committee (TPCC) to issue by September 30, 1993, and annually thereafter, a report containing "a government-wide strategic plan for Federal trade promotion efforts" and describing its implementation. The legislation requires the TPCC to establish in the strategic plan priorities for federal trade promotion and explain the rationale for these priorities. The act also requires the TPCC to include in the plan a strategy for bringing federal trade promotion activities into line with the new priorities and for improving their coordination. The TPCC is also required to propose in the plan a means for eliminating overlap among federal trade promotion activities and increasing cooperation between state and federal trade promotion efforts. The act requires that the

TPCC include in the strategic plan a proposal to the President for an annual unified budget for federal trade promotion activities. This budget is to: (a) reflect the new priorities and improved interagency coordination and (b) eliminate funding for areas of overlap and duplication among federal agencies.

Export Enhancement Program

The EEP, one of four export subsidy programs operated by the Department of Agriculture, is intended to enhance U.S. trade policy strategies and objectives and to expand U.S. agricultural exports. Under the EEP, the Agriculture Department's Commodity Credit Corporation provides bonuses to U.S. exporters to enable them to be price competitive and thereby sell U.S. agricultural products in targeted overseas markets in which competitor countries are making subsidized sales. EEP-eligible commodities have included: wheat, wheat flour, rice, frozen poultry, barley, barley malt, table eggs, feed grains and vegetable oil.

Exporter Data Base

The EDB, operating on a pilot basis in 1992, provides data on the number of exporters, their distribution in cities and states, and their economic characteristics. The EDB, developed by the Commerce Department's International Trade Administration and the Census Bureau links commodity data from millions of U.S. export declarations to the Bureau's various databases on the business characteristics of U.S. firms.

Exporter's Certificate of Origin

The U.S. Customs Service defines an Exporter's Certificate of Origin (also known as Customs Form 353) as a document completed by the exporter, certifying that the goods described therein are eligible for a preferential rate of duty under some trade program such as the U.S.-Canada Free-Trade Agreement.

Exporter's Sales Price

ESP is a statutory term used to refer to the United States sales prices of merchandise which is sold or likely to be sold in the United States, before or after the time of importation, by or for the account of the exporter. Certain statutory adjustments are made to permit a meaningful comparison with the foreign market value of such or similar merchandise, e.g., import duties, United States selling and administrative expenses, and freight are deducted from the United States price.

Export financing interest

Interest income derived from goods manufactured in the US and sold outside the US as long as not more than 50% of the value is imported into the US

Export-import Bank (Ex-IM Bank)

The US federal government agency that extends trade credits to US companies to facilitate the financing of US exports.

Export-Import Bank of Japan

JEXIM is Japan's official provider of export credits. About 10 percent of JEXIM's business is providing export credits. The bank's main role is to disburse about half the funds available under the trade surplus recycling program (the Nakasone facility).

Export-Import Bank of the U.S.

Eximbank was chartered in 1934 as an independent agency to finance the export of U.S. goods and services. Eximbank offers four major export finance support programs: loans, guarantees, working capital guarantees, and insurance. Eximbank undertakes some of the risk associated with financing the production and sale of American-made goods; provides financing to overseas customers for American goods when lenders are not prepared to finance the transactions; and enhances a U.S. exporter's ability to match foreign government subsidies by helping lenders meet lower rates, or by giving financing incentives directly to foreign buyers. Eximbank's information hotline number is 1-800-424-5201.

Export Information System

The EIS is a classified automated system for export licensing operations maintained by the Department of Energy.

Export Legal Assistance Network

The Export Legal Assistance Network, ELAN, sponsored by SBA, is a nationwide group of attorneys with experience in international trade who provide free initial consultations to small businesses on export-related matters. Telephone: 202-778-3080.

Export License

A government document (also known as an "Individual Validated License") authorizing exports of specific goods in specific quantities to a particular destination. This document may be required in some countries for most or all exports and in other countries only under special circumstances.

Export License Voice Information System

ELVIS is a BXA 24-hour on-line service which allows exporters to obtain recorded information on such topics as commodity classifications, emergency handling procedures, and seminars as well as to order information. 202-482-4811

Export Limitation

A provision that limits the recipient country's volume of exports of commodities that are the same as, or like, the commodities being furnished by the United States under a P.L. 480 ("Food for Peace") sales agreement. The export of the actual commodities is also prohibited, with the latter prohibition being termed an export restriction.

Export Limitation Period

The period during which the recipient country must restrict exports of commodities which are considered to be the same as, or like, those supplied under P.L. 480 ("Food for Peace").

Export Management Company

Export Management Company An EMC is a private firm that serves as the export department for several manufacturers, soliciting and transacting export business on behalf of its clients in return for a commission, salary, or retainer plus commission. An EMC maintains close contact with its clients and is supply-driven. An EMC may take title to the goods it sells, making a profit on the markup, or it may charge a commission, depending on the type of products being handled, the overseas market, and the manufacturer-client's needs.

Export Management Consultant (EMC)

A company serving as the export department of other firms. Normally, EMC's work on a commission basis and do not take title to the goods they export. Also see: Export Trading Company.

Export Merchant

A company that buys products directly from manufacturers, then packages and marks the merchandise for resale under its own name.

Export Processing Zones

EPZs are a form of free trade zone which provide incentives for industrial or commercial export activity.

Export processing zones are located in developing countries and are usually in defined areas, industrial parks, or facilities which provide free trade zone benefits and usually offer additional incentives, such as exemption from normal tax and business regulations. The zones, which began appearing around 1975, are sometimes referred to as Special Economic Zones or Development Economic Zones. See: Free Trade Zones.

Export Promotion

Export promotion refers to the collective programs a nation has to help companies sell products abroad. These programs may include business counseling, training, and representational assistance, as well as providing market research information, trade fair opportunities, and export financing assistance.

Export Quotas

Specific restrictions or target objectives on the value or volume of exports of specified goods imposed by the government of the exporting country. These restraints may be intended to protect domestic producers and consumers from temporary shortages of certain materials, or as a means to moderate world prices of specified commodities. Commodity agreements sometimes contain explicit provisions to indicate when export quotas should go into effect among producers. Export quotas are also used in connection with orderly marketing agreements and voluntary restraint agreements.

Export Revolving Line of Credit

The Export Revolving Line of Credit, ERLC, is a form of financial assistance provided by the Small Business Administration (SBA). The ERLC guarantees loans to U.S. firms to help bridge the working capital gap between the time inventory and production costs are disbursed until payment is received from a foreign buyer. SBA guarantees 85 percent of the ERLC subject to a $750,000 guarantee limit. The ERLC is granted on the likelihood of a company satisfactorily completing its export transaction. The guarantee covers default by the exporter, but does not cover default by a foreign buyer; failure on the buyer's side is expected to be covered by letters of credit or export credit insurance.

Under SBA's ERLC program, any number of withdrawals and repayments can be made as long as the dollar limit on the line of credit is not exceeded and disbursements are made within the stated maturity period (not more than 18 months). Proceeds can be used only to finance labor and materials needed for manufacturing, to purchase inventory to meet an export order, and to penetrate or develop foreign markets. Examples of eligible expenses for developing foreign markets include professional export marketing advice or services, foreign business travel, and trade show participation. Under the ERLC program, funds may not be used to purchase fixed assets.

Exports

Goods or services sold to parties in foreign countries.

Export Statistics

Export statistics measure the total physical quantity or value of merchandise (except for shipments to U.S. military forces overseas) moving out of the United States to foreign countries, whether such merchandise is exported from within the U.S. Customs territory or from a U.S. Customs bonded warehouse or a U.S. Foreign Trade Zone.

Export Subsidies

Generally, direct government payments or other economic inducements given to domestic producers of goods that are sold in foreign markets. The GATT recognizes the export subsidies may distort trade, unduly disturb normal commercial competition, and hinder the achievement of GATT fair trade objectives; but it does not clearly define what practices constitute export subsidies.

Export Trade Certificate of Review

A certification of partial immunity from U.S. antitrust laws that can be granted based on the Export Trading Company Act legislation by the Department of Commerce with Department of Justice concurrence. Any prospective or present U.S.-based exporter with antitrust concerns may apply for certification.

Export Trading Company

An ETC is a company doing business in the United States principally to export goods or services produced in the United States or to facilitate such exports by unaffiliated persons. The ETC can be owned by foreigners and can import, barter, and arrange sales between third countries, as well as export. An ETC is demand-driven and transaction-oriented. Generally, an ETC takes title to the products involved, but may work on a commission basis.

Export Trading Company Act

The Export Trading Company Act of 1982: initiates the Export Trade Certificate of Review program that provides antitrust preclearance for export activities; permits bankers' banks and bank holding companies to invest in ETCs; establishes a Contact Facilitation Service within the Commerce Department designed to facilitate contact between firms that produce exportable goods and services and firms that provide export trade services.

Ex post return

Related: Holding-period return

Expost average rate of return

The historical mean percentage an asset has yielded.

Exposure netting

Offsetting exposures in one currency with exposures in the same or another currency, when exchange rates are expected to move in such a way that losses or gains on the first exposed position should be offset by gains or losses on the second currency exposure.

Expropriation

The official seizure by a government of private property. Any government has the right to seize such property, according to international law, if prompt and adequate compensation is given.

Expunge

Used in the context of general equities. Remove any trace of an Auto indication's existence at any time. See: Cancel.

Ex-Quay

"Ex Quay" means that the seller makes the goods available to the buyer on the quay (wharf) at the destination named in the sales contract. The seller has to bear the full cost and risk involved in bringing the goods there. There are two "Ex Quay" contracts in use: (a) Ex Quay "duty paid" and (b) Ex Quay "duties on buyer's account" in which the liability to clear goods for import is to be met by the buyer instead of by the seller.

Ex-rights

Shares of stock that are trading without rights attached.

Ex-rights date

The date on which a share of common stock begins trading ex-rights.

Ex-Ship

"Ex Ship" means that the seller will make the goods available to the buyer on board the ship at the destination named in the sales contract. The seller bears all costs and risks involved in bringing the goods to the destination.

Ex-stock dividends

The time period between the announcement of a stock dividend and its actual payment. The buyer of shares during this time period does is not entitled to the dividend.

Extendable bond

Bond whose maturity can be extended at the option of the lender or issuer.

Extendable notes

Note with maturity that can be extended by mutual agreement between the issuer and investors.

Extended Fund Facility

The EEF is an arrangement by which the International Monetary Fund (IMF) may provide assistance to its members to enable them to meet their balance of payments needs for longer periods and in larger amounts than are available under the IMF's credit tranche policies.

Extension

Voluntary arrangements to restructure a firm's debt, under which the payment date is postponed.

Extension date

The day on which the first option either expires or is extended.

Extension swap

Extending maturity through a swap, e.g. selling a 2-year note and buying one with a slightly longer current maturity.

External finance

Funding that is not generated by a firm's operations: new borrowing or a stock issue.

External funds

Funds originating from a source outside the corporation to increase cash flow and to aid in expansion efforts, e.g., bank loan or bond offering.

External market

Also referred to as the international market, the offshore market, or, more popularly, the Euromarket. A mechanism for trading securities that at issuance (1) are offered simultaneously to investors in a number of countries and (2) are issued outside the jurisdiction of any single country. Related: Internal market.

Extinguish

Retire or pay off debt.

Extra Dividend

A temporary increase in a firm's dividends beyond the normal level.

Extraordinary call

Early redemption of a revenue bond because the revenue source paying the interest on the bond has been eliminated or has disappeared.

Extraordinary item

An unusual and unexpected one-time event that must be explained to shareholders in an annual or quarterly report, e.g., write down for a discontinued operation, employee fraud, a lawsuit, or other one-time events. Results are often presented with and without these items. The logic of excluding these items is that investors a better notion of future performance if one-time events are excluded.

Extra or special dividends

A dividend that is paid in addition to a firm's established or expected quarterly dividend.

Extraordinary positive value

A positive net present value.

Extrapolative statistical models

Models that apply a formula to historical data and project results for a future period. Such models include the simple linear trend model, the simple exponential model, and the simple autoregressive model.

Ex-warrants

Describes a stock sale in which the buyer is not entitled to the warrant accompanying the stock.

Ex-Works

Ex Works Ex Works (EXW) at a named point of origin (examples are: ex factory, ex mill, ex warehouse). Under this term, the price quoted applies only at the point of origin and the seller agrees to place the goods at the disposal of the buyer at a specified place on the date or within the period fixed. All other charges are for the account of the buyer.

F

Fifth letter of a Nasdaq stock symbol specifying that the issue is a foreign company.

FAC

See: Federal Advisory Council.

Face-amount certificate

A debt security issued by face amount. The holder makes payments periodically to the issues, and the issuer promises to pay the purchaser the face value at maturity or the surrendered value if the security is presented by the maturity specified in the certificate.

Face value

See: Par value.

Facilitation

The process of providing a market for a security. Normally, this refers to bids and offers made for large blocks of securities, such as those traded by institutions. Listed options may be used to offset part of the risk assumed by the trader who is facilitation the large block order. See also: Hedge ratio.

Factor

A financial institution that buys a firm's accounts receivable and collects the accounts.

Factor analysis

A statistical procedure that seeks to explain a certain phenomenon, such as the return on a common stock, in terms of the behavior of a set of predictive factors.

Factoring

Factoring is the discounting of a foreign account receivable that does not involve a draft. The exporter transfers title to its foreign accounts receivable to a factoring house (an organization that specializes in the financing of account receivable) for cash at a discount from the face value. Although factoring is often done without recourse to the exporter, the specific arrangements should be verified by the exporter. Factoring of foreign accounts receivables is less common than factoring of domestic receivables.

Factoring Houses

Certain companies which purchase export receivables (e.g., the invoices to foreign buyers) at a discounted price, usually about two to four percent less than their face value.

Factor model

A way of decomposing the forces that influence a security's rate of return into common and firm-specific influences.

Factor portfolio

A well-diversified portfolio constructed to have a beta of 1.0 on one factor and a beta of zero on any other factors.

Factor Return

The return attributable to a particular common factor. We decompose asset returns into a common factor component, based on the asset's exposures to common factors times the factor returns, and a specific return.

Fade

Refers to over-the-counter trading. Fill another OTC dealer's bid for or offer of stock.

Fail

A deal is said to fail if on the settlement date either the seller does not deliver securities in proper form or the buyer does not to deliver funds in proper form.

Fair-and-equitable test

A set of requirements for a plan of reorganization to be approved by the bankruptcy court.

Fair game

An investment prospect that has a zero risk premium.

Fair market price

Amount at which an asset would change hands between two parties, that both have knowledge of the relevant facts. Also referred to as market price.

Fair price

The equilibrium price for futures contracts. Also called the theoretical futures price, which equals the spot price continuously compounded at the cost of carry rate for some time interval. In the context of corporate goverance, Fair-Price provisions limit the range of prices a bidder can pay in two-tier offers. They typically require a bidder to pay to all shareholders the highest price paid to any during a specified period of time before the commencement of a tender offer and do not apply if the deal is approved by the board of directors or a supermajority of the target's shareholders. The goal of this provision is to prevent pressure on the target's shareholders to tender their shares in the front end of a two-tiered tender offer, and they have the result of making such and acquisition more expensive. A majority of states have fair price laws.

Fair price provision

See:Appraisal rights.

Fair rate of return

The rate of return that state governments allow a public utility to earn on its investments and expenditures. Utilities then use these profits to pay investors and provide service upgrades to their customers.

Fair Value

The reference against which U.S. purchase prices of imported merchandise are compared during an anti-dumping investigation. Generally expressed as the weighted average of the exporter's domestic market prices, or prices of exports to third countries during the period of investigation. In some cases fair value is the constructed value. Constructed value is used if there are no, or virtually no, home market or third country sales or if the number of such sales made at prices below the cost of production is so great that remaining sales above the cost of production provide an inadequate basis for comparison.

Fairness opinion

An investment banker's professional opinion as to the price an acquiring firm is offering in a takeover or merger.

Fall Down

In the context of general equities, may not be able to produce as indicated in one's advertised market, due to less help (than anticipated) from other parties or due to changing market conditions.

Fall out of bed

A sudden drop in a stock's price resulting from failed or poor business deals gone bad or falling through.

Fallen angels

Bonds that at the time of issue were considered investment grade but that have dropped below that rating over time.

Fallout risk

A type of mortgage pipeline risk that is generally created when the terms of the loan to be originated are set at the same time the sale terms are established. The risk is that either of the two parties, borrower or investor, fails to close and the loan "falls out" of the pipeline.

Fama, Eugene F.

Finance professor at the University of Chicago. Developer of the Efficient Markets Hypothesis.

Family of funds

Different mutual funds offered by one investment company.

FAPT

Foreign Asset Protection Trust.

Far month

Used in the context of option or futures to refer to the trading month of the contract that is farthest away. Antithesis of nearest month.

Farther out; farther in

Used in the context of options to refer to the relative length of option contract maturities.

FAS

Free alongside ship. A pricing term indicating that the quoted price includes the cost of delivering the goods alongside a designated vessel.

FASB

See: Financial Accounting Standards Board.

FASB No. 8

U.S. accounting standard that requires US firms to translate their foreign affiliates' accounts by the temporal method; that is reporting gains and losses from currency fluctuations in current income. It was in effect between 1975 and 1981 and became the most controversial accounting standard in the US It was replaced by FASB No. 52 in 1981.

FASB No. 52

The US accounting standard that replaced FASB No. 8. US companies are required to translate foreign accounts in terms of the current rate and report the changes from currency fluctuations in a cumulative translation adjustment account in the equity section of the balance sheet.

Fast market

Excessively rapid trading in a specific security that causes a delay in the electronic updating of its last sale and market conditions, particularly in options.

Fast Track

Fast track procedures for approval of trade agreements were included by Congress in trade legislation in 1974, in 1979, and again in the 1988 Trade Act. Fast track provides two guarantees essential to the successful negotiation of trade agreements: (1) a vote on implementing legislation within a fixed period of time, and (2) a vote, up or down, with no amendments to that legislation. Provisions in the Omnibus Trade and Competitiveness Act of 1988 include that the foreign country request negotiation of an FTA and that the President give the Congress a 60-legislative-day notice of intent to negotiate an FTA. During the 60-legislative-day period, either committee can disapprove fast track authority by a majority vote. Disapproval would likely end the possibility of FTA negotiations. The 60-legislative-days can translate into five to ten months of calendar time, depending on the Congressional schedule. Formal negotiations would begin following this 60-day Congressional consideration period.

Favorable Balance of Trade

The value of a nation's exports in excess of the value of its imports.

Favorable trade balance

Condition that total exports of a nation exceed total imports, creating a net export.

FCA

"Free carrier" to named place. Replaces the former term "FOB named inland port" to designate the seller's responsibility for the cost of loading goods at the named shipping point. May be used for multimodal transport, container stations, and any mode of transport, including air.

FCC

Foreign Controlled Corporation.

FCIA

See: Foreign Credit Insurance Association.

FCM

See: Futures commission merchant.

F.C.& S.

Free of Capture & Seizure - Clause excluding war risks from the Marine Policy; war risks can be covered by issuing a separate War Policy with an additional premium being charged.

FDI

See: Foreign direct investment.

FDIC

See: Federal Deposit Insurance Corporation.

Feasible portfolio

A portfolio that an investor can construct, given the assets available.

Feasible set of portfolios

The collection of all feasible portfolios.

Feasible target payout ratios

Payout ratios that are consistent with the level of excess funds available to make cash dividend payments.

F.E.C.

See under Foreign Exchange Certificate.

FED Pass

A Federal Reserve action adding more reserves to the banking system, increasing the money available for lending, and making credit easier to attain.

Federal Advisory Council (FAC)

Advisory group made up of one representative (in most cases a banker) from each of the 12 Federal Reserve districts. Established by the Federal REserve Act, the council meets periodically with the Board of Governors to discuss business and financial conditions and make recommendations.

Federal agency bond

Fixed-income security issued by a government agency such as FNMA.

Federal agency securities

Securities issued by corporations and agencies created by the US government, such as the Federal Home Loan Bank Board and Ginnie Mae.

Federal Agricultural Mortgage Corporation (Farmer Mac)

A federal agency chartered in 1988 to provide a secondary market for farm mortgage loans.

Federal credit agencies

Agencies of the federal government set up to supply credit to various classes of institutions and individuals, e.g., S&Ls, small business firms, students, farmers, and exporters.

Federal deficit (surplus)

When federal government expenditures are exceeded by federal government revenue.

Federal Deposit Insurance Corporation (FDIC)

A federal institution that insures bank deposits.

Federal Farm Credit Bank

An institution created by the government with the purpose of uniting the financing activities of the federal land banks, the federal intermediate credit banks, and the banks for cooperatives. See: Federal Farm Credit System.

Federal Farm Credit System

A system chartered in 1971 through the farm credit act providing farmers with credit services through a federal land bank, a federal intermediate credit bank, and a bank for cooperatives. See: Federal Farm Credit Bank.

Federal Financing Bank

A federal institution that lends to a wide array of federal credit agencies funds it obtains by borrowing from the US Treasury.

Federal funds

Noninterest-bearing deposits held in reserve for depository institutions at their district Federal Reserve Bank. Also, excess reserves lent by banks to each other.

Federal funds market

The market in which banks can borrow or lend reserves, allowing banks temporarily short of their required reserves to borrow reserves from banks that have excess reserves.

Federal funds rate

The interest rate that banks with excess reserves at a Federal Reserve district bank charge other banks that need overnight loans. The Fed funds rate, as it is called, often points to the direction of US interest rates. The most sensitive indicator of the direction of interest rates, since it is set daily by the market, unlike the prime rate and the discount rate.

Federal Grain Inspection Service

FGIS certifies that grain produced in the United States meets the official United States Standards for Grain. As part of its responsibilities, FGIS works with international traders. Before any grain can be exported from the United States, it must first be certified by FGIS as having met a specific standard. FGIS staff explain the national inspection system, U.S. grain standards, and commodity inspection programs; conduct briefings and tours; assess foreign inspection and weighing techniques; and respond to inquiries about quality and quantity of U.S. grain exports. FGIS agencies in eight states are delegated authority to perform official export services at ports.

Federal gift tax

A federal tax imposed on assets conveyed as gifts to individuals.

Federal Home Loan Banks

The institutions that regulate and lend to savings and loan associations. The Federal Home Loan Banks play a role analogous to that played by the Federal Reserve Banks vis-à-vis member commercial banks.

Federal Home Loan Mortgage Corporation (FHLMC)

See: Freddie Mac

Federal Housing Administration (FHA)

Federally sponsored agency chartered in 1934 whose stock is currently owned by savings institutions across the United States. The agency buys residential mortgages that meet certain requirements, sells these mortgages in packages, and insures the lenders against loss.

Federal Housing Finance Board (FHFB)

US government agency chartered in 1989 to assume the responsibilities formerly held by the Federal Home Loan Bank system.

Federal Intermediate Credit Bank

A bank sponsored by the federal government to provide funds to institutions making loans to farmers.

Federal intrafund transactions

Intrabudgetary transactions in which payments and receipts both occur within the same Federal fund group.

Federal Land Bank

A bank administered under the US Farm Credit Administration that provides long-term mortgage credit to farmers for agriculture-related expenditures.

Federal margin call

A broker's demand upon a customer for cash, or securities needed to satisfy the required Regulation T down payment for a purchase or short sale of securities.

Federal Maritime Commission (FMC)

A U.S. government agency that regulates and administers the shipping industry. This agency also grants freight forwarder licenses.

Federal National Mortgage Association (Fannie Mae)

A publicly owned, government-sponsored corporation chartered in 1938 to purchase mortgages from lenders and resell them to investors. Known by the nickname Fannie Mae, it packages mortgages backed by the Federal Housing Administration, but also sells some nongovernment-backed mortgages.

Federal Open Market Committee (FOMC)

The body that is responsible for setting the interest rates and credit policies of the Federal Reserve System.

Federal Reserve Act of 1913

Federal legislation that established the Federal Reserve System.

Federal Reserve Bank

One of the 12 member banks constituting the Federal Reserve System that is responsible for overseeing the commercial and savings banks of its region to ensure their compliance with regulation.

Federal Reserve District (Reserve district or district)

One of the twelve geographic regions served by a Federal Reserve Bank.

Federal Reserve Board (FRB)

The seven-member governing body of the Federal Reserve System, which is responsible for setting reserve requirements, and the discount rate, and making other key economic decisions.

Federal Reserve float

Float is checkbook money that appears on the books of both the check writer (the payor) and the check receiver (the payee) while a check is being processed. Federal Reserve float is float present during the Federal Reserve's check collection process. To promote efficiency in the payments system and provide certainly about the date that deposited funds will become available to the receiving depository institutions (and the payee), the Federal Reserve credits the reserve accounts of banks that deposit check according to a fixed schedule. However, processing certain checks and collecting funds from the banks on which these checks are written may take more time than the schedule allows. Therefore, the accounts of some banks may be credited before the Federal Reserve is able to collect payment from other banks, resulting in Federal Reserve float.

Federal Reserve notes

Issues by the US government to the public through the Federal Reserve Banks and their member banks. They represent money owed by the government to the public. Currently, the item "Federal Reserve notes amounts outstanding" consists of new series issues. The Federal Reserve note is the only class of currency currently issued.

Federal Reserve System

The monetary authority of the US, established in 1913, and governed by the Federal Reserve Board located in Washington, D.C. The system includes 12 Federal Reserve Banks and is authorized to regulate monetary policy in the US as well as to supervise Federal Reserve member banks, bank holding companies, international operations of US banks, and US operations of foreign banks.

Federal Savings and Loan Association

An institution chartered by the federal government whose primary function is to collect savings deposits and to provide mortgage loans.

Federally related institutions

Arms of the federal government exempt from SEC registration whose securities are backed by the full faith and credit of the US government (with the exception of the Tennessee Valley Authority).

Fedwire

A wire transfer system for high-value payments operated by the Federal Reserve System.

Fee table

Schedule found in a mutual fund's prospectus that discloses and illustrates the expenses and fees a shareholder will incur.

Fee-and-commission compensation

See: Fee-based compensation

Fee-based compensation

Payment to a financial adviser of a set hourly rate, or an agreed-upon percentage of assets under management, for a financial plan. When the plan is implemented, the adviser may also receive commission on some or all of the investment products purchased, which would be fee-and-commission compensation.

Fee-only compensation

Payment to a financial adviser of a set hourly rate, or an agreed-upon percentage of assets under management, for a financial plan.

Feedback Systems

An equation where the output becomes the input in the next iteration. This is much like a public address system where the microphone is placed next to the speakers generating feedback as the signal is looped through the PA system.

FFO

See: Funds from operations.

FHA prepayment experience

The percentage of loans in a pool of mortgages outstanding at the origination anniversary, based on annual statistical historic survival rates for FHA-insured mortgages.

FI

(1) The two-character ISO 3166 country code for FINLAND. (2) Free in. A pricing term indicating that the charterer of a vessel is responsible for the cost of loading and unloading goods from the vessel.

Fiat money

Nonconvertible paper money.

FICO

See: Financing corporation.

Fictitious credit

A margin account's credit balance. Fictitious credit exists after the proceeds from a short sale are accounted for with respect to the margin requirement. The proceeds from the short sale are reflected as a credit, but must stay in the account to serve as security for the loan of securities made in a short sale, and are therefore inaccessible to the client for withdrawal.

Fidelity bond

See: Blanket fidelity bond.

Fiduciary

One who must act for the benefit of another party.

Field warehouse

Warehouse rented by a company on another firm's premises.

FIFO

See: First in, first out.

Figure

Refers to details about price including the bid and ofter. See: Handle

Figuring the tail

Calculating the yield at which a future money market (one available some period hence) is purchased when that future security is created by buying an existing instrument and financing the initial portion of its life with a term repo.

Fill

The price at which an order is executed.

Fill or kill order (FOK)

A trading order that is canceled unless executed within a designated time period. A market or limited price order that is to be executed in its entirety as soon as it is represented in the trading crowd, and, if not so executed, is to be treated as canceled. For purposes of this definition, a stop is considered an execution. Equivalent to AON and IOC simultaneously.

Filter

A rule that stipulates when a security should be bought or sold according to its price action.

FIM

The ISO 4217 currency code for the Finnish Markka.

Final Determination

The International Trade Administration makes a final determination after the investigation of sales at "less than fair value" and the receipt of comments from interested parties. This determination usually is made within 75 days after the date a preliminary determination is made. However, if the preliminary determination was affirmative, the exporters who account for a significant proportion of the merchandise under consideration may request, in writing, a postponement of this determination. If the preliminary determination was negative, the petitioner may likewise request a postponement. In neither case can this postponement be more than 135 days after the date of the preliminary determination. If the final determination is affirmative and follows a negative preliminary determination, the matter is referred to the International Trade Commission for a determination of the injury caused or threatened by the sales at less than fair value. (Had the preliminary determination been affirmative, the ITC would have begun its investigation at that time.) Not later than 45 days after the date the International Trade Administration makes an affirmative final determination, in a case where the preliminary determination also was affirmative, the International Trade Commission must render its decision on injury. Where the preliminary determination was negative, the ITC must render a decision not later than 75 days after the affirmative final determination. A negative final determination by the Assistant Secretary for Import Administration terminates an antidumping investigation.

Finance

A discipline concerned with determining value and making decisions. The finance function allocates resources, including the acquiring, investing, and managing of resources.

Finance charge

The total cost of credit a customer must pay on a consumer loan, including interest.

Finance company

A company whose business and primary function is to make loans to individuals, while not receiving deposits like a bank.

Financial Accounting Standards Board (FASB)

Board composed of independent members who create and interpret Generally Accepted Accounting Principles (GAAP).

Financial adviser

A professional offering financial advice to clients for a fee and/or commission.

Financial analysis

Analysis of a company's financial statement, often by financial analysts.

Financial analysts

Also called securities analysts and investment analysts. Professionals who analyze financial statements, interview corporate executives, and attend trade shows, in order to write reports recommending either purchasing, selling, or holding various stocks.

Financial assets

Claims on real assets.

Financial control

The management of a firm's costs and expenses in relation to budgeted amounts.

Financial distress

Events preceding and including bankruptcy, such as violation of loan contracts.

Financial distress costs

Legal and administrative costs of liquidation or reorganization. Also includes implied costs associated with impaired ability to do business (indirect costs).

Financial engineering

Combining or carving up existing instruments to create new financial products.

Financial future

A contract entered into now that provides for the delivery of a specified asset in exchange for the selling price at some specified future date.

Financial guarantee insurance

Insurance created to cover losses from specified financial transactions.

Financial innovation

Design of any new financial product, such as exotic currency options and swaps.

Financial institution

An enterprise such as a bank whose primary business and function is to collect money from the public and invest it in financial assets such as stocks and bonds.

Financial institution buyer credit policy

Insurance coverage for loans by banks to foreign buyers of exports.

Financial Institutions Reform, Recovery and Enforcement Act of 1989 (FIRREA)

Legislation that established the Office of Thrift Supervision, which was created in the wake of the savings and loan crisis of the late 1980s.

Financial intermediaries

Institutions that provide the market function of matching borrowers and lenders or traders.

Financial lease

Long-term, noncancellable rental agreement.

Financial leverage

Use of debt to increase the expected return on equity. Financial leverage is measured by the ratio of debt to debt plus equity.

Financial leverage clientele

A group of investors who have a preference for investing in firms that adhere to a particular financial leverage policy.

Financial leverage ratios

Common ratios are debt divided by equity a debt divided by the sum of debt plus equity. Related: capitalization ratios.

Financial market

An organized institutional structure or mechanism for creating and exchanging financial assets.

Financial needs approach

A method of establishing the amount of life insurance required by an individual by estimating the financial needs of dependents in the event of the individual's death.

Financial objectives

Goals related to returns that a firm will strive to accomplish during the period covered by its financial plan.

Financial plan

A blueprint relating to the financial future of a firm.

Financial planner

An investment professional who assists individuals with long- and short-term financial goals.

Financial planning

Evaluating the investing and financing options available to a firm. Planning includes attempting to make optimal decisions, projecting the consequences of these decisions for the firm in the form of a financial plan, and then comparing future performance against that plan.

Financial policy

Criteria describing a corporation's choices regarding its debt/equity mix, currencies of denomination, maturity structure, method of financing investment projects, and hedging decisions with a goal of maximizing the value of the firm to some set of stockholders.

Financial position

The account status of a firm's or individual's assets, liabilities, and equity positions as reflected on its financial statement.

Financial press

Media devoted to reporting financial news.

Financial price risk

The chance there will be unexpected changes in a financial price, including currency (foreign exchange) risk, interest rate risk, and commodity price risk.

Financial public relations

Public relations division of a company charged with cultivating positive investor relations and proper disclosure information.

Financial pyramid

A risk structure that spreads investor's risks across low-, medium-, and high-risk vehicles. The bulk of the assets are in safe, low-risk investments that provide a predictable return (base of the pyramid). At the top of the pyramid are a few high-risk ventures that have a modest chance of success.

Financial ratio

The result of dividing one financial statement item by another. Ratios help analysts interpret financial statements by focusing on specific relationships.

Financial risk

The risk that the cash flow of an issuer will not be adequate to meet its financial obligations. Also referred to as the additional risk that a firm's stockholder bears when the firm uses debt and equity.

Financial service income

Income from delivery of financial services such as banking, insurance, leasing, or financial service management fees.

Financial statement

A report of basic accounting data that helps investors understand a firm's financial history and activities.

Financial statement analysis

Evaluation of a firm's financial statements in order to assess the firm's worth and its ability to meet its financial obligations.

Financial strategy

Practices a firm adopts to pursue its financial objectives.

Financial structure

The way in which a company's assets are financed, such as short-term borrowings, long-term debt, and ownership equity. Financial structure differs from capital structure in that capital structure accounts for long-term debt and equity only.

Financial supermarket

A company offering a wide variety of financial services such as a combination of banking services, stock, and insurance brokerage.

Financial tables

Tables found in newspapers listing prices, dividends, yields, price-earnings ratios, trading volume, and other important data on stocks, bonds, mutual funds, and futures contracts.

Financial Times (F-T)-Actuaries indexes

Share price indexes for U.K. companies The denominator in the index formula is the market capitalization at the base date, adjusted for all capital changes affecting the particular index since the base date. See: Footsie (FTSE) (pronounced footsie).

Financing Corporation (FICO)

A government agency chartered in 1987 to bail out the Federal Savings and Loan Insurance Corporation (FSLIC) by issuing bonds.

Financing decisions

Decisions concerning the liabilities and stockholders' equity side of the firm's balance sheet, such as a decision to issue bonds.

Financing Intermediaries

Institutions that effect agreement terms between borrower and lender by reaching separate agreements with the borrower and the lender.

Financing Cost Savings

A source of competitive advantage that depends on access to low cost sources of capital.

Finder's fee

A fee a person or company charges for service as an intermediary in a transaction.

Fines, Penalties, and Forfeitures System

The Fines, Penalties, and Forfeitures System, FPFS, a part of Customs' Automated Commercial System, is used to assess, control, and process penalties resulting from violations of law or Customs regulations. FPFS provides retrieval of case information for monitoring case status.

FINEX

The financial futures and options division of the New York Cotton Exchange (NYCE), with a trading floor in Dublin, FINEX Europe, creating a 24-hour market in most FINEX contracts.

Finish

Used in the context of general equities. See: Fill.

Finite-Life Real Estate Investment Trust (FREIT)

A Real Estate Investment Trust whose priority is to sell its holdings within a specified period to realize capital gains.

Firewall

The legal barrier between banking and broker/dealer operations within a financial institution created to prevent the exchange of inside information.

Firm

Refers to an order to buy or sell that can be executed without confirmation for some fixed period. Also, a synonym for company.

Firm anomalies

Trading strategies that generate abnormal returns based on firm-specific characteristics.

Firm commitment underwriting

An undorwriting in which an investment banking firm commits to buy and sell an entire issue of stock and assumes all financial responsibility for any unsold shares.

Firm market

In the context of general equities, prices at which a security can actually be bought or sold in decent sizes, as compared to an inside market with very little depth. See: Actual market.

Firm order

In the context of general equities, (1) order to buy or sell for the proprietary account of the broker-dealer firm; (2) buy or sell order not conditional upon the customer's confirmation.

Firm quote

A definite price on a round-lot bid or offer declared by a market maker on a given security and not identified as a nominal quotation (therefore is not negotiable).

Firm-specific news

News that affects only a specific firm. Market news by contrast affects many firms.

Firm's net value of debt

Total firm value minus total firm debt.

FIRREA

See: Financial Institutions Reform, Recovery and Enforcement Act of 1989.

First board

The Chicago Board of Trade's established dates for delivery on futures contracts.

First call

With collateralized mortgage obligation (CMOs.), the start of the cash flow cycle for the cash flow window.

First call date

A date stated in an indenture, that is the first date on which the issuer may redeem a bond either partially or completely.

First In, First Out (FIFO)

An accounting method for valuing the cost of goods sold that uses the cost of the oldest item in inventory first.

First market

Exchange-traded securities.

First mortgage

A type of mortgage that through a lien gives precedence to the lender of the first mortgage over all other lenders in case of default.

First notice day

The first day, varying by contracts and exchanges, on which notices of intent to deliver actual financial instruments or physical commodities against futures are authorized.

First-pass regression

A time series regression to estimate the betas of securities portfolios.

First preferred stock

A type of preferred stock that has priority over other preferred issues and common stock when claiming dividends and assets.

Fiscal agency agreement

An alternative to a bond trust deed. Unlike the trustee, the fiscal agent acts as a representative of the borrower.

Fiscal agency services

Services performed by the Federal Reserve Banks for the U.S. government. These include maintaining deposit accounts for the Treasury Department, paying U.S. government checks drawn on the Treasury, and issuing and redeeming savings bonds and other government securities.

Fiscal policy

Government spending and taxing for the specific purpose of stabilizing the economy.

Fiscal year (FY)

Accounting period covering 12 consecutive months over which a company determines earnings and profits. The fiscal year serves as a period of reference for the company and does not necessarily correspond to the calendar year.

Fiscal year-end

The end of a 12-month accounting period.

Fisher effect

A theory that nominal interest rates in two or more countries should be equal to the required real rate of return to investors plus compensation for the expected amount of inflation in each country.

Fisher's separation theorem

The notion that a firm's choice of investments is separate from its owner's attitudes toward investments. Also referred to as portfolio separation theorem.

Fit

The matching of the investor's requirements and needs such as risk tolerance and growth potential preference with a specific investment.

Fitch sheet

Used in the context of general equities. Chronological listing of trades in a security showing the price, size, exchange, and time (to the second) of the trades; obtained by hitting "#M" on Quotron.

Five Cs of credit

Five characteristics that are used to form a judgment about a customer's creditworthiness: character, capacity, capital, collateral, and conditions.

Five hundred dollar rule

A rule of the Federal Reserve that excludes deficiencies of $500 or less in margin requirements as a necessary reason for the firm to liquidate the client's account to cover a margin call.

Five-K Countries .... 5(k) Countries

Those countries as defined under Section 5(k) of the Export Administration Act. Such countries are eligible for some or all of the same treatment as CoCom countries in relation to export control requirements if those countries maintain comparable export control programs.

Five percent rule

A rule of the National Association of Securities Dealers providing ethical guidelines for spreads created by market makers and commissions charged by brokers.

Fixation

The process of setting a price of a commodity, whether in the present or the future. See: Gold fixing.

Fixed asset

Long-lived property owned by a firm that is used by a firm in the production of its income. Tangible fixed assets include real estate, plant, and equipment. Intangible fixed assets include patents, trademarks, and customer recognition.

Fixed asset turnover ratio

The ratio of sales to fixed assets.

Fixed annuities

Contracts in which an insurance company or issuing financial institution pays a fixed dollar amount of money per period.

Fixed benefits

Payments to a beneficiary that are paid in fixed preset amounts and are not variable.

Fixed-charge coverage ratio

A measure of a firm's ability to meet its fixed-charge obligations: the ratio of (net earnings before taxes plus interest charges paid plus long-term lease payments) to (interest charges paid plus long-term lease payments).

Fixed cost

A cost that is fixed in total for a given period of time and for given production levels.

Fixed dates

In the Euromarket, the standard periods for which Euros are traded (one month out to a year out) are referred to as the fixed dates.

Fixed-dollar obligations

Conventional bonds for which the coupon rate is set at a fixed percentage of the par value.

Fixed-dollar security

A nonnegotiable debt security that can be redeemed at some fixed price or according to some schedule of fixed values, e.g., bank deposits and government savings bonds.

Fixed exchange rate

A country's decision to tie the value of its currency to another country's currency, gold (or another commodity), or a basket of currencies.

Fixed for floating swap

An interest rate swap in which the fixed rate payments are traded for a floating rate.

Fixed income equivalent

Also called a busted convertible. Convertible security that is trading like a straight security because the optioned common stock is trading well below the conversion price.

Fixed income instruments

Assets that pay a fixed dollar amount, such as bonds and preferred stock.

Fixed income market

The market for trading bonds and preferred stock.

Fixed-income securities

Investments that have specific interest rates, such as bonds.

Fixed premium

Payments of a fixed, equal amounts paid to an insurance company for insurance or an annuity.

Fixed price basis

An offering of securities at a fixed price.

Fixed-price tender offer

A one-time offer to purchase a stated number of shares at a stated fixed price, usually at a premium over the current market price.

Fixed rate

A traditional approach to determining the finance charge payable on an extension of credit. A predetermined and certain rate of interest is applied to the principal.

Fixed-rate loan

A loan whose rate is fixed for the life of the loan.

Fixed-rate payer

In an interest rate swap, the counterparty who pays a fixed rate, usually in exchange for a floating-rate payment.

Fixed-term reverse mortgage

A mortgage in which the lending institution provides payments to a homeowner for a fixed number of years.

Fixed trust

A unit investment trust consisting of securities that were agreed upon at the time of investment and do not change.

FJ

The two-character ISO 3166 country code for FIJI.

FJD

The ISO 4217 currency code for the Fijian Dollar.

FK

The two-character ISO 3166 country code for FALKLAND ISLANDS (MALVINAS).

FKP

The ISO 4217 currency code for the Falkland Islands Pound.

Flag

A pattern reflecting price fluctuations within a narrow range, generating a rectangular area on a graph both prior to and after sharp rises or declines.

Flag of Convenience

A ship registered under the flag of a nation which offers conveniences in the areas of taxes, crew, and safety requirements.

Flash

Value of a security displayed, or flashed across the tape, when the tape display cannot keep up with volume on an exchange and lags the current price is lagged more than approximately five minutes.

Flat

Convertibles: Earning interest on the date of payment only.

General: Having neither a short nor a long position in a stock. Clean.

Market: Characterized by horizontal price movement, usually the result of low activity.

Equities: To execute without commission or markup.

Flat benefit formula

Method used to determine a participant's benefits in a defined benefit plan by multiplying months of service by a flat monthly benefit.

Flat price (also clean price)

The quoted newspaper price of a bond that does not include accrued interest. The price paid by the purchaser is the full price.

Flat price risk

Taking a position either long or short that does not involve spreading.

Flat scale

The pattern for new issues where shorter- and longer-term yields display very little difference over the bond's maturity range.

Flat tax

A tax which is levied at the same rate on all levels of income. Antithesis of progressive tax.

Flat trades

A bond in default trades flat; that is, the price quoted covers both principal and unpaid accrued interest. Any security that trades without accrued interest or at a price that includes accrued interest is said to trade flat.

Flattening of the yield curve

A change in the yield curve when the spread between the yield on long-term and short-term Treasuries has decreased. Compare steepening of the yield curve and butterfly shift.

FLEX Options

Exchange traded equity or index options, where the investor can specify within certain limits, the terms of the options, such as exercise price Expiration date, exercise type, and settlement calculation.

Flexible budget

A budget that shows how costs vary with different rates of output or at different levels of sales volume and projects revenue based on these different output levels.

Flexible expenses

Expenses for an individual or corporation that can be adjusted or completely dispessed with, e.g., luxury goods.

Flexible mutual fund

Fund that invests in a variety of securities in varying proportions in order to maximize shareholder returns while maintaining a low level of risk.

Flight to quality

The tendency of investors to move toward safer investments (often government bonds) during periods of high economic uncertainty.

Flip-flop note

Note that allows investors to switch between two different types of debt.

Flip side

In the context of general equities, opposite side to a proposition or position (buy, if sell is the proposition and vice versa).

Flipping

Buying shares in an initial public offering (IPO), and then selling the shares immediately after the start of public trading to turn an immediate profit.

Float

Currency: Exchange rate policy that does not limit the range of the market rate.

Equities: Number of shares of a corporation that are outstanding and available for trading by the public, excluding insiders or restricted stock on a when-issued basis. A stock's volatility is inversely correlated to its float.

Floater

A bond whose interest rate varies with the interest rate of another debt instrument, e.g., a bond that has the interest rate of the Treasury bill +.25%.

Floating debt

Short-term debt that is renewed and refinanced constantly to fund capital needs of a firm or institution.

Floating exchange rate

A country's decision to allow its currency value to change freely. The currency is not constrained by central bank intervention and does not have to maintain its relationship with another currency in a narrow band. The currency value is determined by trading in the foreign exchange market.

Floating exchange rate system

Purchase or sale of the currencies of other nations by a central bank for the purpose of influencing foreign exchange rates or maintaining orderly foreign exchange markets. Also called foreign-exchange market intervention.

Floating lien

General attachment against a company's assets or against a particular class of assets.

Floating Policy

See Open policy.

Floating-rate contract

An guaranteed investment instrument whose interest payment is tied to some variable (floating) interest rate benchmark, such as a specific-maturity Treasury yield.

Floating-rate note (FRN)

Note whose interest payment varies with short-term interest rates.

Floating-rate payer

In an interest rate swap, the counterparty who pays a rate based on a reference rate, usually in exchange for a fixed-rate payment.

Floating-rate preferred

Preferred stock paying dividends that vary with short-term interest rates.

Floating securities

Securities bought in a broker's name and resold quickly to attain a profit in a short amount of time.

Floating supply

The aggregate of securities believed to be available for immediate purchase, that is, in the hands of dealers and investors wanting to sell.

Floor

The area of a stock exchange where active trading occurs. Also the price at which a stop order is activated (when the price drops low enough to activate such an order).

Floor broker

Member of an exchange who is an employee of a member firm and executes orders, as agent, on the floor of the exchange for clients.

Floor official

An employee of a stock exchange who settles disputes related to the auction process on the floor of the stock exchange.

Floor picture

Details of the trading crowd for a stock, such as the major players, their sizes, and the outside market +/- an eighth.

Floor planning

Arrangement used to finance inventory. A finance company buys the inventory, which is then held in trust for the user.

Floor ticket

Summary of a stock or commodities exchange order ticket by the registered representative on receipt of a buy or sell order from a client; gives the floor broker the information needed to execute a securities transaction.

Floor trader

A stock exchange member who generally trades only for his own account or for an account controlled by him, or who has such a trade made for him. Also referred to as a "local."

Flotation (rotation) cost

The costs associated with creating capital through the issue of new stocks or bonds, including the compensation earned by the investment banker plus legal, accounting and printing expenses.

Flow of funds

In the context of municipal bonds, refers to the statement displaying the priorities by which municipal revenue will be applied to the debt.

In the context of mutual funds, refers to the movement of money into or out of a mutual funds or between or among various fund sectors.

Flow-through basis

An account for an investment credit to show all income statement benefits of the credit in the year of acquisition, rather than spreading them over the life of the asset.

Flow-through method

The practice of reporting to shareholders using straight-line depreciation but using accelerated depreciation for tax purposes and "flowing through" the lower income taxes actually paid to financial statements prepared for shareholders.

Flower bond

Government bonds that when owned at the time of death are acceptable at par in payment of federal estate taxes.

Fluctuation

A price or interest rate change.

Fluctuation limit

The limit created by the commodity exchange that halts trading on a future if the price of the future changes, in either direction, more than a previously set amount.

Flurry

A drastic volume increase in a specific security.

FM

The two-character ISO 3166 country code for MICRONESIA, FEDERATED STATES OF.

FO

(1) The two-character ISO 3166 country code for FAROE ISLANDS. (2) Free out. A pricing term indicating that the charterer of a vessel is responsible for the cost of loading goods from the vessel.

FOB (Free On Board)

A pricing term indicating that the quoted price for a good includes the cost of delivering the good onto a vessel provided by or for the purchaser in the U.S. port. The term "f.o.b." must be qualified by a name of location, such as shipping point, destination, name of a city, etc. The stated "f.o.b. point" is usually the location where the title to the goods passes from the seller to the buyer. The seller is liable for the risks of loss or damage to the goods up to the point where title passes to the buyer. The buyer is liable for such charges and risks after passing of title. Identification of which party is liable for transportation charges is a separate item.

FOB Airport

FOB Airport is based on the same principle as the ordinary FOB term. The seller's obligations include delivering the goods to the air carrier at the airport of departure. The risk of loss of or damage to the goods is transferred from the seller to the buyer when the goods have been so delivered.

F.O.B./F.A.S. Endorsement

If a merchant sells on F.O.B., F.A.S., C&F or similar terms, it is the buyer's responsibility to place the insurance.

Focus list

Used in the context of general equities. Investment banks published list of buy and sell recommendations from its research department; signified by a flashing "F" on Quotron.

FOK

See: Fill or kill order.

Food and Agricultural Organization

The FAO was established in 1945, as a specialized agency of the United Nations to combat hunger and malnutrition. The FAO serves as a coordinating body between government representatives, scientific groups, and non-governmental organizations to carry out development programs relating to food and agriculture. Headquarters are in Rome, Italy.

Food for Peace

The "Food for Peace" program (also known as "P.L. 480), originally established by the 1954 Agricultural Trade and Development Act, is the primary means by which the U.S. provides foreign food assistance. The three primary objectives of the program are to:

(a) expand U.S. agricultural exports,
(b) provide humanitarian relief, and
(c) aid the economic development of developing countries.

Commodities are transferred in two ways:

- By government-to-government long-term concessional financing or for local currencies in which priority is given to developing countries which demonstrate the greatest need for food, are undertaking measures to improve their food security and agricultural development, and are potential commercial markets for U.S. agricultural commodities — Title I, administered by the Department of Agriculture; and
- Donations or grants, including:
+ Donations of food commodities for distribution in meeting either emergency conditions or international cooperative non-emergency assistance — Title II, administered by AID; and
+ Providing food assistance on a grant basis to least developed countries through government-to-government agreements.

Proceeds derived from sales on the local market may be used to support a variety of economic development and related activities in the recipient countries — Title III, administered by AID. This assistance is sometimes known as "Food For Development."

Food For Progress

The "Food for Progress" program, established by the 1985 Farm Bill, is carried out by the Department of Agriculture, using the authority of either Public Law 480 or Section 416 of the Agricultural Act of 1949. The program donates surplus government-owned agricultural commodities or Title I (of P.L. 480) funds to needy countries for development and agricultural reform purposes. Food for Progress operates in a less restrictive manner than either P.L. 480 or Section 416.

Footsie (FTSE)

Financial Times (FT)-Actuaries 100 index: "Dow average" of London.

For/At

Used in the context of general equities. Conjunctions used in an order, market summary, or trade recap that signify a bid or an offer, respectively. See: On.

For a number

Used in the context of general equities. Implies that the quantity mentioned is not his total but instead is only approximate, and to open him up more will obligate one to participate.

Forbes 500

Forbes magazine's list of the largest publicly owned corporations in the United States according to sales, assets, profits, and market value.

Force majeure risk

The risk that there will be prolonged interruption of operations for a project finance enterprise due to fire, flood, storm, or some other factor beyond the control of the project's sponsors.

Forced conversion

Occurs when a convertible security is called in by the issuer, usually when the underlying stock is selling well above the conversion price. The issuer thus assures the bonds will be retired without requiring any cash payment. Upon conversion into common, the carrying value of the bonds becomes part of a corporation's equity, thus strengthening the balance sheet and enhancing future debt capability.

Forecasting

Making projections about future performance on the basis of historical and current conditions data.

Foreclosure

Process by which the holder of a mortgage seizes the property of a homeowner who has not made interest and/or principal payments on time as stipulated in the mortgage contract.

Force Majeure

The title of a standard clause in marine contract exempting the parties for non-fulfillment of their obligations as a result of conditions beyond their control, such as earthquakes, floods, or war.

Foreign Access Zone

FAZ is a term adopted by Japan for its form of free trade zone. FAZs are the outgrowth of Japan's effort to improve its trade balance and to stimulate regional economic areas. FAZs are intended to be established around airports and seaports, with facilities (warehouses, cargo-sorting, distribution, import processing, wholesale, design-in centers, exhibition halls) on an international scale. The FAZ concept — which emphasizes imports rather than the processing and job creation — extends from the July 1992 Law on Extraordinary Measures for the Promotion of Imports and the Facilitation of Foreign Direct Investment in Japan. Passage of the law is linked to the Structural Impediments Initiative (SII).

Foreign Affiliate of a Foreign Parent

A foreign affiliate of a foreign parent is, with reference to a given U.S. affiliate, any member of the affiliated foreign group owning the U.S. affiliate that is not a foreign parent of the U.S. affiliate.

Foreign Agricultural Service

The FAS, an agency of the U.S. Department of Agriculture, collects foreign market information regarding agricultural production and trade, develops foreign markets for U.S. agricultural products, and represents U.S. agricultural interests overseas and in multilateral flora. FAS maintains over 60 counselor and attache posts, located in U.S. embassies and consulates, and about fifteen Agricultural Trade Offices (ATOs) which provide market development and trade promotion services in overseas locations. FAS also administers USDA's export credit and concessional sales programs. FAS headquarters are located in Washington, D.C.

Foreign and Commonwealth Office

The FCO, equivalent to the U.S. State Department, is Britain's Diplomatic Service, with posts in about 170 countries. Among its functions, the FCO supports overseas trade and export promotion services in cooperation with Britain's Department of Trade and Industry.

Foreign Assets Control

The Treasury Department's Office of Foreign Assets Control, OFAC, administers sanctions programs involving specific countries and restricts the involvement of U.S. persons in third country strategic exports.

Foreign Assistance Act of 1991

This Act replaced the Support for East European Democracy (SEED) Act. The Foreign Assistance Act allows support to 26 countries, including all East European nations and most of the Soviet republics, but not to the Soviet Union itself.

Foreign Availability

The Bureau of Export Administration conducts reviews to determine the foreign availability of selected commodities or technology subject to export control. The reviews use four criteria to determine foreign availability: comparable quality, availability-in-fact, foreign source, and adequacy of available quantities that would render continuation of the U.S. control ineffective in meeting its intended purpose. A positive determination of foreign availability means that a non-U.S. origin item of comparable quality may be obtained by one or more proscribed countries in quantities sufficient to satisfy their needs so that U.S. exports of such item would not make a significant contribution to the military potential of such countries. A positive determination may result in the decontrol of a U.S. product that has been under export control, or the approval of an export license. However, the control may be maintained if the President invokes the national security override provision of the Act. Beginning with the 1977 amendments to the Export Administration Act, the Congress directed that products with foreign availability be identified and decontrolled unless essential to national security. In January 1983, a program to assess the foreign availability of specific products was established within the Office of Export Administration, now the Bureau of Export Administration, or BXA. Further, 1985 amendments to the Act directed that an Office of Foreign Availability be created.

Foreign banking market

That portion of domestic bank loans supplied to foreigners for use abroad.

Foreign Bank Supervision Enhancement Act

The FBSEA, passed in 1991, increased the Federal Reserve's supervisory powers over foreign banks by: (a) requiring Federal Reserve review before a foreign bank enters or expands in the United States; (b) tightening the standards for entry and expansion that must be considered by the Federal Reserve; (c) requiring Federal Reserve Board approval of U.S. representative offices of foreign banks; and (d) requiring that each U.S. office of a foreign bank be examined at least once a year by the Federal Reserve.

Foreign base company income

A category of Subpart F income that includes foreign holding company income and foreign base company sales and service income.

Foreign bond

A bond issued on the domestic capital market of another company.

Foreign bond market

In the domestic bond market Issues floated by foreign companies or government.

Foreign branch

A foreign affiliate that is legally a part of the parent firm. According to the U.S. tax code, foreign branch income is taxed as it is earned in the foreign country.

Foreign Buyer Program

The Foreign Buyer Program, FBP, is a joint industry-International Trade Administration program to assist exporters in meeting qualified foreign purchasers for their product or service at trade shows held in the United States. ITA selects leading U.S. trade shows in industries with high export potential. Each show selected for the FBP receives promotion through overseas mailings, U.S. embassy and regional commercial newsletters, and other promotional techniques. ITA trade specialists counsel participating U.S. exhibitors.

Foreign Claims Settlement Commission

The FCSC is authorized to determine claims of United States nationals for loss of property in specific foreign countries. These losses have occurred either as a result of nationalization of property by foreign governments or from damage and loss of property as a result of military operations in specific conflicts. The Commission is an independent quasi-judicial agency within the Justice Department.

Foreign corporation

A corporation conducting business in another country from the one it is chartered in and that abides by the laws of another country. See: Alien corporation.

Foreign Corrupt Practices Act

The FCPA prohibits U.S. individuals, companies and direct foreign subsidiaries of U.S. companies from offering, promising, or paying anything of value to any foreign government official in order to obtain or retain business.

Foreign Credit Insurance Association (FCIA)

A private consortium of US insurance companies that offers trade credit insurance to US exporters in conjunction with the US Export-Import Bank.

Foreign crowd

NYSE members who trade in foreign bonds on the floor.

Foreign currency

Money of another country from one's own.

Foreign currency forward contract

Agreement that obligates its parties to exchange given quantities of currencies at a prespecified exchange rate on a certain future date.

Foreign currency futures contract

Standardized and easily transferable obligation between two parties to exchange currencies at a specified rate during a specified delivery month; standardized contract on specified underlying currencies, in multiples of standard amounts. Purchased and traded on a regulated exchange on which margins are posted.

Foreign currency option

An option that conveys the right (but not the obligation) to buy or sell a specified amount of foreign currency at a specified price within a specified time period.

Foreign currency translation

The process of restating foreign currency accounts of subsidiaries into the reporting currency of the parent company in order to prepare consolidated financial statements.

Foreign direct investment (FDI)

The acquisition abroad of physical assets such as plant and equipment, with operating control residing in the parent corporation.

Foreign Disclosure and Technical Information System

FORDTIS is a classified information system that contains an automated database of munition and dual-use export licenses. The system is maintained by the Defense Department's Defense Technology Security Administration.

Foreign Economic Trends

FETs are reports prepared by U.S. embassies abroad to describe foreign country economic and commercial trends and trade and investment climates. The reports describe current economic conditions; provide updates on the principal factors influencing developments and the possible impacts on American exports; review newly announced foreign government policies as well as consumption, investment, and foreign debt trends.

Foreign equity market

Issues floated by foreign companies in the domestic equity market.

Foreigner

All institutions and individuals living outside the United States, including US citizens living abroad, and branches, subsidiaries, and other affiliates abroad of US banks and business concerns; also central governments, central banks, and other official institutions of countries other than the United States, and international and regional organizations, wherever located. Also refers to persons in the United States to the extent that they are known by reporting institutions to be acting for foreigners.

Foreign Exchange

The currency or credit instruments of a foreign country. Also, transactions involving purchase or sale of currencies.

Foreign exchange broker

Intermediaries in the foreign exchange market that do not put their own money at risk.

Foreign Exchange Certificate (FEC)

China's currency. The FEC is convertible into foreign currency at government controlled rates and was designed to be used for the purchase of imported goods. See also Renminbi (RMB) which is a part of two tiered currency system

Foreign exchange controls

Various forms of controls imposed by a government on the purchase/sale of foreign currencies by residents or on the purchase/sale of local currency by nonresidents.

Foreign exchange dealer

A firm or individual that buys foreign exchange from one party and then sells it to another party. The dealer makes the difference between the buying and selling prices, or the spread.

Foreign exchange market

Largely banks that serve firms and consumers who may wish to buy or sell various currencies.

Foreign Exchange Option

A foreign exchange option is an arrangement in which a purchaser and a seller of foreign currencies agree on a specific rate of exchange at a future date. The purchaser may choose to exercise or pass up the option — thus setting a limit on unfavorable exchange rates. The seller is given a fee for tendering the option. Purchasers may exercise the option at any time — in the European option, currency exchange is made on the originally established date; in the American option, exchange is made within a couple of days of the purchaser exercising the option.

F ign exchange risk

The risk that a long or short position in a foreign currency might have to be closed out at a loss due to an adverse movement in exchange rates.

Foreign exchange swap

An agreement to exchange stipulated amounts of one currency for another currency at one or more future dates.

Foreign Exports

Exports of foreign merchandise (re-exports), consist of commodities of foreign origin which have entered the United States for consumption or into Customs bonded warehouses or U.S. Foreign Trade Zones, and which, at the time of exportation, are in substantially the same condition as when imported.

Foreign Flag

A reference to a carrier not registered in the United States that flies the American flag. The term applies to air and sea transportation.

Foreign holdings

The percentage of a portfolio's investments represented by stocks or American Depository Receipts (ADRs) of companies based outside the United States.

Foreign Investment Advisory Service

FIAS was established in 1986 as a joint facility of the International Finance Corporation and the Multilateral Investment Guarantee Agency to help developing countries increase the inflow of foreign investment. The Service provides advice at the request of member governments on formulating a general framework of legal, accounting, and regulatory policies and institutions and procedures to attract and assess investment interest.

Foreign investment risk matrix (FIRM)

Graph that displays financial and political risk by intervals on which countries may be compared according to risk ratings.

Foreign Market Development Program

FMD (also known as the Cooperator Program) is one of several Department of Agriculture (USDA) programs designed to encourage development, maintenance and expansion of commercial export markets for U.S. agricultural commodities and products. Under FMD, USDA considers proposals with preference given to activities promising early results and lasting benefits in commercial export markets. Funds may be used for trade servicing, consumer promotion, market research, and to provide technical assistance to actual or potential foreign purchasers. While agreements under the Cooperator Program may extend from one to five years, types of activities and amounts of funds are annually negotiated between the Foreign Agricultural Service (FAS) and participants (cooperators) and authorized in annual marketing plans. The marketing plans must set forth the objectives and describe the specific project in detail. The amount of funding provided by FAS varies, dependent upon circumstances and whether the activities are characterized as generic or market promotion.

Foreign official institutions

Central governments of foreign countries, including all departments and agencies of national governments; central banks, exchange authorities, and all fiscal agents of foreign national governments that undertake activities similar to those of a treasury, central bank, or stabilization fund; diplomatic and consular establishments of foreign national governments; and any international or regional organization, including subordinate and affiliate agencies, created by treaty or convention between sovereign states.

Foreign market

Part of a nation's internal market, representing the mechanisms for issuing and trading securities of entities domiciled outside that nation. Compare external market and domestic market.

Foreign market beta

A measure of foreign market risk that is derived from the capital asset pricing model.

Foreign Market Value

The price at which merchandise is sold, or offered for sale, in the principal markets of the country from which it is exported. If information on foreign home market sales is not useful, the foreign market value is based on prices of exports to third countries or constructed value. Adjustments for quantities sold, circumstances of sales, and differences in the merchandise can be made to those prices to ensure a proper comparison with the prices of goods exported to the United States.

Foreign-Owned Affiliate in the U.S.

A business in the United States in which there is sufficient foreign investment to be classified as direct foreign investment. To determine fully the foreign owners of a U.S. affiliate, three entities must be identified: the foreign parent, the ultimate beneficial owner, and the foreign parent group. All these entities are "persons" in the broad sense: thus, they may be individuals, business enterprises; governments; religious, charitable, and other nonprofit organizations; estates and trusts; and associated groups.

A U.S. affiliate may have an ultimate beneficial owner (UBO) that is not the immediate foreign parent; moreover, the affiliate may have several ownership chains above it, if it is owned at least 10 percent by more than one foreign person. In such cases, the affiliate may have more than one foreign parent, UBO, and/or foreign parent group.

Foreign Parent

The first foreign person or entity outside the United States in an affiliate's ownership chain that has direct investment in the affiliate. The foreign parent consists only of the first person or entity outside the United States in the affiliate's ownership chain; all other affiliated foreign persons are excluded.

Foreign Parent Group

A foreign parent group, FPG, consists of: (1) the foreign parent, (2) any foreign person or entity, proceeding up the foreign parent's ownership chain, that owns more than 50 percent of the party below it, up to and including the ultimate beneficial owner (UBO), and (3) any foreign person or entity, proceeding down the ownership chain(s) of each of these members, that is owned more than 50 percent by the party above it. A particular U.S. affiliate may have several ownership chains above it, if it is owned at least 10 percent by more than one foreign party. In such cases, the affiliate may have more than one foreign parent, UBO, and/ or foreign parent group.

Foreign Person

A foreign person is any person resident outside the United States or subject to the jurisdiction of a country other than the United States. "Person" is any individual, branch, partnership, association, associated group, estate, trust, corporation, or other organization (whether or not organized under the laws of any State), and any government (including a foreign government, the U.S. Government, a State or local government, and any agency, corporation, financial institution, or other entity or instrumentality thereof, including a government sponsored agency.)

Foreign Policy Controls

Foreign policy controls are distinct from national security controls (CoCom or other international agreements) and are imposed to further U.S. foreign policy. The controls are typically imposed in response to developments in a country or countries — such as considerations regarding terrorism and human rights — or to developments involving a type or types of commodities and their related technical data. Foreign policy controls expire annually, unless extended.

Foreign public borrower

Foreign official institutions; the corporations and agencies of foreign central governments, including development banks and institutions, and other agencies that are majority owned by the central government or its departments; and state, provincial and local governments of foreign countries and their departments and agencies.

Foreign Sales Agent.

An individual or firm that serves as the foreign representative of a domestic supplier and seeks sales abroad for the supplier.

Foreign Sales Corporation

An FSC is a corporation created to secure U.S. tax exemption on a portion of earnings derived from the sale of U.S. products in foreign markets. To qualify for special tax treatment, an FSC must be a foreign corporation, maintain an office outside the U.S. territory, maintain a summary of its permanent books of account at the foreign office, and have at least one director resident outside of the U.S. There are some variations:

— Small FSCs are the same as FSCs, except that small FSCs must file an election with the IRS, and have their tax exemption limited to the income generated by $5 million or less in gross export revenues. Small FSCs do not have to meet foreign management or foreign economic process requirements but must fulfill other requirements.

— Shared FSCs are FSCs which are "shared" by 25 or fewer unrelated exporter "shareholders" for the purpose of reducing costs while obtaining the full tax benefits of an FSC.

Foreign Service

The Foreign Service supports the President and the Secretary of State in pursuing America's foreign policy objectives. Foreign service functions include: representing U.S. interests; operating U.S. overseas missions; assisting Americans abroad; public diplomacy and reporting; communicating and negotiating political, economic, consular, administrative, cultural, and commercial affairs. The Foreign Service comprises officers from the Departments of State, Commerce, and Agriculture and the United States Information Service.

Foreign-source income

Income earned from international operations.

Foreign-targeted issue

Notes sold between October 1984 and February 1986 to foreign institutions, foreign branches of US institutions, foreign central banks or monetary authorities, and to international organizations in which the United States held membership. Sold as companion issues, they could be converted to domestic (normal) Treasury notes with the same maturity and interest rates. Interest was paid annually.

Foreign tax credit

Home country credit against domestic income tax. Received in return for foreign taxes paid on foreign derived earnings.

Foreign Trade Division

FTD is the division in the Commerce Department's Census Bureau which compiles and disseminates official U.S. import and export statistics. The division also maintains international commodity classification systems and conducts methods research, including international comparability of trade statistics.

Foreign Trade Zone

FTZs are the U.S. form of free trade zones. These zones are restricted-access sites in or near ports of entry, that operate under public utility principles to create and maintain employment by encouraging operations in the U.S. which might otherwise have been carried on abroad. Goods brought into a zone for a bona fide Customs reason are exempt from state and local ad valorem tax. The zones are licensed by the Commerce Department's Foreign-Trade Zones Board and operate under the supervision of the Customs Service. Quota restrictions do not normally apply to foreign goods stored in zones, but the Board can limit or deny zone use in specific cases on public interest grounds. Domestic goods moved into a zone for export may be considered exported upon entering the zone for purposes of excise tax rebates and drawback. A foreign trade "subzone" is a non-contiguous zone site located at a manufacturing plant.

Foreign Traders Index

The foreign traders index is the U.S. and Foreign Commercial Service headquarters compilation of overseas contact files, intended for use by domestic businesses. The FTI includes background information on foreign companies, address, contact person, sales figures, size of company, and products by SIC code.

Forex

See: Foreign exchange.

Forfaiter

Purchaser of promises to pay issued by importers.

Forfaiter (Primary)

An individual or financial entity that arranges a forfaiting transaction directly with an exporter and then holds or sells on the payment obligations of the importer/ guarantor.

Forfaiter (Secondary)

An individual or financial entity that buys or sells the payment obligations of the importer/ guarantor.

Forfait Financing

Nonrecourse financing based on discounting of bills of exchange or promissory notes by a financing institution that absorbs the risk of collecting payment from the buyer without recourse to the supplier.

Forfaiting

Forfaiting is a form of supplier credit in which an exporter surrenders possession of export receivables, which are usually guaranteed by a bank in the importer's country, by selling them at a discount to a "forfaiter" in exchange for cash. These instruments may also carry the guarantee of the foreign government. In a typical forfaiting transaction, an exporter approaches a forfaiter before completing a transaction's structure. Once the forfaiter commits to the deal and sets the discount rate, the exporter can incorporate the discount into the selling price. Forfaiters usually work with bills of exchange or promissory notes, which are unconditional and easily transferable debt instruments that can be sold on the secondary market. Three primary differences between export factoring and forfaiting are:

— Factors usually want access to a large percentage of an exporter's business, while most forfaiters will work on a one-shot basis;

— Forfaiters generally work with medium and long-term receivables (180 days to seven years), while factors work with short-term receivables (up to 180 days). Payment terms usually reflect the type of product involved: forfaiters usually work with capital goods, commodities, and large projects; factors work mostly with consumer goods.

— Most factors do not have strong capabilities in developing regions of the world where legal and financial frameworks are inadequate and credit information is not readily available through affiliate factors. However, since forfaiters usually require a bank guarantee, most are willing to work with receivables from these countries.

Forfeiting

Method of financing international trade of capital goods.

Forfeiture

The loss of rights to an asset outlined in a legal contract if a party fails to fulfill obligations of the contract.

Form 8-K

The form required by the SEC when a publicly held company incurs any event that might affect its financial situation or the share value of its stock.

Form 4

The form required by the SEC for a change in the holdings of an individual owning 10% or more of the outstanding stock or in the holdings of a company officer.

Form S-3

A shorter form of registration statement than the Form S-1 that can be used by certain already-public companies to sell additional shares. It is also the form most often used to cover resales of restricted securities by selling stockholders.

Form S-8

A very brief form of registration statement filed with the SEC, registers shares to be issued under a stock plan.

Form T

The form required by the NASD to report equity transactions after the market's regular hours.

Form 10-K

A report required by the SEC from exchange-listed companies that provides for annual disclosure of certain financial information.

Form 3

A form required by the SEC and the stock exchange from all holders of 10% or more of a company's stock and all directors and officers, which details securities owned.

Formula basis

A method of selling a new issue of common stock in which the SEC declares the registration statement effective on the basis of a price formula rather than on a specific range.

Formula investing

A formula-based investment technique in which investment decisions are made using predetermined timing or asset allocation models, e.g., dollar cost averaging.

Fortune 500

Fortune magazine's listing of the top 500 US corporations determined by an index of 12 variables.

48-hour rule

PSA Uniform Practices requirement that all pool information in a to be announced (TBA) transaction be communicated by the seller to the buyer before 3 p.m. EST on the business day 48 hours prior to the agreed-upon trade date.

Forward

See: Forward contract

Forward averaging

A method of calculating taxes on a lump-sum distribution from a qualified retirement plan that enables the tax payer to pay less than the current tax rate.

Forward contract

A contract that specifies the price and quantity of an asset to be delivered on in the future. Forward contracts are not standardized and are not traded on organized exchanges

Forward cover

The purchase in the cash market of the difference between what you are obligated to deliver in a forward contract and the amount of the asset you own. For example, if you agreed to sell 100,000 bushels of corn in September in a forward contract, but you only have 60,000, you need to purchase 40,000 to cover your obligation.

Forward currency contract

An agreement to buy or sell a country's currency at a specific price, usually 30, 60, or 90 days in the future. This guarantees an exchange rate on a given date.

Forward delivery

A transaction in which the settlement will occur on a specified date in the future at a price agreed upon on the trade date.

Forward differential

Annualized percentage difference between spot and forward rates.

Forward discount

A currency trades at a forward discount when its forward price is lower than its spot price.

Forward exchange

A type of foreign exchange transaction whereby a contract is made to exchange one currency for another at a fixed date in the future at a specified exchange rate. By buying or selling forward exchange, business protect themselves against a decrease in the value of a currency they plan to sell at a future date.

Forward Exchange Rate

A forward exchange rate is the price set between two parties for delivery of a foreign currency on an agreed future date. If that date will occur within a week, the agreement is called a spot transaction; if the date is more than a week in the future, the arrangement is called a forward exchange transaction.

Forward exchange transaction

Foreign currency purchase or sale at the current exchange rate but with payment or delivery of the foreign currency at a future date.

Forward foreign exchange contract

Agreement that obligates an investor to deliver a specified quantity of one currency in return for a specified amount of another currency.

Forward foreign exchange rate

The exchange rate available today to exchange currency at some specified date in the future.

Forward forward contract

In Eurocurrencies, a contract under which a deposit of fixed maturity is agreed to at a fixed price for future delivery.

Forward interest rate

Interest rate fixed today on a loan to be made at some future date.

Forward-looking multiple

A truncated expression for a P/E ratio that is based on forward (expected) earnings rather than on trailing earnings.

Forward market

A market in which participants agree to trade some commodity, security, or foreign exchange at a fixed price for future delivery.

Forward parity

Notion that the forward rate is an unbiased predictor of future spot exchange rates.

Forward premium

A currency trades at a forward premium when its forward price is higher than its spot price.

Forward pricing

Practice mandated by the SEC that open-end investment companies establish all incoming buy and sell orders on the next net asset valuation of fund shares.

Forward rate

A projection of future interest rates calculated from either spot rates or the yield curve.

Forward rate agreement (FRA)

Agreement to borrow or lend at a specified future date at an interest rate that is fixed today.

Forward sale

A method for hedging price risk that involves an agreement between a lender and an investor to sell particular kinds of loans at a specified price and future time.

Forward trade

A transaction for which settlement will occur on a specified date in the future at a price agreed upon on the trade date.

Forwarder

Acts as a travel agent for cargo. A forwarder specializes in arranging the transport and completing required shipping documentation. Some are affiliated with NVOCC services. In the United States they are licensed by the Federal Maritime Commission.

For your information (FYI)

A prefix to a security price indicating that the quote is for information purposes only, and not an offer to trade.

Foul Bill of Lading

A bill of lading that contains a notation indicating damage or shortage. Also called claused and are the opposite of clean bills of lading.

401(K)

Under section 401(K) of the Internal Revenue Code, a deferred compensation plan set up by an employer so that employees can set aside money for retirement on a pre-tax basis. Employers may match a percentage of the amount that employees contribute to the plan. Contributions by both employees and employersn as well as investment earnings and interest, are not taxed until the employee withdraws the money; if the employee withdraws the money before retirement age, he or she pays an early withdrawal penalty tax. Currently, employees are allowed to annually contribute up to 15 percent of their salary but no more than $11,000 ($12,000 for people 50 or older). Many employers now offer these deferred compensation plans in lieu of or in addition to pensions.

Fourth market

Refers to the practice of institutional investors trading large blocks of securities directly to avoid brokerage commissions. See: Instinet.

FPA

Abbreviation for the insurance term Free of Particular Average.

FPT

Family Limited Partnership.

FR

The two-character ISO 3166 country code for FRANCE.

FRA

See: Forward rate agreement.

Fractal

An object in which the parts are in some way related to the whole. That is, the individual components are "self-similar." An example is the branching network in a tree. While each branch, and each successive smaller branching is different, they are qualitatively similar to the structure of the whole tree.

Fractal Dimension

A number that quantitatively describes how an object fills its space. In Euclidean, or Plane geometry, objects are solid and continuous. That is, they have no holes or gaps. As such, they have integer dimensions. Fractals are rough and often discontinuous, like a wiffle ball, and so have fractional, or fractal dimensions.

Fractal Distribution

A probability density function that is statistically self-similar. That is, in different increments of time, the statistical characteristics remain the same.

Fractal Market Hypothesis

The fractal market hypothesis states that (1) a market consists of many investors with different investment horizons, and (2) the information set that is important to each investment horizon is different. As long as the market maintains this fractal structure, with no characteristic time scale, the market remains stable. When the market's investment horizon becomes uniform, the market becomes unstable because everyone is trading based upon the same information set. Theory due to Ed Peters.

Fractional Brownian Motion

A biased random walk. Unlike standard Brownian motion, the odds are biased in one direction or the other. It is like playing with loaded dice.

Fractional coins

Metal currency minted in denominations of 50, 25, and 10 cents, and minor coins (5 cents and 1 cent).

Fractional discretion order

A type of order that gives the broker discretion to alter the price, up or down, within a specific fractional range in order to guarantee an execution.

Fractional Noise

A noise which is not completely independent of previous values. See Fractional Brownian Motion, 1/f Noise, White Noise.

Fractional share

Stocks amounting to less than one full share, usually resulting from splits, acquisitions, exchanges, or dividend reinvestment programs.

Framework Agreement

Tokyo Round: The Tokyo Round called for consideration to be given "to improvements in the international framework for the conduct of world trade." Four separate agreements make up what is known as the "framework agreement." They concern:

(1) differential and more favorable treatment for, and reciprocity and fuller participation by, developing countries in the international framework for trade;

(2) trade measures taken for balance of payments purposes;
(3) safeguard actions for development purposes; and
(4) an understanding on notification, consultation, dispute settlement, and surveillance in the GATT.

Enterprise for the Americas Initiative: Under the umbrella of the Enterprise for the Americas Initiative the United States and interested Western hemisphere countries are negotiating bilateral framework agreements which establish agreed upon stages for eliminating counter-productive barriers to trade and investment. They also provide a forum for bilateral dispute settlement.

Generally, the bilateral framework agreements contain similar objectives. They are based on a statement of agreed principles regarding the benefits of open trade and investment, increased importance of services to economies, the need for adequate intellectual property rights protection, the importance of observing and promoting internationally-recognized worker rights, and the desirability of resolving trade and investment problems expeditiously. The parties establish a Council on Trade and Investment to monitor trade and investment relations, hold consultations on specific trade and investment matters of interest to both sides, and work toward removing impediments to trade and investment flows. Framework agreements do not bind signatories to implement specific trade liberalization measures.

Franchise agreement

Contract by which a domestic company (franchisor) licenses its trade name and/or business system and practices for a fee to an independent company (franchisee) in a foreign market.

Franchising

Provision of a specialized sales or service strategy, support assistance, and possibly an initial investment in the franchise in exchange for periodic fees.

Franc Zone

The Franc Zone (French: Zone Franc, ZF) is a monetary union among countries whose currencies are linked to the French franc at a fixed rate of exchange: Benin, Burkina, the Cameroon, Central African Republic, Chad, Comoros, Congo, Equatorial Guinea, France, Gabon, Cote d'Ivoire, Mali, Niger, Senegal, and Togo. These countries have agreed to hold their reserves primarily in French francs and to transact exchanges on the Paris market. The zone was established in May 1951 under the auspices of a French government agency: Comit, Montaire de ZF.

Frankfurt Stock Exchange

The largest of Germany's eight securities exchanges, operated by Deutsche Borse AS.

Freddie Mac (Federal Home Loan Mortgage Corporation)

A Congressionally chartered corporation that purchases residential mortgages in the secondary market from S&Ls, banks, and mortgage bankers and securities these mortgages for sale in the capital markets.

Free Alongside Ship (FAS)

An Incoterm (FAS) that means the seller is responsible for the cost of transporting and delivering goods alongside a vessel in a port in his or her country. Since the buyer has responsibility for export clearance under FAS, it is not a practical Incoterm for U.S. exports. FAS should be used only for ocean shipments since risk and responsibility shift from seller to buyer when the goods are placed within the reach of the ship's tackle (crane).

Free on board (FOB)

Implies that distribution services like transport and handling performed on goods up to the customs frontier (of the economy from which the goods are classed as merchandise.) are included in the price.

Free box

A bank vault or other suitable storage place for the securities of a firm's customer.

Free Carrier

Free Carrier, FCA, to a named place. This term replaces the former "FOB named inland port" to designate the seller's responsibility for the cost of loading goods at the named shipping point. It may be used for multimodal transport, container stations, and any mode of transport, including air.

Free cash flows

Cash not required for operations or for reinvestment. Often defined as earnings before interest (often obtained from the operating income line on the income statement) less capital expenditures less the change in working capital. In terms of a formula.

Free cash flows =

Sales (Revenues from operations)

—COGS (Cost of goods sold-labor, material, book depreciation)

—SG&A (Selling, general administrative costs)
EBIT (Earnings before interest and taxes or Operating Earnings)

—Taxes (Cash taxes) EBIAT (Earnings before interest after taxes)

+ DEP (Book depreciation)

—CAPX (Capital expenditures)

—ChgWC (Change in working capital) C (Free cash flows)

There is an issue as to whether you want to define the FCFs to the firm as a whole (the cash flow to all of its security holders), or the FCFs only to the firm's equity holders. For firm valuation, you want the former; for stock valuation you want the latter. To value the firm, calculate the stream of FCFs to the firm and discount this stream by the firm's WACC (Weighted average cost of capital). This will give you the value of a levered firm, including the tax benefits of debt financing. Alternatively, you can discount the firm's FCFs by its unlevered cost of capital and add separately the present value of the tax benefits. To value the firm's equity, you can either take the above number and subtract the market value of all outstanding debt (liabilities) or you can calculate the FCFs to the firm's equity holders and discount this stream by the firm's levered equity cost of capital. Notice that changes in working capital have the same effect on free cash flows as do changes in physical capital, i.e., capital expenditures. For example, suppose you had to spend $XX to increase the capacity of your plant. This expenditure would be a reduction in free cash flow in the year it was made. Likewise, if you had to increase the level of your cash balance, inventory or receivables by $XX to accommodate greater sales, then this too would result in a like reduction in free cash flows in the year the level of working capital was increased.

Free-Choice Clause

Clause in a countertrade contract that authorizes the primary supplier or its delegate to place orders for any products manufactured in the primary importer's country, without restrictions as to the sectors or companies that are entitled to receive these orders.

Free delivery

Securities industry procedure whereby delivery of securities sold is made to the buying customer's bank without requiring immediate payment; thus a credit agreement of sorts. Antithesis of delivery vs. payment.

Freedom Support Act

The FSA, signed into law in October 1992, authorizes a range of programs to support free market and democratic reforms in Russia, Ukraine, Armenia, and other states of the former Soviet Union.

Freed up

A term used to indicate that an underwriting syndicate's members are no longer restricted to the fixed price agreed upon in the agreement among underwriters and are permitted to trade the security on a free market basis.

Free float

An exchange rate system characterized by the absence of government intervention. Also known as clean float.

Free In

A pricing term indicating that the charterer of a vessel is responsible for the cost of loading goods onto the vessel.

Free In and Out

A pricing term indicating that the charterer of a vessel is responsible for the cost of loading and unloading goods from the vessel.

Freely floating exchange rate system

Monetary system in which exchange rates are allowed to move due to market forces without intervention by country governments.

Free of Particular Average

Marine cargo insurance that does not cover partial losses or partial damage unless caused by the vessel being sunk, stranded, burned, on fire, or in a collision.

Free on Board

Free On Board (FOB) at a named port of export. The seller quotes the buyer a price that covers all costs up to and including delivery of goods aboard a vessel at a port. FOB is also a method of export valuation.

Free on Rail/Free on Truck

These terms are synonymous, since the word "truck" relates to the railway wagons. The terms should only be used then the goods are to be carried by rail.

Free Out

A pricing term indicating that the quoted prices includes the cost of unloading the goods from the vessel.

Free Ports

Free Ports Free ports are a form of free trade zone that usually encompass an entire port area (examples include Hong Kong and Singapore).

Free reserves

Excess reserves minus member bank borrowings at the Fed.

Free rider

A follower who avoids the cost and expense of finding the best course of action simply by mimicking the behavior of a leader who made these investments.

Free-riding

A forbidden practice in which the member of an underwriting syndicate retains a portion of an initial public offering (IPO) and resells the securities at a higher price determined by the market at a later time.

Also forbidden is a brokerage customer's rapid buying and selling of a security without putting up money for the purchase.

Free right of exchange

An investor's right to transfer securities from one name to another name without paying charges that accompany a sales transaction.

Free stock

A stock that is paid for in full and is not pledged in any way as collateral.

Free to trade

Used in the context of general equities. Not subject to any internal (restricted list) or external restrictions on trading; hence, the trader is free to solicit interest.

Free Trade Agreement

An FTA is an arrangement which establishes unimpeded exchange and flow of goods and services between trading partners regardless of national borders. An FTA does not (as opposed to a common market) address labor mobility across borders, common currencies or uniform standards or other common policies such as taxes. Member countries of a free trade area apply their individual tariff rates to countries outside the free trade area.

Free Trade Area

A free trade area is a cooperative arrangement among two or more nations, pursuant to the General Agreement on Tariffs and Trade, whereby trade barriers are removed among the members. The arrangement generally includes a customs union with a common external tariff, although there are exceptions in which members maintain individually separate tariff schedules for external countries.

Free Trade Zones

"Free Trade Zones" (sometimes called "customs free zones" or "duty free zones") is a generic term referring to special commercial and industrial areas at which special customs procedures allow the importation of foreign merchandise (including raw materials, components, and finished goods) without the requirement that duties be paid immediately. If the merchandise is later exported, duty free treatment is given to reexports. The zones are usually located in or near ports of entry. Merchandise brought into these zones may be stored, exhibited, assembled, processed or used in manufacture prior to reexport or entry into the national customs territory. When manufacturing activity occurs in free trade zones, it usually involves a combination of foreign and domestic merchandise, and usually requires special governmental authority. Types of free trade zones include: foreign trade zones (and foreign trade subzones); free ports; and transit zones.

Freeze out

The action of pressurizing shareholders with relatively minor amounts of stock to sell their shares after a takeover.

Freight

A transportation term meaning either goods being transported, and/or charges incurred for such transport.

Freight All Kinds

FAK is a shipping classification. Goods classified FAK are usually charged higher rates than those marked with a specific classification and are frequently in a container which includes various classes of cargo.

Freight Carriage ... paid to

Like C & F, "Freight/Carriage paid to ..." means that the seller pays the freight for the carriage of the goods to the named destination. However, the risk of loss of or damage to the goods, as well as of any cost increases, is transferred from the seller to the buyer when the goods have been delivered into the custody of the first carrier and not at the ship's rail. The term can be used for all modes of transport including multi-modal operations and container or "roll on-roll off" traffic by trailer and ferries. When the seller has to furnish a bill of lading, waybill or carrier's receipt, he duly fulfills this obligation by presenting such a document issued by the person with whom he has contracted for carriage to the named destination.

Freight Carriage ... and insurance paid to

This term is the same as "Freight/Carriage Paid to ..." but with the addition that the seller has to procure transport insurance against the risk of loss of damage to the goods during the carriage. The seller contracts with the insurer and pays the insurance premium.

Freight Forwarder

An independent business which handles export shipments for compensation. At the request of the shipper, the forwarder makes the actual arrangements and provides the necessary services for expediting the shipment to its overseas destination. The forwarder takes care of all documentation needed to move the shipment from origin to destination, making up and assembling the necessary documentation for submission to the bank in the exporter's name. The forwarder arranges for cargo insurance, makes the necessary overseas communications, and advises the shipper on overseas requirements of marking and labeling. The forwarder operates on a fee basis paid by the exporter and often receives an additional percentage of the freight charge from the common carrier. An export freight forwarder must be licensed by the Federal Maritime Commission to handle ocean freight and by the International Air Transport Association (IATA) to handle air freight. An ocean freight forwarder dispatches shipments from the United States via common carriers, books or arranges space for the shipments, and handles the shipping documentation.

Freight shippers

Agents who coordinate the logistics of transportation.

FREIT

See: Finite-Life Real Estate Investment Trust.

Frequency distribution

The organization of data to show how often certain values or ranges of values occur.

Fresh picture

Updated estimation of a stock or market, usually following recent trading activity or news that has changed the previous look.

Fresh signal

Piece of information (fundamental or technical) leading one to believe a stock will move in a certain manner.

FRF

The ISO 4217 currency code for the French Franc.

Friction costs

Costs, both implied and direct, associated with a transaction. Such costs include time, effort, money, and associated tax effects of gathering information and making a transaction.

Frictional cost

The difference between an index fund return and the index it represents. The typically lower rate of return from the fund results from transactions costs.

Frictionless market

Ideal trading environment that imposes no costs or restraints on transactions.

Frictions

The "stickiness" involved in making transactions; the total process including time, effort, money, and tax effects of gathering information and making a transaction such as buying a stock or borrowing money.

Friendly Merger

A business combination that the management of both firms believes will be beneficial to stockholders.

Friendly takeover

Merger when the target firm's management and board of directors is in favor of the takeover. Antithesis of hostile takeover.

FRN

See: Floating-rate note.

Front-end load

The fee applied to an investment at the time of initial purchase, e.g., on a mutual fund purchased from a broker or mutual fund company.

Front fee

The fee initially paid by the buyer upon entering a split-fee option contract.

Front office

Refers to revenue generating sales personnel in a brokerage, insurance, or other financial services operation.

Front running

Entering into options or futures contracts with advance knowledge of a block transaction that will influence the price of the underlying security to capitalize on the trade. This practice is expressly forbidden by the SEC.

Frozen account

A disciplinary action taken by the Federal Reserve Board for some violation of Regulation T, an individual investor cannot sell securities until they are paid for in full and certificates delivered.

Fry a bigger fish

Used in the context of general equities. Work on a trade of larger size than a trade just disclosed.

FSC

See: Foreign Sales Corporation.

F.T.A.A.

See under Free trade Area of the Americas.

Full

Handle.

Full compensation

Payment for delivery of goods to one party by buying back more than 100 % of the value that was originally sold.

Full coupon bond

A bond with a coupon equal to the going market rate; the bond is therefore selling at par.

Full disclosure

Describes exchange and government regulations providing for the release and free exchange of all information pertinent to a given security.

Full Employment and Balance Growth Act of 1978(Humphrey-Hawkins Act)

Federal legislation that, among other things, specifies the primary objectives of U.S. economic policy-maximum employment, stable prices, and moderate long-term interest rates.

Full faith-and-credit obligations

The security pledges for larger municipal bond issuers, such as states and large cities that have diverse funding sources.

Full-payout lease

See: Financial lease.

Full price

Also called dirty price; the price of a bond including accrued interest. Related: Flat price.

Full-service broker

A broker who provides clients an all-inclusive selection of services such as advice on security selection and financial planning.

Full-service lease

Also called rental lease. Arrangement in which lessor promises to maintain and insure the equipment leased.

Full Set of Bills of Lading

All originals of an ocean bill of lading.

Full trading authorization

Indication that a broker with a discretionary account can operate free of all trading guidelines from the client.

Fully depreciated

An asset that has already been charged with the maximum amount of depreciation allowed by the IRS for accounting purposes.

Fully diluted earnings per shares

Earnings per share expressed as if all outstanding convertible securities and warrants have been exercised.

Fully distributed

A new stock issue that has been completely resold to the investing public and is no longer held by dealers.

Fully invested

Used to describe an investor whose assets are totally committed to investments, typically stock.

Fully modified pass-throughs

Agency pass-throughs that guarantee the timely payment of both interest and principal. Related: Modified pass-throughs.

Fully valued

Used in the context of general equities. Said of a stock that has reached a price at which analysts think the underlying company's fundamental earnings power has been fully recognized by the market.

Functional currency

As defined by FASB No. 52, an affiliate's functional currency is the currency of the primary economic environment in which the affiliate generates and expends cash.

Fund assets

The total value of a portfolio's securities, cash, and other holdings, minus any outstanding debts.

Fund family

Set of funds with different investment objectives offered by one management company. In many cases, investors may move their assets from one fund to another within the family at little or no cost.

Fund of funds

A mutual fund or hedge fund that invests in other funds.

Fund manager

The person whose responsibility it is to oversee the allocation of the pool of money invested in a particular mutual fund. The fund manager is charged with investing the money to attain the returns and level of risk of the mutual fund investors.

Fund switching

Moving money within a mutual fund family from one mutual fund to another.

Fun money

Money that can be used to invest in risky investments with high potential return.

Fundamental analysis

Security analysis that seeks to detect misvalued securities through an analysis of the firm's business prospects. Research often focuses on earnings, dividend prospects, expectations for future interest rates, and risk evaluation of the firm. Antithesis of technical analysis. In macroeconomic analysis, information such as interest rates, GNP, inflation, unemployment, and inventories is used to predict the direction of the economy, and therefore the stock market. In microeconomic analysis, information such as balance sheet, income statement, products, management, and other market items is used to forecast a company's imminent success or failure, and hence the future price action of the stock.

Fundamental beta

The product of a statistical model to predict the fundamental risk of a security using not only price data but also other market-related and financial data.

Fundamental descriptors

In the model for calculating fundamental beta, ratios in risk indexes other than market variability, which rely on financial data other than price data.

Fundamental forecasting

Analyzing the future on the basis of fundamental relationships between economic variables and exchange rates.

Fundamental Information

Information relating to the economic state of a company or economy. In market analysis, fundamental information is related to the earnings prospects of the firm only.

Funded debt

Debt maturing after more than one year.

Funded Liability

A source of funds that a firm must take overt action to arrange and that carries an interest cost.

Funded pension plan

A pension plan in which all liabilities, including payments to be made to pensioners in the immediate future, are completely funded.

Funding

Used to describe the refinancing of a debt prior to its maturity (the same as refunding). In corporate finance refers to the floating of bonds to raise finance and levels of capital. See also: refunding.

Funding ratio

The ratio of a pension plan's assets to its liabilities.

Funding risk

Related: Interest rate risk.

Funds From Operations (FFO)

Used by real estate and other investment trusts to define the cash flow from trust operations; earnings with depreciation and amortization added back. A similar term increasingly used is funds available for distribution (FAD), which is FFO less capital investments in trust property and the amortization of mortgages.

Fungibility

The substitutability of listed options, which is dependent upon their common expiration dates and strike prices. The congruence of expiration dates and strike prices lets investors close positions by offsetting transactions through the options clearing corporation.

Furthest month

Used in the context of commodities or options trading to refer to the month that is away from the contract's date of settlement.

FUTOP

The Danish derivatives market, merged with the Copenhagen Stock Exchange in 1997.

Future

A term used to designate all contracts covering the sale of financial instruments or physical commodities for future delivery on a commodity exchange.

Future investment opportunities

The identification of additional, more valuable, investment opportunities in the future that result from a current opportunity or operation.

Futures

A term used to designate all contracts covering the sale of financial instruments or physical commodities for future delivery on a commodity exchange.

Futures commission merchant (FCM)

A firm or person engaged in soliciting or accepting and handling orders for the purchase or sale of futures contracts, subject to the rules of a futures exchange and, who, in connection with such solicitation or acceptance of orders, accepts any money or securities to provide margin for any resulting trades or contracts. The FCM must be licensed by the CFTC. Related: Commission house, omnibus account.

Futures contract

A legally binding agreement to buy or sell a commodity or financial instrument in a designated future month at a price agreed upon today by the buyer and seller. Futures contracts are standardized according to the quality, quantity, and delivery time and location for each commodity. A futures contract differs from an option because an option is the right to buy or sell, while a futures contract is the promise to actually make a transaction. A future is part of a class of securities called derivatives, so named because such securities derive their value from the worth of an underlying investment.

Futures contract multiple

A constant set by an exchange, which when multiplied by the futures price gives the dollar value of a stock index futures contract.

Futures market

A market where contracts for future delivery of a commodity or a security are bought or sold.

Futures option

An option on a futures contract. Related: Options on physicals.

Futures price

The price at which parties to a futures contract agree to transact upon the settlement date.

Future value

The amount of cash at a specified date in the future that is equivalent in value to a specified sum today.

Fuzzy Logic

A system which mathematically models complex relationships which are usually handled in a vague manner by language. Under the title of "Fuzzy Logic" falls formal fuzzy logic (a multi-valued form of logic), and fuzzy sets. Fuzzy sets measure the similarity between an object and a group of objects. A member of a fuzzy set can belong to both the set, and its compliment. Fuzzy sets can more closely approximate human reasoning than traditional "crisp" sets. See: Crisp sets.

FVO (for valuation only)

See: For your information.

G

Fifth letter of a Nasdaq stock symbol specifying that the issue is the first convertible bond of the company.

G-7

See Group of Seven.

GA

The two-character ISO 3166 country code for GABON.

GAAP

See: Generally Accepted Accounting Principles.

Gadfly

A nickname for a "professional" securityholder who owns stock in various companies, attends annual meetings and asks senior management hard and often embarrassing questions.

Gaijin

Japanese term used to describe a non-Japanese investor in Japan (outside person). A more polite version of the same word is gaikokujin which means outside country person.

Gain

A profit on a securities transaction recognized by selling a security for more than the security originally cost. The gain is the difference between the cost and the sale.

Gambia River Basin Development Organization

The Organization (French: Organisation pour la Mise en Valeur du Fleuve Gambie, OMVG) promotes the construction of dams for hydroelectric and irrigation purposes. The organization was established in June 1978; headquarters are in Dakar, Senegal. Members include: the Gambia, Guinea, Guinea-Bissau, and Senegal.

Gamma

The ratio of a change in the option delta to a small change in the price of the asset on which the option is written.

Gap

Financing that is required, but for which no provision has been made. The difference in total funding needed for a proposal and the amount of funding already made available.

Gap opening

In the context of general equities, opening price that is substantially higher or lower than the previous day's closing price, usually because of some extraordinarily positive or negative news.

Garage

The floor of the NYSE, which is situated on the north side of the main trading floor.

Garbatrage

Rising stock prices and increased market activity in an entire sector caused by a psychology change stemming from a major takeover involving two companies in the sector. Speculators feel other takeovers are likely in the sector. See: Rumortrage.

Garman-Kohlhagen option pricing model

A model widely used to price foreign currency options.

Gateway

In the context of travel activities, gateway refers to a major airport or seaport. Internationally, gateway can also mean the port where customs clearance takes place.

Gather in the stops

A market strategy in which investors sell stocks to drive prices to a level that breaks through stop orders known to exist. Once the price is low enough, the stop orders become market orders and are executed, to create snowballing.

GATS

See General Agreement on Trade in Services.

GATT

See General Agreement on Tariffs and Trade. A multilateral treaty intended to help reduce trade barriers between signatory countries and to promote trade through tariff concessions.

GATT Panel

A panel of neutral representatives that may be established by the GATT Secretariat under the dispute settlement provisions of the GATT to review the facts of a dispute and render findings of GATT law and recommend action.

Gaussian

A system whose probabilities are well described by the normal distribution, or bell shaped curve.

GB

The two-character ISO 3166 country code for UNITED KINGDOM.

GBP

Pound Sterling currency.

GBP

The ISO 4217 currency code for the United Kingdom Pound.

GCC-5

The five countries of the GULF COOPERATION COUNCIL: Bahrain, Kuwait, Oman, Qatar and the United Arab Emirates (UAE) which lie in the Arabian Gulf region.

GD

The two-character ISO 3166 country code for GRENADA.

GDP

See: Gross Domestic Product.

GDP implicit price deflator

An economic technique used to account for inflation by comparing the current-dollar gross domestic product GDP to constant-dollar GDP as a ratio. The ratio accounts for price changes of goods and services that make up GDP and changes in the composite of GDP.

GE

The two-character ISO 3166 country code for GEORGIA.

Gearing

Financial leverage.

GEM (growing equity mortgage)

Mortgage in which annual increases in monthly payments are used to reduce outstanding principal and to shorten the term of the loan.

General Average

Provision in maritime law where all shippers on a given voyage would reimburse the ship line in the event of vessel sinking or catastrophic damage. It also provides for the reimbursement to those shippers whose cargo was thrown overboard in order to save the vessel.

General Average Contribution

The amount of money paid by each shipper involved in a General Average.

General account

Federal Reserve Board's term for a margin account provided to a customer by a brokerage firm. Governed by Regulation T of the FED.

General Agreement on Tariffs and Trade

The GATT is a binding contract among over 100 governments. GATT was established in 1947 as an interim measure pending the establishment of the International Trade Organization, under the Havana Charter. The International Trade Organization (ITO) was never ratified by Congress. Operating in the absence of an explicit international organization, GATT has provided the legal framework for international trade with its primary mission being the reduction of trade barriers. Headquarters offices are in Geneva, Switzerland.

General Agreement on Trade in Services (GATS)

This agreement, a part of the Uruguay Round, is designed to promote more open laws and regulations, provide national treatment to service providers, set up dispute settlement and enforcement procedures, and provide for progressive liberalization through future trade round.

General Arrangements to Borrow

The GAB, established in 1962 and amended several times, is an agreement under which the International Monetary Fund may borrow monies from major industrial nations (Belgium, Canada, France, Germany, Italy, Japan, the Netherlands, the United Kingdom, the United States, Sweden, and Switzerland). The GAB were originally designed to enable the participants to strengthen the Fund by lending to it specified amounts of their currencies. These loans would be made when supplementary resources were needed to help finance purchases by GAB participants in circumstances where such financing would forestall or cope with an impairment of the international monetary system. The GAB were amended to include an associated agreement with Saudi Arabia and to permit the Fund to use the arrangements to finance transactions with nonparticipants under certain conditions on purchases involving upper credit tranche conditionality

General Average (G.A.)

Ancient principle of equity in which all parties in a sea adventure (ship, cargo, and freight) proportionately share losses resulting from a voluntary and successful sacrifice of part of the ship or cargo to save the whole adventure from an impending peril, or extraordinary expenses necessarily incurred for the joint benefit of ship and cargo.

General Average Security

Documents the cargo owner presents to the General Average Adjuster to replace the vessel owner's maritime lien on cargo for its share of General Average and to obtain release of the goods by the Steamship Company. G.A. Security consists of a G.A. Bond and either a cash deposit or an Underwriter's Guarantee.

General cash offer

A public offering made to investors at large.

Generic credit spread

Refers to the corporate bond spread for a particular credit rating and expiry. For example, 10-year single A corporates were priced or trading at 130 basis points above Treasuries last night, or said diffrently, 130 is the generic credit spread for 10-year single A corporates.

General Exception

CoCom controls exports at three levels, depending on the item and the proposed destination. At the highest or "general exception" level, unanimous approval by CoCom members is necessary.

General Export License

Any of various export licenses covering export commodities for which Individually validated export licenses are not required. No formal application or written authorization is needed to ship exports under a general export license

Generalized System of Preferences

The Generalized System of Preferences, GSP, is a framework under which developed countries give preferential tariff treatment to manufactured goods imported from certain developing countries. GSP is one element of a coordinated effort by the industrial trading nations to bring developing countries more fully into the international trading system. The U.S. GSP scheme is a system of nonreciprocal tariff preferences for the benefit of these countries. The U.S. conducts annual GSP reviews to consider petitions requesting modification of product coverage and/or country eligibility. United States GSP law requires that a beneficiary country's laws and practices relating to market access, intellectual property rights protection, investment, export practices, and workers rights be considered in all GSP decisions.

General Imports

"General Imports" measure the total physical arrivals of merchandise from foreign countries, whether such merchandise enters consumption channels immediately or is entered into bonded warehouses or Foreign Trade Zones under Customs custody.

General ledger

Accounting records that show all the financial statement accounts of a business.

General lien

An attachment that gives the lender the right to seize the personal property of a borrower who has not fulfilled the obligations of the loan, but prevents the lender from seizing real property.

General License

These are licenses, authorized by the Bureau of Export Administration, that permit the export of goods and technology to specified countries without the need for a validated license. No prior written authorization is required and no individual validated license is issued. There are over twenty different types of general licenses, each represented by a symbol. The reason so many general licenses exist is to accommodate the various exporting situations that the Bureau of Export Administration has determined should not require an Individual Validated License.

Generally Accepted Accounting Principles (GAAP)

The overall conventions, rules, and procedures that define accepted accounting practice at a particular time in the U.S.

General loan and collateral agreement

The agreement governing the broker-dealer's borrowing against listed securities from a bank for the purpose of carrying on business and making transactions. See: Broker loan rate.

General mortgage

A type of obligation that covers all a borrower's mortgageable properties, not just one specific property.

General obligation bonds

Municipal securities secured by the issuer's pledge of its full faith, credit, and taxing power.

General Order

A penalty imposed on imported goods that are not promptly cleared through customs.

General partner

A participant who has unlimited liability for the obligations of a partnership.

General partnership

A partnership in which all participants are general partners.

General revenue

The sum of taxes, charges, and miscellaneous income taken in at the state and local level while neglecting overlapping revenue which may be erroneously counted twice.

General System of Preferences (GSP)

A system of tariff preferences designed to encourage the expansion of manufactured and semi-manufactured exports from developing countries. It is part of the tariff structures of numerous developed countries. Under the GSP program, the United States offers preferential duty-free entry on approximately 4,290 products from 134 countries. The program covers a broad spectrum of agricultural, manufactured, and semimanufactured products, but stipulates that certain products may not be designated duty-free eligible due to the import sensitivity of U.S. domestic industries.

General Tariff

A tariff that applies to countries that do not enjoy either preferential or most-favored-nation tariff treatment. Where the general tariff rate differs from the most-favored-nation rate, the general tariff rate is usually the higher rate.

Generation-skipping transfer or trust

A trust in which a principal amount is placed in a trust on the death of person A and is transferred to A's grandchildren when A's children die. The income from the trust goes to the children of person A while they survive.

Generic

Describes the characteristics and/or experience of the total universe of a coupon of MBS sector type; that is, in contrast to a specific pool or collateral group, as in a specific CMO issue.

Genetic Algorithms

Models that optimize rules by mimicking the Darwinian Law of survival of the fittest. A set of rules are chosen by those that work the best. The weakest are discarded. In addition, two successful rules can be combined (the equivalent to genetic cross-overs) to produce offspring rules. The offspring can replace the parents, or they will be discarded if less successful than the parents. Mutation is also accomplished by randomly changing elements. Mutation and cross-over occur with low probability, as in nature.

Geographic risk

Risk that arises when an issuer issues policies concentrated within certain geographic areas, such as the risk of damage from a hurricane or an earthquake.

Geometric mean return

Also called the time-weighted rate of return, a measure of the compound rate of growth of the initial portfolio market value during the evaluation period, assuming that all cash distributions are reinvested in the portfolio. It is computed by taking the geometric average of the portfolio subperiod returns.

Gesellschaft mit beschr„nker Haftung

The GmbH (German, meaning: "limited liability company") is a corporation with separate legal personality. Its shareholders participate in the original share capital with their initial contributions but are not liable to the company's creditors. One person alone can form a limited liability company but legal entities may also be shareholders. The firm name of a limited liability company must either be derived from the purpose of its business or — as in the case of limited partnerships — from the name of the shareholder or a combination of both. It must always state "with limited liability" (mbH).

Gestation repo

A reverse repurchase agreement between mortgage firms and securities dealers. Under the agreement, the firm sells federal agency-guaranteed MBS and simultaneously agrees to repurchase them at a future date at a fixed price.

Get hit

Go lower in price, when bids in the stock or market are hit, causing those bids to vanish and be replaced by lower ones. Come in. Antithesis of on the take.

Get out

Used in the context of general equities. Sell interest ("We could get out big size in Humana.")

GF

The two-character ISO 3166 country code for FRENCH GUIANA.

GH

The two-character ISO 3166 country code for GHANA.

Ghosting

The illegal practice that one firm drives a stock's price higher or lower, while other conspiring firms follow its lead to influence up the price of the stock.

GI

The two-character ISO 3166 country code for GIBRALTAR.

GIC

See: Guaranteed Investment Contract.

Gift splitting

A technique used to avoid a gift tax in which a large sum of money to be given by two parents to a child is halved and given to the child separately For example, a husband and wife each donate $10,000 to their child rather than one parent donating $20,000.

Gift tax

A tax assessed on the giver of a property or asset as a gift. A $10,000 federal gift tax exemption exists per recipient. See: Gift splitting.

Gift inter vivos

A piece of property or asset given from one living person to another.

Gilt-edged securities

British and Irish government securities. Blue Chip.

Gilts

British and Irish government securities. Blue Chip.

Ginnie Mae

See: Government National Mortgage Association

Ginnie Mae pass-through

A security guaranteed by the Government National Mortgage Association that is backed by a collection of mortgages, in which the investor receives the interest and principal payments of participating homeowners.

Give up

Used for listed equity securities. (1) Term used in a securities transaction involving three brokers, as follows: Broker A, a floor broker, executes a buy order for broker B (a member firm broker who has too much business at the time to execute the order). The broker with whom broker A completes the transaction (the sell-side broker) is broker C. Broker A "gives up" the name of broker B, so that the record shows a transaction between broker B and broker C even though the trade is actually executed between broker A and broker C; (2) distribution of commissions to brokerage houses not participating in a trade. This is a grey area of the law governing reimbursement of a broker for services (e.g., research). See: Directed brokerage.

GL

The two-character ISO 3166 country code for GREENLAND.

Glamor stock

A popular stock characterized by high earnings growth rate and a price that rise is faster than the market average in a bull market.

Global Depository Receipt

A receipt denoting ownership of foreign-based corporation stock shares which are traded in numerous capital markets around the world.

Glass-Steagall Act

1933 legislation prohibiting commercial banks to own, underwrite, or deal in corporate stock and corporate bonds.

Global bonds

Bonds designed to qualify for immediate trading in any domestic capital market and in the Euromarket.

Global Export Manager

The Global Export Manager, GEM, is an electronic system for collecting and disseminating trade leads and business opportunities. GEM is maintained by the National Association of State Development Agencies (NASDA).

Global fund

A mutual fund that can invest anywhere in the world, including the U.S.

Globalization

Tendency toward a worldwide investment environment, and the integration of national capital markets.

Global Quota

A global quota is a quota on the total imports of a product from all countries.

GM

The two-character ISO 3166 country code for GAMBIA.

GMC

See: Guaranteed Mortgage Certificate.

GN

The two-character ISO 3166 country code for GUINEA.

GNMA-I

Mortgage-backed securities (M.B.S.) on which registered holders receive separate principal and interest payments on each of their certificates, usually directly from the servicer of the M.B.S. pool. GNMA-I mortgage-backed securities are single-issuer pools.

GNMA-II

Mortgage-backed securities (M.B.S.) on which registered holders receive an aggregate principal and interest payment from a central paying agent on all their certificates. Principal and interest payments are disbursed on the 20th day of the month. GNMA-II M.B.S. are backed by multiple-issuer pools or custom pools (one issuer but different interest rates that may vary within one percentage point). Multiple-issuer pools are known as "jumbos." Jumbo pools are generally longer and offer certain mortgages that are more geographically diverse than single-issuer pools. Jumbo pool mortgage interest rates may vary within one percentage point.

GNMA Midget

A GNMA pass-through certificate backed by fixed-rate mortgages with a 15-year maturity. GNMA Midget is a dealer term and is not used by GNMA in the formal description of its programs.

Gnomes

Freddie Mac's 15-year fixed-rate pass-through securities issued under its cash program.

GNP

See: Gross National Product.

Go along

Used for listed equity securities. Buy or sell at prices that randomly occur on the floor, participating in what trades the specialist and other players will allow.

Go around

Describes the N.Y. Federal Reserve Bank's trading desk practice of communicating with primary dealers to establish a market of bids and offers on behalf of the Federal Open Market Committee.

Goal

An individual's or institution's financial objective.

Godfather offer

An aggressive takeover technique in that the proposed offer of the acquiring company is so large that management of the target company cannot refuse, out of fear of lawsuits or shareholder revolt.

Go-go fund

A type of mutual fund in highly aggressive growth stocks. The fund has high levels of risk and potential return.

Gold Key Service

The Gold Key Service is an International Trade Administration service that provides customized information for U.S. firms visiting a country — market orientation briefings, market research, introductions to potential business partners, an interpreter for meetings, assistance in developing a market strategy, and help in putting together a follow-up plan. Trade Specialists design an agenda of meetings, screen and select the right companies, arrange meetings with key people, and go with U.S. representatives to ensure that no unforeseen difficulties occur.

Goes

Used in the context of general equities. (1) Trades ("10 IBM goes on at 115 "); see Print; (2) indicates a change in the stock's inside market ("Apple goes 3/4 bid").

Going ahead

A broker-dealer trades in a personal account prior to filling the orders of his or her clients. Prohibited by the NASD rules of fair practice.

Going away

The type of bond purchased by dealers for immediate resale to investors, as opposed to purchasing bond, to hold for some amount of time, and then reselling it at a future date.

Going-concern value

The value of a company to another company or individual in terms of an operating business. The difference between a company's going-concern value and its asset or liquidation value is deemed goodwill and plays a major role in mergers and acquisitions.

Going long

The investor's purchase of a security for investment or speculation that the price will rise resulting in a profit once the security is sold. See:: long position. Antithesis of going short.

Going out

Used in the context of general equities. Soliciting/advertising over the SS1, NASDSAQ, or Autex.

Going private

When publicly owned stock in a firm is replaced with complete equity ownership by a private group. The firm is delisted on stock exchanges and can no longer be purchased in the open markets.

Going public

When a private company first offers shares to the public market and investors. See: IPO.

Going short

Selling stock that an investor does not own by borrowing shares from a broker. The assumption is that the price will fall. The investor then buys (covers the short) the shares at a lower price than what they were sold for, recognizing the difference as a profit. Antithesis of going long.

Going into the trade

Used in the context of general equities. 1) Condition of the traders position in the security and expectations of stock placement with accounts just prior to taking an order to the exchange floor for execution; 2) On the way in. Antithesis of come out of the trade.

Gold bars

Bars with a minimum content of 99.5% gold, which may be held by central banks or traded by investors.

Gold bond

Bonds issued by gold-mining companies and backed by gold. The bonds make interest payments based on the level of gold prices.

Gold bullion

Investment-grade, pure gold, which may be smelted into gold coins or gold bars.

Gold certificate

Certificate of an investor, that shows proof of ownership of gold bullion.

Gold coins

Coin minted in gold, such as the American Eagle or the Canadian Maple Leaf.

Gold exchange standard

A fixed exchange rate system adopted in the Bretton Woods agreement. It required the U.S. to peg the dollar to gold and other countries to peg their currencies to the dollar.

Gold fixing

The process of determining the price of gold based on supply and demand forces of the market; which occurs twice daily in London.

Gold mutual fund

A mutual fund that primarily invests in gold-mining companies' stock.

Gold standard

An international monetary system in which currencies are defined in terms of their gold content, and payment imbalances between countries are settled in gold. It was in effect from about 1870 to 1914.

Goldbug

Analysts who recommends gold as an investment/ hedge.

Golden handcuffs

A contract that binds a broker to a brokerage firm by offering the broker commissions and bonuses, but penalizes the broker if he or she goes to work for another firm.

Golden handshake

A large payment to a senior employee who is forced into retirement or fired as a result of a takeover or simular development.

Golden hello

A bonus a securities firm pays to attract an employee from a competing firm.

Golden parachute

Compensation paid to top-level management by a target firm if a takeover occurs.

Goldilocks economy

A term developed in the mid 1990s to describe the positive performance of the economy as "not too hot, not too cold; just right."

Good delivery

A delivery in which everything - order-endorsement, any necessary attached legal papers.

Good delivery and settlement procedures

Refers to PSA Uniform Practices such as cutoff times on delivery of securities and notification, allocation, and proper endorsement.

Good faith deposit

Used in the context of commodities. Refers to the initial margin account deposit needed when buying or selling a futures contract; approximately 2%-10% of the contract value. Used in the context of securities to describe the deposit required by securities firms engaged in transactions on behalf of a new client. Also used to refer to the deposit with a municipal bond issuer by firms competing for the underwriting business.

Good money

Federal funds that clear on the same day, unlike clearinghouse funds, which require three days to clear.

Goods

Anything purchased other than services or real property.

Good-this-Month order (GTM)

An order to buy or sell securities that continues to be a valid order until the end of the current month.

Good through/until date order

Used in the context of general equities. Market or limited price order that remains viable for a stated period of time unless cancelled, executed, or changed, after which such order or the portion thereof not executed is to be treated as cancelled.

Good 'til cancelled order (GTC)

An order to buy or sell stock that is good until you execute or cancel it. Brokerages usually set a limit of 30-60 days, at which the G.T.C. order expires if not restated. (Different from a day order.)

Goodwill

Excess of purchase price over fair market value of net assets acquired under the purchase method of accounting.

Go to

Used in the context of general equities. Sell interest ("we've got 50 IBM to go".).

Government bond

See: Government securities.

Government National Mortgage Association (Ginnie Mae)

A wholly owned U.S. government corporation within the Department of Housing & Urban Development. Ginnie Mae guarantees the timely payment of principal and interest on securities issued by approved servicers that are collateralized by FHA-issued, VA-guaranteed, or Farmers Home Administration (FmHA)-guaranteed mortgages.

Government obligations

U.S. government-backed debt instruments, which are considered among the safest investments possible, including Treasury bonds, bills, and notes, and savings bonds.

Government Procurement Policies and Practices

The term refers to a nontariff barrier to trade involving the discriminatory purchase by official government agencies of goods and services from domestic suppliers, despite their higher prices or inferior quality as compared with competitive goods that could be imported.

Government securities

Negotiable U.S. Treasury securities.

Government sponsored enterprises

Privately owned, publicly chartered entities, such as the Student Loan Marketing Association, created by Congress to reduce the cost of capital for certain borrowing sectors of the economy including farmers, homeowners, and students.

Governments

U.S. government-issued securities, such as Treasury bills, bonds, and notes, and savings bonds. Governments are considered among the safest investments available as they are backed by the U.S. government. Also used to refer to debt issues of federal agencies, which are not directly backed by the U.S. government.

GP

The two-character ISO 3166 country code for GUADELOUPE.

GPM

See: Graduated Payment Mortgages.

GQ

The two-character ISO 3166 country code for EQUATORIAL GUINEA.

GR

The two-character ISO 3166 country code for GREECE.

Grace period

The time period stipulated in most loan contracts and insurance policies during which a late payment will not result in default or cancellation.

Graduated call writing

Selling covered call options at incrementally rising exercise prices, so that as the price of the underlying stock rises and the options are exercised, the seller receives a higher average price than the original exercise price.

Graduated lease

A type of long-term lease whose payments are variable rather than fixed, and depend upon a benchmark rate, such as changes in the consumer price index.

Graduated payment

Repayment terms calling for gradual increases in the payments on a closed-end obligation. A graduated payment loan usually involves negative amortization.

Graduated-payment mortgage (GPM)

A type of stepped-payment loan in which the borrower's payments are initially lower than those on a comparable level-rate mortgage. The payments gradually increase over a predetermined period (usually 3, 5, or 7 years), and then are fixed at a level-pay schedule, which will be higher than the level-pay amortization of a level-pay mortgage originated at the same time. The difference between what the borrower actually pays and the amount required to fully amortize the mortgage is added to the unpaid principal balance.

Graduated security

A security that has moved from listing on an exchange of less prominence to one of more prominence.

Graham and Dodd method of investing

An investment strategy based on security analysis and identification. Investors buy stocks with undervalued assets speculating that these assets will appreciate to their true value.

Graham-Harvey Measure 1

Performance measure developed by John Graham and Campbell Harvey. The idea is to lever a fund's portfolio to exactly match the volatility of the S&P 500. The difference between the fund's levered return and the S&P 500 return is the performance measure.

Graham-Harvey Measure 2

Performance measure developed by John Graham and Campbell Harvey. The idea is to lever the S&P 500 portfolio to exactly match the volatility of the fund. The difference between the fund's return and the levered S&P 500 return is the performance measure.

Grandfathered activities

Nonbank activities, some of which would normally not be permissible for bank holding companies and foregin banks in the United States, but which were acquired or engaged in before a particular date. Such activities may be continued under the "grandfather" clauses of the Bank Holding Company Act and the International Banking Act.

Grandfather Clause

The General Agreement on Tariffs and Trade (GATT) provision that allows the original contracting parties to exempt from general GATT obligations mandatory domestic legislation which is inconsistent with GATT provisions, but which existed before the GATT was signed. Newer members may also "grandfather" domestic legislation if that is agreed to in negotiating the terms of accession. (U.S. legislation also provides for "grandfather clauses.")

Grant

The issuance of an award under a stock plan, such as a stock option or shares of restricted stock.

Grant Date

The date on which an option or other award is granted.

Grantor

A trader in the options market who makes premium income by selling options.

Grantor Retained Income Trust (GRIT)

A tax-saving trust in which a grantor transfers property to a beneficiary, but receives income until termination, at which time the beneficiary begins receiving the income.

Grantor trust

A mechanism of issuing MBS wherein the mortgages' collateral is deposited with a trustee under a custodial or trust agreement.

Graveyard market

Bear market in which investors who sell are faced with substantial losses, while potential investors prefer to stay liquid; that is, to keep their money in cash or cash equivalents until market conditions improve.

Gray knight

In a merger or acquisitions, a gray knight is an acquiring company that outbids a white knight in pursuit of its own best interests, although it is friendlier than a hostile bidder.

Gray list

Formal roster of stocks that can be traded by the block desks, but not in risk arbitrage because an investment bank is involved with the company on nonpublic activity (e.g., mergers and acquisitions defense). A stock's presence on this list should never be conveyed to anyone outside the trading area, much less outside the firm. See: Restricted list.

Gray market

Describes the sale of securities that have not officially been issued to firms other than the underwriting syndicate. This type of market serves as a good indicator of demand for a new issue in the public market.

Gray Market Imports

This term refers to imports bearing a genuine trademark but imported by a party other than the trademark holder or authorized importer.

Great call

Used in the context of general equities. Potential customer who may have an interest in participating in a particular trade if customer's past inquiry or activity is any indication.

Greater fool theory

An investment notion that even when a stock is fully valued by conventional standards, there is room for upward movement because there are enough buyers to push prices farther upward purely on speculation or hype.

Greenmail

The holding of a large block of stock of a target company by an unfriendly company, with the object of forcing the target company to repurchase the stock at a substantial premium to prevent a takeover.

Greenshoe option

Option that allows the underwriter for a new issue to buy and resell additional shares.

Gross per broker

The dollar amount of commissions generated by a broker or registered representative over a specific period.

Gross Domestic Product (GDP)

A measure of the market value of all goods and services produced within the boundaries of a nation, regardless of asset ownership. Unlike gross national product, GDP excludes receipts from that nation's business operations in foreign countries, as well as the share of reinvested earnings in foreign affiliates of domestic corporations.

Gross earnings

A person's total taxable income prior to adjustments. See: adjusted gross income.

Gross estate

The total value of a person's property and assets before accounting for debts, taxes, and liabilities.

Gross income

A person's total income prior to exclusions and deductions.

Gross interest

Interest earned before taxes are deducted.

Gross lease

A type of property lease in which the lessor (owner of the property being leased) pays expenses associated with ownership such as damages, taxes, and insurance.

Gross National Product (GNP)

Measures and economy's total income. It is equal to G.D.P. plus the income abroad accruing to domestic residents minus income generated in domestic market accruing to non-residents.

Gross parity

Applies mainly to convertible securities and international equities. Antithesis of net parity. For the price of a convertible, including accrued interest. For the price of international security, including commissions, fees, stamp duty, and other transaction costs, translated into U.S. dollar amounts.

Gross profit

Sales minus the cost of goods sold.

Gross profit margin

Gross profit divided by sales, which is equal to each sales dollar left over after paying for the cost of goods sold.

Gross sales

Total sales calculated by summing all sales at invoice values, neglecting any adjustments such as customer discounts or returns.

Gross spread

The fraction of the gross proceeds of an underwritten securities offering that is paid as compensation to the underwriters of the offering.

Gross Weight

The full weight (including goods and packaging) of shipment.

Ground lease

A lease of land, as opposed to a lease of a building.

Group insurance

Insurance coverage for a group, which can usually be obtained at a cheaper rate than insurance for an individual.

Group of Five

Similar to the Group of Seven (G-7), with the exception of Canada and Italy. Seven This term refers to seven major economic powers (Canada. France, Germany, Great Britain, Italy, Japan, and the United States) whose finance ministers seek to promote balanced economic growth and stability among exchange rates.

Group of Seven

The G-5 countries plus Canada and Italy.

Group of Eight

The G-7 countries plus Russia.

Group of Ten

Under the International Monetary Fund's General Agreements to Borrow (GAB), established in 1962, 10 of the wealthiest industrial members of the IMF "stand ready to lend their currencies to the IMF up to specified amounts when supplementary resources are needed." The finance ministers of these countries comprise the Group of 10 (also called the Paris Club). Members include: Belgium, Canada, France, Germany, Italy, Japan, Netherlands, Sweden, Switzerland, the United Kingdom, and the United States. Though numbering 11 with the addition of Switzerland in 1984, the numerical name persists.

Group of Eleven

The G-11 (also known as the Cartagena Group) was established in 1984 and comprises the largest debtor nations in Latin America: Argentina, Bolivia, Brazil, Chile, Colombia, Dominican Republic, Ecuador, Mexico, Peru, Uruguay, and Venezuela.

Group of Fifteen

The G-15, established in 1990, consists of relatively prosperous or large developing countries. The G-15 discusses the benefits of mutual cooperation in improving their international economic positions. Members include: Algeria, Argentina, Brazil, Egypt, India, Indonesia, Jamaica, Malaysia (a very active member), Mexico, Nigeria, Peru, Senegal, Venezuela, Yugoslavia, and Zimbabwe.

Group of Twenty-four

A grouping of finance ministers from 24 developing country members of the International Monetary Fund. The Group, representing eight countries from each of the African, Asian, and Latin American country groupings in the Group of 77, was formed in January 1972 to counterbalance the influence of the Group of 10.

Group of Seventy-Seven

A grouping of developing countries which received its name in connection with 77 countries issuing a joint statement in Geneva, Switzerland in 1964. The G-77's primary focus is serving as a caucus for articulating members' collective interests primarily in areas of promoting economic cooperation among developing countries and in negotiations on economic matters with developing countries. G-77 membership has increased since 1964 to over 125 countries.

Groupement d'Interet Economique

Groupement d'interet Economique (French: "economic interest grouping") is a joint venture which has features of both a partnership and a corporation. The GIE is used by enterprises that wish to set up a joint activity on a trial basis or to cooperate, but not to merge. The GIE must be an extension of some activity of its members, frequently marketing, research, and management. Airbus Industrie is an example of a GIE.

Group rotation

The tendency of stocks in one sector of the market to outperform and then underperform other industries, usually as a result of economic cycles or the conditions in a particular industry.

Group rotation manager

A top-down manager who deduces the phases of the business cycle and allocates assets accordingly.

Group sales

Block sale (of large amounts) of securities to institutional investors.

Group Universal Life Policy (GULP)

Universal life insurance on a group basis. See: Group insurance.

Growing Equity Mortgage (GEM)

Mortgage with a fixed interest rate and payments that increase throughout the term of the mortgage.

Growing perpetuity

A constant stream of cash flows without end that is expected to rise indefinitely.

Growth fund

A mutual fund that invests primarily in stocks with a history of and future potential for capital gains.

Growth and income fund

A mutual fund that invests primarily in stocks with a history of capital gains (growth) and consistent dividend payments (income).

Growth manager

A money manager who seeks to buy stocks that typically sell at relatively high P/E ratios due to high earnings growth, with the expectation of continued high or higher earnings growth.

Growth opportunity

Opportunity to invest in profitable projects.

Growth phase

A phase of development during which a company experiences rapid earnings growth as it produces new products and expands market share.

Growth rates

Compound annual growth rate for the number of full fiscal years shown. If there is a negative or zero value for the first or last year, the growth is N.M. (not meaningful).

Growth stock

Common stock of a company that has an opportunity to invest money and earn more than the opportunity cost of capital.

GS

The two-character ISO 3166 country code for SOUTH GEORGIA AND THE SOUTH SANDWICH ISLANDS.

GSP

See under the Generalized System of Preferences.

GT

The two-character ISO 3166 country code for GUATEMALA.

GTC

See: Good 'til cancelled order.

GU

The two-character ISO 3166 country code for GUAM.

Guarantee

The assumption of responsibility for payment of a debt or performance of some obligation if the liable party fails to perform to expectations.

Guaranteed Credits

Credits that are insured under export insurance programs of government and government-supported agencies.

Guaranteed Freight

Freight payable whether the goods are delivered or not, provided the failure to deliver the goods resulted from causes beyond the carrier's control.

Guarantee Fee

A sum paid by the importer to the guarantor, usually as a percentage per annum of the face value of the bills or notes being guaranteed.

Guarantee letter

A commercial bank's letter assuring payment of the exercise price of a client's put option.

Guaranteed bond

A type of bond for which a firm other than the issuer guarantees its interest and principal payments.

Guaranteed insurability

A life and health insurance policy feature that enables the insured to add coverage at future times and at fixed and agreed-upon rates regardless of health conditions.

Guaranteed insurance contract

A contract promising a stated nominal interest rate over some specific time period, usually several years.

Guaranteed investment contract (GIC)

A pure investment product in which a life company agrees, for a single premium, to pay at a maturity date the principal amount of a predetermined annual crediting (interest) rate over the life of the investment.

Guaranteed Mortgage Certificates (GMC)

First issued by Freddie Mac in 1975, G.M.C.s, like PCs, represent undivided interest in specified conventional whole loans and participations previously purchased by Freddie Mac.

Guardian

An individual or trust institution appointed by a court to care for a minor or an incompetent person and his or her property.

Guaranteed renewable policy insurance

A type of insurance policy that requires the insurer to renew the policy to an individual regardless of health changes. No changes may be made to an individual policyholder unless the same change is applied to all policyholders.

Guaranteed replacement cost coverage insurance

A policy that covers the full cost of replacing damaged property without any allowances or deductions, e.g., depreciation.

Guaranteeing/ Avalising Bank

The person, bank, or financial entity who gives the guarantee for the importer.

Guarantor program

Under the Freddie Mac program, the aggregation by a single issuer (usually an S&L) for the purpose of forming a qualifying pool to be issued as PCs under the Freddie Mac guarantee.

Gulf Cooperation Council

The GCC, established in May 1981, seeks to strengthen cooperation (in areas such as agriculture, industry, investment, security, and trade) among its six members: Bahrain, Kuwait, Quatar, Oman, Saudi Arabia, and the United Arab Emirates. The GCC, created in response to the outbreach of the Iran-Iraq war, established the Gulf Standards Organization in November 1982 and the Gulf Investment Corporation in 1984. The presidency of the GCC rotates yearly among members. Council headquarters are in Riyadh, Saudi Arabia.

Gun jumping

In the context of securities trading, refers to trading in a security on the basis of information that has not been made available to the public. The illegal solicitation of buy orders in an underwriting before completion and finalization of Securities and Exchange Commission registration.

Gunslinger

An aggressive portfolio manager who makes risky investments, typically in margin accounts, in search of high returns.

GW

The two-character ISO 3166 country code for GUINEA-BISSAU.

GY

The two-character ISO 3166 country code for the for GUYANA.

Gypsy Swaps

In the context of Regulation D. A private purchaser wishes to invest directly in an issuer but hopes to acquire unrestricted securities. Through arrangements and understandings with the issuer, a stockholder with shares that are either restricted securities currently eligible for sale under Rule 144 or unrestricted securities sells the shares to the private purchaser. At about the same time, the issuer sells an equivalent number of shares to the stockholder. The Securities & Exchange Commission's view is that the shares taken by the private purchaser from the stockholder will be restricted securities within the meaning of Rule 144(a)(3). The holding period will date to the private acquisition. A public resale of the shares acquired from the stockholder without regard to the conditions of Rule 144 would raise serious issues under Section 5 of the Securities Act for all parties to the transactions.

H

Fifth letter of a Nasdaq stock symbol specifying that the issue is the second preferred bond of the company.

HAB

See: House Air Waybill.

Haircut

The margin or difference between the actual market value of a security and the value assessed by the lending side of a transaction).

Half-life

The point in the life of a mortgage-backed security guaranteed or issued by the Government National Mortgage Association, the Federal National Mortgage Association or the Federal Home Loan Mortgage Corporation when half the principal has been repaid.

Half-stock

Stock, common or preferred, with a $50 par value.

Hammering the market

Heavy selling of stocks by speculators who think that the stock is overvalued and is about to drop.

Handle

The whole-dollar price of a bid or offer is referred to as the handle (e.g., if a security is quoted at 101.10 bid and 101.11 offered, 101 is the handle). Traders are assumed to know the handle. See: Full.

Hands-off investor

An investor who has a large stake in a company, but does not wish to play an active role in the management of the corporation.

Hands-on investor

An investor who has a large stake in a corporation and takes an active role in its management. Antithesis of hands-off investor.

Hang Seng index

The major index in Hong Kong.

Hard call protection

Usually refers to callable bonds. The period of time when a bond cannot be called, no matter what the interest rate is. That is, if the interest rate falls sharply, most callable bonds will be called (so the bond issuer can reissue at a lower interest rate). Hard call protection ensures that the holder of the bond can benefit when rates fall.

Hard capital rationing

A capital budget that under no circumstances can be violated.

Hard Currency

Currency that has sound value, is generally acceptable at face value internationally, and is convertible in the open market. Also known as convertible currency.

Hard dollars

Actual separate payments made by a customer for services, including research, provided by a brokerage firm. Antithesis of soft dollars.

Harmless warrant

Warrant that allows the user to purchase a bond only by surrendering an other bond with similar terms.

The Harmonized Commodity Description and Coding System

Commonly known as Harmonized System. It isa a classification system devised by the Customs Cooperation Council to provide uniformity in tariff classification, trade statistics, and transport documentation among cooperating countries.

Harmonized System

The Harmonized Commodity Description and Coding System (or Harmonized System, HS) is a system for classifying goods in international trade, developed under the auspices of the Customs Cooperation Council. Beginning on January 1, 1989, the new HS numbers replaced previously adhered-to schedules in over 50 countries, including the United States. For the United States, the HS numbers and four additional digits are the numbers that are entered on the actual export and import documents. Any other commodity code classification number (SITC, end-use, etc.) are just rearrangements and transformations of the original HS numbers.

Hart-Scott-Rodino Act

Often used in risk arbitrage. Antitrust act administered by U.S. Department of Justice and the FTC that requires an investor to file a form with the government before he acquires an economic interest in the lesser amount of $15 million or 15% of the capitalization of a specific security. The government has thirty days to respond to the filer.

Harvey, Campbell R.

Author of this glossary. Finance professor at Duke University. Author of research on international finance, asset allocation, and emerging markets.

Head & shoulders

In technical analysis, a pattern that results where a stock price reaches a peak and declines; rises above its former peak and again declines; and rises a third time but not to the second peak, and then again declines. The first and third peaks are shoulders, while the second peak is the formation's head. Technical analysts generally consider a head and shoulders formation to be a very bearish indication.

Hearing

A hearing which is held at the request of an interested party in antidumping proceedings for the purpose of allowing interested persons to express their views orally to officials of the Commerce Department. The hearing is held prior to the Commerce Department's (International Trade Administration) final determination or before the final results of an administrative review are published.

Heavy

An equities market now dominated by sellers, or oversupply, resulting in falling prices. See: Overbought, resistance level, tired.

Hedge

A transaction that reduces the risk of an investment.

Hedge clause

A clause in a research report or any published document, that attempts to absolve the writer of responsibility for the accuracy of information provided.

Hedge fund

A fund that may employ a variety of techniques to enhance returns, such as both buying and shorting stocks according to a valuation model.

Hedge quality

Measured by the R-square in a regression of spot rate changes on futures price changes.

Hedge ratio (delta)

For options, ratio between the change in an option's theoretical value and the change in price of the underlying stock at a given point in time. For convertibles, percentage of a convertible bond representing the number of underlying common shares sold against the shares into which bonds are convertible. If a preferred is convertible into 2000 common shares, a 75% hedge ratio would be short (long) 1500 common for every 1000 preferred long (short). See: Delta.

Hedge wrapper

An options strategy in which an investor with a long position in an underlying stock buys an out-of-the-money put and sells an out-of-the-money call. The hedge wrapper defines a range where the stock will be sold at expiration of the option, which way the stock moves.

Hedged portfolio

A portfolio consisting of a long position in the stock and a long position in the put option on the stock, so as to be riskless and produce a return that equals the risk-free interest rate.

Hedged tender

An investor sells a portion of a stock holding short a tender offer in the event all shares tendered are not accepted. For example, investor Q has 5000 shares of XYZ. An acquiring company makes a tender offer of $100 a share when the shares are currently worth $80. Investor Q short-sells 2500 shares after the announcement and the price of the stock has approached $100. Company XYZ purchases only 2500 of the original shares at $100. Investor Q has sold all shares at $100 even as the price of the stock drops on a post-news dip.

Hedgie

Slang for a hedge fund.

Hedging

A strategy designed to reduce investment risk using call options, put options, short-selling, or futures contracts. A hedge can help lock in profits. Its purpose is to reduce the volatility of a portfolio by reducing the risk of loss.

Hedging demands

Demands for securities to hedge particular sources of consumption risk, beyond the usual mean-variance diversification motivation.

Held at the opening

Used for listed equity securities. Not open for trading because specialists or regulators are not allowing trading to occur until imbalances dissipate or news is disseminated.

Held order

Order that must be executed without hesitation (Hit the bid or take the offer in line) or if the stock can be bought or sold at that price (held limit order) in sufficient quantity.

Hell-or-high-water contract

A contract that obligates a purchaser of a project's output to make cash payments to the project in all events, even if no product is offered for sale.

Helsinki Accord

The Helsinki Accord deals with the rights of people to migrate freely. The tourism portions of the Accord encourage: (a) tourism and tourism studies, (b) preservation of artistic, historic and cultural heritages of signatories, (c) lowering of fees and documentation needed for international travel, and (d) other efforts to encourage cooperation on tourism among countries. The Accord was signed in 1975.

Helsinki Exchanges (HEX)

The Helsinki Exchanges (HEX Ltd., Helsinki Securities and Derivatives Exchange and Clearing House) was formed at the beginning of 1998 following the merger of the Helsinki Stock Exchange Ltd. and SOM Ltd., the Securities and Derivatives Exchange, and the Clearing House.

Hemline theory

A theory that stock prices move in the same direction as the hemlines of women's dresses. For example, short skirts (1920s and 1960s) are symbolic of bullish markets and long skirts (1930s and 1940s) are symbolic of bearish markets.

Herstatt risk

The risk of loss in foreign exchange trading that one party will deliver foreign exchange but the counterparty financial institution will fail to complete its end of the contract. This is also referred to as settlement risk.

HEX

See: Helsinki Exchange.

H-H page

Quotron display page that shows new listed inquiries/orders received after the block call.

HIBOR

Hong Kong Interbank Offer Rate, the annualized offer rate banks pay to attain Hong Kong three-month deposits in denominated dollars.

Hidden load

A sales charge that is not explicitly disclosed or is buried in the fine print of a mutual fund prospectus or life insurance policy and therefore is not immediately apparent.

Hidden values

Valuable assets owned by a company, that are not accurately reflected in its stock price at a particular time.

High-coupon bond refunding

Replace a high-coupon bond with a new, lower-coupon bond.

High credit

The maximum amount of outstanding loans for a particular customer on a bank's record.

High current income mutual fund

A mutual fund whose primary goal is to produce a high level of income by making higher-risk investments in instruments such as junk bonds.

High flyer

High-priced and highly speculative stock that moves up and down sharply over a short period. Generally glamorous in nature due to the capital gains potential associated with them; also used to describe any high-priced stock. Antithesis of sleeper.

High-grade

Credit quality of AAA or AA.

High-grade bond

A bond with Triple-A or Double-A rating in Standard & Poor's, or Moody's rating system.

High price

The highest (intraday) price of a stock over the past 52 weeks, adjusted for any stock splits.

High-premium convertible debenture

A bond with a long-term, high-premium, common stock conversion feature. It also offers a competitive interest rate. This type of investment vehicle is aimed at bond investors who want to be able to convert into stock to hedge against inflation.

High-tech stock

Stocks of companies operating in high-technology fields.

High withholding tax interest income

Interest income that is subject to a foreign gross withholding tax of 5% or more. Specified in US tax code.

High yield

In the context of hedge funds, a style of management that focuses on low rated fixed income securities.

High-yield bond

See: Junk bond.

Highjacking

Japanese term for a takeover.

Highly confident letter

An investment banking firm's letter indicating that the firm is highly confident it will be able to arrange financing for a securities deal.

Highly leveraged transaction (HLT)

Bank loan to a highly leveraged firm.

Highs

Stocks that have hit an all-time high for the current 52-week time period.

Historical cost

Describes the accounting cost carried in the books for a current cost of the item.

Historical Cost Accounting Convention

An accounting technique that values an asset for balance sheet purposes at the price paid for the asset at the time of its acquisition.

Historical exchange rate

An accounting term that refers to the exchange rate in effect at the time an asset or liability is acquired.

Historical trading range

The range of price over which a security or a commodity has traded since listing on a exchange.

Historical volatility

Fluctuations estimated from a historical time series.

Historical yield

A measure of a mutual fund's yield over a specific period of time, e.g., 1 year, 2 year, 5 year, or year to date.

Hit the bid

A dealer who agrees to sell at the bid price quoted by another dealer is said to "hit" that bid. Antithesis of take the offer.

Hit the ribbon

Used in the context of general equities. See: Print.

HK

The two-character ISO 3166 country code for HONG KONG.

HKD

The ISO 4217 currency code for theHong Kong Dollar.

HKFE

See: Hong Kong Futures Exchange.

HLT

See: Highly leveraged transaction.

HM

The two-character ISO 3166 country code for HEARD ISLAND AND MCDONALD ISLANDS.

HN

The two-character ISO 3166 country code for HONDURAS.

HNL

The ISO 4217 currency code for the Honduras Lempira.

Hold

To maintain ownership of a security over a long period of time. "Hold" is also a recommendation of an analyst who is not positive enough on a stock to recommend a buy, but not negative enough on the stock to recommend a sell.

Holder

The purchaser of an option.

Holder of record date

The date on which holders of record in a firm's stock ledger are designated as the recipients of either dividends or stock rights. Also called date of record.

Holding company

A corporation that owns enough voting stock in another firm to control management and operations by influencing or electing its board of directors.

Holding the market

The illegal practice of maintaining and/or placing a sufficient number of buy orders to create price support for a security or commodity in an amount to of stabilize a downward trend.

Holding period

Length of time a security is held.

Holding-period return

Rate of return on an investment over a given period.

Holding-Period Yield (HPY)

The annual rate of return actually realized on an investment in a bond.

Home asset bias

The tendency of investors to over invest in their own county's assets.

Homemade dividend

Sale of some shares of stock to get cash in an amount similar to that of a cash dividend.

Homemade leverage

Idea that as long as individuals borrow (or lend) on the same terms as the firm, they can duplicate the effects of corporate leverage on their own. Thus, if levered firms are priced too high, rational investors will simply borrow on personal accounts to buy shares in unlevered firms.

Home Market Price

See Foreign Market Value.

Homeowner's equity account

A credit line offered by mortgage lenders allowing a homeowner a second mortgage that uses the equity present in the customer's account as collateral.

Homeowner's insurance policy

An insurance policy protecting a homeowner against damage or loss to property.

Home run

Large capital gain in a stock in a short period of time.

Homogeneity

The degree to which items are similar.

Homogeneous

Exhibiting a high degree of homogeneity.

Homogeneous expectations assumption

An assumption of Markowitz portfolio construction that investors have the same expectations with respect to the inputs that are used to derive efficient portfolios: asset returns, variances, and covariances.

Homologation of an Automobile

Homologation of an automobile is the certification by a country that a vehicle conforms to its safety and emission standards — primarily that a vehicle has been manufactured or modified to meet a country's standards.

Hong Kong Futures Exchange (HKFE)

Established in 1976, the Hong Kong Futures Exchange (H.K.F.E.) operates futures and options markets in index, stock, interest rate, and foreign exchange products.

Horizon analysis

An analysis of returns using total return to assess performance over some investment horizon.

Horizon matching strategy

An income immunization strategy that cash-matches over the next few years and duration-matches the rest.

Horizon return

Total return over a given horizon.

Horizontal acquisition

Merger between two companies producing similar goods or services.

Horizontal analysis

The process of dividing each expense item of a given year by the same expense item in the base year. It allows assessment of changes in the relative importance of expense items over time and the behavior of expense items as sales change.

Horizontal Export Trading Company

An export trading company which exports a range of similar or identical products supplied by a number of manufacturers or other producers. Webb-Pomerene Organizations, trade-grouped organized export trading companies, and an export trading company formed by an association of agricultural cooperatives are the prime examples of horizontally organized export trading companies.

Horizontal merger

A merger involving two or more firms in the same industry that are both at the same stage in the production cycle; that is, two or more competitors.

Horizontal price movement

Stock price movement within a narrow price range over an extended period of time which creates the appearance of a relatively straight line on a graph of the stock's price.

Horizontal spread

The simultaneous purchase and sale of two options that differ only in their expiration dates.

Horn of Africa

The Horn of Africa comprises Djibouti, Ethiopia, Somalia, and Sudan.

Hospital revenue bond

A bond issued to finance construction of a hospital by a municipal or state agency.

Host security

The security to which a warrant is attached.

Hostile takeover

A takeover of a company (usually made by an open tender offer to shareholders) against the wishes of the current management and the board of directors by an acquiring company or raider.

Hot

Used in the context of general equities. Active, usually with positive price implications.

Hot money

Money that moves across country borders in response to interest rate differences and that moves away when the interest rate differential disappears.

House

Firms that conduct business as broker-dealers in securities or in the investment banking field are characterized as houses.

House account

A type of account at a brokerage firm that is given a high level of priority and is handled by the main office or an executive, rather than a traditional salesperson.

House Air Waybill (HAWB)

Freight forwarder's air waybill which refers to consolidated shipments. See Air Cargo Receipt.

House call

Notification by a brokerage house that a customer's margin account is below the minimum maintenance level. The client must provide more cash or equity, or the account will be liquidated.

House of issue

An investment banking firm whose business it is to underwrite stock or bond issues and offer the securities to the public.

House maintenance requirement

The internal rules of a brokerage house that govern the minimum amount of equity that must be present in a customer's margin account.

House poor

People who are short on cash because most of their money is tied up in their homes are "house poor."

House rules

Internal rules of broker-dealer firm that govern the handling of its customers' accounts.

Housing bond

Bonds issued by a local housing authority to finance housing projects.

"How are you making XXX?"

"What is your market in a particular stock?" See: Quotation.

HR

The two-character ISO 3166 country code for CROATIA.

HRK

Croatian Kuna currency. (The ISO 4217 currency code).

HT

The two-character ISO 3166 country code for HAITI.

HTG

The ISO 4217 currency code for the Haiti Gourde.

HU

The two-character ISO 3166 country code for HUNGARY.

Hubris

An arrogance due to excessive pride and an insolence toward others. A classic character flaw of a trader or investor.

HUF

(1) The ISO 4217 currency code for the Hungarian Forint. (2) Hindu United Family.

Hulbert rating

A rating by Hulbert Financial Digest (of Alexandria, Virginia) of how well the recommendations of various investment advisory newsletters have performed.

Human capital

The unique capabilities and expertise of individuals.

Humphrey-Hawkins Act

Informal name for the Full Employment and Balanced Growth Act of 1978, from the names of the act's original sponsors.

Hung up

Used to describe the position of an investor whose stocks or bonds have dropped in value below their original purchase price.

Hunkering down

A term used to describe a trader selling off a big position in a stock.

Hurdle rate

The required return in capital budgeting. For example, if a project has an expected rate of return higher than the hurdle rate, the project may be accepted.

Hurst Exponent(H)

A measure of the bias in fractional Brownian motion. $H=0.50$ for Brownian motion. $0.50<H<1.00$ for persistent, or trend-reinforcing series. $0<H<0.50$ for an anti-persistent, or mean-reverting system. The inverse of the Hurst exponent is equal to alpha, the characteristic exponent for Stable Paretian distributions. The fractal dimension of a time series, D, is equivalent to 2-H.

Hybrid

A package of two or more different kinds of risk management instruments that are usually interactive.

Hybrid annuity

A type of insurance company investment that combines the benefits of both a fixed annuity and a variable annuity.

Hybrid security

A convertible security whose optioned common stock is trading in a middle range, causing the convertible security to trade with the characteristics of both a fixed income security and a common stock instrument.

Hyperinflation

See: Inflation

Hypothecation

In banking, refers to the commitment of property to secure a loan.

In securities, refers to the commitment of securities to serve as collateral for margin loans at the broker-dealer firm.

Hysteresis

Used to characterize a lagging effect. Firms may fail to enter markets that appear attractive, or firms that are once invested in a market may persist in operating at a loss. The effect is characteristic of investments with high entry and exit costs along with high uncertainty.

i

I

Fifth letter of a Nasdaq stock symbol specifying that it is the third preferred bond of the company.

IBC's money fund report average

Report giving the average yield of all major money market funds.

IBES

See: Institutional Brokers Estimate System.

IBF

See: International Banking Facility.

I-bonds

Treasury savings bonds with a 30-year maturity indexed to account for inflation.

IBRD

See: International Bank for Reconstruction and Development.

IC

See: Information Coefficient.

ICC

See: International Chamber of Commerce.

IC-DISC

Interest Charge domestic International Sales Corporation.

Ice Clause

An ice clause is a standard clause in the chartering of ocean vessels. It dictates the course a vessel master may take if the ship is prevented from entering the loading or discharge port because of ice, or if the vessel is threatened by ice while in the port. The clause establishes rights and obligations of both vessel owner and charterer if these events occur.

ICPO

Irrevocable Corporate Purchase Order.

ID

The two-character ISO 3166 country code for INDONESIA.

Identified shares

Stock or mutual fund whose purchase date and price may be identified for capital gains and tax purposes when shares sold.

Idiosyncratic Risk

Unsystematic risk or risk that is uncorrelated to the overall market risk. In other words, the risk that is firm-specific and can be diversified through holding a portfolio of stocks.

IDR

The ISO 4217 currency code for the Indonesian Rupiah.

IDR

See: International Depository Receipt.

IE

The two-character ISO 3166 country code for IRELAND.

IEP

The ISO 4217 currency code for the Irish Punt.

IFB

Invitation For Bid.

IFC

See: International Finance Corporation.

I-I page

In over-the-counter trading, same as H-H page, but exclusively for OTC stocks.

IL

The two-character ISO 3166 country code for ISRAEL.

Illegal dividend

A corporation's dividend that is declared in violation of its charter and/or of state laws, typically because of the way it is calculated.

Illiquid

In the context of finance. absence of cash flow needed to fulfill financial debts and meet obligations. In the context of investments, describes a lightly traded investment such as a stock or bond that is not easily converted into cash.

ILS

The ISO 4217 currency code for the Israeli Shekel.

Imbalance of orders

Used for listed equity securities. Too many market orders of one kind-buy or to sell or limit orders to buy up or sell down, without matching orders of the opposite kind. An imbalance usually follows a dramatic event such as a takeover, research recommendation, or death of a key executive, or a government ruling that will significantly affect the company's business. If it occurs before the stock exchange opens, trading in the stock is delayed. If it occurs during the trading day, the specialist halts and then suspends trading (with floor governor's approval) until enough matching orders can be found to make an orderly market.

IMF

See: International Monetary Fund.

IMM

See: International Monetary Market.

Immediate or canceled order (IOC order)

Market or limited price order that is to be executed in whole or in part as soon as such order is represented in the trading crowd. The portion not executed is to be treated as canceled. A stop is considered an execution in this context. See: AON order, FOK order.

Immediate family

Term used in the NASD rules of fair practice to refer to one's parents, brothers, sisters, children, relatives supported financially, father-in-law, mother-in-law, sister-in-law, and brother-in-law.

Immediate payment annuity

An annuity contract paid by a single payment and with a specified payment plan the starts immediately after the contract is purchased.

Immediate settlement

Delivery and settlement of securities within five business days.

Immunization

The construction of an asset and a liability match that benefits from offsetting changes in value.

Immunization strategy

A bond portfolio strategy whose goal is to eliminate the portfolio's risk, in case of a general change in the rate of interest, through the use of duration.

Impaired capital

When a company's total capital is less than the par value of all its capital stock.

Impaired credit

Result of a borrower's reduced credit rating.

Imperfect market

Economic environment in which the costs of labor and other resources used for production encourage firms to use substitute inputs that less costly.

Implicit Bankruptcy Costs

Opportunity costs incurred prior to the bankruptcy process such as the loss of sales or financing.

Implicit tax

Lower or higher before-tax required returns on assets that are subject to lower or higher tax rates.

Implied call

The right of the homeowner to prepay, or call, a mortgage at any time.

Implied repo rate

The rate that a seller of a futures contract can earn by buying an issue and then delivering it at the settlement date. Related: Cheapest to deliver issue.

Implied volatility

The expected volatility in a stock's return derived from its option price, maturity date, exercise price, and riskless rate of return, using an option pricing model such as Black-Scholes.

Import Certificate

The import certificate is a means by which the government of the country of ultimate destination exercises legal control over the internal channeling of the commodities covered by the import certificate.

Import/export letters of credit

Bank or financial institution issuance's of funds in a certain amount provided to facilitate international trade.

Importer

The U.S. Customs Service defines "importer" as a person primarily liable for the payment of duties on the merchandise, or an authorized agent acting on the importer's behalf. The importer may be: (a) a consignee, (b) the importer of record, or (c) the actual owner of the merchandise if the actual owner has filed with Customs a declaration acknowledging ownership along with a superseding bond.

Importer of Record

The U.S. Customs Service defines the importer of record as the owner or purchaser of the goods; or, when designated by the owner, purchaser, or consignee, a licensed Customs broker.

Import License

A document required and issued by some national governments authorizing the importation of goods into their individual countries.

Import Quota

A means of restricting imports by the issuance of licenses to importers, assigning each a quota, after determination of the total amount of any commodity which is to be imported during a period. Import licenses may also specify the country from which the importer must purchase the goods.

Import Quota Auctioning

The process of auctioning the right to import specified quantities of quota-restricted goods.

Import Restrictions

Import restriction, applied by a country with an adverse trade balance (or for other reasons), reflect a desire to control the volume of goods coming into the country from other countries may include the imposition of tariffs or import quotas, restrictions on the amount of foreign currency available to cover imports, a requirement for import deposits, the imposition of import surcharges, or the prohibition of various categories of imports.

Imports

Imports of merchandise include commodities of foreign origin as well as goods of domestic origin returned to the United States with no change in condition or after having been processed and/or assembled in other countries. For statistical purposes, imports are classified by type of transaction:

- — Merchandise entered for immediate consumption. ("duty free" merchandise and merchandise on which duty is paid on arrival);

— Merchandise withdrawn for consumption from Customs bonded warehouses, and U.S. Foreign Trade Zones;

— Merchandise entered into Customs bonded warehouses and U.S. Foreign Trade Zones from foreign countries.

Imports for Consumption

"Imports for Consumption" measure the total of merchandise that has physically cleared through U.S. Customs either entering consumption channels immediately or entering after withdrawal for consumption from bonded warehouses under Customs custody or from Foreign Trade Zones. Many countries use the term "special imports" to designate statistics compiled on this basis.

Import Substitution

A strategy which emphasizes the replacement of imports with domestically produced goods, rather than the production of goods for export, to encourage the development of domestic industry.

Import substitution development strategy

A development strategy followed by many Latin American countries and other LDCs that emphasize import substitution-accomplished through protectionism-as the route to economic growth.

Imputation tax system

Arrangement by which investors who receive a dividend also receive a tax credit for corporate taxes that the firm has paid.

Imputed interest

Used in accounting to refer to interest that has effectively been paid to a bondholder, even though no money has actually been paid.

Imputed value

Refers to the value of an asset, service, or company that is not physically recorded in any accounts but is implicit in the product, e.g., the opportunity cost of cash remaining in a savings account and not invested.

IN

The two-character ISO 3166 country code for INDIA.

Inactive asset

Asset not used in a productive manner at all times.

Inactive post

Trading post on NYSE floor where inactive, lightly traded stocks are traded in 10-share lots as opposed to 100-share lots.

Inactive stock/bond

A security that trades in very small volume on a daily basis. See:: Illiquid.

In-and-out trader

A daytrader, or a speculator who buys and sells the same security on the same day.

In & out

Refers to over-the-counter trading. Trade in which the trader has both the buyers and sellers lined up for a clean trade. See: Cross

In between

Used in the context of general equities. Priced higher than the bid price but lower than the offer price. See: In the middle

In Bond

A term applied to the status of merchandise admitted provisionally to a country without payment of duties

— either for storage in a bonded warehouse or for trans-shipment to another point, where duties will eventually be imposed.

In-Bond System

The In-Bond System, a part of Customs' Automated Commercial System, controls merchandise from the point of unloading at the port of entry or exportation. The system works with the input of departures (from the port of unlading), arrivals, and closures (accountability of arrivals).

In the box

Means that a dealer has a wire receipt for securities, indicating that effective delivery on them has been made.

Incentive fee

Compensation paid to commodities trading advisers or to any practitioner who achieves above-average returns. Sometimes called performance fee.

Incentive Stock Option (ISO)

An Option that has met certain tax requirements entitling the optionee to favorable tax treatment. Such an option is free from regular tax at the date of grant and the date of exercise (when a non-qualified option would become taxable). If two holding period tests are met (two years between grant date and sale date and one year between the exercise date and sale date), the profit on the option qualifies as a long term capital gain rather than ordinary income. If the holding periods are not met, there has been a "disqualifying disposition".

Incestuous share dealing

Trading of shares between companies in order to create a tax or financial benefit for the companies involved.

Income baskets

Category to which certain income is allocated. Losses in one basket may not be used to offset gains in another basket. Specified in U.S. tax code.

Income beneficiary

One who receives income from a trust.

Income bond

A bond whose payment of interest is contingent on sufficient earnings. These bonds are commonly used during the reorganization of a failed or failing business.

Income dividend

Any payout to mutual fund shareholders resulting from interest, dividends, or other income.

Income exclusion rule

The IRS rule that excludes certain types of income from taxation, e.g., welfare payments.

Income fund

A mutual fund that seeks to provide to liberal current income from investments.

Income immunization strategies

Methodologies adopted to insure adequate future cash flow.

Income investment company

A management company focused on managing a mutual fund whose primary purpose is income generation, typically investing in bonds and high dividend yielding stocks.

Income limited partnership

A limited partnership whose main goal is income generation, e.g., real estate, oil equipment.

Income property

Real estate purchased for the reasons of income generation.

Income risk

The possibility that a portfolio's dividends will decline as a result of falling interest rates. Income risk is generally greatest for money market instruments and short-term bonds, and least for long-term bonds.

Income statement (statement of operations)

A statement showing the revenues, expenses, and income (the difference between revenues and expenses) of a corporation over some period of time.

Income stock

Common stock with a high dividend yield and few profitable investment opportunities.

Income tax

A state or federal government's levy on individuals as personal income tax and on the earnings of corporations as corporate income tax.

In competition

Indication that the customer has revealed trading interest to multiple brokers and that the trade will take place with the firm having the highest bid or lowest offer. Antithesis of exclusive.

Incontestability clause

Clause in a life insurance contract preventing the insurer from revoking the policy after it has been in force for a year or two if the life insurance company discovers any important facts that the policyholder may have concealed, such as experiencing a stroke.

Incorporation

This is the act of forming a company and giving it a separate legal existence, and is usually associated with gaining limited liability.

Incoterms

Trade terms used worldwide to specify seller and buyer obligations in shipments against international sales contracts. These terms are adopted by the International Chamber of Commerce (ICC) for international movement of merchandise. Since they in themselves are not law, they must be specified if desired in quotations, sales contracts, purchase orders and commercial invoices.

Incremental cash flows

Difference between the firm's cash flows with and without a project.

Incremental cost of capital

Average cost applicable to the issue of each additional unit of debt and equity.

Incremental costs and benefits

Costs and benefits that would occur if a particular course of action is taken, compared to those that would have obtained if that course of action had not been taken.

Incremental internal rate of return

Internal rate of return (I.R.R.) on the incremental investment from choosing a larger instead of a smaller project.

Indemnify

Used in insurance policy agreements as to compensation for damage or loss. Hold harmless

Indemnification

Used in insurance policy agreements as to compensation for damage or loss. In the context of corporate governance, Director Indemnification uses the bylaws and/or charter to indemnify officers and directors from certain legal expenses and judgements resulting from lawsuits pertaining to their conduct.

Indenture

Agreement between lender and borrower that details specific terms of the bond issuance. Specifies legal obligations of bond issuer and rights of bondholders. An indenture spells out the specific terms of a bond, as well as the rights and responsibilities of both the issuer of the security and the holder.

Independent auditor

A certified public accountant operating outside the company who can provide an accountant's opinion.

Independent broker

NYSE member who executes orders for floor brokers and firms other than its own.

Independent European Program Group

The IEPG is an intergovernmental organization that is not formally part of NATO but whose membership includes all the EC members of the alliance, plus Norway and Turkey. Established in 1976, IEPG's objectives are to promote European cooperation in research, development, and production of defense equipment; improve transatlantic armaments cooperation; and maintain a healthy European defense industrial base.

Independent investments

Investments available to a firm that may be selected individually or in groups because each investment is different in its nature and purpose.

Independent project

A project whose acceptance or rejection is independent of the acceptance or rejection of other projects.

Independent variable

Term used in regression analysis to represent the element or condition that is expected to influence another (so-called dependent) variable.

Index

Statistical composite that measures changes in the economy or in financial markets, often expressed in percentage changes from a base year or from the previous month. Indexes measure the ups and downs of stock, bond, and some commodities markets, in terms of market prices and weighting of companies the index.

Index arbitrage

An investment/trading strategy that exploits divergences between actual and theoretical futures prices. An example is the simultaneous buying (selling) of stock index futures (i.e., S&P 500) while selling (buying) the underlying stocks of that index, capturing as profit the temporarily inflated basis between these two baskets. Often, the point at which profitability exists is expressed at the block call as the number of points the future must be over or under the underlying basket for an arbitrage opportunity to exist. See: Program trading.

Indexed bond

Bond whose payments are linked to an index, e.g., the consumer price index.

Indexed Currency Option Note

An ICON is a debt repayment instrument whose value is partially determined by the exchange rate between two currencies. Interest payments, made in one currency, are lowered if the rate of exchange exceeds a pre-arranged rate.

Indexed Stock Options

Options that have an exercise price which may fluctuate above or below market value at performance options in that the exercise price of indexed options typically remains variable until the option is exercised.

Index fund

Investment fund designed to match the returns on a stock market index. Mutual fund whose portfolio matches that of a broad-based index such as the S&P 500 and whose performance therefore mirrors the market as represented by that index.

Index futures

A futures contract on an index (such as a foreign stock index) in the futures market.

Indexing

A passive instrument strategy calling for construction of a portfolio of stocks designed to track the total return performance of an index of stocks.

Indexing plus

See: Enhanced indexing.

Index method

Technique to calculate rates of return that is based on initial and terminal values.

Index model

A model of stock returns using a market index such as the S&P 500 to represent common or systematic risk factors.

Index option

A call or put option based on a stock market index.

Index and Option Market (IOM)

A division of the CME established in 1982 for trading stock index products and options.

Index swap

A swap of a market index for some other asset, such as a stock-for-stock or debt-for-stock swap.

Index warrant

A stock index option issued by either a corporate or a sovereign entity as part of a security offering, and guaranteed by an option clearing corporation.

Indicated dividend

Total amount of dividends that would be paid on a share of stock over the next 12 months if each dividend were the same amount as the most recent dividend. Usually represented by the letter "e" in stock tables.

Indicated yield

The yield, based on the most recent quarterly rate times four. To determine the yield, divide the annual dividend by the price of the stock. The resulting number is represented as a percentage. See: Dividend yield.

Indication

(1) Notice given by a dealer (through Autex) or customer of an interest in buying or selling stock, sometimes including specific volume and price; (2) approximation of where a specialist sees buy and sell interest to tighten the range to an opening price.

Indication of interest

A dealer's or investor's interest in purchasing (not commitment to buy) securities that are still in the underwriting stage and are being registered by the Securities and Exchange Commission.

Indication pricing schedule

A statement of rates for an interest rate or currency swap.

Indicator

Used in the context of general equities. Technical or fundamental measurement that securities analysts use to forecast the market's direction, such as investment advisory sentiment, volume of stock trading, direction of interest rates, and buying or selling by corporate insiders.

Indifference curve

The expression in a graph of a utility function, where the horizontal axis measures risk and the vertical axis measures expected return. The curve connects all portfolios with the same utility.

Indirect Claim

Claim of a financial intermediary; the intermediary relends funds to the deficit unit to enable it to acquire real assets.

Indirect costs of financial distress

Costs such as lost business as a result of bankruptcy or liquidation.

Indirect diversification benefits

Diversification benefits provided by the multinational corporation that are not available to investors through their portfolio investment.

Indirect Exchange Rate

The foreign currency price of one unit of the home currency.

Indirect method

Reporting in the statement of cash flow that adjusts or reconciles net income to cash from operations.

Indirect quote

For foreign exchange, the number of units of a foreign currency needed to buy one US dollar.

Indirect terms

The price of a unit of domestic currency in foreign currency terms. See: Direct terms.

Individually Validated Export License

A required document issued by the U.S. Government authorizing the export of specific commodities. This license is for a specific transaction or time period in which the exporting is to take place. Compare General export license.

Individual Retirement Account (IRA)

A retirement account that may be established by an employed person. IRA contributions are tax deductible according to certain guidelines, and the gains in the account are tax-deferred.

Individual Retirement Account (IRA) rollover

A provision of the law governing IRA's that enables a retiree or anyone receiving a lump-sum payment from a pension, profit-sharing, or salary reduction plan to transfer the amount into an IRA.

Individual tax return

A tax return filed by an individual to account for their personal income and taxes payable.

Individual Validated License

An IVL is written approval by which the U.S. Department of Commerce grants permission, which is valid for 2 years, for the export of a specified quantity of products or technical data to a single recipient. IVLs also are required, under certain circumstances, as authorization for the reexport of U.S.-origin commodities to new destinations abroad.

Inductive reasoning

The attempt to use information about a specific situation to draw a conclusion.

Industrialization Fund for Developing Countries

The IFU invests in joint venture companies in the developing countries, together with Danish companies. It is a revolving Fund whose resources were made available by the Danish government. IFU takes part in joint ventures as a shareholder and can provide loans or guarantees for loans. The Fund was established by Denmark in 1967; headquarters are in Copenhagen. Since 1978, Fund operations have been funded solely from the return on investments in developing countries and from other financial assets, with no public financial subsidy.

Industrial production

A statistic determined by the Federal Reserve Board focusing on the total output of all US factories and mines on a monthly basis. Used as an economic indicator.

Industrial revenue bond (IRB)

A bond issued by local government agencies on behalf of corporations.

Industrials

General term used in the financial markets to refer to

companies manufacturing, producing, or distributing goods and services.

Industry

The category describing a company's primary business activity. This category is usually determined by the largest portion of revenue.

Industry allocation

Investment of certain proportions of a portfolio in certain industries. Sometimes called sector allocation.

Industry Consultations Program

The Industry Consultations Program for Trade Policy Matters is an advisory committee structure created by the Trade Act of 1974; expanded by the Trade Agreements Act of 1979; and amended by the Omnibus Trade and Competitiveness Act of 1988. The program is operated jointly by Commerce and the U.S. Trade Representative. Members of the committees are appointed by the Secretary of Commerce and the U.S. Trade Representative. The present structure consists of 17 Industry Sector Advisory Committees (ISACs), 3 Industry Functional Advisory Committees (IFACs), a Committee of Chairs, and an Industry Policy Advisory Committee (IPAC). The focus of the 3 Functional Advisory Committees are: (1) Customs Matters, (2) Standards, and (3) Intellectual Property Rights.

Inefficient portfolio

Group of assets dominated by at least one other portfolio under the mean variance rule. For example, if A has both lower return and higher volatility than B, we say A is dominated by B.

Infant industry argument

Argument that industries in the developing and emerging sectors of the economy need protection against international competition in order to establish themselves.

Inflation

The rate at which the general level of prices for goods and services is rising.

Inflation accounting

Accounting practices allowing for the effects of inflation.

Inflation-escalator clause

A clause in a contract providing for increases or decreases in inflation depending on fluctuations in the cost of living, production costs, and so forth.

Inflation hedge

Investments designed to hedge against inflation and the loss of purchasing power associated with it.

Inflation-indexed securities

Securities such as bonds or notes that guarantee a return higher than the rate of inflation if the security is held to maturity.

Inflation risk

Also called purchasing power risk, the risk that changes in the real return the investor will realize after adjusting for inflation will be negative.

Inflation uncertainty

The fact that future inflation rates are not known. It is a possible contributing factor to the makeup of the term structure of interest rates.

Inflexible expenses

Expenses that cannot be adjusted or eliminated such as car payments or rental payments. Antithesis of flexible expenses.

Information Agent

Agent whose primary task is to disseminate and explain the details of capital transactions.

Informational efficiency

The speed and accuracy with which prices reflect new information.

Information asymmetry

Condition that information is known to some, but not all, participants.

Information Coefficient (IC)

The correlation between predicted and actual stock returns, sometimes used to measure the contribution of a financial analyst. An IC of 1.0 indicates a perfect linear relationship between predicted and actual returns, while an IC of 0.0 indicates no linear relationship.

Information content effect

The rise in the stock price following a dividend signal, or publication of some other related news.

Information costs

Transactions costs that include the assessment of the investment merits of a financial asset. Related: Search costs.

Information Highway

A network, consisting of many connected networks, which has the capacity to carry high-speed, broadband services, including interactive and voice, data, image and video communication. The network will allow customers to reach offices, homes, schools, hospitals and a variety of other institutions.

Information-motivated trades

Trades in which an investor believes he or she possesses pertinent information not currently reflected in the stock's price.

Information Ratio

The ratio of annualized expected residual return to residual risk. A central measurement for active management, value added is proportional to the square of the information ratio.

Information services

Organizations that furnish investment and other types of information, such as information that helps a firm monitor its cash position.

Information Signaling

Conveying intelligence through a firm's actions. A firm's dividend policy, for example, provides signals to investors concerning the value of the firm's stock.

Informational efficiency

The degree to which market prices correctly and quickly reflect information and thus the true value of an underlying asset.

Informationless trades

Trades that are the result of either a reallocation of wealth or an implementation of an investment strategy that acts only on existing information. That is, an investor might sell a large block of stock — not because they have information that leads them to think the stock will fall in value — but because they might need the cash for some other investment.

Infotainment

The integration of information, education and entertainment services.

Infrastructure

A country's fundamental system of transportation, communications, and other aspects of its physical capabilities.

Infrequent Exporter

The Commerce Department's International Trade Administration defines an "infrequent exporter" as a company that has some export experience — usually averaging between 1 and 50 export shipments per year — but which still needs assistance to increase the size of its export market or to expand into new ones.

Ingot

A bar of metal such as the type that the Federal Reserve System uses to store gold reserves.

In hand

Used in the context of general equities. Firm indicating control of a bid, offer, or order.

Inherent Vice

An insurance term referring to any defect or other characteristics of a product which could result in damage to the product without external cause. Insurance policies may specifically exclude losses caused by inherent vice.

Inheritance tax return

Tax form required to determine the amount of state tax due on an inheritance.

In the hole

Used in the context of general equities. Below the inside market when one is attempting to sell the stock; at a significant discount. Antithesis of premium.

In-house

In the context of general equities, keeping an activity within the firm. For example, rather than go to the marketplace and sell a security for a client to anyone, an attempt is made to find a buyer to complete the transaction with the firm. Although a listed trade must be taken to the floor of the stock exchange, matching supply with demand within the confines of the firm results in higher commissions for the firm.

In-house processing float

The time it takes the receiver of a check to process a payment and deposit it in a bank for collection.

Initial filing

Has various meanings. It could refer to a form that is filed with the Securities and Exchange Commission in advance of a major event, such as a public offering or a share repurchase. It could also refer to filings that occur before legal inside transactions.

Initial margin

(1) Amount of money deposited by both buyers and sellers of futures contracts to ensure performance of the terms of the contract; (2) amount of cash or eligible securities required to be deposited with a broker before engaging in margin transactions.

Initial margin requirement

When buying securities on margin, the proportion of the total market value of the securities that the investor must pay for in cash. The Security Exchange Act of 1934 gives the Board of Governors of the Federal Reserve the responsibility to set initial margin requirements, but individual brokerage firms are free to set higher requirements. In futures contracts, initial margin requirements are set by the exchange.

Initial Negotiating Right

A right held by one GATT country to seek compensation for an impairment of a given bound tariff rate by another GATT country. INRs stem from past negotiating concessions and allow the INR holder to seek compensation for an impairment of tariff concessions regardless of its status as a supplier of the product in question.

Initial public offering (IPO)

A company's first sale of stock to the public. Securities offered in an IPO are often, but not always, those of young, small companies seeking outside equity capital and a public market for their stock. Investors purchasing stock in IPOs generally must be prepared to accept considerable risks for the possibility of large gains. IPOs by investment companies (closed-end funds) usually include underwriting fees that represent a load to buyers.

Initial Public Offering Spinning

The practice of an investment bank setting aside portions of a corporation's Initial Public Offering for senior management of that corporation.

Initiate coverage

(1) Firm is now followed by analysts at a particular securities house; (2) Indication to cover short position by purchasing the underlying stock (this cancels out the short position).

Injury

In U.S. law, a finding by the International Trade Commission that imports are causing, or are likely to cause, harm to a U.S. industry. An injury determination is the basis for a Section 201 case. It is also a requirement in all antidumping and most countervailing duty cases, in conjunction with Commerce Department determinations on dumping and subsidization.

Inland Bill of Lading

A bill of lading used in transporting goods overland to the exporter's international carrier. Although a through bill of lading can sometimes be used, it is usually necessary to prepare both an inland bill of lading and an ocean bill of lading for export shipments. Compare Air waybill, Ocean bill of lading, and Through bill of lading.

In-line

Used in the context of general equities. (1) An order or market in a specific security within the inside market; 2) any announcement (earnings) that adheres closely to Wall Street analysts' expectations.

In the middle

Used in the context of general equities. At a price exactly in between the bid and offer prices.

In-the-money

A put option that has a strike price higher than the underlying futures price, or a call option with a strike price lower than the underlying futures price. For example, if the March COMEX silver futures contract is trading at $6 an ounce, a March call with a strike price of $5.50 would be considered in the money by $0.50 an ounce. Related: Put. Antithesis of out-of-the-money.

In-the-money option

An option that has value.

In play

Often used in risk arbitrage. Company that has become the target of a takeover, and whose stock has now become a speculative issue.

Input-output tables

Tables that indicate how much each industry requires of the production of each other industry in order to produce each dollar of its own output.

Inquiry

Used in the context of general equities. In-line expression of interest in a particular stock, usually asking the firm to bid for or offer stock.

INR

The ISO 4217 currency code for the Indian Rupee.

In-service withdrawal

A participant-initiated withdrawal from an employer-sponsored retirement plan while the participant is still employed by the company.

Inside market

Refers to over-the-counter trading. Best (highest) bid and best (lowest) offer, often used in the O.T.C. Market. See: In-line.

Insider information

Material information about a company that has not yet been made public. It is illegal for holders of this information to make trades based on it, however received.

Insider trading

Trading by officers, directors, major stockholders, or others who hold private inside information allowing them to benefit from buying or selling stock.

Insider Trading Sanctions Act of 1984

Act imposing civil and criminal penalties for insider trading violations.

Insider Trading & Securities Fraud Enforcement Act of 1988 (ITSFEA)

Federal legislation that greatly increased the penalties for trading on material inside information.

Insiders

These are directors and senior officers of a corporation-in effect, those who have access to inside information about a company. An insider also is someone who owns more than 10% of the voting shares of a company.

Insolvency risk

The risk that a firm will be unable to satisfy its debts. Also known as bankruptcy risk.

Insolvent

A firm that is unable to pay debts (its liabilities exceed its assets).

Inspection Certification

Some purchasers and countries may require a certificate of inspection attesting to the specifications of the goods shipped, usually performed by a third party. Inspection certificates are often obtained from independent testing organizations.

Inspector(s) of Election

The person(s) appointed by the Corporation to act as a judge on voting matters brought before a shareholder meeting. The inspector determines which proxies and ballots are in good form, and acceptable to be voted. They also count and record the votes, supervise and inspect the counting process and attest to the final results. They cannot be overruled on these matters, although they have no voice in the procedural aspects of the meeting itself.

Inspector's or Judge's Certificate

A form provided by the Corporation, and completed by the Inspectors of Election, attesting to the final voting results and percentages of a shareholder meeting.

Installment payments

Distribution of plan assets to beneficiaries based upon a regular schedule.

Installment sale

The sale of an asset in exchange for a specified series of payments (the installments).

Instinet (Institutional Networks Corporation)

Computerized subscriber service that serves as a vehicle for the fourth market. "Instinet" is registered with the SEC As a stock exchange it numbers among its subscribers a large number of mutual funds and other institutional investors linked to each other by computer terminals. The system permits subscribers to display bids and offers (which are exposed system wide for whatever length of time the initiating party specifies) and to consummate trades electronically. Instinet is largely used by market makers, but, nonmarket makers and customers have equal access.

institution

An organization, probably very large, engaged in professional investing in securities. Normally a bank, insurance company, or mutual fund.

Institutional broker

A broker who buys and sells securities for institutional investors such as banks, and mutual funds, pensions.

Institutional Brokers' Estimate System (IBES)

Service that assembles analysts' estimates of future earnings for thousands of publicly traded companies, detailing how many estimates are available for each company and the high, low, and average estimates for each.

Institutional investors

Organizations that invest, including insurance companies, depository institutions, pension funds, investment companies, mutual funds, and endowment funds.

Institutionalization

The gradual domination of financial markets by institutional investors, as opposed to individual investors. This process has occurred throughout the industrialized world.

Instrumentality

Notes issued by a federal agency whose obligations are guaranteed by the full-faith-and-credit of the government, even though the agency's responsibilities are not necessarily those of the US government.

Instruments

Financial securities, such as money market instruments or capital market instruments.

Instruments of International Traffic

Lift vans, cargo vans, shipping tanks, skids, pallets, caul boards, and cores for textile fabrics, arriving (whether loaded or empty) in use or to be used in the shipment of merchandise in international traffic are designated as "instruments of international traffic" (IIT) within the meaning of section 322(a0, Tariff Act of 1930, as amended. Upon Customs acceptance of a type 3 bond, covering these IIT types, such instruments may be released without entry or the payment of duty, subject to the provisions of 19 CFR 10.41a.

In-substance defeasance

Process through which debt is removed from the balance sheet but not canceled.

Insurable interest

An insurance term referring to the relationship between a policy's insured person or property and the potential beneficiary. The beneficiary must have an insurable interest in the insured person or property to receive payment of the policy if the insured died while the policy was in force.

Insurance

Guarding against property loss or damage making payments in the form of premiums to an insurance company, which pays an agreed-upon sum to the insured in the event of loss.

Insurance agent

The insurance company representative and adviser who sells insurance policies.

Insurance broker

A broker, independent of any insurance company, who represents the interests of the buyer in searching for insurance coverage at the lowest cost and providing the highest benefit to the buyer.

Insurance Certificate

This certificate is used to assure the consignee that insurance is provided to cover loss of or damage to the cargo while in transit.

Insurance claim

A claim for reimbursement from the insurance company when the insured has suffered a loss that is covered under an insurance policy.

Insurance dividend

Money paid annually to policyholders participating in cash value life insurance policies.

Insurance policy

A contract detailing an insurance policy and outlining what risks are insured, what insurance premiums are to be paid by the policyholder, what deductibles prevail, and all the details associated with a policy.

Insurance premium

Payments calculated by the insurance company based on risk factors that must be made by the insured to guarantee protection of property loss under an insurance policy.

Insurance principle

The law of averages. The average outcome for many independent trials of an experiment will approach the expected value of the experiment.

Insurance settlement

The payment of proceeds by an insurance company to the insured to settle an insurance claim within the guidelines stipulated in the insurance policy.

Insured

The property or persons covered by an insurance policy.

Insured account

A bank or financial account that is insured for the benefit of the depositor, protecting against loss in the event that the savings institution becomes insolvent. See: FDIC.

Insured bond

A municipal bond backed both by the credit of the

municipal issuer and by commercial insurance policies.

Insured plans

Defined benefit pension plans that are guaranteed by life insurance products. Related: Non-insured plans

Insured Trade Acceptance

A trade acceptance where the buyer's ability to pay is insured.

Intangible asset

A legal claim to some future benefit, typically a claim to future cash. Goodwill, intellectual property, patents, copyrights, and trademarks are examples of intangible assets.

In the tank

.Used in the context of general equities. Slang expression meaning market prices are dropping rapidly.

Integer programming

Variant of linear programming in which the solution values must be integers.

Integrated Carriers

Carriers that have both air and ground fleets; or other combinations, such as sea, rail, and truck. Since they usually handle thousands of small parcels an hour, they are less expensive and offer more diverse services than regular carriers.

Integrated financial market

A market in which there are no barriers to financial flows, and the same risk asset commands the same expected return, irrespective of domicile.

Integrated Services Digital Network (ISDN).

Offers integrated voice, data, image and video services over the digital telephone network at high speeds allowing users to process a wide range of applications using a single telephone line. ISDN is based on a series of internationally accepted telecommunications standards.

Integrated Tariff of the European Community

TARIC is a publication which presents the regulations pertaining to import of products into the EC as well as for some exports. TARIC adopts the provisions of Community legislation, the harmonized system, and the combined nomenclature (CN).

Intellectual Property Rights (IPR)

IPR is a generic phrase encompassing intangible property rights, including, among others, patents, trade and service marks, copyrights, industrial designs, rights in semiconductor chip layout designs, and rights in trade secrets.

Intelsat

See: International Telecommunications Satellite Organization.

Interagency Group on Countertrade

The IGC, established in December 1988 under Executive Order 12661, reviews policy and negotiates agreements with other countries on countertrade and offsets. The IGC operates at the Assistant Secretary level, with the Department of Commerce as chair. Membership includes 11 other agencies: Agriculture, Defense, Energy, Justice, Labor, State, Treasury, the Agency for International Development, the Federal Emergency Management Agency, the U.S. Trade Representative, and the Office of Management and Budget.

Inter-American Commercial Arbitration Commission

The IACAC administers a system for arbitrating and conciliating international commercial disputes throughout the Western Hemisphere. The Commission, associated with the Organization of American States, follows provisions of the United Nations Commission on International Trade Law. IACAC was originally established in 1934; headquarters are in Washington, D.C.

Inter-American Development Bank

IADB, or IDB, (Spanish: Banco Interamericano de Desarrollo, BID), is a regional financial institution which helps accelerate economic and social development in Latin America and the Caribbean. The Bank was established in 1959 (began operations in October 1960); headquarters are in Washington, D.C. The twenty-eight regional members include: Argentina, Bahamas, Barbados, Belize, Bolivia, Brazil, Canada, Chile, Colombia, Costa Rica, Dominican Republic, Ecuador, El Salvador, Guatemala, Guyana, Haiti, Honduras, Jamaica, Mexico, Nicaragua, Panama, Paraguay, Peru, Suriname, Trinidad and Tobago, United States, Uruguay, and Venezuela. The IDB also includes 16 non-regional members: Austria, Belgium, Denmark, Finland, France, Germany, Israel, Italy, Japan, the Netherlands, Norway, Portugal, Spain, Sweden, Switzerland, and the United Kingdom.

Inter-American Investment Corporation

The IIC is a multilateral investment corporation that promotes the economic development of the regional member countries by stimulating the establishment, expansion, and modernization of private enterprises, especially those of medium and small scale, in Latin America and the Caribbean. The IIC works directly with private enterprises in these countries and neither seeks nor requires government guarantees. The Corporation makes direct investments such as equity participation, loans and purchases of debt instruments, as well as direct investment through other financial institutions. The Corporation also finances feasibility studies, underwrites securities, provides technical and managerial assistance, and helps entrepreneurs in mobilizing additional capital. The IIC is affiliated with the Inter-American Development Bank; it was established in 1986; headquarters are in Washington, D.C.

Inter-Arab Investment Guarantee Corporation

The IAIGC promotes Arab development by stimulating capital transfers among members, by providing investment risk coverage, and by supporting development studies. The Corporation was established in 1965; headquarters are in Kuwait; nearly all Arab countries are members.

Interbank market

Financial institutions exchange of currencies between and among themselves.

Interbank rate

See: LIBOR.

Interbank Offered Rate

IBOR is the rate of interest at which banks lend to other prime banks. Terms are established for the length of loan and individual foreign currencies. A number of financial centers offer an IBOR, including: Abu Dhabi (ADIBOR), Bahrain (BIBOR), Brussels (BRIBOR), Hong Kong (HKIBOR), London (LIBOR), Luxembourg (LUXIBOR), Madrid (MIBOR), Paris (PIBOR), Saudi Arabia (SAIBOR), Singapore (SIBOR), and Zurich (ZIBOR).

Interbank spread

The difference between a bank's offer and bid rates for deposits in the Eurocurrency market.

Intercommodity spread

In the commodities market, a spread consisting of a long position and a short position in different but related commodities for example, speculating that the price relationship between the two commodities will change, e.g., platinum and gold.

Intercompany loan

Loan made by one unit of a corporation to another unit of the same corporation.

Intercompany transaction

Transaction carried out between two units of the same corporation.

Interdelivery spread

Used in futures or options market to refer the purchase of one month of a contract and selling another month in the same contract, in the hope that the price difference will widen or narrow, depending on the investment.

Interest

The price paid for borrowing money. It is expressed as a percentage rate over a period of time and reflects the rate of exchange of present consumption for future consumption. Also, a share or title in property

Interest coverage ratio

The ratio of earnings before interest and taxes to annual interest expense. This ratio measures a firm's ability to pay interest.

Interest coverage test

A debt limitation that prohibits the issuance of additional long-term debt if the issuer's interest coverage would, as a result of the issue, fall below some specified minimum.

Interest deduction

An interest expense, such as interest on a margin account, that is allowed as a deduction for tax purposes.

Interest equalization tax

Tax on foreign investment by residents of the US which was abolished in 1974.

Interest expense

Interest expense is the money the corporation or individual pays out in interest on loans.

Interest in Arrears

Interest that is due only at the maturity date rather than periodically over the life of the loan.

Interest on interest

Interest earned on reinvestment of each interest payment on money invested. See: compound interest.

Interest-only loan

A loan in which payment of principal is deferred and interest payments are the only current obligation.

Interest-only strip (IO)

A security based solely on the interest payments from a pool of mortgages, Treasury bonds, or other bonds. Once the principal on the mortgages or bonds has been repaid, interest payments stop, and the value of the IO falls to zero.

Interest payments

Contractual debt payments based on the coupon rate of interest and the principal amount.

Interest rate

The monthly effective interest rate. For example, the periodic rate on a credit card with an 18% annual percentage rate is 1.5% per month.

Interest rate agreement

An agreement whereby one party, for an up-front premium, agrees to compensate the other at specific time periods if a designated interest rate (the reference rate) is different from a predetermined level (the strike rate).

Interest rate cap

An interest rate agreement in which payments are made when the reference rate exceeds the strike rate. Also called an interest rate ceiling.

Interest rate on debt

The firm's cost of debt capital.

Interest rate ceiling

See: Interest rate cap.

Interest rate floor

An interest rate agreement in which payments are made when the reference rate falls below the strike rate. Related: Interest rate cap.

Interest rate futures contract

A futures contract based on an interbank deposit rate or an underlying debt security. The value of the contract rises and falls inversely to changes in interest rates.

Interest rate parity theorem

Expression that the interest rate differential between two countries is equal to the difference between the forward foreign exchange rate and the spot rate.

Interest rate parity line (IRP)

Diagonal line on a graph that characterizes interest rate parity.

Interest rate risk

The chance that a security's value will change due to a change in interest rates. For example, a bond's price drops as interest rates rise. For a depository institution, also called funding risk: The risk that spread income will suffer because of a change in interest rates.

Interest rate swap

A binding agreement between counterparties to exchange periodic interest payments on some predetermined dollar principal, which is called the notional principal amount. For example, one party will pay fixed and receive variable.

Interest-sensitive insurance policy

A cash value life insurance policy whose insurance dividend rates vary with respect to inflation, enabling the policyholder to avoid the loss of purchasing power associated with inflation.

Interest-sensitive stock

Stocks whose earnings are dependent upon and change with the interest rate, e.g., bank stocks.

Interest subsidy

The value of a firm's deduction of the interest payments on its debt from its earnings before calculation of its tax bill under current tax law.

Interest tax shield

The reduction in income taxes that results from the tax-deductibility of interest payments.

Interfund transactions

Financial arrangements effected by payments made from one fund group (either Federal funds or trust funds) to another group.

Interim dividend

The declaration and payment of a dividend prior to annual earnings determination.

Interim financing

A short-term loan made to a company on the condition that a takeout will follow with long-term or intermediate financing.

Interim rate of return

The rate of return earned between cash flows.

Interim statement

A financial statement that reflects only a limited period of a company's financial statement, not the entire fiscal year.

Interlocking directorate

Describes cross-memberships of directors on each other's company Board of Directors.

Intermarket sector spread

The spread between the interest rate offered in two sectors of the bond market for issues of the same maturity.

Intermarket spread swaps

An exchange of one bond for another based on the manager's projection of a realignment of spreads between sectors of the bond market.

Intermarket Surveillance Information System (ISIS)

A database that distributes information from all the major stock exchanges in the United States.

Intermarket Trading System (ITS)

Electronic communications network linking the trading floors of seven registered exchanges to permit trading among them in stocks listed on either the NYSE or AMEX and one or more regional exchanges. Through ITS, any broker or market maker on the floor of any participating exchange can reach other participants for an execution whenever the nationwide quote shows a better price available. A floor broker on the exchange can enter an ITS order to assure excecution of all of an offering or bid, instead of splitting it with competing brokers.

Intermediary

See: Financial intermediary.

Intermediate Consignee

An intermediate consignee is the bank, forwarding agent, or other intermediary (if any) that acts in a foreign country as an agent for the exporter, the purchaser, or the ultimate consignee, for the purpose of effecting delivery of the export to the ultimate consignee.

Intermediate targets

An intermediate target is a variable (such as the money supply) that is not directly under the control of the central bank, but that does respond fairly quickly to policy actions, is observable frequently and bears a predictable relationship to the ultimate goals of policy.

Intermediate-term

Typically one-ten years.

Intermediate trend

General movement in price data that lasts from three weeks to six months.

Intermediated market

A financial market in which some financial institution stands between counterparties to financial transactions.

Intermediation

Investment through a financial institution. Related: Disintermediation.

Intermittency

When a non-linear dynamical system alternates between periodic and chaotic behavior. See: Chaos, Dynamical Systems.

Intermodal Container Transfer Facility

ICTF is a site where cargo is transferred from one form of transit to another, such as rail to ship.

Internal auditor

An employee of a company who analyzes the company's accounting records to that the company is following and complying with all regulations.

Internal expansion

Growth of assets resulting from internal financing or internally generated cash flow.

Internal finance

Finance generated within a firm by retained earnings and depreciation.

Internal growth rate

Maximum rate a firm can expand without outside sources of funding. Growth generated by cash flows retained by company.

Internal market

The mechanisms for issuing and trading securities within a nation, including its domestic market and foreign market. Compare: External market.

Internal measure

The number of days that a firm can finance operations without additional cash income.

Internal rate of return (IRR)

Dollar-weighted rate of return. Discount rate at which net present value (NPV) investment is zero. The rate at which a bond's future cash flows, discounted back to today, equal its price.

Internal Revenue Code

The various statutes and regulations making up federal tax law.

Internal Revenue Service (IRS)

The federal agency responsible for the collection of federal taxes, including personal and corporate income taxes, Social Security taxes, and excise and gift taxes.

Internal Revenue Service Restructuring and Reform Act of 1998

The legislation targeted at IRS reform, particularly related to the time period required for capital gains and taxpayer protection and rights.

Internally efficient market

See: Operationally efficient market.

International arbitrage

Simultaneous buying and selling of foreign securities and ADRs to capture the profit potential created by time, currency, and settlement inconsistencies that vary across international borders.

International Accounting Unit

NATO infrastructure projects are usually denominated in International Accounting Units. The IAU is a unit of measure based on the exchange rates of the 16 NATO member countries and is reevaluated every six months.

International Agreements

An international agreement is governed by international law; the term refers to a broad classification of legally binding arrangements between states. The arrangements include: treaties, conventions, protocols, annexes, accords, and memoranda of understanding. Other common titles include notes, pact, declaration, statute, constitution and process-verbal. The title is not a controlling factor in making distinctions among arrangements. Some titles are not used consistently; and titles are often used as synonyms, with subtlety in differentiation and resulting in an inability to apply certitude in definition. In this context, the following general characteristics apply:

— Treaties are international agreements and are equivalent to conventions. The Vienna Convention on the Law on Treaties defines a treaty as "an international agreement concluded between States in written form and governed by international law, whether embodied in a single instrument or in two or more related instruments and whatever its particular designation." In its restricted sense in the United States, a treaty denotes an international agreement made by the President with the advice and consent of the Senate in accordance with Article II, section 2 of the Constitution. During a year, the U.S. may be a signatory to approximately 400 international agreements; only about a dozen are treaties. Under U.S. law a treaty (or other international agreement, however designated) becomes the law of the land and is binding on federal, state and local government. This is not always the case in other nations which may require legislative action before a treaty takes the same effect as domestic law. The term "plurilateral" is sometimes used to differentiate between a treaty embracing a restricted number of states in contrast with "multilateral" as a reference to a treaty which is open to all nations.

— Conventions are essentially the same as treaties. In the 1980s and beyond, the term convention has been used more in connection with multilateral, than bilateral, arrangements. Depending on the nature of the convention, the President may or may not consult the Senate.

— Protocols may be any sort of international agreement. A protocol can stand alone or, more generally, it may be a supplementary agreement, or an amendment, of some sort.

— Annexes are subsidiary agreements which are additional to a previously established arrangement. However, there is flexibility; the General Agreement on Tariffs and Trade (GATT) uses the term "annex" to indicate a free-standing agreement.

— Accords are further from treaties than conventions. If there is any distinction to be made, an accord may suggest a non-binding agreement; there are exceptions.

— Memoranda of Understanding are very detailed documents devised by Executive Branch agencies (such as aviation or major fishery agreements). An MOU may be less significant; it takes into account U.S. practice and the requirements of the other government. When a treaty or an executive agreement is first published by the United States, it is assigned a TIAS number and published in slip form in the Treaties and other International Acts Series. TIAS, published by the Department of State, is a series of individual pamphlets.

International Asset Pricing Model (IAPM)

The international version of the CAPM assuming that investors in each country share the same consumption basket and purchasing power parity holds.

International Bank for Reconstruction and Development

The International Bank for Reconstruction and Development, a part of the World Bank, was established in December 1945 to help countries reconstruct their economies after World War II. IBRD assists developing member countries by lending to government agencies and by guaranteeing private loans for such projects as agricultural modernization or infrastructural development. Bank headquarters are in Washington, D.C.

International Banking Act

The IBA, passed in 1978, established a federal legislative framework for governing the activities of foreign banks, which previously had been governed only by state laws. The IBA established a policy of national treatment for U.S. offices of foreign banks by:

(a) limiting any new multistate branching activities to activities more comparable to those of U.S. banks;

(b) placing the foreign bank offices under the same reserve requirements that apply to U.S. banks;

(c) limiting foreign bank involvement in U.S. securities; and

(d) making federal deposit insurance available to U.S. offices of foreign banks if they chose to engage in retail banking.

International Banking Facility

An IBF is one of four categories of foreign banking in the United States. An IBF may be a domestic bank or an office of a foreign bank. In either circumstance, the IBF maintains asset and liability accounts that are segregated from domestic activity and limited to financing international trade. IBFs are exempted from such requirements as: reserve levels and obligations to make some insurance premiums. In the U.S., eligibility requirements limit IBFs to business with other IBFs and with non-U.S. residents. U.S. banks may structure operations to draw foreign customer deposits and loans to their domestic offices.

International bonds

A collective term that refers to global bonds, Eurobonds, and foreign bonds.

International Business Opportunities Service

IBOS is a World Bank subscription package which includes information on upcoming projects and business opportunities. The Service includes:

(a) the Monthly Operational Summary (MOS) listing all projects in the pipeline;

(b) Technical Data Sheets (TDS), published for each approved loan, listing identifying information, procurement methods, cofinancing and similar data;

(c) general procurement notices, issued for projects involving international competitive bidding;

(d) specific procurement notices describing specific items to be procured and bidding requirements; and

(e) major contract award notices identifying successful bidders for contracts which were recently awarded.

International Centre for Settlement of Investment Disputes

ICSID, an affiliate of the World Bank, is a public international organization which provides facilities for the conciliation and arbitration of investment disputes between Contracting States and nationals of other Contracting States. The Centre's objective is to promote an atmosphere of mutual confidence between States and foreign investors conducive to increasing the flow of private international investment. The Centre does not itself engage in conciliation or arbitration but assists in the initiation and conduct of conciliation and arbitration proceedings. Recourse to conciliation and arbitration under the ICSID Convention is entirely voluntary. However, once the parties have consented, they are bound to carry out their undertakings and, the case of arbitration, to abide by the award. All Contracting States, whether or not parties to the dispute, are required to recognize awards rendered pursuant to the Convention as binding and to enforce the pecuniary obligations imposed thereby. The Centre also conducts and publishes research in foreign investment law. ICSID was created under a treaty, the Convention on the Settlement of Investment Disputes Between States and Nationals of Other States (the ICSID Convention) which entered into force in October 1966. The Centre's headquarters are in Washington, D.C.

International Chamber of Commerce (ICC)

A business organization with membership from over 80 countries. They work to harmonize trade practices worldwide by establishing agreed upon rules such as

Incoterms and Uniform Customs and Procedures for Documentary Credits.

International Commodity Agreement

An ICA is an international understanding, usually reflected in a legal instrument, relating to trade in a particular basic commodity, and based on terms negotiated and accepted by most of the countries that export and import commercially significant quantities of the commodity. Some commodity agreements (such as exists for coffee, cocoa, natural rubber, sugar, and tin) center on economic provisions intended to defend a price range for the commodity through the use of buffer stocks or export quotas or both. Other commodity agreements (such as existing agreements for jute and jute products, olive oil, and wheat) promote cooperation among producers and consumers through improved consultation, exchange of information, research and development, and export promotion.

International Competitive Bidding

ICB is one of several forms of procurement made with World Bank financing. While the World Bank provides financing from its loans for the contracts and ensures that agreed procurement procedures are observed, the borrower, not the World Bank, is always responsible for procurement. ICB requires that:

(a) all goods or works to be procured through ICB be internationally advertised through the United Nations (in the publication: Development Business) and at least one major local newspaper;

(b) bids be entertained in the bidder's or other currencies in which expenses would normally be occurred on in an international currency specified by the borrower;

(c) payments be made in the currencies in the bids, without requirement to accept any portion of payment in countertrade;

(d) documents be in an international language (English, French, or Spanish);

(e) bids be openly reviewed; and

(f) contracts be awarded to the lowest evaluated responsive bid. ICB permits a margin of preference to be given to domestic goods and, under certain conditions, to domestic contracting services in developing countries.

International Confederation of Free Trade Unions

ICFTU was established in 1949 to promote the trade union movement by recognizing workers' organizations and through other means of support for the rights of workers to bargain. Members include more than 140 national organizations from nearly 100 countries. ICFTU organizes and educates free trade unions in the developing world primarily through its three regional organizations: APRO for Asia and the Pacific located in New Delhi, India; AFRO in Africa, and ORIT in Latin America, located in Mexico City. ICFTU headquarters are in Brussels, Belgium.

International Court of Justice

The ICJ, established in 1945, is the principal judicial organ of the UN. The ICJ decides cases submitted to it by states and gives advisory opinions on legal questions submitted to it by the General Assembly or Security Council or by UN specialized agencies. The court is composed of 15 judges elected by the General Assembly and the Security Council from a list of persons nominated by the national groups in the Permanent Court of Arbitration. The seat of the Court is in The Hague, Netherlands.

International Data Base

The IDB, which is maintained by the Center for International Research, is an automated data bank containing statistical tables of demographic, economic, and social data for all countries of the world. Data categories include: population; vital statistics; health and nutrition; fertility, migration; foreign-born and refugee statistics; provinces and cities; marital status; family planning; ethnic, religious and language groups; literacy and education; labor force, employment, income and gross national product; and household size and housing indicators. IDB data users include the U.S. government, private firms, research institutions, and international organizations.

International Depository Receipt (IDR)

A receipt issued by a bank as evidence of ownership of one or more shares of the underlying stock of a foreign corporation that the bank holds in trust. The advantage of the IDR structure is that the corporation does not have to comply with all the issuing requirements of the foreign country where the stock is to be traded. The US version of the IDR is the American Depository Receipt (ADR).

International Development Association (IDA)

Association established to stimulate country development; it was especially suited for less prosperous nations, since it provided loans at low interest rates.

International diversification

The attempt to reduce risk by investing in more than one nation. By diversifying across nations whose economic cycles are not perfectly correlated, investors can typically reduce the variability of their returns.

International Electrotechnical Commission (IEC)

This is a non-governmental federation of national committees from around 50 countries, representing all the industrial countries in the world. It was established in 1906 to "promote international cooperation on all questions of standardization and related matters in the fields of electrical and electronic engineering and thus to promote international understanding."

International Finance Corporation (IFC)

A corporation owned by the World Bank that produces a number of well-known stock indexes for emerging markets. Its major role is to provide financing for projects in less developed countries.

International finance subsidiary

A subsidiary incorporated in the US, usually in Delaware, whose sole purpose once was to issue debentures overseas and invest the proceeds in foreign operations, with the interest paid to foreign bondholders not subject to US withholding tax. Elimination of the corporate withholding tax has ended the need for this type of subsidiary.

International Fisher effect

States that the interest rate differential between two countries should be an unbiased predictor of the future change in the spot rate.

International Fisher relationship

Theory that nominal interest rates and inflation rates in different countries are connected. The Fisher equation says the nominal interest rate is the product of one plus the real interest rate times one plus the expected rate of inflation.

International Freight Forwarder

See Freight Forwarder.

International fund

A mutual fund that can invest only outside the United States.

International market

Related: External market.

International market index

An index listed on the American Stock Exchange tracking the performance of 50 American Depository Receipts traded on the AMEX, NYSE, and NASDAQ.

International Monetary Fund (IMF)

International Monetary Fund The IMF, established in December 1945, promotes international monetary harmony, monitors the exchange rate and monetary policies of member nations, and provides credit for member countries which experience temporary balance of payments deficits. Each member has a quota, expressed in Special Drawing Rights, which reflects both the relative size of the member's economy and that member's voting power in the Fund. Quotas also determine members' access to the financial resources of, and their shares in the allocation of Special Drawing Rights by, the Fund. The IMF, funded through members' quotas, may supplement resources through borrowing. IMF membership is approximately 175 countries.

International Monetary Market (IMM)

A division of the CME established in 1972 for trading financial futures. Related: Chicago Mercantile Exchange (CME)

International monetary system

The global network of government and commercial institutions within which currency exchange rates are determined.

International mutual fund

A mutual fund that invests strictly in securities markets throughout the world, excluding the United

States. A global fund, on the other hand, invests in both foreign and domestic securities.

International Organization for Standardization

ISO is not an acronym but the name of a standards setting organization chartered by the United Nations. The name ISO is derived from Greek and connotes equality, i.e. each member country regardless of size or wealth gets only one vote. The ISO 4217 are the standard three letter currency codes. These codes are usually composed of the ISO 3166 two letter country code plus a third letter representing the name of the currency.

International Petroleum Exchange (IPE)

Energy futures and options exchange based in London.

International Security Market Association (ISMA)

Swiss law association located in Zurich that regroups all the participants on the Eurobond primary and secondary markets. Establishes uniform trading procedures in the international bond markets.

International Stock Exchange of the U.K. and the Republic of Ireland (ISE)

Organization that replaced the London stock exchange after its merger with the International Securities Regulatory Organization (ISRO).

International Swap Dealers Association (ISDA)

Formed in 1985 to promote uniform practices in the writing, trading, and settlement of swaps and other derivatives.

International Telecommunications Satellite Organization

INTELSAT, created in 1964 under a multilateral agreement, is a nonprofit cooperative of about 120 countries that jointly own and operate a global communications satellite system serving the world. The system is used primarily for international communications, and by many countries for domestic communications. In 1991, the INTELSAT system comprised a network of 16 satellites in geosynchronous orbit over the Atlantic, Indian, and Pacific Ocean regions, with service to about 1,500 international and domestic earth station antennas. COMSAT is the United Statess representative to and participant in Intelsat.

International Telecommunications Union (ITU)

The International Telecommunications Union is an organization established to promote worldwide standards and the development of interworking telecommunications networks throughout the world.

International Trade Commission

An independent U.S. Government agency concerned with imports, import duties, and the effect of imports on U.S. industry. The Commission has six commissioners who review and make recommendations concerning countervailing duty and antidumping petitions submitted by U.S. industries seeking relief from imports that benefit unfair trade practices. Known as the U.S. Tariff Commission before its mandate was broadened by the Trade Act of 1974.

Interpolation

A method of approximating a price or yield that is unknown by using numbers that are known.

Interpositioning

The practice of using a second broker in a securities transaction, which is considered illegal it is if used to generate additional commission.

Inter vivos trust

A trust created between living persons. Antithesis of a testamentary trust.

In touch with

Used in the context of general equities. Having a sell inquiry in a stock (not a firm customer sell order), often entailing a capital commitment. Antithesis of looking for.

Intrabudgetary transactions

Effected when payment and receipt both occur within the budget, or when payment is made from off-budget federal entities whose budget authority and outlays are excluded from the budget totals.

Intracommodity spread

Used in the context of futures trading to refer to a trader holding, buying, and selling contracts in the same commodity on the same exchange, but for different months.

Intracompany trade

Transactions between or among subsidiaries that are part of the same parent company.

Intraday

Term meaning "within the day," often to refer to the high and the low price of a stock.

Intramarket sector spread

The spread between two issues of the same maturity within a market sector. For instance, the difference in interest rates offered for five-year industrial corporate bonds and five-year utility corporate bonds.

Intrastate offering

A securities offering limited to just one state in the United States.

Intrinsic value

The value of an option if it were to expire immediately with the underlying stock at its current price; the amount by which an option is in-the-money. For call options, this is the difference between the stock price, if that difference is a positive number, or zero otherwise. For put options it is the difference between the striking price and the stock price, if that difference is positive, and zero otherwise. See also: In-the-Money, Time Value Premium, Parity.

Intrinsic value of an option

The amount by which an option is in the money. An option that is not in the money has no intrinsic value.

Intrinsic value of a firm

The present value of a firm's expected future net cash flows discounted by the required rate of return.

Inventory

For companies: Raw materials, items available for sale or in the process of being made ready for sale. They can be individually valued by several different means, including cost or current market value, and collectively by FIFO (First in, first out), LIFO (Last in, first out) or other techniques. The lower value of alternatives is usually used to preclude overstating earnings and assets. For securities firms: Securities bought and held by a broker or dealer for resale.

Inventory financing

Used in the context of factoring and general finance to refer to loans to consumer product producers that use inventory as collateral. See also: Inventory loan.

Inventory loan

A secured short-term loan to purchase inventory. The three basic forms are a blanket inventory lien, a trust receipt, and field warehousing financing.

Inventory turnover

A measure of how often the company sells and replaces its inventory. It is the ratio of annual cost of sales to the lastest inventory. One can also interpret the ratio as the time to which inventory is held. For example a ratio of 26 implies that investory is held, on average, for two weeks. It is best to use this ratio to compare companies within an industry (high turnover is a good sign) because there are huge differences in this ratio across industries.

Inverse floater

A derivative instrument whose coupon rate is linked to the market rate of interest in an inverse relationship.

Inverse floating-rate note

A variable-rate security whose coupon rate increases as a benchmark interest rate declines.

Inverted market

A futures market in which the nearer months are selling at price premiums to the more-distant months. Related: Premium.

Inverted scale

A serial bond offering whose bonds with earlier maturity dates have higher yields than bonds with later maturity dates.

Inverted yield curve

When short-term interest rates are higher than long-term rates. Antithesis of positive yield curve.

Investment

The creation of more money through the use of capital.

Investment adviser

A person or an organization that makes the day-to-day decisions regarding a portfolio's investments. Also called a portfolio manager.

Investment Advisers Act

Legislation passed in 1940 requiring financial advisers to register with the Securities and Exchange Commission. The measure was enacted to protect the public from fraud or misrepresentation by investment advisers.

Investment advisory service

A business that specializes in providing investment advice for a fee. All advisers of an advisory service must be registered with the Securities and Exchange Commission.

Investment agreement

An contract specifying the rights and responsibilities of a host government and a corporation in the structure and operation of an investment project.

Investment analysts

Related: Financial analysts.

Investment bank

Financial intermediaries who perform a variety of services, including aiding in the sale of securities, facilitating mergers and other corporate reorganizations, acting as brokers to both individual and institutional clients, and trading for their own accounts. See: Underwriters.

Investment certificate

A document that serves as proof that an individual has an investment in a savings and loan association.

Investment climate

Factors such as economic, monetary, and other conditions that affect the performance of investments.

Investment club

A group of people who combine their money into a larger pool, then invest collectively in stocks and bonds, making decisions as a group.

Investment company

A firm that that invests the funds of investors in securities appropriate for their stated investment objectives in return for a management fee. See also: Mutual fund.

Investment Company Act of 1940

Legislation that requires investment companies to register with the SEC and that outlines standards by which they must operate.

Investment Company Institute (ICI)

A national industry group of investment companies, including mutual funds, founded in 1940.

Investment decisions

Decisions concerning the asset side of a firm's balance sheet, such as the decision to offer a new product.

Investment-grade bonds

A bond that is assigned a rating in the top four categories by commercial credit rating companies. S&P classifies investment-grade bonds as BBB or higher, and Moody's classifies investment grade bonds as Baa or higher. Related: High-yield bond.

Investment history

The history of a member firm that establishes certain norms in respect of its investment practice.

Investment income

The revenue from a portfolio of invested assets.

Investment letter

A letter of intent between the issuer of new securities and the buyer, in the private placement of these new securities. The letter of intent establishes that the securities are being bought for a minimum time period and are treated as an investment, not for resale. If no such letter exists, the securities must be registered with Securities and Exchange Commission.

Investment management

The process of managing money. Also called portfolio management and money management.

Investment manager

The individual who manages a portfolio of investments. Also called a portfolio manager or a money manager.

Investment objective

The financial objective of an investor. Whether the investor requires income or capital appreciation, for example. The investor's objective governs the investment strategy.

Investment opportunity set

The universe of choices as to investments available to an individual or corporation.

Investment philosophy

The style and general ideology of investment practiced by an investor. Certain investors favor small-capitalization stocks, while others prefer large blue-chip stocks, for example.

Investment policy

Statement of objectives and constraints for an individual's or organization's approach.

Investment product line (IPL)

The line of required returns for investment projects as a function of beta (nondiversifiable risk).

Investment Risk

Uncertainty about the future benefits to be realized from an investment.

Investment Valuation Model (IVM)

The basic mathematical technique of finance that calculates the value of an investment as the present value of all future cash flows expected to be generated by the investment.

Investments

As a discipline, the study of financial securities, such as stocks and bonds, from the investor's viewpoint.

Investment software

Computer software that helps investors make investment decisions by identifying situations that meet programmed parameters.

Investment strategy

A strategy, or plan of attack, an investor uses when deciding how to allocate capital among several options including stocks, bonds, cash equivalents, commodities, and real estate. The strategy should take into account the investor's tolerance for risk as well as future needs for capital.

Investment strategy committee

A committee within a brokerage firm that conducts research and makes recommendations on the firm's stated investment strategy.

Investment Tax Credit

Proportion of new capital investment that could be used to reduce a company's tax bill (abolished in 1986).

Investment trust

A closed-end fund regulated by the Investment Company Act of 1940. These funds have a fixed number of shares that are traded on the secondary markets, like corporate stock. The market price may exceed the net asset value per share, in which case shares are selling at a premium. When the market price falls below the (NAV)/share, shares are selling at a discount. Many closed-end funds are of a specialized nature; the portfolio represents a particular industry or, country. These funds are usually listed on US and foreign exchanges.

Investment value

Applies mainly to dealer securities. Fixed income value of a convertible, the price at which the convert would have to sell as a straight debt instrument relative to the yield of other bonds of like maturity, or size, and quality; represents a presumed floor to the bond, assuming the continued creditworthiness of the issuer and the general level of interest rates. Bond value. See: conversion value.

Investor

The owner of a financial asset.

Investor fallout

In the mortgage pipeline, risk that occurs when the originator commits loan terms to the borrowers and gets commitments from investors at the time of application, or if both sets of terms are made at closing.

Investor relations

The process by which the corporation communicates with its investors.

Investor's equity

The balance of a margin account. Related: Buying on margin, initial margin requirement.

Investors service bureau

NYSE service that deals with all general inquiries concerning securities investments.

Invisibles

This refers to areas of non-merchandise "invisible trade" that include expenses such as freight and insurance and most types of services and investment.

Invitation For Bids

A request, verbal or written, which is made to prospective bidders requesting the submission of a bid on specifically described commodities or services.

Invoice

Bill written by a seller of goods or services and submitted to a purchaser for payment.

Invoice billing

Billing system in which invoices are sent off at the time of customer orders and are all separate bills to be paid.

Invoice date

Usually the date when goods are shipped. Payment dates are set relative to the invoice date.

Invoice price

The price that the buyer of a futures contract must pay the seller when a Treasury bond is delivered.

Involuntary liquidation preference

A premium that must be paid to preferred or preference stockholders if the issuer of the stock is forced into involuntary liquidation.

IO

(1) The two-character ISO 3166 country code for BRITISH INDIAN OCEAN TERRITORY. (2) See: Interest-only strip

IOC order

See: Immediate or canceled order.

IOM

See: Index and Option Market.

IPO

See: Initial Public Offering.

IPO Spinning

See Initial Public Offering Spinning.

I.P.R.

See Intellectual Property Rights.

IQ

The two-character ISO 3166 country code for IRAQ.

IQD

The ISO 4217 currency code for the Iraqi Dinar.

IR

The two-character ISO 3166 country code for IRAN, ISLAMIC REPUBLIC OF.

IRA/Keogh accounts

Special accounts that allow saving taxes deferred until money is withdrawn. These plans are subject to frequent changes in law with respect to the deductibility of contributions. Withdrawals of tax-deferred contributions are taxed as income, including the capital gains from such accounts.

IRB

See: Industrial Revenue Bond.

IRR

(1) The ISO 4217 currency code for the Iranian Rial.
(2) See: Internal rate of return.

Irredeemable bond

A bond lacking a call feature or a right of redemption. Also refers to a perpetual bond.

Irrational call option

The implied call imbedded in a MBS. Irrational because the call is sometimes not exercised when it is in the money (interest rates are below the threshold to refinance), and sometimes exercised when it is not in the money. Option exercise like this affects payments on the MBS.

Irrelevance result

The Modigliani and Miller theorem that a firm's capital structure is irrelevant to the firm's value.

Irrevocable letter of credit

Assurance of funds issued by a bank that cannot be canceled or amended without the beneficiary's approval.

Irrevocable trust

A trust that is unable to be amended, altered, or revoked.

IS

The two-character ISO 3166 country code for ICELAND.

ISDA

See: International Swap Dealers Association.

ISK

The ISO 4217 currency code for the Icelandic Krona.

Islamic Development Bank

The IsDB (sometimes IDB) finances economic aid and social development in member countries. The Bank also supports Muslim communities in non-member countries. Membership is open to all countries which are members of the Islamic Conference. Members include: Afghanistan, Algeria, Bahrain, Bangladesh, Benin, Brunei, Burkina, the Cameroon, Chad, Comoros, Djibouti, Egypt, Gabon, The Gambia, Guinea, Guinea-Bissau, Indonesia, Iran, Iraq, Jordan Kuwait, Lebanon, Libya, Malaysia, Maldives, Mali, Mauritania, Morocco, Niger, Oman, Pakistan, the Palestine Liberation Organization, Qatar, Saudi Arabia, Senegal, Sierra Leone, Somalia, Sudan, Syria, Tunisia, Turkey, Uganda, the United Arab Emirates, and Yemen. The Bank was created in 1973 (began operations in October 1975); headquarters are in Jeddah, Saudi Arabia.

ISMA

See: International Security Market Association.

ISO

See: International Organization for Standardization.

Issue

A particular financial asset.

Issued share capital

Total amount of shares that have been issued. Related: Outstanding shares.

Issuer

An entity that puts a financial asset in the marketplace.

Issuing bank

Bank that issues a letter of credit.

Istanbul Stock Exchange

The sole securities exchange in Turkey.

IT

The two-character ISO 3166 country code for ITALY.

Italian Derivatives Market (IDEM)

A derivatives market operated by the Italian Stock Exchange Council. It trades futures and options on the 30 index and individual stock options. See: Italian Stock Exchange.

Italian Exchange (Borsa Italiana)

Italy's major securities exchange.

Italian Stock Exchange (ISE)

The Milan-based stock exchange, which came into effect after the unification of Italy's ten national exchanges in 1991. All listed securities are traded electronically. The main indexes are the MIB and the MIBTEL, based on the prices of all listed shares, and the MIB 30, based on a sample of the 30 most liquid and highly capitalized shares.

Itemized deduction

Specific deductions allowed by the IRS outlined in the tax return.

ITL

The ISO 4217 currency code for the Italian Lira.

ITM

See: In-the-money.

ITS

See: Intermarket Trading System.

"It's us,"

Used in the context of general equities. "The firm, and not a customer, is the party involved."

ENCYCLOPAEDIC DICTIONARY OF INTERNATIONAL BUSINESS MANAGEMENT

ENCYCLOPAEDIC DICTIONARY OF INTERNATIONAL BUSINESS MANAGEMENT

Vol. 3

by

A.S. SUDAN

ANMOL PUBLICATIONS PVT. LTD.
NEW DELHI-110 002 (INDIA)

ANMOL PUBLICATIONS PVT. LTD.
4374/4B, Ansari Road, Daryaganj
New Delhi-110 002
Phones: 23261597, 23278000, 23255577
Email: anmolpublications@vsnl.com

Encyclopaedic Dictionary of International Business Management

First Edition 2003
ISBN 81-261-1508-4 (Set)

PRINTED IN INDIA

Published by J.L. Kumar for Anmol Publications Pvt. Ltd., New Delhi-110 002 and Printed at Mehra Offset Press, Delhi.

PREFACE

Conventionally, 'Business' is understood as a trade or profession; an industrial, commercial, or professional operation; purchase and sale of goods and services; a commercial or industrial establishment; commercial activity; volume or quantity of commercial activity; commercial policy or procedure etc. Business operations are mainly divided into—technical, commercial, financial, security, accounting and managerial activities. Till recently managerial skills had been most neglected aspect of business operations. The term 'managing' consists of various functions, main among which are—planning, organising, commanding, coordinating and controlling.

Amidst the various schools of management thought Business Management can rightly considered as an art, a science and a profession.

As is obvious from the name of the title, the present work contains judiciously selected and well explained terms covering the International Business Management in entirety. This encyclopaedic dictionary will prove a reliable asset to one and all in the field.

—A.S. Sudan

j

J

Fifth letter of a Nasdaq stock symbol specifying the issue is the voting stock of the company.

Jakarta Stock Exchange

Established in 1977, the largest securities exchange in Indonesia.

January effect

Refers to the historical pattern that stock prices rise in the first few days of January. Studies have suggested this holds only for small-capitalization stocks. In recent years, there is less evidence of a January effect.

Japanese Association of Securities Dealers Automated Quotation System (Jasdaq)

Japanese equivalent of Nasdaq.

Japan Corporate Program

The Japan Corporate Program was initiated (by the U.S. Department of Commerce) to help increase U.S. exports to Japan. The program was initiated in January 1991, following selection of 20 companies to participate in a five-year pilot project to improve U.S.

knowledge of, and access to, the Japanese market. As part of the five-year commitment to the program, the companies arrange four visits a year to Japan, including two by their chief executives; publish their product literature in Japanese; participate in at least one trade promotion event in Japan each year; and modify products to enhance consumer acceptance and promote sales in Japan. Commerce supports the 20 firms with market data, arranges introductory meetings with prospective Japanese buyers, and recommends market development strategies.

Japan Development Bank

The Japan Development Bank was founded in 1951 to aid in developing and diversifying the Japanese economy. The JDB is a non-profit organization owned entirely by the Japanese Government. U.S. companies may participate in JDB funding activity under the Bank's Loan Division in the International Department. The International Department disburses loans to foreign companies under two primary loan programs: Promotion of Foreign Direct Investment in Japan and Facilities for Import Products. The other loan programs of JDB are also available to foreign-owned companies under the principle of equal treatment of clients regardless of nationality.

Japan Export Information Center

The Japan Export Information Center (JEIC) provides information on doing business in Japan, market entry alternatives, market information and research, product standards and testing requirements, tariffs and non-tariff barriers. The Center maintains a commercial library and participates in private- and government-sponsored seminars on doing business in Japan. JEIC is operated by the International Trade Administration of the Department of Commerce. (202-482-2425 and 202-482-4524; fax: 202-482-0469)

Japan External Trade Organization

Although legally under the aegis of the Ministry of International Trade and Industry (MITI), JETRO administers the export programs of the Japanese Government independently. MITI subsidizes about 60 percent of JETRO's total annual expenditures and, technically, has final decision-making authority over JETRO management and programs. Originally established to help Japanese firms export, JETRO also assists American companies seeking to export to Japan and promotes Japanese direct investment in the United States and U.S. direct investment in Japan.

Japan International Cooperation Agency

JICA administers the bilateral grant portion of Japan's Official Development Assistance (ODA). JICA covers both: (a) grant aid cooperation (offered without the obligation of repayment) and (b) technical cooperation (offering trainees, experts, equipment, project-type technical cooperation, and development studies). The Agency was established in August 1974; headquarters are in Tokyo, Japan. See: Export-Import Bank of Japan Overseas Economic Cooperation Fund.

JCCT

The U.S.-China Joint Commission on Commerce and Trade.

J-curve

Theory that says a country's trade deficit will initially worsen after its currency depreciates because higher prices on foreign imports will more than offset the reduced volume of imports in the short run.

"J" Curve and Real Exchange Rates

The current account may initially worsen before improving in response to real depreciation in exchange rates, because it takes time for the growth of import volumes to decline in response to higher import prices. This phenomenon is known as the "J-curve effect," because the downward movement followed by an upward movement in the current account resembles the letter "J."

Jensen index

An index that uses the capital asset pricing model to determine whether a money manager outperformed a market index. The alpha of an investment or investment manager.

JEXIM

Japan Export Import Bank.

JM

The two-character ISO 3166 country code for JAMAICA.

JMD

The ISO 4217 currency code for the Jamaican Dollar.

JO

The two-character ISO 3166 country code for JORDAN.

Jobber

A term for a market maker used on the London Stock Exchange.

JOD

The ISO 4217 currency code for the Jordanian Dinar.

Johannesburg Stock Exchange (JSE)

Established in 1886, the Johannesburg Stock Exchange is the only stock exchange in South Africa. Gold and mining stocks form the majority of shares listed.

Joint account

An agreement between two or more firms to share risk and financing responsibility in purchasing or underwriting securities, or an account owned jointly by two or more persons at a bank or brokerage house.

Joint and survivor annuity

A type of annuity opened by and intended for two people, that makes payments for the entire lifetime of both beneficiaries, even if one of them dies.

Joint bond

A bond that is guaranteed by the issuer and a party other than the issuer.

Joint clearing members

Firms that clear on more than one exchange.

Joint Committee for Investment and Trade

The JCIT, was established in October 1990 to demonstrate U.S. and Mexican commitment to greater economic cooperation. The Committee identifies trade and investment opportunities and coordinates trade promotion events.

Joint float

An arrangement by which a group of currencies maintain a fixed relationship relative to each other, but move jointly relative to another currency in response to supply and demand conditions in the exchange market.

Jointly and severally

Municipal bond underwriting in which the account is undivided and syndicate members are responsible for unsold bonds in proportion to their participation, regardless of how many bonds they may have already sold. A firm with 20% of the account is responsible for selling 20% of the unsold bonds even if has already sold 25% of the total debt issue, for example. See: Severally but not jointly.

Joint stock company

A form of business organization that falls between a corporation and a partnership. The company sells stock, and its shareholders are free to sell their stock, but shareholders are liable for all debts of the company.

Joint tax return

Tax return filed by two people, usually spouses.

Joint Technical Committee 1 (JTC1)

A technical committee set up jointly by ISO and IEC to oversee all international standardization activities in the field of information technology.

Joint tenants with right of survivorship

In the case of a joint account, on the death of one account holder, ownership of the account assets is transferred to the remaining account holder or holders.

Joint Venture

An international business collaboration between foreign interests and private parties from the host country (or the host government in some cases) in which two or more parties establish a new business enterprise to which each contributes, and in which ownership and control are shared.

Populated or unpopulated joint ventures. A legally independent entity joint venture is populated when it has its own management and staff personnel, and is unpopulated or a "shell company" when partner companies loan the temporary services of their own management and staff to share in the work of the venture.

Jonestown defense

An extreme defensive tactic employed by the management of a target corporation to prevent a hostile takeover. The defensive tactics are so extreme that they typically lead to the destruction of the target corporation. See: Suicide.

Joseph Effect

The tendency for persistent time series ($0.50<H<1.00$), to have trends and cycles. The term "Joseph Effect" was coined by Mandelbrot in reference to Joseph's interpretation of Pharaoh's dream of seven fat years followed by seven lean years.

JP

The two-character ISO 3166 country code for JAPAN.

JPY

The ISO 4217 currency code for the Japanese Yen.

JSE

See: Johannesburg Stock Exchange.

Jumbo certificate of deposit

A certificate of deposit in increments of $100,000.

Jumbo loan

Loans of $1 billion or more. Or, loans that exceed the statutory size limit eligible for purchase or securitization by the federal agencies.

Jump ball

Used in the context of general equities. (1) Deal in which no trading house has exclusivity (each firm is in direct competition for a piece of business); (2) no preference in picking a particular side (buy/sell) of a stock as profile, indicated during the block call, indicate that the sales force could have the stock either way.

Junior debt (subordinate debt)

Debt whose holders have a claim on the firm's assets only after senior debtholder's claims have been satisfied. Subordinated debt.

Junior issue

A debt or equity issue from one corporation over which the issue of another firm takes precedence with respect to dividends, interest, principal, or security in the event of liquidation.

Junior mortgage

A mortgage that will be satisfied only after more senior mortgages have been satisfied. E.g., a first mortgage will be satisfied prior to a second or a third mortgage.

Junior refunding

Issuing of new securities to refinance government debt that matures in one to five years.

Junior security

A security that has a lower-priority claim on a company's assets and income than a senior security. For example common stock is junior to preferred stock.

Junk bond

A bond with a speculative credit rating of BB (S&P) or Ba (Moody's) or lower. Junk or high-yield bonds offer investors higher yields than bonds of financially sound companies. Two agencies, Standard & Poors and Moody's Investor Services, provide the rating systems for companies' credit.

Jurisdiction

Offshore Jurisdiction. Offshore Jurisdiction/Location is a country, or special area within a country, in which the legislation applicable to the formation, management and taxation of companies is geared towards international business rather than the governance of domestic business within the country. Such countries are competing for this international business and, as a result, the legislation and taxation are often 'favourable' to companies incorporated in these countries.

Onshore Jurisdiction. This refers to a country in which the legislation applicable to the formation, management and taxation of companies is geared towards the regulation of the domestic economy and the control of companies trading and investing within it. Such jurisdictions are, in general, less favourable to a company and its owners than offshore jurisdictions, whose legislation and taxation is geared more to attracting international business which does not have specific location requirements.

Jury of executive opinion

A method of forecasting using a composite forecast prepared by a number of individual experts. The experts form their own opinions initially from the data given, and revise their opinions according to the others' opinions. Finally, the individuals' final opinions are combined.

"Just me asking"

Used in the context of general equities. "Not a customer request for information."

Just-in-time inventory systems

Systems that schedule materials to arrive exactly when they are needed in the production process.

Justified price

The fair market price of an asset.

k

K

Fifth letter of a Nasdaq stock symbol specifying the issue has no voting rights.

Kaffirs

South African gold mining shares that trade on the London Stock Exchange.

Kangera Basin Organization

The KBO promotes integrated exploitation and management of water and land resources in the Kangera Basin. Officially known as the Organization for the Managment and Development of the Kangera Basin (French: Organisation pour l'Amnagement et le Dveloppement du Bassin de la Riviere Kagera), the KBO was established in 1978; headquarters are in Kigali, Rwanda. BKO members inlcude: Burundi, Rwanda, Tanzania, and Uganda.

Kansas City Board of Trade (KCBT)

The U.S.-based futures and options exchange for no. 2 red wheat futures and, options, Value Line Index futures and Mini Value Line futures and options.

Kappa

The ratio of the dollar price change in the price of an option to a 1% change in the expected volatility.

Karachi Stock Exchange

The major securities exchange of Pakistan.

KCBT

See: Kansas City Board of Trade.

K.D. (Knocked Down)

An abbreviation meaning the article described is supplied unassembled.

KE

The two-character ISO 3166 country code for KENYA.

Keidanren

Keidanren (the Japanese Federation of Economic Organizations) was established in 1946 as a private, nonprofit economic organization representing virtually all branches of economic activity in Japan.

Keiretsu

Keiretsu refers to the horizontally and vertically linked industrial structure of post-war Japan. The horizontally linked groups include a broad range of industries linked via banks and general trading firms. There are eight major industrial groups, sometimes referred to as "Kigyo Shudan": Mitsubishi, Mitsui, Sumitomo, Fuyo, DKB, Sanwa, Tokai, and IBJ. The vertically linked groups (such as Toyota, Matshushita, and Sony) are centered around parent companies, with subsidiaries frequently serving as suppliers, distributors, and retail outlets. Common characteristics among the groups include crossholding of company shares, intragroup financing, joint investment, mutual appointment of officers, and other joint business activities.

The keiretsu system emphasizes mutual cooperation and protects affiliates from mergers and acquisitions. Ties within groups became looser after the oil shocks of the 1970s as a result of decreasing dependence on banks for capital.

Keogh plan

A type of pension account in which taxes are deferred. Available to those who are self-employed.

KES

The ISO 4217 currency code for the Kenyan Shilling.

Key industry

An industry that plays a critical role in a nation's economy.

Key man (or woman) insurance

A life insurance policy purchased by a company to insure the life of a key executive. The company is the beneficiary in case of the executive's death.

Keynesian economics

An economic theory of British economist, John Maynard Keynes that active government intervention is necessary to ensure economic growth and stability.

KG

The two-character ISO 3166 country code for KYRGYZSTAN.

KGS

The ISO 4217 currency code for the Kyrgyzstan Som.

KH

The two-character ISO 3166 country code for CAMBODIA.

KHR

The ISO 4217 currency code for the Cambodian Riel.

KI

The two-character ISO 3166 country code for KIRIBATI.

"Kick it out"

Used in the context of general equities. "Liquidate a position (sell a long/cover a short) without regard to price."

Kickback

In the context of finance, refers to compensation of dealers by sales finance companies for discounting installment purchase paper. In the context of contracts, refers to secret payments made to insure that the contract goes to a specific firm.

Kicker

An additional feature of a debt obligation that increases its marketability and attractiveness to investors.

Kiddie tax

Tax owed for the investment income of children if the amount is more than $1,400.

Killer bees

Those who aid a company in fending off a takeover bid, usually investment bankers who devise strategies to make the target less attractive or more difficult to acquire.

Kiting

Used in of banking to refer to the practice of depositing and drawing checks at two or more banks and taking advantage of the time it takes for the second bank to collect funds from the first bank. Also refers to illegally increasing the face value of a check by changing the numbers on the check. In the context of securities, refers to the manipulation and inflation of stock prices.

KLCE

See: Kuala Lumpur Commodities Exchange.

KLOFFE

See: Kuala Lumpur Options and Financial Futures Exchange.

KLSE

See: Kuala Lumpur Stock Exchange.

KM

The two-character ISO 3166 country code for COMOROS.

KMF

The ISO 4217 currency code for the Comoros Franc.

KN

The two-character ISO 3166 country code for SAINT KITTS AND NEVIS.

Knock-out option

An option that- is worthless at expiration if the underlying commodity or currency price reaches a specific price level.

Know your customer

An ethical foundation of securities brokers that an adviser who recommends the purchase or sale of any security to a customer, must believe that the recommendation is suitable for the customer, given the customer's financial situation.

Kokusai Denshin Denwa

The Kokusai Denshin Denwa Company, KDD, was established in 1953 but traces its history back to 1871 and the establishment of its predecessor organizations. For more than a century, the company was Japan's sole supplier of international telecommunications services and today remains Japan's leading international carrier. KDD is Japan's signatory to INTELSAT and INMARSAT.

Kommanditgesellschaft

KG (German, meaning: "limited partnership") differs from the general partnership in that only the general partner (Komplementaer) has full personal liability for the liabilities of the partnership while the remaining (limited) partners' (Kommanditist) liability is limited to the specific amount of their contribution. The company must carry the name of one personally liable partner with reference to the existence of a company. The name of the general partner with unlimited liability may not be left out.

Kommanditgesellschaft auf Aktien

KGaA (German, meaning: "limited partnership by shares") is a combination of the elements of a stock company and a limited partnership. There is at least one general partner whose liability is unlimited while limited shareholders have an interest in the stated capital divided into shares without being personally liable for the debts of the company.

Kondratieff Wave

An economic theory of the Soviet economist Kondratieff stating that the economies of the western world are susceptible to major up-and-down "supercycles" lasting 50 to 60 years.

Korea Foreign Trade Association

KFTA, a non-profit, private business organization of Korean companies, provides information and services concerning trade both for members and for foreign businesses. KFTA, with headquarters are in Seoul, maintains some U.S. offices.

Korea Stock Exchange

The major securities market of Korea.

Korea Trade Promotion Corporation

KOTRA, a non-profit organization, was established by the Korean government in 1962 to promote foreign trade. The corporation now also serves as an import promotion center offering a variety of free services in trade, investment, and international economic cooperation. KOTRA, with headquarters in Seoul, has a network of domestic and overseas offices, including several U.S. sites. KOTRA's U.S. telephone: 1-800-568-7248.

KP

The two-character ISO 3166 country code for KOREA, DEMOCRATIC PEOPLE'S REPUBLIC OF.

KPW

The ISO 4217 currency code for the North Korean Won.

KR

The two-character ISO 3166 country code for KOREA, REPUBLIC OF.

Kreditanstalt fur Wiederaufbau

The KfW (English: Reconstruction Loan Corporation) provides assistance to developing countries in the form of loans, grants, materials, or services. The KfW determines volume and use of funds, repayment conditions, interest rates, fund-release procedures, and monitoring requirements. It promotes the establishment of German companies in developing countries and promotiong new technologies by German companies in developing countries. See also Deutsche Finanzierungsgesellschaft fur Beteilgungen in Entwicklungsl„ndern GmbH Deutsche Gesellschaft fur Technische Zusammenarbeit.

Kruggerand

A gold coin minted by the republic of South Africa that typically sells for slightly higher prices than the market value of the gold it contains.

KRW

The ISO 4217 currency code for the South Korean Won.

Kuala Lumpur Commodities Exchange (KLCE)

The Malaysian commodity exchange for trading futures in crude palm oil, crude palm kernel oil, tin, rubber, and cocoa.

Kuala Lumpur Options and Financial Futures Exchange (KLOFFE)

Established in 1995, the Kuala Lumpur Options and Financial Futures Exchange offers equity derivative products based on underlying instruments traded on the Kuala Lumpur Stock Exchange (KLSE).

Kuala Lumpur Stock Exchange (KLSE)

Established in 1973, the Kuala Lumpur Stock Exchange (KLSE) is the only stock exchange in Malaysia.

Kurtosis

Measures the fatness of the tails of a probability distribution. A fat-tailed distribution has higher-than-normal chances of a big positive or negative realization. Kurtosis should not be confused with skewness, which measures the fatness of one tail. Kurtosis is sometimes referred to as the volatility of volatility.

Kuwait Fund for Arab Economic Development

The KFAED is a Kuwaiti independent public institution which assists Arab and other developing countries in developing their economies by granting them concessional loans for development programs and by financing pre-investment studies of ways to expand production capacities. Fund operations, originally restricted to Arab countries, were extended to cover other developing countries in July 1974. In March 1981, the objectives of the Fund were extended to include participation in the capital and resources of development institutions and other types of establishments. These recipients have included: the Arab Fund for Economic and Social Development, the African Development Bank, the African Development Fund, the Arab Bank for Economic Development in Africa, the Inter-Arab Investment Guarantee Corporation, the International Development Association, the International Fund for Agricultural Development, and the Special Program of Assistance for African Countries. KFAED was established in December 1961; its headquarters are in Safat, Kuwait.

KW

The two-character ISO 3166 country code for KUWAIT.

KWD

The ISO 4217 currency code for the Kuwait Dinar.

KY

The two-character ISO 3166 country code for CAYMAN ISLANDS.

KYD

The ISO 4217 currency code for the Cayman Islands Dollar.

Kyoto Convention

See: International Convention on the Simplification and Harmonization of Customs Procedures.

KZ

The two-character ISO 3166 country code for KAZAKSTAN.

KZT

The ISO 4217 currency code for the Kazakhstan Tenge.

L

L

Fifth letter of a Nasdaq stock symbol specifying that the issue is a class of stock such as third preferred class of warrants, foreign preferred, sixth class of preferred stock, or preferred when issued stock.

LA

The two-character ISO 3166 country code for LAO PEOPLE'S DEMOCRATIC REPUBLIC.

Ladder strategy

A bond portfolio construction strategy that invests approximately equal amounts in every maturity within a given range.

Lady Macbeth Strategy

Strategy in which a third party poses as a white knight in a takeover bid, and then joins forces with an unfriendly bidder.

Laffer curve

A curve conjecturing that economic output will increase if marginal tax rates are cut. Named after economist Arthur Laffer.

Lag

Payment of a financial obligation later than is expected or required, as in lead and lag. Also, the number of periods that an independent variable in a regression model is "held back" in order to predict the dependent variable.

Lag response of prepayments

A delay of typically about three months between the time the weighted-average coupon of an MBS pool crosses the threshold for refinancing and observation of an acceleration in prepayment speed is observed.

Lagging

Strategy used by a firm to stall payments, normally in response to exchange rate projections.

Lagging indicators

Economic indicators that follow rather than precede the country's overall pace of economic activity. See also: Leading indicators and coincident indicators.

Laisse-faire

Doctrine that a government should not interfere with business and economic affairs.

Laisser Passer

A document accorded by a host government to foreign diplomatic personnel, which permits them to pass freely across the border of that country.

LAK

The ISO 4217 currency code for Laos New Kip.

Lake Chad Basin Commission

The LCBC recommends plans for developing the Chad Basin and coordinates research programs. The Commission was established in 1964; headquarters are in N'Djamena, Chad. LCBC members include: The Cameroon, Chad, Niger, and Nigeria.

Lambda

The ratio of a change in the option price to a small change in the option volatility. It is the partial derivative of the option price with respect to the option volatility.

Land contract

A method of real estate financing; a mortgage-holding seller finances a buyer by taking a down payment and subsequent payments in installments, but holds the title until the mortgage is fully repaid.

Landlord

A property owner who rents property to a tenant.

Lapsed option

An option that no longer has any value because it has reached its expiration date without being exercised.

Large-cap

A stock with a high level of capitalization, usually at least $5 billion market value.

Lagging indicators

Economic indicators that follow rather than precede the country's overall pace of economic activity. See also: Leading indicators and coincident indicators.

Last in, first out (LIFO)

An accounting method that fixes the cost of goods sold to the most recent purchases. Hence, if prices are generally rising, LIFO will lead to lower accounting profitability.

Last sale

The most recent trade performed in a security.

Last split

After a stock split, the number of shares distributed for each share held and the date of the distribution.

Last trading day

The final day under an exchange's rules during which trading may take place in a particular futures or options contract. Contracts outstanding at the end of the last trading day must be settled by delivery of underlying physical commodities or financial instruments, or by agreement for monetary settlement, depending futures contract specifications.

Late charge

A fee a credit grantor charges a borrower for a late payment.

Late tape

A delay in the display of price changes on the tape of an exchange because of heavy trading. In severe instances the first digit of each price is intentionally deleted.

Latin American Association of Development Financing Institutions

The Association promotes cooperation among members in ways which support the integration of Latin American economies, including efforts to improve the flow of information among members and encouraging studies of problems of common interest. Members include 24 Latin American countries and several countries in Europe and North America. The Association was established in January 1968; headquarters are in Lima, Peru.

Latin American Economic System

LAES (Spanish: Sistema Econ¢mico Latinoamericano, SELA), established in October 1975, promotes economic and social integration among approximately 26 Latin American and Caribbean member states. The System also seeks to present a united view for Latin America before agencies of the European Economic Communities and the United Nations. LAES headquarters are in Caracas, Venezuela.

Latin American Integration Association

LAIA (Spanish: Asociaci¢n Latinoamericana de Integraci¢n, ALADI) was originally created in 1960 as the Latin American Free Trade Association (LAFTA). LAFTA was restructured by the 1980 Montevideo Treaty as a more flexible alternative to LAIA. LAIA, whose membership included Argentina, Bolivia, Brazil, Chile, Colombia, Ecuador, Mexico, Paraguay, Peru, Uruguay, and Venezuela, has been declining as a major Latin American integration effort in favor of regional efforts, such as Mercosur. Association headquarters are in Montevideo, Uruguay.

Launder

To move illegally acquired cash through financial systems so that it appears to be legally acquired.

Law

There are two general types of legal system that have developed throughout the world: Common law is based on the English legal system and is the basis of the legal systems in many countries that were historically part of the British Empire, including many Caribbean countries that now operate as offshore entities. Civil Law is based primarily on the French and Spanish legal systems and tends to refer to the constitution of the country rather than past legal precedent.

Law of large numbers

The mean of a random sample approaches the mean (expected value) of the population as sample size increases.

Law of one price

An economic rule stating that a given security must have the same price no matter how the security is created. If the payoff of a security can be synthetically created by a package of other securities, the implication is that the price of the package and the price of the security whose payoff it replicates must be equal. If it is unequal, an arbitrage opportunity would present itself.

Layoffs

Layoffs are the termination of employees with or without advance notice and for reasons other than performance. Layoffs are one of many tools used to implement a downsizing strategy to reduce the size of the workforce. Downsizing can be done with or without layoffs. Downsizing includes an array of other tools to reduce the workforce.

Layup

Used in the context of general equities. Easily executed trade or order. See: Lead pipe.

LB

The two-character ISO 3166 country code for LEBANON.

LBO

See: Leveraged buyout.

LBP

The ISO 4217 currency code for Lebanese Pound.

LC

The two-character ISO 3166 country code for SAINT LUCIA.

LCL

See: Less Than Container Load.

LDC

See: Less developed countries.

Lead

Payment of a financial obligation earlier than is expected or required.

Lead manager

The commercial or investment bank with the primary responsibility for organizing syndicated bank credit or bond issued. The lead manager recruits additional lending or underwriting banks, negotiates terms of the issue with the issuer, and assesses market conditions.

Lead pipe

Used in the context of general equities. Virtually certain that trade will take place; lead pipe cinch. See: Layup.

Lead regulator

A leading self-regulatory organization that over sees compliance with a particular section of the law, such as the NYSE, ASE, or NASDAQ

Lead Time

The period of time from the date that the goods or services are requisitioned to the time when goods can be delivered, allowing for the public bidding and ordering.

Lead underwriter

The head of a syndicate of financial firms that are sponsoring an initial public offering of securities or a secondary offering of securities. Could also apply to bond issues.

Leader

A stock or group of stocks that is the first to move in a market upsurge or downturn.

Leading

Strategy used by a firm to accelerate payments, normally in response to exchange rate expectations.

Leading economic indicators

Economic series that tend to rise or fall in advance of the rest of the economy.

Leading indicator

A change in a measurable economic factor that is evident before the economy starts to follow a specific trend.

Leading and lagging

Refers to timing of cash flows within a corporation.

Leading the market

In the context of general equities, this is a stock or group of stocks moving with the market as a whole, but moving in advance of the general market.

League of Arab States

The League of Arab States (or Arab League) is a regional grouping aimed at improving relations among Arab nations. Members include: Algeria, Bahrain, Djibouti, Egypt, Iraq, Jordan, Kuwait, Lebanon, Libya, Mauritania, Morocco, Oman, Palestine, Qatar, Saudi Arabia, Somalia, Sudan, Syria, Tunisia, United Arab

Emirates, Yeman Arab Republic, Yemen People's Democractic Republic. The League was established in March 1945; headquarters are in Cairo, Egypt.

Leakage

Release of information selectively or not before official public announcement.

LEAPS

See: Long-Term Anticipation Securities.

Lease

A long-term rental agreement, and a form of secured long-term debt.

Lease acquisition cost

The legal fees and other expenses incurred when acquiring a lease.

Leasehold

An asset providing the right to use property under a lease agreement.

Leasehold improvement

An improvement made to leased property.

Lease-purchase agreement

An agreement that allows for portions of lease payments to be used to purchase the leased property.

Lease rate

The payment per period stated in a lease contract.

Leaseback

A transaction that involves the sale of some property, and an agreement by the seller to lease the property back from the buyer after the sale.

Leasing

Financing under which the customer (or lessee) pays for the use of assets (capital goods and equipment) in regular installments as the asset produces revenues. Under a finance lease, a lessee can acquire use of an asset for most, if not all, of its useful life. Under an operating lease, a lessee acquires use of an asset for a fraction of its useful life. Sometimes the lessee has the option to purchase the asset at residual value upon termination of the lease term.

Leaves

Used in the context of general equities. Remains to buy or sell of a previously entered order after a report of partial execution has been given. If the floor broker to buy 20M IBM at $115, and he then buys 6M at this price, his report would be, "You bought 6M IBM at $115; leaves 14."

Ledger cash

A firm's cash balance as reported in its financial statements. Also called book cash.

Leg

A prolonged trend in stock market prices, such as a multiple-period bull market; or, an option that is one side of a spread transaction. See: Lifting a leg.

Leg up

Used in the context of general equities. (1)Have a portion of the offsetting side of a trade in your pocket (spoken for) so your capital risk in the transaction is reduced. (Purchase of 10,000 of a 50,000 buy order leaves the trader a "leg up".) (2) Complete one side of a two-sided transaction, as in a swap or contingency order.

LEGAL

A computerized database maintained by the NYSE to keep track of enforcement actions, audits, and complaints against member firms. This term is not an acronym but is referred to in capitals.

Legal capital

Value at which a company's shares are recorded in its books.

Legal bankruptcy

A legal proceeding for liquidating or reorganizing a business.

Legal defeasance

The deposit of cash and permitted securities, as specified in the bond indenture, into an irrevocable trust sufficient to enable the issuer to fully discharge its obligations under the bond indenture.

Legal entity

A person or organization that can legally enter into a contract, and may therefore be sued for failure to comply with the terms of the contract.

Legal investments

Investments that a regulated entity is permitted to make under the rules and regulations that govern its conduct.

Legal list

A list of high-quality debt and equity securities chosen by a state agency that are acceptable holdings for fiduciary institutions.

Legal monopoly

A government-regulated firm that is legally entitled

to be the only company offering a particular service in a particular area.

Legal opinion

A statement, usually written by a specialized law firm, required for a new municipal bond issue stating that the issue is legally acceptable.

Legal transfer

A stock transaction that requires special documentation in addition to standard stock or bond power to be legally valid.

Legislative risk

The risk that new or changed legislation will have a large positive or negative effect on an investment.

Legitimate

Used in the context of general equities. Real interest in trading as compared to a profile stance. See: Natural.

Lehman Brothers Adjustable-Rate Mortgage Index

A benchmark index that includes all agency-guaranteed securities with coupons that periodically adjust based on a spread over a published index.

Lehman Brothers Aggregate Bond Index

A benchmark index made up of the Lehman Brothers Government/Corporate Bond Index, Mortgage-Backed Securities Index, and Asset-Backed Securities Index, including securities that are of investment-grade quality or better, have at least one year to maturity, and have an outstanding par value of at least $100 million.

Lehman Brothers California Municipal Bond Index

A benchmark index that includes investment-grade, tax-exempt, and fixed-rate bonds issued in California.

All securities have long-term maturities (greater than two years) and are selected from issues larger than $50 million.

Lehman Brothers Corporate Bond Index

A benchmark index that includes all publicly issued, fixed-rate, nonconvertible, dollar-denominated, SEC-registered, investment-grade corporate debt.

Lehman Brothers Government Bond Index

A benchmark index made up of the Treasury Bond Index and the Agency Bond Index as well as the 1-3 Year Government Index and the 20+ Year Treasury Index.

Lehman Brothers Government/Corporate Bond Index

A benchmark index made up of the Lehman Brothers® Government and Corporate Bond indexes, including U.S. government Treasury and agency securities as well as corporate and Yankee bonds.

Lehman Brothers Mortgage-Backed Securities Index

A benchmark index that includes 15- and 30-year fixed-rate securities backed by mortgage pools of the Government National Mortgage Association (GNMA), Federal Home Loan Mortgage Corporation (FHLMC), and Federal National Mortgage Association (FNMA).

Lehman Brothers Municipal Bond Index

A benchmark index that includes investment-grade, tax-exempt, and fixed-rate bonds with long-term maturities (greater than two years) selected from issues larger than $50 million.

Lehman Brothers New York Municipal Bond Index

A benchmark index that includes investment-grade, tax-exempt, and fixed-rate bonds issued in the state of New York. All securities have long-term maturities (greater than two years) and are selected from issues larger than $50 million.

Lemon

An investment with poor results.

Lemons problem

Named after 2001 Nobel Laureate George Akerlof's 1970 paper "The Market for Lemons". His original example had to do with used cars. Why does the seller want to get rid of the car? It might be a lemon. The buyer and seller have asymmetric information. Hence, the buyer will demand a deep discount on the car because of the possibility it is a lemon.

Lend

To provide money temporarily on the condition that it or its equivalent will be returned, often with an interest fee.

Lendable funds

The pool of funds available to borrows; typically categorized by currency and maturity.

Lender

Businesses that provide loans to others.

Lender of last resort

Traditionally the Federal Reserve Bank in the US, which assists banks that face large withdrawals of funds and in so doing stabilizes the banking system.

Lender liability lawsuits

Legal action of debtor against creditors that alleges unfair enforcement of loan covenants or violation of implied terms of a loan agreement.

Lending agreement

A contract regarding funds transferred between a lender and a borrower.

Lending at a premium

A loan from one broker to another of securities to cover a customer's short position, with a borrowing fee included. A fee is unusual since securities are normally lent freely between brokers.

Lending at a rate

Interest paid to a customer on the credit balance received from a short sale.

Lending securities

Securities borrowed from a broker's inventory, from another customer's margin account, or from another broker, when a customer is required to deliver on a short sale.

Leptokurtosis

The condition of a probability density curve to have fatter tails and a higher peak at the mean than the normal distribution.

Less Developed Country

An LDC is a country with low per capita gross national product. Terms such as third world, poor, developing nations, and underdeveloped have also been used to describe less developed countries.

Lessee

An entity that leases an asset from another entity.

Lesser Developed Countries

The classification LLDC (sometimes also known as "Least" Developed Countries) was developed by the

United Nations to give some guidance to donor agencies and countries about an equitable allocation of foreign assistance. The criteria for designating a country an LLDC, originally adopted by the UN Committee for Development Planning in 1971, have been modified several times. Criteria have included low: per-capita-income, literacy, and manufacturing share of the country's total gross domestic product. There is continuing concern that the criteria should be more robust and less subject to the possibility of easy fluctuation of a country between less developed and least developed status.

Lessor

An entity that leases an asset to another entity.

Less Than Container Load

Shipments of less than container load size (<$50,000).

Letter of Administration

A certificate issued by the Court evidencing the appointment of the Administrator of an Estate.

Letter of comment

A communication to the firm from the SEC that suggests changes to its registration statement.

Letter of Credit

(Also called Documentary credits). A document issued by a bank at the buyer's request in favor of the seller, promising to pay an agreed amount of money upon receipt by the bank of conforming documents with a specified time.

Irrevocable Letter of Credit - a letter in which the issuing bank waives all right to cancel or in any way amend without consent of the beneficiary or seller.

Confirmed Irrevocable Letter of Credit - a letter to which has been added the responsibility of a bank other than the issuing bank.

Revocable Letter of Credit - a letter in which the issuing bank reserves the right to cancel or amend such portion of the amount involved as has not been availed of prior to the actual payment or negotiation of drafts drawn thereunder.

Revolving Credit - a letter in which the issuing bank notifies the seller of the merchandise that the amount involved when utilized will again become available, usually under the same terms and without issuance of another letter.

Special clauses:

1. Red Clause: a clause authorizing the drawing of clean drafts (without documents) accompanied by a statement that the shipping documents concerned will be furnished later.
2. Telegraphic Transfer Clause: a clause containing an undertaking on the part of the issuing bank to pay the invoiced amount to the order of the negotiating bank upon receipt of an authenticated cablegram (telex) from the latter that the required documents have been received by it and are being forwarded.
3. Green Clause: an endorsement authorizing the drawing of clean drafts without documents by the beneficiary, but requiring the covered merchandise to be stored in the name of the paying bank until the documents are received.

Letter of Guarantee

A letter from a bank to a brokerage firm which states that a customer (who has written a call option) does indeed own the underlying stock and the bank will guarantee delivery if the call is assigned. Thus the call can be considered covered. Not all brokerage firms accept letters of guarantee. Also: letter issued to Option Clearing Corporation by member firms covering a guarantee of any trades made by one of its customers, (a trader or broker on the exchange floor).

Letter of intent

An assurance by a mutual fund shareholder that a certain amount of money will be invested monthly, in exchange for lower sales charges. In mergers, a preliminary merger agreement between companies after significant negotiations.

Letter of Undertaking

See Link Contract.

Letter stock

Privately placed common stock, so-called because the SEC requires a letter from the purchaser stating that the stock is not intended for resale.

Letter of Testamentary

A certificate issued by the court evidencing the appointment of an executor of estate.

Letter of Transmittal

A document used by security holder to accompany certificates surrendered in an exchange or other corporate action.

Level

Used in the context of general equities. Price measure of an indication.

Level-coupon bond

Bond with a stream of coupon payments that remain the same throughout the life of the bond.

Level debt service

A municipal charter provision that debt payments must be relatively equal from year to year so that required revenue projections are easier.

Level load

A mutual fund that charges a permanent sales charge, usually at some fixed percentage. See: Front-end loads and back-end loads.

Level pay

Scheduling principal and interest payments (P&I) due under a mortgage so that total monthly payment of P&I is the same. Different from the typical mortgage for which the principal payment component of the monthly payment becomes gradually greater while the monthly interest component shrinks.

Level term insurance

A life insurance policy with a fixed face value and increasing premiums.

Leverage

The use of debt financing, or property of rising or falling at a proportionally greater amount than comparable investments. For example, an option is said to have high leverage compared to the underlying stock because a given price change in the stock may result in a greater increase or decrease in the value of the option.

Leverage clientele

A group of shareholders who, because of their personal leverage, seek to invest in corporations that maintain a compatible degree of corporate leverage.

Leverage ratios

Measures of the relative value of stockholders, capitalization, and creditors obligations, and of the firm's ability to pay financing charges. Value of firm's debt to the total value of the firm (debt plus stockholder capitalization).

Leverage rebalancing

Making transactions to adjust (rebalance) a firm's leverage ratio to a target ratio.

Leveraged beta

The beta of a leveraged required return; that is, the beta as adjusted for the degree of leverage in the firm's capital structure.

Leveraged buyout (LBO)

A transaction used to take a public corporation private that is financed through debt such as bank loans and bonds. Because of the large amount of debt relative to equity in the new corporation, the bonds are typically rated below investment-grade, properly referred to as high-yield bonds or junk bonds. Investors can participate in an LBO through either the purchase of the debt (i.e., purchase of the bonds or participation in the bank loan) or the purchase of equity through an LBO fund that specializes in such investments.

Leveraged company

A company that has debt in its capital structure.

Leveraged equity

Stock in a firm that relies on financial leverage. Holders of leveraged equity experience the benefits and costs of using debt.

Leveraged investment company

An investment company or mutual fund entitled to borrow capital for its operations. Also, an investment company that issues both income shares and capital shares.

Leveraged lease

A lease arrangement under which the lessor borrows a large proportion of the funds needed to purchase the asset. The lender has a lien on the assets and a pledge of the lease payments to secure the borrowing.

Leveraged portfolio

A portfolio that includes risky assets purchased with funds borrowed.

Leveraged recapitalization

Often used in risk arbitrage. A public company takes on significant additional debt with the purpose of either paying an extraordinary dividend or repurchasing shares, leaving the public shareholders with a continuing interest in a more financially leveraged company. Popular form of shark repellent See: Stub.

Leveraged required return

The required return on an investment when the investment is financed partially by debt.

Leveraged stock

Stocks financed with credit, such as that purchased on a margin account.

Levered portfolio

Investment at least partially financed by borrowing.

LI

The two-character ISO 3166 country code for LIECHTENSTEIN.

Liability

A financial obligation, or the cash outlay that must be made at a specific time to satisfy the contractual terms of such an obligation.

Liability funding strategies

Investment strategies that select assets so that cash flows will equal or exceed the client's obligations.

Liability insurance

Insurance guarding against damage or loss that the policyholder, may cause another person in the form of bodily injury or property damage.

Liability swap

An interest rate swap used to alter the cash flow characteristics of an institution's liabilities so as to provide a better match with its assets.

LIBOR

See: London Interbank Offered Rate.

License

Official or legal permission from the owners to do, use, or own specified things of value such as intellectual property, service and trade marks, technology transfers and know-how. International license agreements between companies in different countries are subject to the applicable laws in each country which may differ in their effect and enforcement and accordingly affect the rights and liabilities of the parties.

License agreement

A contract by which a domestic company (the licensor) allows a foreign company (the licensee) to market its products in a foreign country in return for royalties, fees, or other forms of compensation.

Licensed production.

(Also one of the means of implementing Offsets - see under *Offsets*). Overseas production of a U.S.-origin article based upon transfer of technical information under direct commercial arrangements beteen a U.S. manufacturer and a foreign government or producer.

Licensing

A business arrangement in which the manufacturer of a product (or a firm with proprietary rights over certain technology, trademarks, etc.) grants permission to some other group or individual to manufacture that product (or make use of that proprietary material) in return for specified royalties or other payment.

Lien

A security interest in one or more assets that lenders hold in exchange for secured debt financing.

Life annuity

An annuity that pays a fixed amount for the lifetime of the annuitant.

Life cycle

The lifetime of a product or business, from its creation to its demise or transformation.

Life-Cycle Processing

An accounting approach in which a company sets product prices based on recovering costs over the life cycle of the product. U.S. authorities dispute the validity of this approach because projections of future yield improvements cannot be verified at the time of dumping calculations.

Life expectancy

The length of time that an average person is expected to live, which is used by insurance companies use to make projections of benefit payouts.

Life insurance

An insurance policy that pays a monetary benefit to the insured person's survivors after death.

Life insurance in force

The dollar amount of life insurance that a company has issued, measured as the sum of policy face values and dividends paid.

Life insurance policy

The contract that sets out the terms of life insurance coverage.

Lifetime reverse mortgage

A type of mortgage in which a homeowner borrows against the value a home, while retaining title, and making no payments while residing in the home. When the owner ceases living in the house, the property is sold, and the loan repaid.

LIFFE

See: London International Financial Futures and Options Exchange.

LIFO

See: Last in, first out.

Lift

An increase in securities prices, as shown by some economic indicator.

Lifted

Refers to over-the-counter trading. Having an offer taken in a stock, followed by the market maker raising the offer price.

Lifting a leg

Closing out one side of a long-short arbitrage before the other is closed.

Lighten up

Selling some part of a stock or bond position in a portfolio to realize capital gains or to losses or increase cash assets.

Lighter

An open or covered vessel which transfers cargo between ship and shore, used mainly in harbors and inland waterways. Lighters are generally used for shorter hauls than barges.

Lima Stock Exchange

Peru's major securities market.

Limit

See Trading Limit.

Limit Cycles

An attractor for non-linear dynamic systems which has periodic cycles or orbits in phase space. An example is an undamped pendulum which will have a closed circle orbit equal to the amplitude of the pendulum's swing. See: Attractor, Phase Space.

Limitation on asset dispositions

A bond covenant that restricts in some way a firm's ability to sell major assets.

Limitation on conversion

Applies mainly to convertible securities. Possible delay in convertibility. More frequently, the right to convert may be terminable prior to a redemption date, preventing the holder from receiving a final coupon or dividend. See: Accrued interest.

Limitation on liens

A bond covenant that restricts in some way a firm's ability to grant liens on its assets.

Limitation on merger, consolidation, or sale

A bond covenant that restricts in some way a firm's ability to merge or consolidate with another firm.

Limitation on sale-and-leaseback

A bond covenant that restricts in some way a firm's ability to enter into sale-and-leaseback transactions, financing techniques that could affect creditor thinness..

Limitation on subsidiary borrowing

A bond covenant that restricts in some way a firm's ability to borrow at the level of firm subsidiary.

Limited Appointment

Limited appointees to the U.S. and Foreign Commercial Service (or to other foreign services) are persons from the private sector or from the Federal Government who are non-career officers assigned overseas for a limited time.

Limited company

A form of business commonly used in the U.K. comparable to incorporation in the U.S.

Limited discretion

Permission by a client that allows a broker to make certain stock and option trades without first consulting the client about the trade.

Limited flexibility exchange rate system

The International Monetary Fund's name for an exchange rate system with a managed float.

Limited International Bidding

LIB is one of several forms of procurement made with World Bank financing. In some circumstances (such as: small purchases, urgent need, or few suppliers), suppliers or contractors of specialized goods and services participate by invitation rather than in response to an advertisement.

Limited Liability

This is associated with the identity of a company being distinct from the members that own it, and reflects the position that owners of the company are only liable for the acts of the company to the extent of any unpaid share capital. In the United Kingdom there are two types of limited companies:

(a) a private limited company in which the public cannot be invited to subscribe to any share issue and

(b) a public limited company (plc) which can raise funds through share issues.

Before a limited company can "go public," it must have a minimum share capital. A private limited company requires no minimum share capital.

Limited-liability instrument

A security, such as a call option, in which the owner can lose only the initial investment.

Limited partner

A partner who has limited legal liability for the obligations of the partnership.

Limited partnership

A partnership that includes one or more partners who have limited liability.

Limited payment policy

Life insurance providing full life protection but requiring premiums for only part of the customer's lifetime.

Limited risk

The risk inherent in options contracts, which is much lower than that of a futures contract, which has unlimited risk. The maximum loss in buying a call option, for example, is the premium paid for the option.

Limited price order

Used in the context of general equities. See: Limit order.

Limited-tax general obligation bond

A general obligation bond of a government backed by specified or constrained revenue sources.

Limited warranty

A warranty with certain conditions and limitations on the parts covered, type of damage covered, and/or time period for which the agreement is good.

Limit on close order

An order to buy or sell stock at the closing price only if the price is at a predetermined level or better.

Limit order

An order to buy a stock at or below a specified price, or to sell a stock at or above a specified price. For instance, you could tell a broker "buy me 100 shares of XYZ Corp at $8 or less" or "sell 100 shares of XYZ at $10 or better" The customer specifies a price, and the order can be executed only if the market reaches or betters that price. A conditional trading order designed to avoid the danger of adverse unexpected price changes.

Limit order book

A record of unexecuted limit orders maintained by the specialist. These orders are treated equally with other orders in terms of priority of execution.

Limit order information system

The electronic system supplying information about securities traded on participating exchanges so that the best securities prices can be found.

Limit price

See: Maximum price fluctuation.

Limit up, limit down

The maximum price change allowed for a commodity futures contract per trading day.

Linear programming

Technique for finding the maximum value of some equation, subject to stated linear constraints.

Linear regression

A statistical technique for fitting a straight line to a set of data points.

Line of credit

An informal loan arrangement between a bank and a customer allowing the customer to borrow up to a prespecified amount.

Line Release System

The Line Release System, a part of Customs' Automated Commercial System, is designed for the release and tracking of shipments through the use of personal computers and bar code technology. To qualify for line release, a commodity must have a history of invoice accuracy, and be selected by local Customs districts on the basis of high volume. To release the merchandise, Customs reads the bar code into a personal computer, verifies that the bar code matches the invoice data, and enters the quantity. The cargo release is transmitted to the Automated Commercial System, which establishes an entry and the requirement for an entry summary, and provides the Automated Broker Interface system participants with release information.

Link Contract

As used in this publication, a generic name for the side document that links the import/export components of a countertrade transaction. The link contract specifies conditions under which a primary supplier irrevocably commits to purchase, or cause to be purchased, goods and/or services from sources designated by the primary buyer. It also prescribes penalties or remedial procedures in case of nonperformance. The document is sometimes referred to as a letter of undertaking, a protocol, a framework contract, or just a countertrade contract.

Linking method

Method for calculating rates of return that multiplies one plus the interim rate of return.

Lintner's observations

John Lintner's work (1956) suggests that dividend policy is related both a target level, and to the speed of adjustment of change in dividends.

Lipper Mutual Fund Industry Average

The average level of performance for all mutual funds, as reported by Lipper Analytical Services.

Liquid asset

Asset that is easily and cheaply turned into cash-notably, cash itself and short-term securities.

Liquidation System

The Liquidation System, a part of Customs' Automated Commercial System, closes the file on each entry and establishes a batch filing number which is essential for recovering an entry for review or enforcement purposes. An entry liquidation is a final review of the entry. P.L. 95-410 (Customs Procedural Reform and Simplification Act of 1978) requires that all liquidations be performed within one year from the date of consumption entry or final withdrawal on a warehouse entry. Three one-year extensions are permitted.

Liquid market

A market allowing the buying or selling of large quantities of an asset at any time and at low transactions costs.

Liquid yield option note (LYON)

Zero-coupon, callable, putable, convertible bond developed by Merrill Lynch & Co.

Liquidating dividend

Payment by a firm to its owners from capital rather than from earnings.

Liquidation

Occurs when a firm's business is terminated. Assets are sold, proceeds are used to pay creditors, and any leftovers are distributed to shareholders. Any transaction that offsets or closes out a long or short position. Related: Buy in, evening up, offset liquidity.

Liquidation by assignment

Sale or realization of a debtor firm's assets voluntarily agreed to by its creditors who estimate that the firm's liquidation value exceeds its going-concern value.

Liquidation rights

The rights of a firm's securityholders in the event the firm liquidates.

Liquidation value

Net amount that could be realized by selling the assets of a firm after paying the debt.

Liquidator

Person appointed by an unsecured creditor in the United Kingdom to oversee the sale of an insolvent firm's assets and the repayment of its debts.

Liquidity

A high level of trading activity, allowing buying and selling with minimum price disturbance. Also, a market characterized by the ability to buy and sell with relative ease. Antithesis of illiquidity.

Liquidity diversification

Investing in a variety of maturities to reduce the price risk to which holding long bonds exposes the investor.

Liquidity Fund

A California company that buys real estate limited partnership interests at 25% to 35% lower than the current value of the real estate assets.

Liquidity preference hypothesis

The argument that greater liquidity is valuable, all else equal. Also, the theory that the forward rate exceeds expected future interest rates.

Liquidity premium

Forward rate minus expected future short-term interest rate.

Liquidity ratios

Ratios that measure a firm's ability to meet its short-term financial obligations on time, such as the ratio of current assets to current liabilities.

Liquidity risk

The risk that arises from the difficulty of selling an asset in a timely manner. It can be thought of as the difference between the "true value" of the asset and the likely price, less commissions.

Liquidity theory of the term structure

A biased expectations theory that asserts that the implied forward rates will not be a pure estimate of the market's expectations of future interest rates because they embody a liquidity premium.

Lisbon Stock Exchange (LSE)

Stock exchange trading stocks, bonds, and unit trusts. The BVL general index is the exchange's official index.

Listed firm

A company whose stock trades on a stock exchange, and conforms to listing requirements.

Listed option

An option that has been accepted for trading on an exchange.

Listed security

Stock or bond that has been accepted for trading by one of the organized and registered securities exchanges in the United States. Generally, the advantages of being listed are that exchanges provide: (1) an orderly marketplace; (2) liquidity; (3) fair price determination; (4) accurate and continuous reporting on sales and quotations; (5) information on listed companies; and (6) strict regulation for the protection of securityholders. Antithesis of OTC Security.

Listed stocks

Stocks that are traded on an exchange.

Listing

In the context of real estate, written agreement between a property owner and a real estate broker that gives the broker permission to find a buyer or tenant for some property. See: Listing broker.

Listing broker In the context of equity, when a stock is traded in exchange it is said to be listed.

A licensed real estate broker who completes a listing of a property for sale.

Listing requirements

Requirements, including minimum shares outstanding, market value, and income, that are laid down by an exchange for any stock to be listed for trading.

Living benefits

Life insurance benefits from which the insured can draw cash while still living, usually in the case of some high-cost illness.

Living trust

A trust that an individual establishes during the individual's lifetime, enabling the person to control the assets contributed to the trust. Also known as an inter vivos trust.

Living will

A document specifying the kind of medical care a person wants-or does not want-in the event of terminal illness or incapacity.

LK

The two-character ISO 3166 country code for SRI LANKA.

LKR

The ISO 4217 currency code for Sri Lankan Rupee.

LLC

Limited Liability Company.

Lloyds of London

A marketplace in London for underwriting syndicates.

LLP

Limited Liability Partnership.

Load

The sales fee charged to an investor when shares are purchased in a load fund or annuity. See: Bank-end load; front-end load; level load.

Load fund

A mutual fund that sells shares with a sales charge-typically 4% to 8% of the net amount indicated. Some no-load funds also levy distribution fees permitted by Article 12b-1 of the Investment Company Act; these are typically 0. 25%. A true no-load fund has neither a sales charge nor

Load-to-load

Arrangement whereby the customer pays for the last delivery when the next one is received.

Load spread option

A method of allocating the annual sales charge on load funds, often through percentage deductions from a customer's periodic fixed payments.

Loan

Temporary borrowing of a sum of money. If you borrow $1 million you have taken out a loan for $1 million.

Loan amortization schedule

The timetable for repaying the interest and principal on a loan.

Loan commitment

Assurance by a lender to make money available to a borrower on specific terms in return for a fee.

Loan crowd

Historical term. In the 1920's and 1930's, it refers to the group of member firms that lend or borrow securities needed to cover the positions of customers who have sold short securities. The crowd could be found around the loan post.

Loan Preference Principle

The theory that a covered loan is less expensive when its cost is calculated in one currency, it will also be less expensive in all other currencies.

Loan Receipt

Document signed by the Assured where he acknowledges receipt of money advanced by the insurance company as an interest-free loan (instead of payment of a loss) repayable to the insurance company only if the loss is recovered from a third party and then only to the extent of the recovery.

Loan syndication

Group of banks sharing a loan. See: Syndicate.

Loan value

The maximum percentage of the value of securities that a broker can lend to a margin account customer, as dictated by the Federal Reserve Board in Regulation T.

Loan-to-value ratio (LTV)

The ratio of money borrowed on a property to the property's fair market value.

Loaned flat

Securities lent interest-free between brokers to cover customers' short sale positions.

LOC

See: Letter of credit.

Local

A futures exchange member who trades securities for his or her own account.

Local Competitive Bidding

LCB is one of several forms of procurement made with World Bank financing. LCB is generally used for contracts involving: (a) labor intensive activities; (b) small value; (c) locally procurable services or goods priced below the world market; (d) intermittant work; or (e) activities to be performed at numerous sites.

Local expectations hypothesis (LEH)

Theory that bonds similar in all aspects except maturity will have the same holding-period rate of return.

Local expectations theory

A form of the pure expectations theory that suggests that the returns on bonds of different maturities will be the same over a short-term investment horizon.

Local taxes

Property, sewer, school, or other community paid to a locality. Local taxes are usually deductible for federal income tax purposes.

Location-specific advantages

Advantages (natural and created) that are available only or primarily in a particular place.

Locational arbitrage

Attempt to exploit discrepancies in exchange rates between banks.

Lock

Used in the context of general equities. Make a market both ways (bid and offer) either on the bid, offering, or an in-between price only. Locking on the offering occurs to attract a seller, since the trader is willing to pay (and ask) the offering side when others only ask it. Locking on the bid side attracts buyers for similar reasons. Typically, the sell side requires a plus tick to comply with short sale rules.

Lock in

To ensure that an individual transacts all his or her business with a sole broker by providing superior services, such as accommodating block buy and sell needs or preparing excellent research (soft-dollar lock). This usually guarantees a certain volume of business.

Lock-out

With PAC bond CMO classes, the period before the PAC sinking fund becomes effective. With multifamily loans, the period of time during which prepayment is prohibited.

Lock-up CDs

CDs that are issued with the tacit understanding that the buyer will not trade the certificate. Quite often, the issuing bank will insist that it hold the certificate for safekeeping by it to ensure that the buyer holds the understanding.

Lockup option

Often used in risk arbitrage. Privilege offered a white knight (friendly acquirer) by a target company to buy crown jewels or additional equity. The aim is to discourage a hostile takeover. See: Shark repellent.

Lockbox

A collection and processing service provided to firms by banks, which collect payments from a dedicated postal box to which the firm directs its customers to send payment to. The banks make several collections per day, process the payments immediately, and deposit the funds into the firm's bank account.

Locked in

When an investor is unable to take advantage of preferential tax treatment because of time remaining on a required holding period. Also, a commodities position in which the market has a limit up or limit down day and investors are unable to move in to or out of the market.

Locked market

A market is locked if the bid price equals the ask price. This can occur, for example, if the market is brokered and one side pays brokerage only, in over-the-counter trading the initiator of the transaction. Highly competitive market environment with inside bid and offering at the same price. Often occurs when an OTC dealer has not updated the market.

Log-linear least-squares method

A statistical technique for fitting a curve to a set of data points. One of the variables is transformed by taking its logarithm, and then a straight line is fitted to the transformed set of data points.

Lognormal distribution

Pattern of frequency of occurrence in which the logarithm of the variable follows a normal distribution.

Lognormal distributions are used to describe returns calculated over periods of a year or more.

LOI

Letter of Intent.

Lombard Rate

The Lombard rate is one of the official interest rates in Germany used to regulate the money market. Other countries use the term Lombard to describe rates which function somewhat like the Lombard rate. The Swiss, for example, have their own Lombard rate. In France, it's called the Central Bank Intervention rate but performs the same function.

Lome Convention

The Convention is an agreement concluded at Lom,, Togo in February 1975 and which entered into force in April 1976. The orginal Convention has been followed by several additional Lom, Conventions which expanded the scope of the original agreement. The Convention is between the European Community (EC) and 62 African, Caribbean, and Pacific states (mostly former colonies of the EC members). The agreement covers some aid provisions as well as trade and tariff preferences for the ACP countries when shipping to the EC. Lom, grew out of the 1958 Treaty of Rome's "association" with the 18 African colonies/countries that had ties with Belgium and France. The ACP members are: Angola, Bahamas, Barbados, Benin, Botswana, Burkina Faso, Burundi, Cameroon, Cape Verde, Central African Republic, Chad, Comoros, Congo, Cote d'Ivoire, Djibouti, Dominica, Equatorial Guinea, Ethiopia, Fiji, Gabon, Gambia, Ghana, Grenada, Guinea, Guinea-Bissau, Guyana, Jamaica, Kenya, Lesotho, Liberia, Madagascar, Malawi, Mali, Mauritius, Mauritania, Mozambique, Namibia, Niger, Nigeria, Papua New Guinea, Rwanda, Saint Lucia,

Saint Vincent, Samoa, Sao Tome and Principe, Senegal, Seychelles, Sierra Leone, Solomon Islands, Somalia, Sudan, Suriname, Swaziland, Tanzania, Togo, Trinidad and Tobago, Uganda, Zaire, Zambia, and Zimbabwe.

London Club

The London Club, a creditor cartel of commercial banks, evolved in the early 1980s. Debt rescheduling (i.e., constructing new repayment profiles over a specific period of time) was a primary function of the club. The Brady deals on debt restructuring (i.e., renegotiating the entire stock of outstanding debt at a discount), obviated the need to reschedule repayments every couple of years. In some respect, the Bank Advisory Committee has replaced the London Club. The Paris Club, also concerned with debt repayment, is an association of official creditors.

London Commodity Exchange (LCE)

Merged with the London International Financial Futures and Options Exchange in 1996.

London Interbank Bid Rate

LIBID is the rate of interest paid for funds in the London interbank market. The bid to Libor's offer has been used as a reference for floating rate payments for especially strong borrowers.

London Interbank Mean Rate

Abbreviated as LIMEAN, this is the midpoint of the LIBOR-LIBID spread. LIMEAN has been used as a reference for floating rate payments.

London Interbank Offered Rate

LIBOR, the most prominent of the interbank offered rates, is the rate of interest at which banks in London lend funds to other prime banks in London. LIBOR is frequently used as a basis for determining the rate of interest payable on Eurodollars and other Eurocurrency loans. The effective rate of interest on these Eurocredits is LIBOR plus a markup negotiated between lender and borrower.

London International Financial Futures and Options Exchange

LIFFE, Europe's leading exchange, trades in futures contracts including short-term interest rates, government bonds, stock indices, and traded options on these instruments. The Exchange was established in 1982 to provide a means for hedging interest rates and currency exposures against volatility. Originally called the London International Financial Futures Exchange, LIFFE merged in March 1992 with the London Traded Options Market (LTOM) and retained the original acronym.

London Metal Exchange (LME)

A market for trading base metals, where traded options contracts are available against the underlying futures contract.

London Stock Exchange (LSE)

The U.K.'s six regional exchanges joined together in 1973 to form the stock exchange of Great Britain and Ireland, later named the LSE. The FTSE 100 index (known as the footsie) is its dominant index.

Long

One who has bought a contract to establish a market position and who has not yet closed out this position through an offsetting sale; the opposite of short.

Long bonds

Bonds with a long current maturity. The "long bond" is the 30-year US Treasury bond.

Long coupons

(1) Bonds or notes with a long current maturity. (2) A bond on which one of the coupon periods, usually the first, is longer than the other periods or the standard period.

Long-Dated Forward

The long-dated forward is a foreign exchange contract whose maturity exceeds one year; a few have extended over ten years.

Long hedge

The purchase of a futures contract in anticipation of actual purchases in the cash market. Used by processors or exporters as protection against an advance in the cash price. Related: hedge, short hedge

Long leg

The part of an option spread in which an agreement to buy the underlying security is made.

Long market value

The market value of a security, excluding options, as of the close of the last business day.

Long position

Owning or holding options (i.e., the number of contracts bought exceeds the number of contracts sold). For equities, a long position occurs when an individual owns securities. An owner of 1,000 shares of stock is said to be "Long the stock." Related: Short position.

Long position in an option

Purchase of an options.

Long run

A period of time in which all costs are variable; longer than one year.

Long straddle

Taking a long position in both a put and a call option.

Long-term

In accounting terms, one year or longer.

Long-term assets

Value of property, equipment, and other capital assets minus the depreciation. This is an entry in the bookkeeping records of a company. It is usually established on a "cost" basis, and thus does not necessarily reflect the market value of the assets.

Long-term capital gain

A profit on the sale of a security or mutual fund share that has been held for more than one year.

Long-term debt

An obligation having a maturity of more than one year from the date it was issued. Also called funded debt.

Long-term debt/capitalization

Indicator of financial leverage. Shows long-term debt as a proportion of the capital available. Determined by dividing long-term debt by the sum of long-term debt, preferred stock and common stockholder's equity.

Long-term debt-to-equity ratio

A capitalization ratio comparing long-term debt to shareholders' equity.

Long-term debt ratio

The ratio of long-term debt to total capitalization.

Long-Term Anticipation Securities (LEAPS)

Long-term options.

Long-term financial plan

Financial plan covering two or more years of future operations.

Long-term financing

Liabilities repayable in more than one year plus equity.

Long-term forward contracts

Contracts that state exchange rate at which a specified amount of a particular currency can be exchanged at a future date (more than one year from today).

Long-term gain

A profit on the sale of a capital assets held longer than 12 months, and eligible for long-term capital gains tax treatment.

Long-term goals

Financial goals expected to be accomplished in five years or longer.

Long-term investor

A person who makes investments for a period of at least five years in order to finance his or her long-term goals.

Long-term liabilities

Amount owed for leases, bond repayment, and other items due after 1 year.

Long-term loss

A loss on the sale of a capital asset held less than 12 months that can be used to offset a capital gain.

Look

Used for listed equity securities.

Look-thru

A method for calculating US taxes owed on income from controlled foreign corporations that was introduced by the Tax Reform Act of 1986.

Lookback option

An option that allows the buyer to choose as the option strike price any price of the underlying asset that has occurred during the life of the option. For a call option, the buyer will choose the minimum price; for a put option, the buyer will choose the maximum price. This option will always be in the money.

Looking for

In the context of general equities, this describing a buy interest in which a dealer is asked to offer stock, often involving a capital commitment. Antithesis of in touch with.

Loophole

A technicality in some legislation or regulation that makes it possible to avoid certain consequences or circumvent a rule without breaking the law, such as in the use of a tax shelter.

Loose credit

Policy by the Federal Reserve Board to make loans less expensive and more available by reducing interest rates through open market operations.

Loss

The opposite of gain.

Loss Carry-Back (Carry-Forward)

A tax provision that allows operating losses to be used as a tax shield to reduce taxable income in prior and future years. Losses can be carried backward for up to three years and forward for up to 15 years under current tax codes.

Loss-control activities

Actions that an insured person or company takes at the instigation of an insurance company in order to prevent accidents or losses.

Loss-of-income insurance

Insurance coverage that will pay out income that a policyholder loses as a result of a disability, injury, or business disruption.

Loss of Market

A situation in which, for one reason or another, sound cargo is no longer wanted by the consignee when it arrives. This is a "business loss" not recoverable under a Marine Cargo Policy; e.g., Christmas trees arriving in January undamaged.

Loss ratio

The ratio of losses paid or accrued by an insurer to premiums collected over a year.

Lots

In the context of general equities, this blocks or portions of trades. Can express a specific transaction in a stock at a certain time, often implying execution at the same price (e.g., "I traded 40m in two lots of 10 and four lots of 5.").

Louvre Accord

The Louvre Accord (February 1987) attempted to stop the dollar's fall and stabilize currency relationships by introducing reference ranges among the G-7 currencies

Low

In the context of general equities, this is a specific minimum limit required by a seller in execution an order ("I'll sell 50 with an eighth low."); implies a not-held limit order. Antithesis of top.

Low balance method

A method of calculating interest on the basis of the lowest balance of an account over the applicable period.

Low ball

Slang for making an offer well below the fair value of an asset in hopes that the seller may be desperate to sell.

Low-coupon bond refunding

Refunding of a low-coupon bond with a new, higher-coupon bond.

Lowest Responsible Bidder

That bidder who is awarded a contract because his bid in unit price, total cost of operation, or value per dollar is lower than any of the bidders and whose reputation, past performance and financial capabilities are such, that they would be judged to be capable of satisfying the needs of a specific contract.

Low grade

A bond with a rating of B or lower.

Low-load fund

A mutual fund that charges a sales commission of 3.5% or less for the purchase of shares.

Low price

The day's lowest price of a security that has changed hands between a buyer and a seller.

Low price-earnings ratio effect

The tendency of portfolios of stocks with a low price-earnings ratio to outperform portfolios of stocks with high price-earnings ratios.

LR

The two-character ISO 3166 country code for LIBERIA.

LRD

The ISO 4217 currency code for the Liberian Dollar.

LS

The two-character ISO 3166 country code for LESOTHO.

LSL

The ISO 4217 currency code for the Lesotho Loti.

LT

The two-character ISO 3166 country code for LITHUANIA.

LTL

The ISO 4217 currency code for the Lithuanian Litas.

LTV

See: Loan-to-value ratio.

LU

The two-character ISO 3166 country code for LUXEMBOURG.

LUF

The ISO 4217 currency code for the Luxembourg Franc.

Lump sum

A large one-time payment of money.

Lump-sum distribution

A single payment that represents an employee's interest in a qualified retirement plan. The payment must be prompted by retirement (or other separation from service), death, disability, or attainment of age 59-1/2, and must be made within a single tax year to avoid the federal government's 10% penalty tax.

Lusophone Countries

Lusophone countries are those in which the official language is Portuguese: Angola, Brazil, Cape Verde, Guinea-Bissau, Mozambique, Portugal, and Sao-Tome and Principe.

LV

The two-character ISO 3166 country code for LATVIA.

LVL

The ISO 4217 currency code for the Latvian Lats.

LY

The two-character ISO 3166 country code for LIBYAN ARAB JAMAHIRIYA.

Lyapunov Exponents

A measure of the dynamics of an attractor. Each dimension has a Lyapunov exponent. A positive exponent measures sensitive dependence on initial conditions, or how much our forecasts can diverge based upon different estimates of starting conditions. Another way to view Lyapunov exponents is the loss of predictive ability as we look forward into time. Strange Attractors are characterized by at least one positive exponent. A negative exponent measures how points converge towards one another. Point Attractors are characterized by all negative variables. See: Attractor, Limit Cycle, Point Attractor, Strange Attractor.

LYD

The ISO 4217 currency code for the Libyan Dinar.

LYON

See: Liquid yield option note.

M

M

Fifth letter of a NASDAQ stock symbol specifying that the issue is the company's fourth class of preferred shares.

M1

Measure of the U.S. money stock that consists of currency held by the public, travelers checks, demand deposits and other checkable deposits including NOW (negotiable order of withdrawal) and ATS (automatic transfer service) account balances and share draft account balances at credit unions.

M2

Measure of the U.S. money stock that consists of M1, certain overnight repurchase agreements and certain overnight Eurodollars, savings deposits (including money market deposit accounts), time deposits in amounts of less that $100,000 and balances in money market mutual funds (other than those restricted to institutional investors).

M3

Measure of the U.S. money stock that consists of M2, time deposits of $100,000 or more at all depository institutions, term repurchase agreements in amounts of $100,000 or more, certain term Eurodollars and balances in money market mutual funds restricted to institutional investors.

MA

The two-character ISO 3166 country code for MOROCCO.

Maastricht Treaty

The Maastricht Treaty (named for the Dutch town in which the treaty was signed) is also known as the Treaty of European Union. The treaty creates a European Union by:

(a) commiting the 12 member states of the European Economic Community to both European Monetary Union (EMU) and political union;

(b) introducing a single currency (European Currency Unit, ECU);

(c) establishing a European System of Central Banks (ESCB);

(d) creating a European Central Bank (ECB); and

(e) broadening EEC integration by including both a common foreign and security policy (CFSP) and cooperation in justice and home affairs (CJHA).

The treaty, negotiated in 1991 and signed in February 1992, entered into force on November 1, 1993. The Maastricht Treaty envisioned EMU being achieved in three stages:

— A first stage (encompassing treaty negotiations and lasting through January 1, 1994) concludes with ratification of treaty amendments needed to establish EMU, including participation by all 12 EEC member states in the Exchange Rate Mechanism;

— A second stage (January 1, 1994 through no later than January 1, 1999) involves establishment of the European Monetary Institute (EMI) to support development of a single currency (the ecu) and development of the ECB;

— A third stage (starting no later than January 1, 1999) involves irrevocable fixing of exchange rates and the debut of the ECB with transfer of powers necessary for administering economic and monetary union.

MAB

See: Master Air Waybill.

Macaroni defense

A tactic used by a corporation that is the target of a hostile takeover bid involving the issue of a large number of bonds that must be redeemed at a higher value if the company is taken over.

Macaulay duration

The weighted-average term to maturity of the cash flows from a bond, where the weights are the present value of the cash flow divided by the price.

Macro

In the context of hedge funds, a style of management that takes long term strategic bets. For example, the manager might believe that the Yen will appreciate relative to the dollar over the next six months and alter the portfolio to capture this potential profit opportunity.

Macro country risks

Country risks or political risks that affect all foreign firms in a host country.

Macroassessment

Overall risk assessment of a country without consideration of an MNC's business.

Macroeconomics

Analysis of a country's economy as a whole.

MAD

The ISO 4217 currency code for the Moroccan Dirham.

Madrid Stock Exchange (Bolsa de Madrid)

The largest of Spain's four stock exchanges.

Maghreb States

The Maghreb states include the three nations of Algeria, Morocco, and Tunisia. The European Community concluded a trade and aid agreement in 1976 with these states. The term Maghreb states sometimes also includes Libya and Mauritania. The five Maghreb states created the Arab Maghreb Union.

Magic of diversification

The effective reduction of risk (variance) of a portfolio, achieved without reduction to expected returns through the combination of assets with low or negative correlations (covariances). Related: Markowitz diversification.

Mail Delay

Time a payment spends in the postal system before delivery.

Mail float

Time period that checks for payment spend in the postal system.

Mailing Date

A specific date set for the mailing of certain material

to security holders such as interim reports, proxy material and dividend checks.

Maintenance

Appropriate ongoing adjustments to security holder records.

Maintenance call

A call for additional money or securities when a margin account falls below its exchange-mandated required level.

Maintenance fee

A yearly charge to maintain brokerage accounts, such as asset management accounts or IRAs.

Maintenance margin

The dollar amount required to be kept at the OCC throughout the life of an option contract; percentage of the dollar amount of securities that must always be kept as margin.

Maintenance margin requirement

A sum, usually smaller than but part of the original margin, that must be maintained on deposit at all times. If a customer's equity in any futures position drops to or below, the maintenance margin level, the broker must issue a margin call for the amount at money required to restore the customer's equity in the account to the original margin level. Related: Margin, margin call.

Majority shareholder

A shareholder who is part of a group that controls more than half the outstanding shares of a corporation.

Majority voting

Voting system under which corporate shareholders

vote for each director separately. Related: Cumulative voting.

Make a market

Dealers are said to make a market when they quote bid and offered prices at which they stand ready to buy and sell.

Make whole provision

Related to the lump-sum payments made when a loan or bond is called, equal to the NPV of future loan or coupon payments not paid because of the call. The payment can be significant and negate the attractiveness of a call.

Making delivery

Refers to the seller's actually turning over to the buyer the assets agreed upon in a forward contract.

Malaysia Commodity Exchange

A subsidiary of the KLSE that trades interest rate futures on the three-month Kuala Lumpur Interbank offered rate.

Maloney Act

1938 legislation amending the Securities Exchange Act that regulates the OTC market.

Managed account

An investment portfolio one or more clients entrusted to a manager who decides how to invest it.

Managed float

Also known as "dirty" float, this is a system of floating exchange rates with central bank intervention to reduce currency fluctuations.

Managed Futures

In the context of hedge funds, a style of management that focuses on short-term trading in the futures market.

Management

The people who administer a company, create policies, and provide the support necessary to implement the owners' business objectives.

Management buying

The acquisition of a controlling interest in a promising business by an outside investment group that retains existing management and places representatives on the board of directors.

Management buyout (MBO)

Leveraged buyout whereby the acquiring group is led by the firm's management.

Management/closely held shares

Percentage of shares held by persons closely related to a company, as defined by the Securities and Exchange Commission. Part of these percentages often are included in "institutional holdings"—making the combined total of these percentages over 100. There is overlap as institutions sometimes acquire enough stock to be considered by the SEC to be closely allied to the company.

Management contract

An agreement by which a company will provide its organizational and management expertise in the form of services.

Management fee

An investment advisory fee charged by the financial adviser to a fund typically on the basis of the fund's average assets, but sometimes determined on a sliding scale that declines as the dollar amount of the fund increases.

Management's discussion and analysis (MD&A)

A report from management to shareholders that accompanies the firm's financial statements in the annual report. It explains the period's financial results and enables management to discuss topics that may not be apparent in the financial statements in the annual report.

Manager

The person or persons responsible for the overall investment decisions of a mutual fund.

Managerial decisions

Decisions concerning the operation of the firm, such as the choice of firm size, firm growth rates, and employee compensation.

Managerial flexibility

Flexibility in the timing and scale of investment provided by a real investment option.

Managing underwriter

The leading firm in an underwriting group, which originates the deal and acts as an agent for the group.

Mandatory convertibles

A debt instrument that is exchangeable at some point for equity in the form of common stock or a new issue.

Mandatory redemption schedule

Schedule according to which bond sinking fund payments must be made.

Manifest

See Ship's manifest.

Manipulation

Dealing in a security to create a false appearance of active trading, in order to bring in more traders. Illegal.

Manufactured housing securities (MHS)

Loans on manufactured homes-that is, factory-built or prefabricated housing, including mobile homes.

Manufactured Imports Promotion Organization

MIPRO is a non-profit organization, established in 1978 by the joint efforts of the Japanese Government and the private sector to promote imports of foreign manufactured products by hosting exhibitions and providing a wide range of market information. MIPRO's activities are broadly classified into three categories:

(a) holding imported product trade exhibitions for buyers and the general public;

(b) disseminating information regarding imported products and the Japanese market; and

(c) promoting sales of foreign products to Japanese consumers to promote recognition of the quality of imported goods.

Maple Leaf

A gold, silver, or platinum coin minted in Canada that usually trades at slightly more than its current bullion value.

Maquiladora

The maquiladora (or "in-bond" industry) program allows foreign manufacturers to ship components into Mexico duty-free for assembly and subsequent reexport. Industry established under the maquiladora program is Mexico's second largest source of foreign revenue (following oil exports). The maquiladora programs was established in 1965; in December 1989, the Mexican government liberalized the maquiladora program to make this a more attractive and dynamic sector of the economy. As a result, maquiladora operations may import, duty and import license free, products not directly involved in production, but that support production, including computers and other administrative materials and transportation equipment.

Margin

Allows investors to buy securities by borrowing money from a broker. The margin is the difference between the market value of a stock and the loan a broker makes. Related: Security deposit (initial).

Margin account (stocks)

A leverageable account in which stocks can be purchased for a combination of cash and a loan. The loan in the margin account is collateralized by the stock; if the value of the stock drops sufficiently, the owner will be asked to either put in more cash, or sell a portion of the stock. Margin rules are federally regulated, but margin requirements and interest may vary among broker/dealers.

Margin requirement

A performance bond paid upon purchase of a futures contract that protects the exchange clearinghouse from loss.

Margin stock

Any stock listed on a national securities exchange, any over-the-counter security approved by the SEC for trading in the national market system, or appearing on the Board's list of over-the-counter margin stock and most mutual funds.

Margin trading

Buying securities, in part, with borrowed money.

Marginal

Incremental.

Margin agreement

The agreement governing customers' margin accounts.

Marginal cost

The increase or decrease in a firm's total cost of production as a result of changing production by one unit.

Marginal efficiency of capital

The percentage yield earned on an additional unit of capital.

Marginal revenue

The change in total revenue as a result of producing one additional unit of output.

Marginal tax rate

The tax rate that would have to be paid on any additional dollars of taxable income earned.

Marginal utility

The change in total satisfaction as a result of consuming one additional unit of a specific good or service.

Margin call

A demand for additional funds because of adverse price movement. Maintenance margin requirement, security deposit maintenance.

Margin department

The department in a brokerage firm that monitors customers' margin accounts, ensuring that all short sales, stock purchases, and other positions are covered by the margin account balance.

Margin of profit

Gross profit divided by net sales. Used to measure a firm's operating efficiency and pricing policies in order to determine how competitive the firm is within the industry.

Margin of safety

With respect to working capital management, the difference between (1) the amount of long-term financing and (2) the sum of fixed assets and the permanent component of current assets.

Margin requirement (options)

The amount of cash an uncovered (naked) option writer is required to deposit and maintain to cover his daily position valuation and reasonably foreseeable intraday price changes.

Margin security

A security that may be bought or sold in a margin account as defined in Regulation T.

Marine Cargo Insurance

Broadly, insurance covering loss of, or damage to, goods at sea. Marine insurance typically compensates the owner of merchandise for losses in excess of those which can be legally recovered from the carrier that are sustained from fire, shipwreck, piracy, and various other causes. Three of the most common types of marine insurance coverage are "free of particular average" (f.p.a.), "with average" (w.a.), and "All Risks Coverage."

Marital deduction

A tax deduction that allow spouses to transfer unlimited amounts of property to one another.

Marital trust

A trust created to allow one spouse to transfer, during life or upon death, an unlimited amount of property to his/her spouse without incurring gift or estate tax.

Markdown

The amount subtracted from the selling price of securities when they are sold to a dealer in the OTC market. Also, the discounted price of municipal bonds after the market has shown little interest in the issue at the original price.

Marked-to-market

An arrangement whereby the profits or losses on a futures contract are settled each day.

Market

Usually refers to the equity market. "The market went down today" means that the value of the stock market dropped that day.

Market Access

Market access refers to the openness of a national market to foreign products. Market access reflects a government's willingness to permit imports to compete relatively unimpeded with similar domestically produced goods.

Market analysis

An analysis of technical corporate and market data used to predict movements in the market.

Market-based forecasting

Analyzing future spot rates on the basis of a market-determined exchange rate (such as the current spot rate or forward rate).

Market-based corporate governance system

Organization of a corporation whereby the supervisory board represents a dispersed set of largely equity shareholders.

Market-book ratio

Market price of a share divided by book value per share.

Market break

See: Break.

Market capitalization

The total dollar value of all outstanding shares. Computed as shares times current market price. Capitalization is a measure of corporate size.

Market capitalization rate

Expected return on a security. The market-consensus estimate of the appropriate discount rate for a firm's cash flow.

Market clearing

Total demand for loans by borrowers equals total supply of loans from lenders. The market, any market, clears at the equilibrium rate of interest or price.

Market conversion price

Also called conversion parity price, the price that an investor effectively pays for common stock by purchasing a convertible security and then exercising the conversion option. This price is equal to the market price of the convertible security divided by the conversion ratio.

Market correction

A relatively short-term drop in stock market prices, generally viewed as bringing overpriced stocks back to a level closer to companies' actual values.

Market cycle

The period between the two latest highs or lows of the S&P 500, showing net performance of a fund through both an up and a down market. A market cycle is complete when the S&P is 15% below the highest point or 15% above the lowest point (ending a down market).

Market Disruption

Market disruption refers to the situation which is created when a surge of imports in a given product line causes sales of domestically produced goods in a particular country to decline to an extent that the domestic producers and their employees suffer major economic hardship.

Market Eye

A financial information service based in the U.K. sponsored by the ISE (International Stock Exchange of the UK and the Republic of Ireland) that provides current market and statistical information.

Market failure

The inability of arm's length markets to deliverer goods or services. A multinational corporation's market internalization advantages may take advantage of market failure.

Market-if-touched (MIT)

A price order, below market if a buy or above market if a sell, that automatically becomes a market order if the specified price is reached.

Market impact costs

The result of a bid/ask spread and a dealer's price concession. Also called price impact costs.

Market index

Market measure that consists of weighted values of the components that make up certain list of companies. A stock market tracks the performance of certain stocks by weighting them according to their prices and the number of outstanding shares by a particular formula.

Market interest rate

Rates of interest paid on deposits and other investments, determined by the interaction of the supply of and demand for funds in the money market.

Market internalization advantages

Conditions that allow a corporation to exploit the failure of an arm's length market to deliver goods or services efficiently.

Market jitters

Anxiety among many investors, causing them to sell stocks and bonds, pushing prices down.

Market letter

A newsletter analyzing the market that is written by an SEC-registered investment adviser who sells the letter to subscribers. See: Hulbert Rating.

Market maker

Used in the context of general equities. One who maintains firm bid and offer prices in a given security by standing ready to buy or sell round lots at publicly quoted prices. See: Agent, dealer, specialist.

Market microstructure

The functional setup of a market.

Market model

The market model says that the return on a security depends on the return on the market portfolio and the extent of the security's responsiveness as measured by beta. The return also depends on conditions that are unique to the firm. The market model can be graphed as a line fitted to a plot of asset returns against returns on the market portfolio. This relationship is sometimes called the single-index model.

Market Neutral

In the context of hedge funds, a style of management that has long and short equity exposure with nearly exposure on average to fluctuations in the market. However, the on average qualification is important. The risk of the longs and the shorts could fluctuate through time leading to negative returns when the market falls sharply.

Market Not Held Order

Also a market order, but the investor is allowing the floor broker to use his own discretion as to the exact timing of the execution. If the floor broker expects a decline in price and he is holding a "market not held buy order", he (she) may wait to buy, figuring that a better price will soon be available. There is no guarantee that a "market not held order" will be filled.

Market-on-Close (MOC) order

An order to trade stocks, options, or futures as close as possible to the market close. See also MOC.

Market opening

The start of formal trading on an exchange.

Market order

Used in the context of general equities. Order to buy or sell a stated amount of a security at the most advantageous price obtainable after the order is represented in the trading crowd. You cannot specify special restrictions such as all or none (AON) or good 'til canceled order (GTC) on market orders. See: Limit order.

Market order go-along/participating

Used for listed equity securities. See: Percentage order.

Market-Oriented Cooperation Plan

The MOCP, established in 1990, is aimed at improving long-term business relations between Japan's automotive manufacturers and U.S. auto parts suppliers.

Market-Oriented Sector-Selective

The MOSS talks were begun in January 1985 as bilateral trade discussions between the U.S. and Japan in an effort to remove many trade barriers at once in a given sector. MOSS talks have focused on five sectors: (a) telecommunications, (b) medical equipment and pharmaceuticals, (c) electronics, (d) forest products, and (e) auto parts. Overall, the talks focus high-level attention on reducing certain market obstacles opening communication channels to resolve follow-up disputes.

Market Oriented Sector Specific Negotiations (MOSS)

Sectoral trade negotiations between the governments of the United States and Japan. As of 1995, the only active MOSS negotiations dealt with medical equipment and technology. Remaining MOSS talks occur under the Framework Agreement.

Market out clause

A clause that may appear in an underwriting firm commitment that releases it from its purchase requirement if there are negative securities market developments.

Market overhang

The theory that, in certain situations, institutions wish to sell their shares but postpone the sale because large orders under current market conditions would drive down the share price and that the consequent threat of securities sales will tend to retard the rate of share price appreciation. Support for this theory is largely anecdotal.

Market penetration/share

Used in the context of general equities. Percent of trading volume in a stock that a particular market maker trades.

Market Performance Committee (MPC)

A group of NYSE market oversight specialists who monitor specialists' efficiency in maintaining fair prices and orderly markets.

Marketplace price efficiency

The degree to which the prices of assets reflect the available marketplace information. Marketplace price efficiency is sometimes estimated as the difficulty faced by active management of earning a greater return than passive management would, after adjusting for the risk associated with a strategy and the transactions costs associated with implementing a strategy.

Market portfolio

A portfolio consisting of all assets available to investors, with each asset held in proportion to its market value relative to the total market value of all assets.

Market price

The last reported price at which a security was traded on an exchange.

Market price of risk

A measure of the extra return, or risk premium, that investors demand to bear risk. The reward-to-risk ratio of the market portfolio.

Market prices

The amount of money that a willing buyer pays to acquire something from a willing seller, when a buyer and seller are independent and when such an exchange is motivated by only commercial consideration.

The Market Promotion Program

(MPP) was authorized by the Food, Agriculture, Conservation, and Trade Act of 1990 and is administered by the U.S. Department of Agriculture's Foreign Agricultural Service. Under the MPP, surplus stocks or funds from the Commodity Credit Corporation are used to partially reimburse agricultural organizations conducting specific foreign market development projects for eligible products in specified countries. Proposals for MPP programs are developed by trade organizations and private firms. Activities financed by the programs vary from commodity to commodity, and include activities such as market research, construction of a three-story wood demonstration building, construction of a model feed mill, and consumer promotion activities. (MPP is broader in scope than the Targeted Export Assistance [TEA] program, repealed by the 1990 Farm Bill, whose purpose was to assist exports of commoditis hurt by unfair foreign trade practices.)

Market research

A technical analysis of factors such as volume, price trends, and market breadth that are used to predict price movement.

Market return

The return on the market portfolio.

Market risk

Risk that cannot be diversified away. Related: Systematic risk

Market RRR (required rate of return) Schedule

A line that indicates the minimum return required by investors at each level of investment risk. The schedule begins at the risk-free interest rate and rises as risk increases.

Market sectors

The classifications of bonds by issuer characteristics, such as state government, corporate, or utility.

Market segmentation theory or preferred habitat theory

A biased expectations theory that asserts that the shape of the yield curve is determined by the supply of and demand for securities within each maturity sector.

Market share

The percentage of total industry sales that a particular company controls.

Market sweep

A second offering following a tender offer, allowing institutional investors to obtain a controlling interest at a price higher than the original offer.

Market timer

A money manager who assumes he or she can forecast when the stock market will go up and down.

Market timing

Asset allocation in which investment in the equity market is increased if one forecasts that the equity market will outperform T-bills and is decreased when the market is anticipated to underperform.

Market timing costs

Costs that arise from price movement of a stock during a transaction period but attributable to other activity in the stock.

Market tone

The general state of well-being of a securities market, based mostly on trading activity.

Market value

(1) The price at which a security is trading and could presumably be purchased or sold. (2) What investors believe a firm is worth; calculated by multiplying the number of shares outstanding by the current market price of a firm's shares.

Market value ratios

Ratios that relate the market price of the firm's common stock to selected financial statement items.

Market value-weighted index

An index of a group of securities computed by calculating a weighted average of the returns on each security in the index, where the weights are proportional to outstanding market value.

Marketability

A negotiable security is said to have good marketability if there is an active secondary market in which it can easily be resold.

Marketable securities

Securities that are easily convertible to cash because there is high demand allowing them to be sold quickly.

Marketable title

A clear, reasonably incontestable title to a piece of real estate that is good for transaction purposes.

Marketed claims

Claims that can be bought and sold in financial markets, such as those of stockholders and bondholders.

Marking (or Marks)

Letters, numbers, and other symbols placed on cargo packages to facilitate identification.

Marking to market

Settling or reconciling changes in the value of futures contracts on a daily basis. Also refers to the practice of reporting the value of assets on a market rather than book value basis.

Marking up or down

The amount by which a securities dealer raises or lowers the price of a stock or bond due to changes in demand and supply.

Markowitz, Harry

Nobel laureate in economics. Father of modern portfolio theory.

Markowitz diversification

A strategy that seeks to combine in a portfolio assets with returns that are less than perfectly positively correlated, in an effort to lower portfolio risk (variance) without sacrificing return. Related: Naive diversification.

Markowitz efficient frontier

The graphical depiction of the Markowitz efficient set of portfolios representing the boundary of the set of feasible portfolios that have the maximum return for a given level of risk. Any portfolios above the frontier cannot be achieved. Any below the frontier are dominated by Markowitz efficient portfolios.

Markowitz efficient portfolio

Also called a mean-variance efficient portfolio, a portfolio that has the highest expected return at a given level of risk.

Markovian Dependence

The condition where observations in a time series are dependent on previous observations in the near term. Markovian dependence dies quickly, while long-memory effects like Hurst dependence, decay over very long time periods.

Markowitz efficient set of portfolios

The collection of all efficient portfolios, which can be graphed as the Markowitz efficient frontier.

Marks and Numbers

Identifying symbols and numbers placed by the shipper on each piece of cargo in a shipment.

Marks of Origin

The physical markings on a product that indicate the country of origin where the article was produced. Customs rules require marks of origin of most countries.

Mark-to-market

Adjustment of the book value or collateral value of a security to reflect current market value.

Marriage penalty

A tax that has the effect of penalizing a married couple because they pay more tax on a joint tax return than they would if they file tax returns individually.

Married put

A put option bought at the same time as its underlying securities in order to hedge the price paid for the securities.

Marrried Put and Stock

The simultaneous purchase of stock and the corresponding number of put options. This is a limited risk strategy during the life of the puts because the stock can be sold at the strike price of the puts.

Married Put Strategy

A put and stock are considered to be married if they are bought on the same day, and the position is designated at that time as a hedge.

Master Air Waybill (MAWB)

An air waybill issued by an airline, not a freight forwarder. MAWB refers to the air waybill governing all MAWBS on a consolidated air shipment.

Master limited partnership (MLP)

A publicly traded limited partnership.

Master pension plan.

See: Prototype plan

Matador market

The foreign market in Spain.

Matched and lost

The outcome of the flip of a coin used to determine which of two brokers who are locked in competition for equal trades may actually execute the trades.

Match-fund

A bank is said to match-fund a loan or other asset when it does so by buying (taking) a deposit of the same maturity. The term is commonly used in the Euromarket.

Matched book

A bank runs a matched book when the of maturities of its assets and liabilities is distribution equal.

Matched maturities

The coordination by a financial institution of the maturities of its assets (loans) and liabilities (deposits) in order to enable it to meet its obligations at the required times.

Matched orders

Used for listed equity securities. Participate in equal amounts of a trade at a certain price, particularly when two parties have the same level of priority on the exchange floor (this requires standing in the trading crowd).

Matched Sale Purchase Transactions

Transaction in which the Federal Reserve sells a government security to a dealer or a foregin central bank and agrees to buy back the security to a dealer or a foreign central bank and agrees to buy back the security on a specified date (usually within seven days) at eh same price (the reverse of a repurchase agreement). Such transaction allow the Federal Reserve to temporarily absorb excess reserves from the banking system, limiting the ability of banks to make new loans and investments.

Matched sale transaction

Applies mainly to convertible securities. Procedure whereby the Federal Reserve Bank of New York sells government securities to a nonbank dealer against payment in federal funds. The agreement requires the dealer to sell the securities back by a specified date, which ranges from 1 to 15 days. The Fed pays the dealer a rate of interest equal to the discount rate. These transactions, also called reverse repurchase agreements, decrease the money supply for temporary periods by reducing dealers' bank balances and thus excess reserves.

Matching concept

The accounting principle that requires the recognition of all costs that are associated with the generation of the revenue reported in the income statement.

Matchmaker Events

Matchmaker trade delegations are organized and led by the International Trade Administration to help new-to-export and new-to-market firms meet prescreened prospects who are interested in their products or services in overseas markets. Matchmaker delegations usually target two major country markets and limit trips to a week or less. This approach is designed to permit U.S. firms to interview a maximum number of prospective overseas business partners with a minimum of time away from their home office. The program includes U.S. embassy support, briefings on market requirements and business practices, and interpreter services. Matchmaker events, based on specific product themes and end-users, are scheduled for a limited number of countries each year.

Material Adverse Change or Effect

Many mergers and acquisitions contracts include a material adverse change clause that allows a company to renegotiate or walk away from a deal if the other company or its subsidiaries announces a significant event that may negatively affect its stock price or operations. See also materiality.

Materiality

The importance of an event or information in influencing a company's stock price. Companies must report any material events within one month by filing SEC form 8-K.

Materials requirement planning

Computer-based systems that plan backward from the

production schedule to make purchases in order to manage inventory levels.

Mathematical programming

An operations research technique that solves problems in which an optimal value is sought subject to specified constraints. Mathematical programming models include linear programming, quadratic programming, and dynamic programming.

Matif SA

The futures exchange of France.

Matrix trading

Swapping bonds in order to take advantage of temporary differences in the yield spread between bonds with different ratings or different classes.

Mature

To cease to exist; to expire.

Mature economy

The economy of a nation with a stable population and slowing economic growth.

Matured noninterest-bearing debt

Outstanding savings bonds and notes that have reached final maturity and no longer earn interest. Includes all Series A-D, F, G, 1, J, and K bonds. Series E bonds (issued between May 1941 and November 1965), Series EE (issued since January 1980), Series H (issued from June 1952 through December 1979), and savings notes issued between May 1967 and October 1970 have a final maturity of 30 years. Series HH bonds (issued since January 1980) mature after 20 years.

Maturity

For a bond, the date on which the principal is required

to be repaid. In an interest rate swap, the date that the swap stops accruing interest.

Maturity date

Usually used for bonds. Date that the bond finishes and is paid off. Date on which the principal amount of a note, draft, acceptance, bond, or other debt instrument becomes due and payable.

Maturity factoring

An arrangement that provides collection and insurance of accounts receivable.

Maturity phase

A stage of company development in which earnings to grow at the rate of the general economy. Related: Three-phase DDM.

Maturity spread

The difference in returns between bonds pfof different time lengths.

Maturity value

Related: Par value.

Maximum capital gains mutual fund

A mutual fund whose objective is to produce capital gains by investing in small or risky rapid-growth companies.

Maximum expected return criterion (MERC)

Standard that one choose the asset with the highest anticipated return.

Maximum price fluctuation

The greatest amount by which the contract price can change, up or down, during one trading session, as fixed by exchange rules in the contract specification Related: Limit price.

Maximum return criterion (MRC)

Standard that one choose the asset with the highest return.

May Day

The date of May 1, 1975, after which brokers were allowed to charge any brokerage commission, rather than a mandatory rate.

May expand

Used in the context of general equities. Warning that the size of the order/total may be increased. See: "more behind it."

MBO

See: Management buyout.

MBS depository

A book-entry depository for GNMA securities. The depository was initially operated by MBSCC and is now a separately incorporated, participant-owned, limited-purpose trust company organized under the State of New York Banking Law.

MBSCC

See: Mortgage-Backed Securities Clearing Corporation.

MBS servicing

The requirement that the mortgage servicer maintain payment of the full amount of contractually due principal and interest payments whether or not actually collected.

MC

The two-character ISO 3166 country code for MONACO.

MD

The two-character ISO 3166 country code for MOLDOVA, REPUBLIC OF.

MDA

See: Multiple discriminant analysis.

MDBs

See under Multilateral Development Banks.

MDL

The ISO 4217 currency code for the Moldovan Leu.

Meals and entertainment expense

A tax deduction allowed for meals and entertainment expenses incurred in the course of business.

Mean

The expected value of a random variable. Arithmetic average of a sample.

Mean of the sample

The arithmetic average; that is, the sum of the observations divided by the number of observations.

Mean return

See: Expected return

Mean-variance analysis

Evaluation of risky prospects based on the expected value and variance of possible outcomes.

Mean-variance criterion

The selection of portfolios based on the means and variances of their returns. The choice of the higher expected return portfolio for a given level of variance or the lower variance portfolio for a given expected return.

Mean-variance efficient portfolio

Related: Markowitz efficient portfolio

Measurement error

Errors in measuring an explanatory variable in a regression, which leads to biases in estimated parameters.

Measurement Noise

See: Observational Noise.

Medallion Stamp Program

A program approved by the Securities Transfer Association that enables participating financial institutions to guarantee signatures. The Medallion programs ensure that the individual signing the certificate or stock,power is in fact the registered owner as it appears on the stock certificate or stock power. Any U.S. financial institution that belongs to a Medallion Stamp Program can provide Medallion guarantees. Such institutions include banks, savings and loans, credit unions and U.S. brokerages.

Median market cap

The midpoint of market capitalization (market price multiplied by the number of shares outstanding) of the stocks in a portfolio. Half the stocks in the portfolio will have higher market capitalizations; half will have lower.

Medium-term bond

A bond maturing in two to ten years.

Medium-Term Guarantee Program

Ex-Im Bank effort encouraging commercial lenders to finance the sale of U.S. capital equipment and services to approved foreign buyers. The Ex-IM Bank guarantees the principal and interest on these loans.

Medium-term note

A corporate debt instrument that is continuously offered to investors over a period of time by an agent of the issuer. Investors can select from maturity bands of: 9 months to 1 year, more than 1 year to 18 months, more than 18 months to 2 years, etc., up to 30 years.

Meff Renta Fija

The derivatives exchange in Barcelona, Spain, listing futures and options on fixed-interest securities and on interest rates, including the MIBOR (Madrid Interbank Offered Rate).

Meff Renta Variable

Stock index and equity derivatives market in Spain trading futures and options on the Iberian Exchange (IBEX)-35 index and on individual stocks.

Member bank

A national- or state-chartered bank that is a member of the Federal Reserve System.

Member firm

Used for listed equity securities. Brokerage firm that has at least one membership on a major stock exchange even though, by exchange rules, the membership in the name of an employee and not of the firm itself.

Membership or a seat on the exchange

A limited number of exchange positions that enable the holder to trade for the holder's own accounts and charge clients for the execution of trades for their accounts. Related: member firm.

Member short sale ratio

The total shares sold short by NYSE members divided by total short sales, which is used to analyze market expectations and bullish or bearish trends.

Menu

Used in the context of general equities. Hierarchy of choices concerning price and volume of bids or offers proposed to a customer (e.g. Menu of offerings to a customer buyer - a) 10m @ 24 1/4; b) 25m @ 24 1/2; or c) 50m @ 24 3/4).

Member short sale ratio

The total shares sold short by NYSE members divided by total short sales, which is used to analyze market expectations and bullish or bearish trends.

Mercantile agency

An organization that supplies credit ratings and reports on firms that are prospective customers.

Mercato Italiano Futures (MIF)

The Italian futures market trading Italian >Treasury bond (BTB) futures.

Merchandise

All movable goods such as cars, textiles, appliances, etc. and 'f.o.b.' means free on board.

Merc, the

Chicago Mercantile Exchange.

Merchant bank

A British term for a bank that specializes not in lending out its own funds, but in providing various financial services such as accepting bills arising out of trade, underwriting new issues, and providing advice on acquisitions, mergers, foreign exchange, portfolio management, etc.

Mercosur

Mercosur (Spanish; Mercosul in Portuguese; or Southern Common Market) is comprised of Argentina, Brazil, Paraguay, and Uruguay. Mercosur is scheduled to enter into force in December 1994 for Argentina and Brazil and to enter into force in December 1995 for Paraguay and Uruguay. Mercosur, modeled similarly to the European Community's Treaty of Rome, will establish a common external tariff and eliminate barriers to trade in services. While in the Southern Cone, Chile has not sought entry to Mercosur, but does have an agreement with Argentina which will provide for some similar benefits.

Merger

(1) Acquisition in which all assets and liabilities are absorbed by the buyer. (2) More generally, any combination of two companies. The firm's activity in this respect is sometimes called M&A (Merger and Acquisition)

Merger Arbitrage

In the context of hedge funds, a style of management that involves the simultaneous purchase of stock in a company being acquired and the sale of stock in its acquirer.

Method of payment

The way a merger or acquisition is financed.

Mexican Stock Exchange

The only stock exchange in Mexico. The Indice de Precios y Cotizaciones, or IPC index, consists of the 35 most representative stocks chosen every two months.

Mezzanine bracket

The members of an underwriting group with involvement large enough to be in the second participation tier from the top.

Mezzanine level

The period in a company's development just before it goes public.

Mezzanine financing

The next stage of financing that follows venture capital financing.

MG

The two-character ISO 3166 country code for MADAGASCAR.

MGF

The ISO 4217 currency code for the Madagascar Franc.

MH

The two-character ISO 3166 country code for MARSHALL ISLANDS.

Micro-cap stock

See: Penny stock.

Micro country risks

Country or political risks that are specific to an industry, company, or project within a host country.

Microassessment

The risk assessment of a country as related to an MNC's type of business.

Microeconomics

Analysis of the behavior of individual economic units such as companies, industries, or households.

Mid cap

A stock with a capitalization usually between $1 billion and $5 billion.

Mid-cap SPDRs

This is the same as a SPDR except the index it tracks is Standard&Poor's Mid-cap 400. This SPDR also trades on the AMEX, under the symbol MDY.

Middle Market Manufacturing Exporter (MMME)

An exporter with the following traits: 1) Manufacturer with less than 500 employees 2) Ships less than $1 Million per year (on average) overseas.

Midget

A 15 year GNMA bond; similar to a Dwarf.

Midmarket

Price around which a market maker derives bid and asked prices.

Milan Stock Exchange

The largest regional stock exchange in Italy, facilitating more than 90% of the country's trading volume.

Military Critical Technologies List

The MTCL is a document listing technologies that the U.S. Defense Department considers to have current or future utility in military systems. The MCTL describes arrays of design and manufacturing know-how; keystone manufacturing, inspection, and test equipment; and goods accompanied by sophisticated operation, application, and maintenance know-how. Military justification for each entry is included in a classified version of the list.

Miller and Modigliani's irrelevance proposition

Theory that if financial markets are perfect, corporate financial policy (including hedging policy) is irrelevant.

Miller, Merton

Nobel Laureate and coauthor of the famous Miller-Modigliani theorems. Finance professor at the University of Chicago.

Mimic

An imitation that sends a false signal.

Mini-manipulation

Trading in the underwriting security of an option contract in order to manipulate its price so that the options will become in-the-money.

Minimum maintenance

The lowest required equity level that must be held with a broker in a margin account. See: margin call.

Minimum price fluctuation

Smallest increment of price movement possible in trading a given contract. Also called point or tick.

Minimum purchases

For mutual funds, the amount required to open a new account (Minimum Initial Purchase) or to deposit into an existing account (Minimum Additional Purchase). These minimums may be lowered for buyers participating in an automatic purchase plan

Minimum-variance frontier

Graph of the lowest possible portfolio variance that is attainable for a given portfolio expected return.

Minimum-variance portfolio

The portfolio of risky assets with lowest variance.

Ministry of Foreign Economic Relations and Trade

The People's Republic of China (PRC) Ministry of Foreign Economic Relations and Trade, MOFERT, was established in March 1982 by combining former separate ministries. MOFERT implements national trade policies through administrative actions, drafting laws and issuing foreign trade regulations. MOFERT does not engage in foreign trade transactions but facilitates the foreign trading corporations (FTCs) which do.

Ministry of Health and Welfare

Under the Pharmaceutical Affairs Law, MHW is Japan's agency responsible for regulating medical products. The Ministry also is charged with determining Japanese healthcare expenditures.

Ministry of International Trade and Industry

MITI occupies a central position in Japan's "economic bureaucracy" and is regarded as one of the three most powerful and prestigious ministries of the central government (along with the Ministry of Finance and the Ministry of Foreign Affairs). In formulating and implementing Japan's trade and industrial policies, MITI is responsible for funding most of Japan's export promotion programs (although operation of these programs is left to JETRO). The Ministry also supervises the export financing programs of Japan's Export-Import Bank, operates several types of export insurance programs, supports research organizations, and facilitates various types of overseas technical and cooperation training programs. Lately, MITI has assumed a role in encouraging imports of foreign products into Japan.

Ministry of Posts and Telecommunications

MPT is Japan's telecommunications regulatory agency. The Ministry is authorized to adjust supply and demand among service providers to ensure that there is not excessive competition in a given market. To do so, MPT issues "administrative guidance" to the industry and recommends "unification" when there appears to be excessive competition in a given market.

Minority interest

An outside ownership interest in a subsidiary that is consolidated with the parent for financial reporting purposes.

Minus

The symbol (-) that precedes the change figure in a stock table to indicate a closing sale lower than that of the previous day.

Minus tick

See: downtick.

MIP

See: Monthly income preferred security.

Misery index

An index that sums the unemployment and inflation rates, used as a political rating or measure of consumer confidence.

Mismatch bond

Floating rate note whose interest rate is reset at more frequent intervals than the rollover period (e.g. a note whose payments are set quarterly on the basis of the one-year interest rate).

Miss the price/market

Used for listed equity securities. 1) Have an order in hand but fail to execute a transaction on terms favorable to a customer and, thus, be negligent as a broker; 2) receive an order just after a print has transpired.

MIT

See: Market-if-touched.

Mixed account

A brokerage account holding both long and short positioned securities.

Mixed bag

Used in the context of general equities. Group of stocks which consists of some which are up, down, and neutral.

Mixed Credit

Mixed credit refers to the practice of combining concessional and market-rate export credit as an export promotion mechanism.

Mixed forecasting

Development of forecasts using a combination of forecasting techniques.

MK

The two-character ISO 3166 country code for MACEDONIA, THE FORMER YUGOSLAV REPUBLIC OF.

MKD

The ISO 4217 currency code for the Macedonian Denar.

ML

The two-character ISO 3166 country code for MALI.

MLP

See: Master limited partnership.

MM

The two-character ISO 3166 country code for MYANMAR.

MMDA

See: Money market demand account.

MMK

The ISO 4217 currency code for the Myanmar (ex-Burma) Kyat.

MMME

See: Middle Market Manufacturing Exporter.

MN

The two-character ISO 3166 country code for MONGOLIA.

MNC

See: Multinational corporation.

MNT

The ISO 4217 currency code for the Mongolian Tugrik.

MO

The two-character ISO 3166 country code for MACAU.

Mob spread

The yield spread between a tax-free municipal bond and a Treasury bond with the same maturity.

MOC

See Market on Close.

Mock trading

The simulated trading of securities used as a learning device in training investors and broker.

Modeling

The process of creating a depiction of reality, such as a graph, picture, or mathematical representation.

Modern portfolio theory

Principals underlying the analysis and evaluation of rational portfolio choices based on risk-return trade-offs and efficient diversification.

Modified Accelerated Cost Recovery System (MACRS)

A 1986 act that set out rules for the depreciation of qualifying assets, allowing for greater acceleration over longer periods of time.

Modified duration

The ratio of Macaulay duration to (1 + y), where y = the bond yield. Modified duration is inversely related to the approximate percentage change in price for a given change in yield.

Modified pass-throughs

Agency pass-throughs that guarantee (1) timely interest payments and (2) principal payments as collected, but no later than a specified time after they are due. Related: fully modified pass-throughs

Modigliani and Miller Proposition I

A proposition by Modigliani and Miller which states that a firm cannot change the total value of its outstanding securities by changing its capital structure proportions. Also called the irrelevance proposition.

Modigliani and Miller Proposition II

A proposition by Modigliani and Miller which states that the cost of equity is a linear function of the firm's debt/equity-ratio.

MOE

Major Office Equipment Justification Form.

MOFERT

China's Ministry of Foreign Economic Relations and Trade - responsible for screening and approving the implementation of the three types of enterprises with foreign investment in China: the Wholly Foreign-Owned Venture, the Contractual Joint Venture and the Equity Joint Venture.

Momentum

The amount of acceleration of an economic, price, or volume movement. A trader that follows a movement strategy will purchase stocks that have recently risen in price.

Momentum indicators

Indicators used in market analysis to quantify the momentum of upward and downward price movements.

MONEP (Marche des Options Negociables de Paris)

A subsidiary of the Paris Bourse that trades stock and index options.

Monetarist

An economist who believes that changes in the money supply are the most important determinants of economic activity and economic cycles.

Monetary assets and liabilities

Assets and liabilities with contractual payoffs.

Monetary Control Act of 1980 (MAC)

Act which requires that all banks and all institutions that accept deposits from the public make periodic reports to the Federal Reserve System. Starting in September 1981, the Fed charged banks for a range of services that it had provided free in the past, including check clearing, wire transfer of funds and the use of automated clearinghouse facilities.

Monetary gold

Gold held by governmental authorities as a financial asset.

Monetary indicators

Economic indicators of the effects of monetary policy, such as the condition of the credit market.

Monetary policy

Actions taken by the Board of Governors of the Federal Reserve System to influence the money supply or interest rates.

Monetary/non-monetary method

Under this translation method, monetary items (e.g. cash, accounts payable and receivable, and long-term debt) are translated at the current rate while non-monetary items (e.g. inventory, fixed assets, and long-term investments) are translated at historical rates.

Monetize the debt

Financing the national debt by printing new money, which causes inflation due to a larger money supply.

Money

Currency and coin that are guaranteed as legal tender by the government, a regulatory agency or bank.

Money base

Composed of currency and coins outside the banking system plus liabilities to the deposit money banks.

Money center banks

Banks that raise most of their funds from the domestic and international money markets , relying less on depositors for funds.

Money management

Related: Investment management.

Money manager

Related: Investment manager.

Money market

Money markets are for borrowing and lending money for three years or less. The securities in a money market can be U.S.government bonds, Treasury bills and commercial paper from banks and companies.

Money market demand account (M.M.D.A.)

An account that pays interest based on short-term interest rates.

Money market fund

A mutual fund that invests only in short term securities, such as bankers' acceptances, commercial paper, repurchase agreements and government bills. The net asset value per share is maintained at $1.00. Such funds are not federally insured, although the portfolio may consist of guaranteed securities and/or the fund may have private insurance protection.

Money market hedge

The use of borrowing and lending transactions in foreign currencies to lock in the home currency value of a foreign currency transaction.

Money market instruments

See: Cash investments.

Money market notes

Publicly traded issues that may be collateralized by mortgages and Mortgage Backed Securities (MBSs).

Money market security

Short-term investment usually of less than one year.

Money market yield

A bond quotation convention based on a 360-day year and semiannual coupons. See: Bond equivalent yield.

Money purchase plan

A defined benefit contribution plan in which the participant contributes some part and the firm contributes at the same or a different rate. Also called an individual account plan.

Money order

A financial instrument backed by a deposit at a certain firm such as a bank that can be easily converted into cash.

Money rate of return

Annual money return as a percentage of asset value.

Money supply

M1-A: Currency plus demand deposits

M1-B: M1-A plus other checkable deposits.

M2: M1-B plus overnight repos, money market funds, savings, and small (less than $100M) time deposits.

M3: M-2 plus large time deposits and term repos.

L: M-3 plus other liquid assets.

Monitor

To seek information about an agent's behavior; a device that provides such information.

Monopoly

Absolute control of all sales and distribution in a market by one firm, due to some barrier to entry of other firms, allowing the firm to sell at a higher price than the socially optimal price

Monopsony

The existence of only one buyer in a market, forcing sellers to accept a lower price than the socially optimal price.

Monte Carlo simulation

An analytical technique for solving a problem by performing a large number of trail runs, called simulations, and inferring a solution from the collective results of the trial runs. Method for calculating the probability distribution of possible outcomes.

Monthly income preferred security (MIP)

Preferred stock issued by a subsidiary located in a tax haven. The subsidiary relends the money to the parent.

Monthly investment plan

A plan in which a certain amount is invested each month in order to benefit from dollar cost averaging.

Montreal Exchange/Bourse de Montreal

The oldest stock exchange in Canada trading stocks, bonds, futures, and options. The Canadian Market Portfolio Index (XXM) tracks the market performance of the 25 highest capitalized stocks traded on at least two Canadian exchanges.

Moody's investment grade

A rating of one through four assigned by Moody's Investors Service to municipal short-term bonds.

Moody's Investors Service

A leading global credit rating, research and risk analysis firm.

MOP

The ISO 4217 currency code for the Macau Pataca.

Moral hazard

The risk that the existence of a contract will change the behavior of one or both parties to the contract, e.g. an insured firm will take fewer fire precautions.

Moral obligation bond

A tax-exempt bond issued by a municipality or a state financial intermediary that is backed by the moral, but not legal, obligation of a state government to appropriate funds in case of default .

"More behind it"

Used in the context of general equities. More stock exists to be bought or sold by the same buyer or seller, respectively. Often, the buyer or seller does not disclose the full size of his buy or sell interest as not to affect the market adversely. See: May expand.

More flexible exchange rate system

The International Monetary Fund's name for an exchange rate system in which rates float freely.

Morgan Stanley Capital International (MSCI)

This firm publishes a number of well known benchmarks, such as the MSCI World Index.

Morgan Stanley Capital International Emerging Markets Global Index

A market capitalization-weighted benchmark index made up of equities from 29 developing countries.

Morgan Stanley Capital International Europe, Australia, Far East Index

See: EAFE Index.

Morgan Stanley Capital International Europe Index

A market capitalization-weighted benchmark index made up of equities from 15 European countries. France, Germany, and the United Kingdom represent about two-thirds of the index.

Morgan Stanley Capital International Pacific Free index

A market capitalization-weighted benchmark index made up of equities from Pacific Basin countries. Japan represents about three-fourths of the index.

Morgan Stanley Capital International World Index

A market capitalization-weighted benchmark index made up of equities from 23 countries, including the United States.

Morgan Stanley REIT Index

A capitalization-weighted benchmark index of the most actively traded real estate investment trusts (REITs), designed to measure real estate equity performance.

Morningstar rating system

A system used in rating mutual funds and annuity by Morningstar Incorporated of Chicago.

Mortality tables

Tables of probability that individuals of various ages will die within one year.

Mortgage

A loan secured by the collateral of some specified real estate property which obliges the borrower to make a predetermined series of payments.

Mortgage-Backed Securities Clearing Corporation (MBSCC)

"Founded" in 1979, MBSCC is the sole provider of automated post-trade comparison, netting, risk management and pool notification services to the mortgage-backed securities market. The organization is a registered clearing agency with the Securities and

Exchange Commission and majority-owned by its members — MBS dealers, inter-dealer brokers and other non-broker/dealers. MBSCC provides its specialized services to major market participants active in various Government National Mortgage Association (GNMA), Fannie Mae(FNMA) and Federal Home Loan Mortgage Corporation (FHLMC) MBS programs.

Mortgage-backed securities (MSBs)

Securities backed by a pool of mortgage loans.

Mortgage banker

A company or individual that originates mortgage loans and sells them to investors, while taking care of borrowers' loan payments, records, taxes, and insurance.

Mortgage bond

A bond in which the issuer has granted the bondholders a lien against the pledged assets. See: Collateral trust bonds

Mortgage broker

A company or individual that places mortgage loans with lenders, but does not originate or service loans like a mortgage banker.

Mortgage duration

A modification of standard duration to account for the impact on duration of MBSs of changes in prepayment speed resulting from changes in interest rates. Two factors are employed: one that reflects the impact of changes in prepayment speed or price.

Mortgagee

The lender of a loan secured by property.

Mortgage interest deduction

A federal tax deduction for interest paid on a mortgage used to acquire, construct, or improve a residence.

Mortgage life insurance

A life insurance policy that pays off the remaining balance of the insured person's mortgage at death.

Mortgage pass-through security

Also called a passthrough, a security created when one or more mortgage holders form a collection (pool) of mortgages and sells shares or participation certificates in the pool. The cash flow from the collateral pool is "passed through" to the security holder as monthly payments of principal, interest, and prepayments. This is the predominant type of MBS traded in the secondary market.

Mortgage pipeline

The period from the taking of applications from prospective mortgage borrowers to the marketing of the loans.

Mortgage-pipeline risk

The risk associated with taking applications from prospective mortgage borrowers who may opt to decline to accept a quoted mortgage rate within a certain grace period.

Mortgage pool

A group of mortgages with similar class, interest rate, and maturity characteristics.

Mortgager

The borrower of a loan secured by property.

Mortgage rate

The interest rate on a mortgage loan.

Mortgage REIT

An REIT that invests in loans secured by real estate which derive income from mortgage interest and fees.

Mortgage servicing

The collection of monthly payments and penalties, record keeping, payment of insurance and taxes, and possible settlement of default , involved with a mortgage loan.

Moscow Interbank Currency Exchange (MICEX)

Established in 1992, the most liquid and best organized financial exchange in Russia.

MOSS

See Market Oriented Sector Specific Negotiations.

Most active list

The stocks with the highest volume of trading on a certain day.

Most distant futures contract

When several futures contracts are considered, the contract settling last. Related: nearby futures contract

Most Favored Nation Treatment

A commitment that a country will extend to another country the lowest tariff rates it applies to any other country. All contracting parties undertake to apply such treatment to one another under Article I of GATT. When a country agrees to cut tariffs on a particular product imported from one country, the tariff reduction automatically applies to imports of this product from any other country eligible for most-favored nation treatment. This principle of nondiscriminatory treatment of imports appeared in numerous bilateral trade agreements prior to establishment of GATT. A country is under no obligation to extend MFN treatment to another country unless both are bilateral contracting parties of the General Agreement on Tariffs and Trade or MFN treatment is specified in a bilateral agreement.

Moving average

Used in charts and technical analysis, the average of security or commodity prices constructed in a period as short as a few days or as long as several years and showing trends for the latest interval. As each new variable is included in calculating the average, the last variable of the series is deleted.

MP

The two-character ISO 3166 country code for NORTHERN MARIANA ISLANDS.

MQ

The two-character ISO 3166 country code for MARTINIQUE.

MR

The two-character ISO 3166 country code for MAURITANIA.

MRO

The ISO 4217 currency code for the Mauritanian Ouguiya.

MRQ

A short-form for Most Recent Quarter. Often used in the context of explaining company performance. MRQ earnings, for example.

MS

The two-character ISO 3166 country code for MONTSERRAT.

MSCI

See: Morgan Stanley Capital International.

MT

The two-character ISO 3166 country code for MALTA.

MTL

The ISO 4217 currency code for the Maltese Lira.

MTN

Medium term notes issued by corporations, much like shorter-term commercial paper.

MU

The two-character ISO 3166 country code for MAURITIUS.

MUD

A municipal utility district, which is a political subdivision that administers utility-related services, sometimes requiring the issue of special assessment bonds.

Multibuyer policy

Ex-Im Bank program that provides credit risk insurance on export sales to many different buyers.

Multicurrency clause

Such a clause on a Euro loan permits the borrower to switch from one currency to another currency on a rollover date.

Multicurrency loans

Gives the borrower the possibility of drawing a loan in different currencies.

Multifactor CAPM

A version of the capital asset pricing model derived by Robert Merton that includes extra-market sources of risk referred to as factors. Related: arbitrage pricing theory

Multifamily loans

Loans usually represented by conventional mortgages on multi-family rental apartments.

Multi-Fiber Arrangement

The MFA is an international umbrella compact, authorized by the General Agreement on Tariffs and Trade (GATT), that allows contracting parties to negotiate bilaterally quantitative restrictions on textile imports (which normally would be considered contrary to GATT provisions) to the extent the importing country considers them necessary to prevent market disruption. The Uruguay Round Agreement on Textiles and Clothing contains an agreed schedule for the gradual phase-out of quotas established pursuant to the MFA over a ten-year transition period, after which textile and clothing trade will be fully integrated into the GATT and subject to the same disciplines as other sectors.

Multilateral Agreement

An international compact in which three or more parties participate.

Multilateral Development Banks

There are five MDBs. See: African Development Bank Asian Development Bank European Bank for Reconstruction and Development Inter-American Development Bank World Bank.

Multilateral Investment Fund

The MIF provides program and project grants to advance investment reform and technical assistance for privatization movements in Latin America and the Caribbean and to encourage domestic and foreign investment in the area. The Fund, an outgrowth of the Enterprise for the Americas Initiative, is administered by the Inter-American Development Bank. MIF was established in January 1993.

Multilateral Investment Guarantee Agency

MIGA was established in April 1988 as a part of the World Bank Group. MIGA encourages equity investment and other direct investment flows to developing countries through the mitigation of noncommercial investment barriers. The agency offers investors guarantees against non-commercial risks; advises developing member governments on the design and implementation of policies, programs, and procedures related to foreign investments; and sponsors a dialogue between the international business community and host governments on investment issues. MIGA provides coverage for equity interests, other forms of direct investment, industrial cooperation such as management and service contracts, licensing and franchising agreements, turnkey contracts, and arrangements concerning transfer of technology and know-how in which the investor assumes a stake in the performance of the venture.

Multilateral netting system

Elimination of offsetting cash flows between a parent and several subsidiaries.

Multilateral Steel Agreement

Attainment of an MSA was an achievement intended as part of the Steel Trade Liberalization Program and resulting the Bilateral Consensus Agreements. The MSA would have addressed the underlying causes of unfair trade in steel by eliminating tariffs, nontariff measures such as quotas, and most subsidies in the steel sector, and established a dispute-settlement mechanism. The United States and 34 other countries participated in negotiations for an MSA under the general auspices of the General Agreement on Tariffs and Trade. MSA negotiations were suspended in March 1992, coincident with the expiration of the steel voluntary restraint agreements.

Multilateral Trade Negotiations

A term describing the eight multilateral rounds of negotiations held under the auspices of the General Agreement on Tariffs and Trade since 1947.

Multinational Corporation

A multinational corporation is a business which owns or controls product or service facilities outside the country in which it is based.

Multinational netting

Elimination of offsetting cash flows within a multinational corporation's books.

Multinational restructuring

Changing the terms of an MNC's assets or liabilities by mutual agreement.

Multi-option financing facility

A syndicated confirmed credit line with attached options.

Multiperiod immunization

A portfolio strategy in which a portfolio is created that will be capable of satisfying more than one predetermined future liability regardless of interest rate changes.

Multiple Arbitrage

In the context of hedge funds, a style of management where by the fund employs more than one arbitrage strategy. Portfolio manager opportunistically allocates capital among the various strategies in order to create the best risk/reward profile for the overall fund. Common strategies include merger arbitrage, convertible arbitrage, fixed income arbitrage, long/short equities pairs trading, and volatility arbitrage. In the context of equity and private equity investment, this refers to an investment in a firm where by standard multiples (earnings/price, book/price) indicate the price is far cheaper than industry averages.

Multiple-discriminant analysis (MDA)

Statistical technique for distinguishing between two groups on the basis of their observed characteristics.

Multiple-issuer pools

Under the GNMA-II program, pools formed through the aggregation of individual issuers' loan packages.

Multiple listing

An agreement used by a broker who is a member of a multiple-listing organization, providing the exclusive right to sell with an additional authority and obligation on the part of the listing broker to distribute the listing to the other brokers.

Multiple peril insurance

insurance policy which covers a wide variety of property damage.

Multiple rates of return

More than one rate of return from the same project that make the net present value of the project equal to zero. This situation arises when the IRR method is used for a project in which negative cash flows follow positive cash flows. For each sign change in the cash flows, there is a different rate of return.

Multiple regression

The estimated relationship between a dependent variable and more than one explanatory variable.

Multiples

Another name for price/earnings ratios.

Multiplier

The investment multiplier which quantifies the overall effects of investment spending on total income. The deposit multiplier which shows the effects of a change in bank deposits on the total amount of outstanding credit and the money supply.

Multirule system

A technical trading strategy that combines mechanical rules, such as the CRISMA (cumulative volume, relative strength, moving average) Trading System of Pruitt and White.

Municipal bond

State or local governments offer muni bonds or municipals, as they are called, to pay for special projects such as highways or sewers. The interest that investors receive is exempt from some income taxes.

Municipal bond insurance

An insurance policy which guarantees payment on municipal bonds in the event of default .

Municipal bond fund

A mutual fund that invests in tax-exempt bonds issued by state, city, and/or local governments. The interest obtained from these bonds is passed through to shareholders and is generally free of federal (and sometimes state and local) income taxes.

Municipal improvement certificate

A certificate used to finance local government projects and services which is financed by a special tax assessment and provides tax-free interest .

Municipal Investment Trust (MIT)

A unit investment trust that buys municipal bonds and usually holds them until maturity, passing the bond income on to shareholders, usually tax-free.

Municipal notes

Short-term notes issued by municipalities in anticipation of tax receipts, proceeds from a bond issue, or other revenues.

Municipal revenue bond

A bond issued to finance a public project that is funded by the revenues of the project.

MUR

The ISO 4217 currency code for the Mauritius Rupee.

Mutilated security

A certificate on which the name of the issue, the issuer, or some other identifying detail cannot be read.

Mutual association

A savings and loan association organized as a cooperative, with members purchasing shares, voting on association affairs, and receiving income in the form of dividends.

Mutual company

A corporation that is owned by a group of members and that distributes income in proportion to the amount of business that members do with the company.

Mutual exclusion doctrine

The doctrine that ruled that municipal bond interest is federal tax-free. In return for this federal tax exemption, states and localities cannot tax interest generated by federal government securities.

Mutual fund

Mutual funds are pools of money that are managed by an investment company. They offer investors a variety of goals, depending on the fund and its investment charter. Some funds, for example, seek to generate income on a regular basis. Others seek to preserve an investor's money. Still others seek to invest in companies that are growing at a rapid pace. Funds can impose a sales charge, or load, on investors when they buy or sell shares. Many funds these days are no load and impose no sales charge. Mutual funds are investment companies regulated by the Investment Company Act of 1940. Related: open-end fund, closed-end fund.

Mutual fund cash-to-assets ratio

The portion of the assets of a mutual fund which exists in cash instruments.

Mutual fund custodian

A commercial bank or trust company that holds securities owned by a mutual fund and sometimes acts as transfer agent for the mutual fund.

Mutual fund theorem

A result associated with the CAPM, asserting that investors will choose to invest their entire risky portfolio in a market-index or mutual fund.

Mutually exclusive investment decisions

Investment decisions in which the acceptance of a project precludes the acceptance of one or more alternative projects.

Mutual offset

A system, such as the arrangement between the Chicago Mercantile Exchange (CME) and Singapore International Monetary Exchange (SIMEX), which allows trading positions established on one exchange to be offset or transferred on another exchange.

Mutual Recognition Agreements

MRAs are negotiated on a sectoral basis (such as: telecommunciations, medicial devices, pharmaceuticals, chemicals, processed foods) and allow countries to accept each other's final test results, although quality assurances may be required. Under MRAs, the entire testing and certification process may occur outside the importing country. Under MRA's with the European Community, a U.S. firm would obtain product certification on an EC-wide basis, enabling the firms to market its products throughout the Community.

Based on private-law contractual negotiations, subcontracting permits a notified body of the EC to delegate some of its testing responsibilities to a third-country testing lab or quality assessment body. However, the notified body retains ultimate responsibility for final decisions relating to EC certification. Formal discussions between representatives of the U.S. Government and the European Economic Community on entering MRSs began in October 1992.

Mutual savings bank

A state-chartered savings bank which is owned by its depositors and managed by a fiduciary board of trustees.

MV

The two-character ISO 3166 country code for MALDIVES.

MVR

The ISO 4217 currency code for the Maldive Islands Rufiyaa.

MW

The two-character ISO 3166 country code for MALAWI.

MWK

The ISO 4217 currency code for the Malawian Kwacha.

MY

The two-character ISO 3166 country code for MALAYSIA.

MYR

The ISO 4217 currency code for the Malaysian Ringgit.

MX

The two-character ISO 3166 country code for MEXICO.

MXN

The ISO 4217 currency code for the Mexican Peso.

MZ

The two-character ISO 3166 country code for MOZAMBIQUE.

MZM

The ISO 4217 currency code for the Mozambique Metical.

n

N

Fifth letter in a Nasdaq stock symbol specifying that the issue is the company's third class of preferred shares.

NA

The two-character ISO 3166 country code for NAMIBIA.

NAD

The ISO 4217 currency code for the Namibian Dollar.

Nacional Financiera

NAFIN promotes growth in Mexico's priority development areas. NAFIN provides financial assistance to small and medium-sized Mexican businesses, encourages foreign investment in Mexico, and supports technological development in Mexico. NAFIN headquarters are in Mexico City, Mexico.

Naive diversification

A strategy whereby an investor simply invests in a number of different assets in the hope that the variance of the expected return on the portfolio is lowered.

In contrast, mathematical programming can be used to select the best possible investment weights. Related: Markowitz diversification.

NAFTA

See North American Free Trade Agreement.

Nagoya Stock Exchange

Established after World War II, one of the three major securities markets in Japan.

Naked option strategies

An unhedged strategy making exclusive use of one of the following: Short call strategy (selling or writing call options), and short put strategy (selling or writing put options). By themselves, these positions are called naked strategies because they do not involve an offsetting or risk-reducing position in another option or the underlying security. Related: Covered option strategies. Antithesis of covered option.

Naked strategies

Writing an option without owning the underlying asset. Holder is naked because holder may have agreed to sell something not owned.

Naked writer

See Uncovered call writing and Uncovered put writing.

Named perils insurance

An insurance policy that names specific risks covered by the policy.

Named Perils Policy

Any marine policy limiting coverage to perils specifically listed in the policy; opposed to All Risks policy. See "All Risks."

Narrow-Based

Generally referring to an index, it indicates that the index is composed of only a few stocks, generally in a specific industry group. See also broad-based.

Narrow market

An inactive market, which displays large fluctuations in prices due to a low volume of trading.

Narrowing the spread

Reducing the difference between the bid and ask prices of a security.

NASD

See: National Association of Securities Dealers.

Nasdaq

See: National Association of Securities Dealers Automatic Quotation System

Nasdaq small-capitalization companies

A group of 2000 companies with relatively small capitalization, which are listed separately and have at least two market makers.

Nasdaq stock market

The first electronic stock market listing over 5000 companies. The Nasdaq stock market comprises two separate markets, namely the Nasdaq National Market, which trades large, active securities and the Nasdaq Smallcap Market that trades emerging growth companies.

NASD form FR-1

A form required by the NASD of foreign dealers to ensure that firms participating in a new distribution of securities make a bona fide public offering.

National Advisory Council on International Monetary and Financial Policies

The NAC is responsbile for coordinating U.S. participation in the international financial institutions and the policies and practices of agencies of the U.S. government that make, or participate in making, foreign loans or that engage in foreign financial, exchange, or monetary transactions. With regard to international financial institutions, the Council seeks to ensure that their operations are conducted in a manner consistent with U.S. policies and objectives and with lending and other foriegn financial activities of U.S. government agencies.

The Council formulates and reviews policies and programs for use by the U.S. representatives to these institutions and advises the Secretary of the Treasury on:

— Policies and selected proposed transactions of the institutions;

— Proposed actions by these institutions requiring U.S. approval on such subjects as the flotation of securities, increases in quotas and subscriptions, and changes in their articles of agreement; and

— Problems relating to the administration and management of the international finnancial institutions.

NAC membership includes: the Departments of the Treasury (as chair), State, and Commerce, the U.S. Trade Representative, the Federal Reserve System, the Export-Import Bank, and the International Development Cooperation Agency.

National Agricultural Library

In its international role, the NAL cooperates in database production, compilation of world lists of journals, publication exchange, cooperative indexing, and intern training. The NAL serves as the U.S. center for the international agricultural information system. The NAL's AGRICOLA database covers all aspects of agriculture via bibliographic records to documents, including international agricultural trade topics such as policy, research, flows of commodities, environmental, taxation, and sociological impacts. AGRICOLA is produced soley by the NAL. The NAL's Agricultural Trade and Marketing Information Center (ATMIC) disseminates information on agribusiness, countertrade (barter), exports, and trade development. The NAL is located in Beltsville, Maryland. See: Agriculture Information System.

National Association of Investors Corporation

A Michigan-based association that helps groups establish investment clubs.

National Association of Securities Dealers (NASD)

Nonprofit organization formed under the joint sponsorship of the investment bankers' conference and the SEC to comply with the Maloney Act, which provides for the regulation of the OTC market.

National Association of Securities Dealers Automatic Quotation System (Nasdaq)

An electronic quotation system that provides price quotations to market participants about the more actively traded common stock issues in the OTC market. About 4000 common stock issues are included in the Nasdaq system.

National Association of State Departments of Agriculture

NASDA is a nonprofit, nonpartisan organization of the 50 state departments of agriculture and those from the trust territories of Puerto Rico, Guam, American

Samoa, and the Virgin Islands. Headquarters are in Washington, D.C.

National Association of State Development Agencies

The National Association of State Development Agencies, NASDA, was formed in 1946 to provide a forum for directors of state economic development agencies to exchange information, compare programs, and deal with issues of mutual interest. NASDA's organization includes International Trade and Foreign Investment components. Trade activities include maintenance of a State Export Program Database.

National bank

A commercial bank approved by the U.S. Comptroller of the Currency, which is required to be a member of and purchase stocks in the Federal Reserve System.

National Credit Union Administration

Federal agency that oversees and insures the federal credit union system, and is funded by its members.

National debt

Treasury bills, notes, bonds, and other debt obligations that constitute the debt owed by the federal government.

National Defense Executive Reserve

The NDER Program, which is operated by the Commerce Department's Bureau of Export Administration, recruits and trains experienced business executives and other qualified civilians to serve in key government positions during periods of emergency. These reservists would augment Department of Commerce staff as required to respond to national security emergencies.

National Foundation for Consumer Credit

A nonprofit organization that seeks to help consumers who have taken on too much debt by helping them work out payment plans and supplying credit counseling.

National Futures Association (NFA)

The futures industry self-regulatory organization established in 1982.

Nationalization

A government takeover of a private company.

National Intelligence Council

The NIC is comprised of the U.S. National Intelligence Officers and concentrates on problems of particular geographic regions and functional areas such as economics and chemical/biological warfare.

National market

Related: Internal market.

National Market Advisory Board

Group that advises the SEC on establishing a national exchange market system, which is a highly automated, continuous national exchange, but that preserves the regional exchanges.

National Market System (NMS)

Refers to over the counter trading. System of trading OTC stocks under the sponsorship of the NASD. Must meet certain criteria for size, profitability and trading activity. More comprehensive information is available for NMS stocks than for non-NMS stocks traded OTC (high, low, and last-sale prices, cumulative volume figures, and bid and ask quotations throughout the day). This is due to the fact that market makers must report the actual price and number of shares in each transaction within 90 seconds verses nonreal-time reporting for non-NMS stocks (thus, last sale prices and minute-to-minute volume updates are not possible).

National Member Body (NB)

Every country that participates in the work of the International Organization for Standardization (ISO) nominates a single body which will represent it within ISO and those of its various sub-committees and working groups that it wishes to be involved with. These national member bodies may choose to participate in any, or all, of the various fields of standardization that are the responsibility of ISO by becoming either a Participting Member or an Observer Member. A similar process applies for countries participating in the work of the International Electrotechnical Commission (IEC).

National Quotation Bureau

A service that publishes bid and offer quotes from market makers in OTC transactions.

National Securities Clearing Corporation (NSCC)

A clearing corporation that facilitates the settlement of accounts among brokerage firms, exchanges, and other clearing corporations.

National Security Controls

National security controls restrict exports of U.S. goods and technology which would make a significant contribution to the military potential of another country and thus be detrimental to Western countries' national security.

National Security Council

The NSC was established by the National Security Act of 1947 to advise the President with respect to the integration of domestic, foreign, and military policies relating to national security.

National Security Override

In some cases, despite a finding of foreign availability of a controlled commodity, control is maintained over exporting the commodity because it is deemed a national security sensitive item. The term national security override is used to describe this circumstance.

National Stock Exchange (NSE)

Second-largest stock exchange based in India.

National tax policy

The way a country chooses to allocate tax burdens.

National Tourism Policy Act

Legislation, passed in 1981, that created the U.S. Travel and Tourism Administration and required the establishment of the Tourism Policy Council and the Travel and Tourism Advisory Board.

National Trade Data Bank

The NTDB contains international economic and export promotion information supplied by 19 U.S. agencies. Data are updated monthly and are presented in one of three standard formats: text, time series, or matrix. The NTDB contains data from the Departments of Agriculture (Foreign Agricultural Service), Commerce (Bureau of the Census, Bureau of Economic Analysis, International Trade Administration, and National Institute for Standards and Technology), Energy, Labor (Bureau of Labor Statistics), the Central Intelligence Agency, Eximbank, Federal Reserve System, U.S. International Trade Commission, Overseas Private Investment Corporation, Small Business Administration, the U.S. Trade Representative, and the University of Massachusetts (MISER data on state origins of exports).

National Trade Estimates Report

An annual report by USTR that identifies significant foreign barriers to and distortions of trade.

National Treatment

National treatment affords individuals and firms of foreign countries the same competitive opportunities, including market access, as are available to domestic parties.

Natural

Used in the context of general equities. Customer buyer or seller, versus a principal or profile interest. Legitimate, real.

Natural logarithm

Logarithm to the base *e* (approximately 2.7183).

Natural Resource Based Products

This GATT Negotiating Group was formed as a direct result of pressure from resource-rich LDCs to have an additional forum to deal with their special concerns, including the removal of barriers to trade in natural resource-based products. There are different interpretations among participants as to whether this group includes only three traditional product areas examined during the early 1980s GATT Work Program on NRBPs: non-ferrous metals and minerals; fish and fish products; and wood and wood products, or whether the Group may also discuss barriers in non-traditional product areas such as energy-based products.

NAV

See: Net asset value.

NC

The two-character ISO 3166 country code for NEW CALEDONIA.

NCDN

Non-Circumvention/Non-Discrimination.

NE

The two-character ISO 3166 country code for NIGER.

Near money

Assets that are easily convertible into cash, such as money market accounts and bank deposits.

Nearby

The nearest active trading month of a financial or commodity futures market. Related: Deferred futures.

Nearby futures contract

When several futures contracts are considered, the contract with the closest settlement date is called the nearby futures contract. The next (or the "next out") futures contract is the one that settles just after the nearby futures contract. The contract farthest away in time from settlement is called the most distant futures contract.

Nearest month

The expiration date of an option or future that is closest to the present.

"Need the tick"

Used for listed equity securities. A stock must trade up/down at least one tick (1/8) in order to comply with regulations governing short sales/corporate repurchases.

Negative amortization

A loan repayment schedule in which the outstanding principal balance of the loan increases, rather than amortizing, because the scheduled monthly payments do not cover the full amount required to amortize the loan. The unpaid interest is added to the outstanding principal, to be repaid later.

Negative NPV tie-in project

A negative-NPV infrastructure development project that a local government requires of a company engaged in a positive NPV investment project elsewhere in the country.

Negative carry

Related: Net financing cost.

Negative cash flow

Occurs when spending in a business is greater than earnings.

Negative convexity

A bond characteristic such that the price appreciation will be less than the price depreciation for a large change in yield of a given number of basis points. For example, a fixed-rate mortgage may lose value as rates go down because of prepayments.

Negative covenant

A bond covenant that limits or prohibits certain actions unless the bondholders agree.

Negative duration

Occurs when the price of an MBS moves in the same direction as interest rates.

Negative income tax

A proposal to assist taxpayer with below-subsistence-level incomes. After filing a tax return, such persons would receive a subsidy to bring them up above the poverty level.

Negative pledge clause

A bond covenant that requires the borrower to grant lenders a lien equivalent to any liens that may be granted in the future to any other currently unsecured lenders.

Negative working capital

Occurs when current liabilities exceed current assets, which can lead to bankruptcy.

Negative yield curve

When the yield on a short-term security is higher than the yield on a long-term security, partially because high interest rates are creating a greater demand for short-term borrowing.

Neglected firm effect

The tendency of firms that are neglected by security analysts to outperform firms that are the subject of considerable attention.

Negotiable

A security whose title is transferable by delivery . See also: Negotiable instrument.

Negotiable bill of lading

Contract that grants title of merchandise to the holder, which allows banks to use the merchandise as collateral.

Negotiable certificates of deposit

Large-denomination bank certificates of deposit that can be traded.

Negotiable instrument

An unconditional order or promise to pay some amount of money, easily transferable from one party to another.

Negotiable order of withdrawal (NOW)

Demand deposits that pay interest.

Negotiable Order of Withdrawal Account (NOW)

An interest-earning account on which chechs may be drawn. Withdrawals from NOW accounts may be offered by commerical banks, mutual savings banks, and savings and loan associations and may be owned only by individuals and certain nonprofit organizations and govermental units.

Negotiated certificate of deposit

A large-denomination CD, generally $1MM or more, that can be sold but cannot be cashed in before maturity.

Negotiated commission

An unfixed broker's commission that is determined through negotiation, depending on the specifics of the trades performed.

Negotiated markets

Markets in which each transaction is separately negotiated between buyer and seller (i.e., an investor and a dealer).

Negotiated offering

An offering of securities for which the terms, including underwriters' compensation, have been negotiated between the issuer and the underwriters.

Negotiated sale

Determining the terms of an offering by negotiation between the issuer and the underwriter rather than through competitive bidding by underwriting groups.

Negotiated underwriting

A securities offering process in which the purchase price paid to the issuer and the public offering price are determined by negotiation rather than through competitive bidding.

NEO

Abbreviation for nonequity options, which are options contracts on foreign currencies, debt issues, commodities, and stock indexes.

Net

The gain or loss on a security sale as measured by the selling price of a security less the adjusted cost of acquisition.

Net adjusted present value

The adjusted present value minus the initial cost of an investment.

Net advantage to leasing

The net present value of entering into a lease financing arrangement rather than borrowing the necessary funds and buying the asset.

Net advantage to merging

The difference in total post- and pre-merger market value minus the cost of the merger.

Net advantage of refunding

The net present value of the savings from a refunding.

Net after-tax gain

Capital gain after income taxes have been paid.

Net asset value (NAV)

The value of a fund's investments. For a mutual fund, the net asset value per share usually represents the fund's market price, subject to a possible sales or redemption charge. For a closed-end fund, the market price may vary significantly from the net asset value.

Net assets

The difference between total assets on the one hand and current liabilities and noncapitalized long-term liabilities on the other hand.

Net benefit to leverage factor

A linear approximation of a number, that enables one to operationalize the total impact of leverage on firm value in the capital market imperfections view of capital structure.

Net book value

The current book value of an asset or liability; that is, its original book value net of any accounting adjustments such as depreciation.

Net capital requirement

SEC requirement that member firms and nonmember securities broker-dealers maintain a maximum ratio of indebtedness to liquid capital of 15 to 1.

Net cash balance

Beginning cash balance plus cash receipts minus cash disbursements.

Net change

This is the difference between a day's last trade and the previous day's last trade.

Net currency exposure

Exposure to foreign exchange risk> after netting all intracompany cash flows.

Net current assets

The difference between current assets and current liabilities, also known as working capital.

Net errors and omissions

In balance of payments accounting, net errors and omissions record the statistical discrepancies that arise in gathering balance of payments data.

Net exposed assets

Exposed assets less exposed liabilities. This term is used with market values or, in translation accounting, with book values.

Net financing cost

Also called the cost of carry or, simply, carry, the difference between the cost of financing the purchase of an asset and the asset's cash yield. Positive carry means that the yield earned is greater than the financing cost; negative carry means that the financing cost exceeds the yield earned.

Net float

Sum of disbursement float and collection float.

Net Foreign Investment

Net foreign investment is the sum of U.S. exports of goods and services, receipts of factor income, and capital grants received by the United States (net), less the sum of imports of goods and services by the United States, payments of factor income, and transfer payments to foreigners (net). It may also be viewed as the acquisition of foreign assets by U.S. residents, less the acquisition of U.S. assets by foreign residents. It includes the BPA statistical discrepancy.

Net income

The company's total earnings, reflecting revenues adjusted for costs of doing business, depreciation, interest, taxes and other expenses.

Net income per share of common stock

See: Earnings per share.

Net interest cost (NIC)

The total amount of interest that will be paid on a debt obligation by a corporate or municipal bond issuer.

Net investment

Gross, or total, investment minus depreciation.

Net investment income per share

Income received by an investment company from dividends and interest on investments less administrative expenses, divided by the number of outstanding shares.

Net lease

A lease arrangement under which the lessee is responsible for all property taxes, maintenance expenses, insurance, and other costs associated with keeping the asset in good working condition.

Net monetary assets

See: Monetary assets less monetary liabilities.

Net operating loss carrybacks

The application of losses to offset earnings in previous years.

Net operating loss carryforwards

Application of losses to offset earnings in future years.

Net operating losses

Losses that a firm can take advantage of to reduce taxes.

Net operating margin

The ratio of net operating income to net sales.

Net parity

Antithesis of gross parity. Convertibles: Price of a convertible security including accrued interest. International: Price of international security including commissions, fees, stamp duty, and other transaction costs, translated into U.S. dollar amounts.

Net period

The period of time between the end of the discount period and the date payment is due.

Net position

The value of the position subtracting the initial cost of setting up the position. For example, if 100 options where purchased for $1 each and the option is currently trading for $9, the value of the net position is $900 - $100 = $800.

Net present value (NPV)

The present value of the expected future cash flows minus the cost.

Net proceeds

Amount received from the sale of an asset after deducting all transaction costs.

Net present value of future investments

The present value of the total sum of NPVs expected to result from all of the firm's future investments.

Net present value of growth opportunities

A model valuing a firm in which net present value of new investment opportunities is explicitly examined.

Net present value rule

An investment is worth making if it has a positive NPV Projects with negative NPVs should be rejected.

Net Price

Price after substracting all discounts, rebates, etc.

Net profit margin

Net income divided by sales; the amount of each sales dollar left over after all expenses have been paid.

Net quick assets

Cash, marketable securities, and accounts receivable less current liabilities.

Net realized capital gains per share

Capital gains realized by an investment company minus any capital losses divided by the total number of the company's outstanding shares.

Net sales

Gross sales less returns and allowances, freight out, and cash discounts allowed.

Net sales transaction

Refers to over-the-counter trading. Securities deal in which the quoted prices include commissions (i.e., OTC); looked at another way, the buyer and seller do not pay fees or commissions in addition to the print or quotation prices.

Net salvage value

The after-tax net cash flow for terminating the project.

Net tangible assets per share

All of a company's assets except patents, trademarks, and other intangible assets minus all liabilities and the par value of preferred stock, divided by the number of shares outstanding.

Net transaction

A securities transaction in which no commissions or

extra fees are paid, such as in an initial public offering.

Net transaction exposure

Offsetting inflows against outflows in a given currency to determine extent of exposure to risk.

Net Weight

Weight of the goods alone without any immediate wrappings; e.g., the weight of the contents of a tin can without the weight of the can. See "Legal Weight."

Net working capital

Current assets minus current liabilities. Often simply referred to as working capital.

Net worth

Common stockholders' equity which consists of common stock, surplus, and retained earnings.

Net yield

The rate of return on a security minus purchase costs, commissions, or markups.

Netting

Reducing transfers of funds between subsidiaries or separate companies to a net amount.

Netting out

To get or bring in as a net; to clear as profit.

Network A/Network B

See: Consolidated tape.

Neutral

Describing an opinion that is neither bearish not bullish. Neutral option strategies are generally designed to perform best if there is little or no net change in the price of the underlying stock or index. See also Bearish and Bullish.

Neutral hedge

Hedge that is expected to yield a dollar-neutral result of the combined position, regardless of price change in any part of the hedge securities. For any convertible trading at a premium, this ratio is less than 100%. The higher the convertible premium, the lower a ratio must be to be neutral. See: Delta.

Neural Nets

Models which mimic the massive parallel processing that occurs in the brain.

Neutral period

In the Euromarket, a period over which Eurodollars are sold is said to be neutral if it does not start or end on either a Friday or the day before a holiday.

Neutral stock

A stock with a beta of 1.0.

New account report

A broker's document including information about a new client. See: Know your customer.

New European Exchange (NEWEX)

A trading market for Central and East Eurpoean securities established by the Deutsche Börse (German Stock Market) and the Wiener Börse (Austrian Stock Market) in 2000.

New high/new low

A stock valued at its highest or lowest price in the last year.

New issue

Securities that are publicly offered for the first time, whether in an IPO or as an additional issue of stocks or bonds by a company that is already public.

New-issues market

The market in which a new issue of securities is first sold to investors. This is not a separate market but refers to a niche of the overall market.

New listing

A security that has just been entered on a stock or bond exchange for trading.

Newly Independent States (NIS)

Twelve of the republics of the former Soviet Union: Armenia, Azerbaijan, Belarus, Georgia, Kazakhstan, Kyrgystan, Moldova, Russia, Tajikistan, Turkmenistan, Ukraine, and Uzbekistan.

Newly Industrialized Economy (NIE)

A developing economy that has reached a relatively advanced stage of economic growth and have experienced rapid growth of GDP, industrial production, and exports in recent years. The term was first applied to Hong Kong, Singapore, South Korea, and Taiwan, but it is often extended to other countries. Also known as NIC (Newly Industrialized Countries.)

New money

In a Treasury auction, the amount by which the par value of the securities offered exceeds that of those maturing.

New-To-Export

As defined by the International Trade Administration, a new-to-export action is one that results from documented assistance to a company that assists the client's first verifiable export sale. Either the company has not exported to any destination during the past 24 months or prior exports have resulted from unsolicited orders or were received through a U.S.-based intermediary.

New-To-Market

As defined by the International Trade Administration, a reportable new-to-market export action is one that results from documented assistance to an exporter that facilitates a verifiable sale in a new foreign market. Either the company has not exported to that market during the past 24 months or previous exports to that market have resulted from unsolicited orders or were received through a U.S. based intermediary.

New York Cotton Exchange (NYCE)

Commodities exchange in New York trading futures and options on cotton, frozen concentrated orange juice, and potatoes, as well as interest rate, currency, and index futures and options.

New York Futures Exchange (NYFE)

A wholly owned subsidiary of the NYSE that trades futures and futures options on the NYSE composite index.

New York Mercantile Exchange (NYMEX)

The world's largest physical commodity futures exchange.

New York Stock Exchange (NYSE)

Also known as the Big Board or the Exchange.

New Zealand Stock Exchange

Automated, screen-based national trading system based in Wellington.

"News out"

Refers to over-the-counter trading. A news story concerning the stock being considered has recently been posted on one of the news services, such as the Dow Jones News Service or Reuters. A courtesy standard in trading is to mention that "news is out," in case the other party is unaware of the new development.

Next day settlement

Transaction in which the contract is settled the day after the trade is executed. See: Settlement date.

Next futures contract

The contract settling immediately after the nearby futures contract.

Nexus (of contracts)

A set or collection of something.

NF

The two-character ISO 3166 country code for NORFOLK ISLAND.

NFA

See: National Futures Association.

NG

The two-character ISO 3166 country code for NIGERIA.

NGN

The ISO 4217 currency code for the Nigerian Naira.

NI

The two-character ISO 3166 country code for NICARAGUA.

NICs

Newly Industrialized Countries, which are countries with high-growth industrial economies, such as Hong Kong and Malaysia.

N.I.E.

See Newly Industrialized Economy.

NIF

See: Note issuance facility.

Nifty Fifty

Institutional investor' 50 most popular stocks.

Niger Basin Authority

The NBA (French: Autorit, du Bassin du Neiger) fosters coordinated development of the Niger Basin area. The Authority regulates navigation, publishes statistics and hydrological forecasts, promotes environmental control and agricultural and infrastructure development. NBA's predecessor organization was established in 1964; headquarters are in Niamey, Niger. NBA members include: Benin, Burkina Faso, the Cameroon, Chad, C"te d'Ivoire, Guinea, Mali, Niger, and Nigeria.

Nigeria Trust Fund

The NTF grants loans on preferential terms to finance projects in Nigeria in cooperation with other lending institutions. The Fund, which is administered by the African Development Bank, was established in February 1976.

Nikkei

The common term for the Nihon Keizai newspaper, Japan's leading financial newspaper. The Nikkei usually refers to the price-weighted average of 225 stocks of the first section of the Tokyo Stock Exchange.

Nikkei stock average

Applies mainly to international equities. Price-weighted average of 225 stocks of the first section of the Tokyo Stock Exchange started on May 16, 1949. Japanese equivalent of the US Dow.

Nine-bond rule

An NYSE rule requiring that orders for nine bonds or fewer stay on the floor for one hour to seek a market.

19c3 stock

A stock listed on a national securities exchange after April 26, 1979, that is exempt from the Securities and Exchange Commission rule that prohibits exchange members from participating in off-board trading.

NIO

The ISO 4217 currency code for the Nicaraguan Cordoba Oro.

N.I.S.

See Newly Independent States.

NL

The two-character ISO 3166 country code for NETHERLANDS.

NLG

The ISO 4217 currency code for the Dutch Guilder.

NM

Abbreviation for "not meaningful".

NMS

See: National Market System.

NO

The two-character ISO 3166 country code for NORWAY.

No-action letter

A letter from the Securities and Exchange Commission agreeing that the commission will take no civil or criminal action against a party, regarding a specific activity.

No Adjournment

Within the text on the proxy, card are the words: "Shares will be voted at this annual meeting or at any adjournment thereof." If a securityholder strikes out this phrase, the proxy cannot be counted at any adjournment (reconvening) of the meeting.

Noah Effect

The tendency of persistent time series ($0.50<H<1.00$) to have abrupt, and discontinuous changes. The normal distribution assumes continuous changes in a system. However, a time series which exhibits Hurst statistics may abruptly change levels, skipping values either up or down. Mandelbrot coined the term "Noah effect" after the biblical story of the deluge. See: Joseph Effect, Hurst Exponent, Persistence, Anti-persistence.

"No Autex"

Used in the context of general equities. "No buy or sell interest should be entered into the Autex (advertising) system." Inquirers do not want exposure of an inquiry to affect the price at which they hope to ultimately transact the trade, hence disturbing the customer's picture.

NOB spread

Notes over bonds spread. This is the difference in yield between Treasury notes (maturing in 2 to 10 years) and Treasury bonds (maturing in 15 or more years), which is traded using Treasury note and bond futures.

NOBO (Non-Objecting Beneficial Owner)

A beneficial ("street") security holder who has not objected to his or her name being released to the Corporation, if the Corporation so requests.

No book

Used for listed equity securities. Not much, if any, stock is being bid for or offered at the present time by customers or the specialist.

No-brainer

A market in which it does not take very complex analysis to figure out how securities are going to perform, such as a strong bull market.

Noise

Price and volume fluctuations that can confuse interpretation of market direction. Used in the context of general equities. Stock market activity caused by program trades, dividend rolls, and other phenomena not reflective of general sentiment. Antithesis of real.

Noisy Chaos

A chaotic dynamical system with either observational or system noise added. See: Chaos, Dynamical Systems, Observational Noise, System Noise.

NOK

The ISO 4217 currency code for the Norwegian Krone.

No-load fund

A mutual fund that does not impose a sales commission. Related: Load fund, no-load mutual fund.

No-load mutual fund

An open-end investment company whose shares are sold without a sales charge. There can be other distribution charges, however, such as Article 12B-1 fees.

A true no-load fund has neither a sales charge nor a distribution fee.

No-load stock

Shares that can be purchased from the issuing companies themselves, so that broker fees and commissions can be avoided.

No-par-value stock

A stock with no par value given in the charter or stock certificate.

Nomenclature of the Customs Cooperation Council

This was known as the "Brussels Classification Nomenclature" prior to January 1, 1975. It is the customs tariff adhered to by most European countries and many other countries throughout the world, but not by the United States.

Nominee Name

A name that is used by the Corporation as a generic registered owner on a stock or bond certificate. The use of nominee names makes the processing of security transfers easier.

Nominal

In name only. Differences in compounding cause the nominal rate to differ from the effective interest rate. Inflation causes the purchasing power of money to differ from one time to another.

Nominal annual rate

An effective rate per period multiplied by the number of periods in a year. Same as annual percentage rate.

Nominal cash flow

A cash flow expressed in nominal terms if the actual dollars to be received or paid out are given.

Nominal dollars

Dollars that are not adjusted for inflation.

Nominal exchange rate

The actual foreign exchange quotation in contrast to the real exchange rate, which has been adjusted for changes in purchasing power.

Nominal exercise price

The exercise price of a GNMA option contract, which equals the unpaid principal balance multiplied by the adjusted exercise price.

Nominal income

Income that has not been adjusted for inflation and decreasing purchasing power.

Nominal interest rate

The interest rate unadjusted for inflation.

Nominal price

Price quotations on futures for a period in which no actual trading took place.

Nominal quotation

Used in the context of general equities. Bid and offer prices given by a market maker for the purpose of valuation, not as an invitation to trade; must be specifically identified as such by prefixing the quotes FYI (for your information) or FVO (for valuation only).

Nominal yield

The income received from a fixed income security in one year divided by its par value. See also: Coupon rate.

Nominee

A person or firm to whom securities or other properties are transferred to facilitate transactions, while leaving the customer as the actual owner.

Nonaccredited investor

Wealthy, sophisticated investors who do not meet SEC net worth requirements. These investors require less protection because of large financial resources, but only 35 nonaccredited investor can be included per investment.

Noncallable

A preferred stock or bond that cannot be redeemed whenever desired by the issuer.

Noncash charge

A cost, such as depreciation, depletion, and amortization, that does not involve any cash outflow. That is, this is treated as an accounting expense — not a real expense that demands cash.

Nonclearing member

An exchange member firm that is not able to clear transactions, and must pay another member firm to carry out its clearing operations.

Noncompete

A provision in a number of employment contracts that prohibits an employee from working for a competing firm for a specified number of years after the employee leaves the firm.

Noncompetitive bid

In a Treasury auction, bidding for a specific amount of securities at the price, whatever it may turn out to be, equal to the average price of the accepted competitive bids.

Noncompetitive tender

Offer by an investor to purchase Treasury securities at a price equivalent to the weighted average discount rate or yield of accepted competitive bids in a Treasury auction. Noncompetitive tenders are always accepted in full.

Noncontributory pension plan

A pension plan that is fully paid for by the employer, requiring no employee contributions.

Noncumulative

Applies mainly to convertible securities. Type of preferred stock on which unpaid or omitted dividends do not accrue. Omitted dividends are, as a rule, gone forever.

Noncumulative preferred stock

Preferred stock whose holders must forgo dividend payments when the company misses a dividend payment. Related: Cumulative preferred stock.

Noncurrent asset

Any asset that is expected to be held for the whole year, not sold or exchanged, such as real estate, machinery, or a patent.

Noncurrent liability

A liability due in one year.

Non-Discretionary Proposal

A proposition on a proxy card requiring a response from the beneficial owner which does not fall under the Ten Day Rule. Therefore, the broker cannot vote on behalf of the beneficial owner, it can only vote after specific instructions have been received from the beneficial owner.

Nondiscretionary trust

A personal trust whose trustee has no discretion in deciding how income will be distributed to the beneficiary.

Nondeductible contribution

A contribution to either a traditional IRA or Roth IRA. Income tax is due on the contribution in the tax year for which the contribution is made.

Nondeliverable Forward Contracts (NDF)

Agreement regarding a position in a specified currency, a specified exchange rate, and a specified future settlement date, that does not result in delivery of currencies. Rather one party in the agreement makes a payment to the other party on the basis of the exchange rate at the future date.

Nondiversifiability of human capital

The difficulty of hedging one's human capital (the unique capabilities and expertise of individuals) and employment effort.

Nondiversifiable risk

Risk that cannot be eliminated by having a large portfolio of many assets.

Non-Equity Option

An option whose underlying entity is not common stock; typically refers to options on physical commodities and index options.

Nonfinancial assets

Physical assets such as real estate and machinery.

Nonfinancial services

Such things as freight, insurance, passenger services, and travel.

Noninsured plans

Defined benefit pension plans that are not guaranteed by life insurance products. Related: Insured plans.

Noninterest-bearing note

A note without periodic interest payment, but selling at a discount and maturing at face value. See: Zero-coupon bond.

Nonmarketed claims

Claims that cannot be easily bought and sold in the financial markets, such as those of the government and litigants in lawsuits.

Nonintermediated debt market

A financial market in which borrowers (government and large corporations) appeal directly to savers for debt capital through the securities markets without using a financial institution as intermediary>.

Nonmarketable security

Securities that cannot be easily bought and sold.

Nonmember bank

Depository institution that is not a member of the Federal Reserve System. Specifically, a state-chartered commercial bank that has elected not to join the System.

Nonmember firm

Used for listed equity securities. Brokerage firm that is not a member of an organized exchange (NYSE). Such firms execute trades either through member firms, or on regional exchanges where they are members, or in the third market.

Nonmonetary assets and liabilities

Assets and liabilities with noncontractual payoffs.

Nonparallel shift in the yield curve

A shift in the yield curve in which yields do not change by the same number of basis points for every maturity. Related: Parallel shift in the yield curve.

Nonparticipating life insurance policy

Life insurance policy whose policyholders do not receive dividends, because they are not participants in the interest, dividends, and capital gains earned by the insurer on premiums paid.

Nonperforming asset

An asset that is not effectively producing income, such as an overdue loan.

Nonproductive loan

A loan that increases spending power, but is used in business that does not directly increase the economy's output, such as a leveraged buyout loan.

Nonpublic information

Information about a company that is not known by the general public, which will have a definite impact on the stock price when released. See: Insider trading.

Nonpurpose loan

A loan with securities pledged as collateral, but which is not to be used in securities trading or transactions.

Nonqualified plan

A retirement plan that does not meet the IRS requirements for favorable tax treatment.

Nonqualifying annuity

An annuity that does not fall under an IRS-approved pension plan. Contributions are made with after-tax dollars, but earnings can accumulate tax-deferred until withdrawal.

Nonqualifying stock option

An employee stock option that does not satisfy IRS qualifying rules and therefore is liable for taxation upon exercise .

Nonrated

A bond that has not been rated by a large rating agency, usually because the issue is too small.

Nonrecourse

In the case of default, the lender has no ability to claim assets over and above what the limited partners contributed.

Nonrecourse loan

A loan for which no partner or related person bears the economic risk of loss. For example, if a partnership fails to repay a non-recourse loan, the lender has no recourse against any partner except to foreclose of the assets used to secure the loan.

Nonrecurring charge

A one-time expense or credit shown in a company's financial statement.

Nonredeemable

Not permitted, under the terms of an indenture, to be redeemed.

Nonrefundable

Not permitted, under the terms of an indenture, to be refundable.

Nonreproducible assets

A tangible asset with unique physical properties, like a parcel of land, a mine, or a work of art.

Nonsterilized intervention

Taking an action in the foreign exchange market without adjusting for changes in money supply.

Nonsystematic risk

Nonmarket or firm-specific risk factors that can be eliminated by diversification. Also called unique risk or diversifiable risk. Systematic risk refers to risk factors common to the entire economy.

Non-Tariff Barriers

NTBs are market access barriers that result from prohibitions, restrictions, conditions or specific requirements and make exporting products difficult and/or costly. The term covers any restriction or quota, charge, or policy, other than traditional customs duties, domestic support programs, discriminatory labeling and health standards, and exclusive business practices which limit the access of imported goods. NTBs may result from government or private sector actions.

Non-Tariff Measures

While there is no specific definition of an NTM, some of the most commonly-used NTMs include import quotas or other quantitative restrictions, non-automatic import licensing, customs surcharges or other fees and charges, customs procedures, export subsidies, unreasonable standards or standards-setting procedures, government procurement restrictions, inadequate intellectual property protection, and investment restrictions. Participants in the Tokyo Round attempted to address these barriers through the negotiations of a number of GATT codes, open for signature to all GATT members. Seven codes were negotiated during the Tokyo Round, covering customs valuations, import licensing, subsidies and countervailing duties, antidumping duties, standards, government procurement, and trade in civil aircraft. Although the Tokyo Round codes had alleviated some of the problems caused by non-tariff measures, overall use of NTMs has increased since conclusion of the Tokyo Round.

Nontradables

Goods and services produced and consumed domestically that are not close substitutes to import or export goods and services.

Non Vessel Operating Common Carriers (NVOCC)

An ocean carrier that does not own or operate their own vessels. They use less than full containerloads which they ship on actual ship lines. They issue their own bills of lading which are backed up by actual on board ocean bills of lading issued to them by the other carrier.

Non-Vessel Owning Carrier

An NVOC is a firm which consolidates and disperses international containers that originate at, or are bound for, inland ports.

Nonvoting stock

A security that does not entitle the holder to vote on the corporation's resolutions or elections.

No Protest

Instructions given to a collecting bank not to protest a specific item in the event of non payment or non acceptance.

Nordic Council

The Nordic Council, established in 1952, is directed toward supporting cooperation among Nordic countries in communications, cultural, economics, environmental,, fiscal, legal, and social areas. Members include: Denmark, Finland, Iceland, Norway, and Sweden. Council headquarters are in Stockholm, Sweden.

Nordic Investment Bank

The NIB, which began operating in December 1975, promotes economic cooperation and development by providing resources and guarantees for exports and for capital investment projects. Bank members include: Denmark, Finland, Iceland, Norway, and Sweden. Bank headquarters are in Helsinki, Finland.

Normal annuity form

The manner in which retirement benefits are paid out.

Normal backwardation theory

Holds that the futures price will be bid down to a level below the expected spot price.

Normal deviate

Related: Standardized value.

Normal Distribution

The well known bell shaped curve. According to the Central Limit Theorem, the probability density function of a large number of independent, identically distributed random numbers will approach the normal distribution. In the fractal family of distributions, the normal distribution only exists when alpha equals 2, or the Hurst exponent equals 0.50. Thus, the normal distribution is a special case which in time series analysis is quite rare. See: Alpha, Central Limit Theorem, Fractal Distribution.

Normal growth firms

Companies whose earnings grow at a constant rate.

Normal investment practice

The investment history of a customer, which is used as a benchmark to test the bona fide public offerings requirement of the allocation of a hot issue.

Normal Market Size (NMS)

A system that categorizes the size of transactions that are normal for a particular security and forces market makers to deal within these sizes.

Normal portfolio

A customized benchmark that includes all the securities from which a manager normally chooses, weighted as the manager would weight them in a portfolio.

Normal probability distribution

A probability distribution for a continuous random variable that forms a symmetrical bell-shaped curve around the mean. This distribution has no skewness or excess kurtosis.

Normal random variable

A random variable that has a normal probability distribution.

Normal retirement

The age or number of working years after which a pension plan beneficiary can retire and receive unreduced benefits immediately.

Normal trading unit

See: Round lot.

Normalized earnings

Earnings that have been adjusted in order to take into account the effect of cycles in the economy.

Normalizing method

Making a change in the income account equivalent to the tax savings realized through the use of different depreciation methods for shareholder and income tax purposes, thus washing out the benefits of the tax savings reported as final net income to shareholders.

North American Free Trade Agreement

NAFTA, which entered into force in January 1994, is a free trade agreement comprising Canada, the United States and Mexico. NAFTA exceeds 360 million consumers and a combined output of $6 trillion —approximately 20 percent larger than the European Community. NAFTA's consumer population is slightly smaller than the European Economic Area which has over 380 million consumers. The Agreement:

- Progressively eliminates almost all U.S.-Mexico tariffs over a 10-year period, with a small number of tariffs for trade-sensitive industries phased out over a 15-year period. Mexico-Canada tariffs are also phased out over a 10-year period. Tariff reduction schedules between the United States and Canada negotiated in the Canadian Free Trade Agreement are retained.

— Eliminates other barriers to trade such as import licensing requirements and Customs user fees.

— Guarantees service providers of the three countries equal treatment in the NAFTA area, including the right to invest and the right to sell services across borders.

— Establishes five basic principles to protect foreign investors and their investment int he free trade area:

(a) nondiscriminatory treatment,

(b) freedom from performance requirements,

(c) free transference of funds related to an investment,

(d) expropriation only in conformity with international law, and

(e) the right to seek international arbitration for a violation of the agreement's protections.

The Agreement contains special provisions for sensitive economic sectors, including agriculture, automotive products, energy, and textiles and apparel. The Agreement also created a Border Environment Cooperation Commission and a North American Development Bank.

North Atlantic Treaty Organization

NATO members include Belgium, Canada, Denmark, France (which has only partial membership), Greece, Iceland, Italy, Luxembourg, Netherlands, Norway, Portugal, Spain, Turkey, United Kingdom, United States, and Germany. With the end of the "cold war," NATO's role, originally defense-oriented is being redefined.

Norwegian Agency for Development Cooperation

NORAD provides financing of project exports from Norway to developing countries for development undertakings which contribute to development and which can be sustained without future external assistance. About 50 percent of Norwegian assistance is bilateral aid; the balance is channelled as multialteral aid through UN specialized agencies and financial institutions, including regional development banks. NORAD bilaterial aid includes provisions for Norwegian private industrial sector participation as suppliers of capital equipment and services and technology.

A portion of assistance may involve concessional financing for Norwegian project exports, including mixed credits, export credit guarantees, support for training in connection with project exports, and tied co-financing on grant basis with the World Bank, the African Development Bank, and the Asian Development Bank. NORAD assistance is subject the OECD's Development Assistance Committee guidelines for development assistance and associated financing.

NORAD was established in 1968; headquarters are in Oslo, Norway.

No Substitution

Within the text on a proxy card are the words: "The shareholder appoints certain people (collectively, the proxy committee) with full power of substitution to vote the shares." If the security holder strikes out this phrase, the proxy cannot be voted if there is a change in the designated proxy committee.

Not a name with us

Refers to over-the-counter trading. Not a registered market maker in the security, especially in OTC and convertibles, or having nothing real to do.

Not-for-profit

An organization established for charitable, humanitarian, or educational purposes that is exempt from some taxes and in which no one in profits or losses.

Not rated

A rating service indicator, neither positive nor negative, showing that a security or company has not been rated.

Not-sufficient-funds check

A bank check having insufficient funds to back it.

Not held order (NH order)

Applies mainly to international equities. Market or limit order in which the customer does not desire to transact automatically at the inside market (market held) but instead has given the trader or floor broker (listed stock) time and price discretion in transacting on a best-efforts basis. This will not hold the broker responsible for missing the price within the limits (limit not held) or obtaining a worse price (market not held). The order is marked "not held, disregard tape/ DRT, take time" or bears any such qualifying notation, excluding "or better." See: Held order.

Note

Debt instruments with initial maturities longer than one year and shorter than 10 years.

Note agreement

A contract for privately placed debt.

Note issuance facility (NIF)

An agreement by which a syndicate of banks indicates a willingness to accept short-term notes from borrowers and resell these notes in the Eurocurrency markets.

Notes to the financial statements

A detailed set of notes immediately following the financial statements in an annual report that explain and expand on the information in the financial statements.

Notice day

A day on which notices of intent to deliver pertaining to a specified delivery month may be issued. Related: Delivery notice.

Notice of Meeting

The legal one page notice to security holders stating the date, time and place of the shareholder meeting. This page is normally attached to the front of the proxy statement.

Notice Period

The time during which the buyer of a futures contract can be called upon to accept delivery. Typically, the 3 to 6 weeks preceding the expiration of the contract.

Notification date

The day the option is either exercised or expires.

Notifying Bank

See: Advising Bank.

Notional principal amount

In an interest rate swap, the predetermined dollar principal on which the exchanged interest payments are based.

Nouveau Marche

An equity market unit of the Paris Bourse that deals solely in innovative, high-growth companies.

Novation

Defeasance whereby the firm's debt is cancelled.

NOW

See: Negotiable Order of Withdrawal.

NP

The two-character ISO 3166 country code for NEPAL.

NPR

The ISO 4217 currency code for the Nepalese Rupee.

NPV

See: Net present value.

NPV profile

A graph of NPV as a function of the discount rate.

NR

The two-character ISO 3166 country code for NAURU.

NRA (Non-Resident Alien) Tax

The tax which must be withheld by the corporation or

its disbursing agent (usually 15% or 30%, depending on the holder's citizenship).

NU

The two-character ISO 3166 country code for NIUE0.

Nugget

A 15 year Gold FHLMC (Freddie Mac) bond; similar to a Dwarf.

Numismatist

Collector of historical coins and currencies.

NYSE

See: New York Stock Exchange.

NYSE composite index

Composite index covering price movements of all new world common stocks listed on the New York Stock Exchange. It is based on the close of the market on December 31, 1965, at a level of 50.00, and is weighted according to the number of shares listed for each issue. Print changes in the index are converted to dollars and cents so as to provide a meaningful measure of changes in the average price of listed stocks. The composite index is supplemented by separate indexes for four industry groups: industrial, transportation, utility, and finance.

NZ

The two-character ISO 3166 country code for NEW ZEALAND.

NZD

The ISO 4217 currency code for the New Zealand Dollar.

O

Fifth letter of a Nasdaq stock symbol specifying that it is the company's second class of preferred shares.

OAS

See: Option adjusted spread.

Oath of Inspectors

A sworn statement signed by the Inspectors of Election, usually notarized, wherein they swear they will impartially and faithfully execute their duties as Inspectors of Election at the annual or special meeting of shareholders.

Objective (mutual funds)

The fund's investment strategy category as stated in the prospectus. There are more than 20 standardized categories. E.g. Aggressive growth, balanced.

Objective probability

The true unobservable underlying odds that something is so.

Obligation

A legal responsibility, such as to repay a debt.

Obligation bond

A municipal bond with a face value greater than the value of the underlying property. The difference is designed to compensate the lender for costs exceeding the mortgage value.

Obligor

A person who has an obligation to pay off a debt.

Observational Noise

The error between the true value in a system and its observed value due to imprecision in measurement. Also called Measurement Noise. See: Dynamical Noise.

OCC

See: Options Clearing Corporation.

Ocean Bill of Lading

A receipt for the cargo and a contract for transportation between a shipper and the ocean carrier. It may also be used as an instrument of ownership which can be bought, sold, or traded while the goods are in transit. To be used in this manner, it must be a negotiable "Order" Bill-of-Lading.

— A Clean Bill-of-Lading is issued when the shipment is received in good order. If damaged or a shortage is noted, a clean bill-of-lading will not be issued.

— An On Board Bill-of-Lading certifies that the cargo has been placed aboard the named vessel and is signed by the master of the vessel or his representative. On letter of credit transactions, an On Board Bill-of-Lading is usually necessary for the shipper to obtain payment from the bank. When all Bills-of-Lading are processed a ship's manifest is prepared by the steamship line. This summarizes all cargo aboard the vessel by port of loading and discharge.

— An Inland Bill-of-Lading (a waybill on rail or the "pro forma" bill-of-lading in trucking) is used to document the transportation of the goods between the port and the point of origin or destination. It should contain information such as marks, numbers, steamship line, and similar information to match with a dock receipt.

Ocean Freight Differential

OFD is the amount by which the cost of the ocean freight bill for the portion of commodities required to be carried on U.S. flag vessels exceeds the cost of carrying the same amount on foreign flag vessels. When applied to agricultural commodities shipped under Food for Peace, OFD is the amount paid by the Commodity Credit Corporation.

Odd lot

A trading order for less than 100 shares of stock. Compare round lot.

Odd-Lot Buy Back

An offer made by the corporation or its agent to purchase shares from odd-lot shareholders.

Odd-lot dealer

A broker who combines odd lots of securities from multiple buy or sell orders into round lots and executes transactions in those round lots.

Odd-Lot Resale

An offer made by the corporation or its agent to purchase shares from odd-lot shareholders and immediately resell them in the market, usually in round-lots to institutions, thus saving the corporation the expense of merely buying shares back.

Odd-lot short-sale ratio

The percentage of total odd-lot sales that is composed of short sales.

Odd-lot theory

The theory that profits can be made by making trades contrary to odd-lot trading patterns, since odd-lot investors have poor timing. This theory is no longer popular.

OECD

See: Orgainization for Economic Cooperation and Development.

OECF

Japan's Overseas Economic Cooperation Fund.

OEX index

Applies to derivative products. Quotron symbol for the S&P 100 index option.

Off-balance-sheet financing

Financing that is not shown as a liability on a company's balance sheet.

Off-board

Used for listed equity securities. Transacted away from a national securities exchange even though the stock itself is listed, such as on the NYSE, and instead of on the OTC market, a regional exchange, or in the third or fourth markets (between customers directly). After 9:30 a.m., if the stock has not opened due to the exchange's discretion, trading can occur elsewhere, but the trader must assume the role of a quasi-specialist in the process.

Off-budget Federal entities

Federally owned and controlled entities whose transactions are excluded from the budget totals under provisions of law. Their receipts, outlays, and surplus or deficit are not included in budget receipts, outlays or deficits. Their budget authority is not included in totals of the budget.

Offene Handelsgesellschaft - OHG

German, meaning: "general partnership": is characterized by the unlimited and direct liability of all partners who are jointly and severally liable. Their liability cannot be restricted. The partnership must carry the family name of at least one partner with reference to the kind of partnership (such as "& Co.").

Offer

Indicates a willingness to sell at a given price. Related: Bid.

Offer price

See: Offer.

Offer wanted

Used in the context of general equities. Notice by a potential buyer of a security that he or she is looking for supply from a potential seller of the security, often requiring a capital commitment. Antithesis of bid wanted.

Offering date

Date on which a new set of stocks or bonds will first be sold to the public.

Offering memorandum

A document that outlines the terms of securities to be offered in a private placement.

Offering scale

The range of prices offered by the underwriter of a serial bond issue with different maturities.

Offering statement

A shortened registration statement required by the Securities and Exchange Commission on debt issues with less than a nine-month maturity.

Offerings

Often refers to initial public offerings. When a firm goes public and makes an offering of stock to the market.

Off-floor order

Used for listed equity securities. (1) Order to buy or sell a security that originates off the floor of an exchange; customer orders originating with brokers, as distinguished from orders placed by floor members trading for their own accounts. Exchange rules require that an off-floor order be executed before orders initiated on the floor. Upstairs order. Antithesis of on-floor order; (2) order not handled on the floor but instead upstairs.

Office of International Cooperation and Development

The Department of Agriculture's OICD is responsible for cooperative international research, scientific and technical exchanges, and liaison with international agricultural organizations. OICD also directs training and technical assistance in efforts in approximately 80 development countries.

Office of Munitions Control

See: Defense Trade Controls.

Office of Thrift Supervision (OTS)

An agency of the U.S. Treasury department responsible for the US savings and loan industry.

Official Development Assistance

Financial flows to developing countries and multilateral institutions provided by official agencies of national, state, or local governments. Each transaction must be:

- administered with the promotion of the economic development and welfare of developing countries as its main objective; and
- concessional in character and contain a grant element of at least 25 percent.

Official reserves

Holdings of gold and foreign currencies by official monetary institutions.

Official statement

A statement published by an issuer of a new municipal security describing itself and the issue.

Official settlements balance (overall balance)

An overall measurement of a country's private financial and economic transactions with the rest of the world.

Official unrequited transfers

Include a variety of subsidies, military aid, voluntary cancellation of debt, contributions to international organizations, indemnities imposed under peace treaties, technical assistance, taxes, or fines.

Offsets

The term offsets is an umbrella label for a broad range of industrial and commercial compensation practices required as a condition of purchase in commercial or government-to-government sales of either military or high-cost civilian hardware. Whether commercial or military, offsets involve overseas production that results in the creation or expansion of industrial capacity in the importer's country. The compensatory forms of offset include coproduction, licensed production, subcontractor production, overseas investment, and technology transfer.

Coproduction permits a foreign government or producer to acquire the technical information to manufacture all or part of a U.S.-origin article. Licensed production of a U.S.-origin article involves transfer of technical information under direct commercial arrangements between a U.S. manufacturer and a foreign government or producer. Subcontractor production of a U.S.-origin article usually involves a direct commercial arrangement between the U.S. manufacturer and a foreign producer but does not necessarily involve license of technical information.

Overseas investment arising from an offset agreement involves capital contribution toward the establishment or expansion of a subsidiary or joint venture in a foreign country. Technology transfer arises from agreement to conduct research and development abroad, to provide technical assistance to a subsidiary or joint venture of overseas investment, or to perform other activities under direct commercial arrangement between a U.S. manufacturer and a foreign entity.

Countries require offsets for a variety of reasons: to ease (or "offset") the burden of large defense purchases on their economies, to increase domestic employment, to obtain desired technology, or to promote targeted industrial sectors. Governments sometimes impose offset requirements on foreign exporters, as a condition for approval of major sales agreements in an effort to either reduce the adverse trade impact of a major sale or to gain specified industrial benefits for the importing country. In these circumstances, offset requirements may be direct or indirect, depending on whether the goods and services are integral parts of the product. In a direct offset, a U.S. manufacturer selling a product uses a component that is made in the purchasing country. In an indirect offset, the exporter would buy products that are peripheral to the manufacture of its product. See: Countertrade.

Offshore Banking Center

See: Offshore Banking Unit.

Offshore Banking Unit

An OBU is normally a foreign bank which conducts domestic moneymarket, Eurocurrency, and foreign exchange settlements. OBUs cannot accept domestic depostis but their activities are unrestricted by domestic authorities. OBUs are located in major financial centers (known as offshore banking centers) with liberal reserve, tax, and capital market requirements.

Offshore Dollars

See: Eurodollars.

Offshore finance subsidiary

A wholly owned affiliate incorporated overseas, usually in a tax haven country, whose function is to issue securities abroad for use in either the parent's domestic or foreign business.

Offshore fund

A mutual fund whose headquarters is based outside the United States.

Offshore Manufacturing

Offshore manufacturing is the foreign manufacture of goods by a domestic firm primarily for import into its home country.

OID

See: Original issue discount debt.

"O.K. to cross"

Used for listed equity securities. "Legal to cross the buy and sell orders on the exchange floor because transactor is not a principal in the transaction."

Old-line factoring

Factoring arrangement that provides collection, insurance, and finance for accounts receivable.

Old-To-Market

As defined by the International Trade Administration, old-to-market is a term which refers to committed/experienced larger-scale firms. A significant portion of manufacturing capability may be foreign sourced. Export sales volume is often in excess of 15 percent of total sales.

Oligopoly

A Market characterized by a small number of producers who often act together to control the supply of a particular good and its market price.

Oligopsony

A Market characterized by a small number of large buyers who control all purchases and therefore the market price of a good or service.

OM

The two-character ISO 3166 country code for OMAN.

OMR

The ISO 4217 currency code for the Oman Rial.

OM Stockholm AB

The derivatives market of Sweden, trading a wide variety of interest rate and bond futures. The exchange trades futures and options on the OMX equity index.

Omitted dividend

A dividend that was scheduled to be declared, but that is not voted by the board of directors probably because the company is experiencing financial difficulties.

Omnibus account

An account carried by one futures commission merchant with another futures commission merchant in which the transactions of two or more persons are combined and carried in the name of the originating broker, rather than designated separately. Related: Commission house.

Omnibus Proxy

A list issued by depositories detailing their participants, and their holdings, and authorizing the participants to vote their proxies directly. This type of proxies are issued by Cede & Co. and by certain bank custodians.

On

Used in the context of general equities. Conjunction that denotes trade execution /indication, usually during a pre-opening look. "Looks 6 on 6000 shares at opening." See: for/at.

On balance

Used for listed equity securities. Left over after pairing off other market buy and sell orders, usually before the opening of a stock or market but at times at the close (especially during index expirations). See: Imbalance of orders.

On board

Used in the context of general equities. Long.

On Board Bill Of Lading

A bill of lading in which a carrier certifies that goods have been placed on board a certain vessel.

On Board Ocean Bill of Lading

An ocean bill of lading bearing an on board notation, or words indicating that the merchandise is located aboard the vessel for transportation. These notations must be initialed or signed by an authorized employee or agent of the ship line.

On Carriage

Freight costs arising after the cost of principal international freight costs. These are usually inland freight charges for delivery within the buyer's country.

On a clean up

Used in the context of general equities. Willingness to participate in part of a trade if all of the stock available is spoken for except for the "clean up amount."

One-decision stock

A quality stock that is not actively traded, but rather held for its growth potential.

One-factor APT

A special case of the arbitrage pricing theory that is derived from the one-factor model by using diversification and arbitrage. It shows that the expected return on any risky asset is a linear function of a single factor.

144 stock

Used in the context of general equities. Restricted stock.

One-man picture

When both bid and the offered prices of a broker come from the same source.

1/f Noise

See: Anti-Persistence.

One-share-one-vote rule

The principle that all shareholders should have equal voting rights in public companies and each shareholder should have one vote.

One-way market

(1) A market in which only one side, the bid or asked, is quoted or firm. (2) A market that is moving strongly in one direction.

On-floor order

Used for listed equity securities. Security order originating with a member on the floor of an exchange when dealing with his or her own account, versus an upstairs order. Antithesis of off-floor order.

On the close order

A market order that is to be executed as close as possible to the closing price of the day.

On the money

Used in the context of general equities. In-line, or at the same price, as the last sale.

On the opening order

A market order that is to be executed at the price of the first trade of the day.

On the print

Used in the context of general equities. To participate in a block trade that has already transpired, as if that customer had been part of the trade originally; often used by a new party looking to participate in a trade that has just happened. See: Open on the print.

On the run

The most recently issued (and typically the most liquid) government bond in a particular maturity range.

On the sidelines

An investor who decides not to invest due to market uncertainty.

On the take

Used in the context of general equities. Price moving upward, because more buyers are taking offerings, causing offerings to vanish and be replaced by higher ones. Antithesis of come in, get hit.

On the tape

Used in the context of general equities. (1) Trade printed on the ticker tape; (2) news displayed on Reuters or the Dow Jones News Service.

OPD

Tape symbol showing either the first transaction of the day in a security after a delayed opening or the opening transaction in a security whose price has experienced a large rise or fall from the previous day's closing price.

OPEC

See: Organization of Petroleum Exporting Countries.

Open

Used in the context of general equities. Having either buy or sell interest at the indicated price level and side of a preceding trade. "Open on the buy/sell side" means looking for buyers/sellers (for someone who is a seller/buyer). Antithesis of clean.

Open Account

A trade arrangement in which goods are shipped to a foreign buyer without guarantee of payment. The obvious risk this method poses to the supplier makes it essential that the buyer's integrity be unquestionable.

Open book

See: Unmatched book.

Open contracts

Contracts that have been bought or sold without completion of the transaction by subsequent sale or purchase, or by making or taking actual delivery of the financial instrument or physical commodity.

Open depending on the floor

Used for listed equity securities. Having room for a customer buyer or seller contingent on the results of a trade being executed on the floor (i.e., satisfying the specialist book and the orders the trader opened up). See: Open on the print, subject.

Open-End Contract

An open purchase order with a definite amount of money limit for specific material that remains open over a stated contract period such as three, six or twelve months. Vendor to be selected by public bid and material to be ordered in writing or by phone as needed.

Open-end credit

Revolving line of credit that is extended with every purchase or cash advance.

Open-end fund

Used in the context of general equities. Mutual fund that continually creates new shares on demand. Mutual fund shareholders buy the funds at net asset value and may redeem them at any time at the prevailing market prices. Antithesis of closed-end fund.

Open-end lease

A lease agreement that provides for an additional payment at the expiration of the lease to adjust for any change in the value of the property.

Open-end mortgage

Mortgage against which additional debts may be issued. Related: Closed-end mortgage.

Open Insurance Policy

A marine insurance policy that applies to all shipments made by an exporter over a period of time rather than to one shipment only.

Open interest

The total number of derivatives contracts traded that have not yet been liquidated either by an offsetting derivative transaction or by delivery. Related: Liquidation.

Open-market operation

Purchase or sale of government securities by the monetary authorities to increase or decrease the domestic money supply.

Open-market purchase operation

A systematic program of repurchasing shares of stock in market transactions at current market prices, in competition with other prospective investors.

Open-market rates

Interest rates that are determined in the open market by supply and demand, as opposed to being set by the Federal Reserve Board.

Open (good-till-cancelled) order (GTC order)

Order to buy or sell a security that stays active until it is completed or the investor cancels it.

Open-outcry

The method of trading used at futures exchanges, typically involving calling out the specific details of a buy or sell order, so that the information is available to all traders.

Open Policy

A cargo policy with no expiration date that provides automatic coverage of cargo to or from an Assured in a specified trade at agreed rates, terms, and conditions. Usually consists of separate Marine and War policies.

Open position

A net long or short position whose value will change with a change in prices.

Open on the print

Used in the context of general equities. Block trader's term for a block trade that has been completed with an institutional client and printed on the consolidated tape, but leaves the block trader with stock available (because the trader has taken a long or short position to complete the trade) for new customers who are on the opposite side of the market to the initiating customer.

Open repo

A repurchase agreement with no definite term. The agreement is made on a day to day basis, and either the borrower or the lender may choose to terminate. The rate paid is higher than on overnight repo and is subject to adjustment if rates move.

Open up

Used in the context of general equities. Disclose more information (e.g., the exact price and quantity of one's potential interest). See: Put pants on it.

Opening

The period at the beginning of the trading session officially designated by an exchange, during which all transactions are considered made "at the opening." Related: Close.

Opening Bank

A bank which establishes a letter of credit.

Opening price

The range of prices at which the first bids and offers are made or the first transactions are completed on an exchange.

Opening purchase

Creation of or increase in a long position in a given series of options.

Opening sale

Creation of or increase in a short position in a given series of options.

Opening transaction

Applies to derivative products. (1)Buy or sell transaction that creates a position out of a flat one (writing an option short or buying an option long). Antithesis of closing transaction. (2) First transaction of the day in a stock.

Operating Assets

Another term for working capital.

Operating cash flow

Earnings before depreciation minus taxes. Measures the cash generated from operations, not counting capital spending or working capital requirements.

Operating Committee

The Operating Committee (chaired by the Commerce Department) is the first step in resolving interagency disputes over the disposition of license applications for dual-use items not reviewed by one of the other interagency working groups. The other working groups include: (a) the Subgroup on Nuclear Export Coordination (SNEC), chaired by State for applications involving nuclear concerns; (b) the Missile Technology Export Control Group (MTEC), chaired by State for applications involving missile technology concerns; and (c) the "Shield," chaired by State for applications involving chemical or biological warfare concerns. These committees review applications and participate in the dispute resolution. Prior to any escalation to the Advisory Committee on Export Policy (ACEP), all applications must be reviewed by one of these working groups. See: Advisory Committee on Export Policy.

Operating cycle

The average time between the acquisition of materials or services and the final cash realization from that acquisition.

Operating Differential Subsidy

ODS is a payment which the U.S. government makes to vessels carrying the American flag to offset the difference in operating costs between U.S. and foreign carriers.

Operating expenses

The amount paid for asset maintenance or the cost of doing business. Earnings are distributed after operating expenses are deducted.

Operation Exodus

Operation Exodus is a U.S. Customs Service export enforcement program that was developed in 1981 to help stem the flow of the illegal export of U.S.-sourced arms and technology to the Soviet bloc and other prohibited destinations.

Operating exposure

Degree to which exchange rate changes, in combination with price changes, will alter a company's future operating cash flows.

Operating lease

Short-term, cancelable lease. A type of lease in which the contact period is shorter than the life of the equipment, and the lessor pays all maintenance and servicing costs.

Operating leverage

Fixed operating costs, which are characterized as leverage because they accentuate variations in profits.

Operating profit (or loss)

Revenue from a firm's regular activities less costs and expenses and before income deductions.

Operating profit margin

The ratio of operating profit to net sales.

Operating rate

The percentage of total production capacity of a company, industry, or country that is being used.

Operating ratio

A ratio that measures a firm's operating efficiency.

Operating in the red

Doing business while losing money.

Operating risk

The inherent or fundamental risk of a firm, without

regard to financial risk. The risk that is created by operating leverage. Also called business risk.

Operationally efficient market

Market in which investors can obtain transactions services that reflect the true costs associated with furnishing those services. Also called an internally efficient market.

Operations department

See: Back office.

Opinion shopping

Attempts by a corporation to attain reporting objectives by following questionable accounting principles, with the help of an auditor willing to sanction the practices. Prohibited by the SEC.

OPM

Stands for "other people's money," which refers to borrowed funds used to increase the return on invested capital.

Oporto

Portugal's derivatives exchange (Bolsa de Derivados do Oporto) trading futures on the ten-year government bond, Portuguese stock index, and three-month interbank deposit rate LISBOR (Lisbon Interbank Offered Rate).

Opportunity cost of capital

Expected return that is forgone by investing in a project rather than in comparable financial securities.

Opportunity costs

The difference in the actual performance of a particular investment and some other desired investment adjusted for fixed costs and execution costs. It often refers to the most valuable alternative that is given up.

Opportunity line

Slope of a graph representing portfolios achieved by combining different levels of borrowing and lending with a single risky portfolio. Sometimes called investment opportunity set.

Opportunity set

The possible expected return and standard deviation pairs of all portfolios that can be constructed from a given set of assets.

Optimal contract

The contract that balances the three types of agency costs (contracting, monitoring, and misbehavior) against one another to minimize the total cost.

Optimal portfolio

An efficient portfolio most preferred by an investor because its risk/reward characteristics approximate the investor's utility function. A portfolio that maximizes an investor's preferences with respect to return and risk.

Optimal redemption provision

Provision of a bond indenture that governs the issuer's ability to call the bonds for redemption prior to their scheduled maturity date.

Optimization approach to indexing

An approach to indexing that seeks to optimize some objective, such as to maximize the portfolio yield, to maximize convexity, or to maximize expected total returns.

Optimum capacity

The amount of manufacturing output that creates the lowest cost per unit.

Optimum Leverage Ratio

The borrowing level that maximizes the value of the firm. The cost of capital to the firm is minimized at that same level.

Option

Gives the buyer the right, but not the obligation, to buy or sell an asset at a set price on or before a given date. Investors, not companies, issue options. Buyers of call options bet that a stock will be worth more than the price set by the option (the strike price), plus the price they pay for the option itself. Buyers of put options bet that the stock's price will drop below the price set by the option. An option is part of a class of securities called derivatives, which means these securities derive their value from the worth of an underlying investment.

Option account

A brokerage account that is approved to hold option positions or trades.

Option-adjusted spread (OAS)

(1) The spread over an issuer's spot rate curve, developed as a measure of the yield spread that can be used to convert dollar differences between theoretical value and market prices. (2) The cost of the implied call embedded in an MBS, defined as additional basis-yield spread. When added to the base yield spread of an MBS without an operative call produces the option-adjusted spread.

Option agreement

A form that an options investor opening an option account fills out guarantees the investor will follow trading regulations and has the financial resources to settle possible losses.

Option cycle

The cycle of option expiration months. The most common cycles are: January, April, July, and October (JAJO); February, May, August, and November (FMAN); and March, June, September, and December (MJSD).

Option elasticity

The percentage increase in an option's value, given a 1 percentage point change in the value of the underlying security.

Option holder

A person who has an option that has not been exercised.

Option margin

The margin requirement for options described in Regulation T and in brokers' individual policies.

Option mutual fund

A mutual fund that buys and sells options for aggressive or conservative investment.

Option not to deliver

In the mortgage pipeline, an additional hedge placed in tandem with the forward or substitute sale.

Option premium

The option price.

Option price

Also called the option premium; the price the buyer of the options contract pays for the right to buy or sell a security at a specified price in the future.

Option Pricing Curve

A graphical representation of the projected price of an option at a fixed point in time. It reflects the amount of time value premium in the option for various stock prices, as well. The curve is generated by using a mathematical model. The delta (or hedge ratio) is the slope of a tangent line to the curve at a fixed stock price. See also Delta and Hedge Ratio

Option seller

Also called the option writer; the party who grants a right to trade a security at a given price in the future.

Option series

A group of options on the same underlying security with the same exercise price and maturity month.

Option spread

The trading of options of the same class at the same time in order to profit from changes in the size of the spread between different options.

Option writer

See: Option seller.

Optional dividend

A dividends that the shareholder can elect to receive either in cash or in stock.

Optional payment bond

A bond whose principal and/or interest may be paid in foreign or domestic currency at the discretion of the bondholder.

Options Clearing Corporation (OCC)

Applies to derivative products. Financial institution that is the actual issuer and guarantor of all listed option contracts.

Options contract

A contract that, in exchange for the option price, gives the option buyer the right, but not the obligation, to buy (or sell) a financial asset at the exercise price from (or to) the option seller within a specified time period, or on a specified date (expiration date).

Options contract multiple

A constant, set at $100, that when multiplied by the cash index value gives the dollar value of the stock index underlying an option. That is the dollar value of the underlying stock index = Cash index value x $100 (the options contract multiple).

Options on physicals

Interest rate options written on fixed income securities, as opposed to those written on interest rate futures contracts.

Oral contract

A contract not recorded on paper or on computer, buy made vocally which is usually enforceable.

Or better

Used in the context of general equities. Indication on the order ticket of a limit order to buy or sell securities at a price better than the specified limit price if a better price can be obtained. Does not imply a not-held order, but rather puts more emphasis on executing at the limit if available.

Order

Instruction to a broker/dealer to buy, sell, deliver, or receive securities or commodities that commits the issuer of the "order" to the terms specified. See: indication, inquiry, bid wanted, offer wanted.

Order Bill Of Lading

A negotiable bill of lading made out to the order of the shipper.

Order Book Official

The exchange employee in charge of keeping a book of public limit orders on exchanges utilizing the "marker-maker" system, as opposed to the "specialist system", of executing orders. See also Market-Marker and Specialist.

Order imbalance

Orders of one kind for a stock not offset by the opposite orders, which causes a wide spread between bid and offer prices.

Ordering Costs

Costs that occur when an order is placed regardless of the size of the order.

Orderly Marketing Agreement

A bilateral agreement between governments by which one government limits exports to the other. Similar to a voluntary export restriction agreement or a voluntary restraint agreement. Used to address injury to a domestic industry.

Contracts negotiated between two or more governments, in which the exporting nation undertakes to ensure that international trade in specified "sensitive" products will not disrupt, threaten, or impair competitive industries or workers in importing countries.

Order Parameter

In a nonlinoar dynamic system, a variable-acting link a macrovariable, or combination of variables-that summarizes the individual variables that can affect a system. In a controlled experiment, involving thermal convection, for example, temperature can be a control parameter; in a large complex system, temperature can be an order parameter, because it summarizes the effect of the sun, air pressure, and other atmospheric variables. See: Control parameter.

Order room

The brokerage firm department receives and processes all orders to buy and sell securities.

Order splitting

Breaking up orders so that they can be processed as small orders for execution by SOES. Prohibited by NASD.

Order ticket

A form detailing an order instruction that a customer gives an account executive.

Ordinary income

The income derived from the regular operating activities of a firm or individual.

Ordinary interest

Interest based on a 360-day year instead of a 365-day year, resulting in what can be a significant difference.

Ordinary shares

Apples mainly to international equities. Shares of non-U.S. companies traded in their individual home markets. Usually cannot be delivered in the US See: ADR.

Organisation Mondiale de la Propriete Intellectuelle

See: World Intellectual Property Organization.

Organisation pour la Mise en Valeur du Fleuve Gambie

See: Gambia River Basin Development Organization.

Organisation pour la Mise en Valeur du Fleuve Sénégal

See: Organization for the Development of the Senegal River.

Organization chart

A chart showing the hierarchical interrelationships of positions within an organization.

Organizacion de los Estados Americanos

See: Organization of American States.

Organization for the Development of the Senegal River

The Organization (French: Organisation pour la Mise en Valeur du Fleuve S,n,gal, OMVS) promotes hydroelectric, irrigation and navigation use of the Senegal river. The organization was established in March 1972; headquarters are in Dakar, Senegal. Members include: Guinea-Bissau, Mali, Mauritania, and Senegal.

Organization for Economic Cooperation and Development

OECD provides a forum for discussion of common economic and social issues facing the United States, Canada, Western Europe, Japan, Australia, and New Zealand. OECD was founded in September 1960 as successor to the Organization for European Economic Cooperation (OEEC) which had administered European participation in the Marshall Plan. OECD seeks "to achieve the highest sustainable economic growth and employment and a rising standard of living in member countries while maintaining financial stability and thus contribute to the world economy." Members include: Australia, Austria, Belgium, Canada, Denmark, Finland, France, Germany, Greece, Iceland, Ireland, Italy, Luxembourg, Japan, the Netherlands, New Zealand, Norway, Portugal, Spain, Sweden, Switzerland, Turkey, the United Kingdom, and the United States. OECD headquarters are in Paris, France. See: Arrangement on Guidelines for Officially Supported Export Credits.

Organization of African Trade Union Unity

OATUU is recognized as the sole representative of African organized labor by the Organization of African Unity (OAU) and the International Labor Organization (ILO). OATUU is formally non-aligned and independent of all international trade union organizations, but maintains relations with trade unions worldwide. OATUU headquarters are in Accra, Ghana.

Organization of African Unity

The OAU, founded in May 1963 with 32 African countries, has since grown beyond 5 members. The Organization aims to further African unity and solidarity, to coordinate political, economic, cultural, scientific, and defense policies; and to eliminate colonialism in Africa. Members include: Algeria, Angola, Benin, Botswana, Burkina Faso, Burundi, Cameroon, Cape Verde, Central Africa Republic, Chad, Comoros, Congo, Cote d'Ivoire, Egypt, Equatorial Guinea, Ethopia, Gabon, the Gambia, Ghana, Guinea, Guinea-Bissau, Kenya, Lesotho, Liberia, Libya, Madagascar, Malawi, Mali, Mauritania, Mauritius, Morocco, Mozambique, Namibia, Niger, Nigeria, Rwanda, Sao Tome and Principe, Senegal, Seychelles, Sierra Leone, Somalia, Sudan, Swaziland, Tanzania, Togo, Tunisia, Uganda, Zaire, Zambia, Zimbabwe. OAU headquarters are in Addis Ababa, Ethiopia.

Organization of American States

The OAS (Spanish: Organizacion de los Estados Americanos, OEA), or the Pan American Union, is a regional organization created in Bogota, Colombia in April 1948 (entered into force in December 1951) which promotes Latin American economic and social development. Members include the United States, Mexico, and most Central American, South American, and Caribbean nations. Members include: Antigua and Barbuda, Argentina, the Bahamas, Barbados, Belize, Bolivia, Brazil, Canada, Chile, Colombia, Costa Rica, Cuba (participation suspended), Dominica, Dominican Republic, Ecuador, El Salvador, Grenada, Guatemala, Guyana, Haiti, Honduras, Jamaica, Mexico, Nicaragua, Panama, Paraguay, Peru, St. Christopher-Nevis, St. Lucia, St. Vincent and the Grenadines, Suriname, Trinidad and Tobago, the United States, Uruguay, and Venezuela. The U.S. accredits an Ambassador to the OAS. The OAS secretariat is located in Washington, D.C. See: Sistema de Informacion al Comercio Exterior.

Organization of Arab Petroleum Exporting Countries

OAPEC was created in 1968; members include: Algeria, Bahrain, Egypt, Iraq, Kuwait, Libya, Qatar, Saudi Arabia, Syria, and the United Arab Emirates. Headquarters are in Cairo, Egypt. See: Organization of Petroleum Exporting Countries.

Organization of Eastern Caribbean States

OECS was intended to promote territorial integrity; changing focus includes the recent founding of an export development agency. The Organization was established in 1981; headquarters are in St. Lucia. Members include: Antigua and Barbuda, Dominica, Grenada, Montserrat, Saint Christopher and Nevis, Saint Lucia, Saint Vincent, and the Grenadines.

Organization of the Islamic Conference

The OIC, established in May 1971, promotes cooperation in cultural, economics, scientific and social areas among Islamic nations. Headquarters are located in Jeddah, Saudi Ar abia. About half the ICO members are also members of the Organization of African Unity. OIC members include: Afghanistan, Algeria, Bahrain, Bangladesh, Benin, Brunei, Burkina Faso, Cameroon, Chad, Comoros, Cyprus, Djibouti, Egypt, Gabon, the Gambia, Guinea, Guinea-Bissau, Indonesia, Iran, Iraq, Jordan, Kuwait, Lebanon, Libya, Malaysia, Maldives, Mali, Mauritania, Morocco, Niger, Nigeria, Oman, Pakistan, Qatar, Saudi Arabia, Senegal, Sierra Leone, Somalia, Sudan, Syria, Tunisia, Turkey, Uganda, the United Arab Emirates, and Yemen.

Organization of Petroleum Exporting Countries (OPEC)

An association of 12 oil-exporting countries: Algeria, Gabon, Indonesia, Iran, Iraq, Kuwait, Libya, Nigeria, Qatar, SAudi Arabia, the United Arab Emirates, and Venezuela. Formed in 1960, its major purpose is to coordinate the petroleum production and pricing policies of its members.

Organised exchange

A securities marketplace where purchasers and sellers regularly gather to trade securities according to the formal rules adopted by the exchange.

Orientation Visits

See: Trade and Development Agency.

Original face value

The principal amount of a mortgage as of its issue date.

Original issue discount debt (OID debt)

Debt that is initially offered at a price below par.

Original Issue Discount securities (OIDS)

Bonds on which the coupon rate is set considerably below the yield to maturity at the time of issuance so that the bonds are issued at a discount from a par value.

Original margin

The margin needed to cover a specific new position. Related: Margin, security deposit (initial).

Original maturity

Maturity at issue. For example, a five-year note has an original maturity of five years; one year later it has a maturity of four years.

Origination

The making of mortgage loans.

Organization for Economic Cooperation and Development (OECD)

An organization of industrialized countries formed to promote the economic health of its members and to contribute to worldwide development.

Originator

A bank, savings and loan, or mortgage banker that initially made a mortgage loan that is part of a pool. Also, an investment bank that has worked with the issuer of a new securities offering from the beginning and is usually appointed manager of the underwriting syndicate.

Orphan stock

A stock that is ignored by research analysts and as a result may be trading at low price earnings ratios.

Osaka Securities Exchange (OSE)

Established after World War II, one of the three major securities markets in Japan.

Oslo Stock Exchange

An exchange founded in 1819 and trading stocks, bonds, and stock options that is considered the options market of Norway.

OTC

See: Over-the-counter.

OTC Bulletin Board

An electronic quotation listing of the bid and asked prices of OTC stocks that do not meet the requirements to be listed on the NASDAQ stock-listing system.

OTC margin stock

Shares traded over-the-counter that can be used as margin securities under Regulation T.

Other capital

In the balance of payments, other capital is a residual category that groups all the capital transactions that have not been included in direct investment, portfolio investment, and reserves categories. It is divided into long-term capital and short-term capital and, because of its residual status, can differ from country to country. Generally speaking, other long-term capital includes most nonnegotiable instruments of a year or more, like bank loans and mortgages. Other short-term capital includes financial assets that can be liquidated in less than a year such as currency, deposits, and bills.

Other current assets

Value of noncash assets, including prepaid expenses and accounts receivable, due within one year.

Other income

Income from activities that are not undertaken in the ordinary course of a firm's business.

Other long-term liabilities

Value of leases, future employee benefits, deferred taxes, and other obligations not requiring interest payments that must be paid over a period of more than one year.

Other sources

Amount of funds generated during the period from operations by sources other than depreciation or deferred taxes. Part of free cash flow calculation.

OTM

See: Out of the money.

Out

Used in the context of general equities. (1) No longer obligated to an order, as it has already been canceled: (2) advertised on Autex.

Out-of-favor industry or stock

An unpopular industry or stock that usually has a low price-earnings ratio.

Out of line

A stock price that is too high or too low in comparison with similar-quality stocks in the same industry, according to its price/earnings ratio.

Out-of-the-money option

A call option is out of the money if the strike price is greater than the market price of the underlying security. That is, you have the right to purchase a security at a price higher than the market price, which is not valuable. A put option is out of the money if the strike price is lower than the market price of the underlying security.

Out of the name

Used in the context of general equities. To no longer have an active trading profile/ position in the stock.

Out of print

Not open on the print. See: Clean.

Out there

Used in the context of general equities. Indication gained from their trading and inquiry activity that buyers and/or (more often) sellers are in the market and should be found to get their order. "Feels like IBM is 'out there'."

Out with

Used in the context of general equities. Showing of an inquiry to another broker by a customer ("he's out with....").

Outlays

Payments on obligations in the form of cash, checks, the issuance of bonds or notes, or the maturing of interest coupons.

Outright quote

A quote in which all the digits of the bid and offer prices are quoted. See: Points quote.

Outright rate

Actual forward rate expressed in dollars per currency unit, or vice versa.

Outside director

A director of a company who is not an employee of that company and brings in outside experience to help make board decisions.

Outside market

Used in the context of general equities. Outside the inside market (above the lowest offering and below the highest bid).

Outside of you

Used for listed equity securities. Another order bidding for or offering stock at the same price that the trader has put on the floor himself, represented by another broker in the trading crowd. These orders may have different price limits (possible top or low on floor mentioned to floor broker but not announced in the crowd). See: Matching orders.

Outsourcing

Purchasing a significant percentage of intermediate components from outside suppliers.

Outstanding

Used in the context of general equities. Stock held by shareholders (verses the company's treasury stock).

Outstanding Dividends

Dividend checks which have been mailed to shareholders of record but not yet cashed. Funds are held until the check is paid, reissued or escheated to the state as abandoned property.

Outstanding share capital

Issued share capital less the par value of shares that are held as the company's treasury stock.

Outstanding shares

Shares that are currently owned by investors.

Overage

Apples mainly to convertible securities. Difference between how much common stock one party must sell and the other wishes to buy for the same amount of convertible in a swap.

Overall FTC limitation

A limitation on the FTC equal to foreign source income times US tax on worldwide income divided by worldwide income.

Overall market price coverage

Total assets less intangibles divided by the total of the market value of the security issue and the book value of liabilities and issues having a prior claim. This is used to determine how much of the market value of a certain class of securities would be covered in liquidation.

Overbought

Used in the context of general equities. Technically too high in price, and hence a technical correction is expected. See: Heavy. Antithesis of oversold.

Overbought-oversold indicator

An indicator that attempts to define when prices have moved too far and too fast in either direction and thus are vulnerable to reaction.

Overcapitalization

Said to occur when a firm cannot service its debt even though its debt/equity ratio is not excessive.

Overdraft

Provision of instant credit by a lending institution.

Overdraft checking account

A checking account associated with a line of credit that allows a person to write checks for more that the actual balance in the account, with a finance charge on the overdraft.

Overfunded pension plan

A pension plan that has a positive surplus (i.e., assets exceed liabilities).

Overhang

Used in the context of general equities. Sizable block of securities or commodities contracts that, if released on the market, would put downward pressure on prices; prohibits buying activity that would otherwise translate into upward price movement. Examples include shares held in a dealer's inventory, a large institutional holding, a secondary distribution still in registration, and a large commodity position about to be liquidated.

Overhanging Bond

A convertible bond issue that investors do not convert into common stock because the stock has not appreciated in value.

Overhead

The expenses of a business that are not attributable directly) the production or sale of goods.

Overheating

An economy that is growing very quickly, with the risk of high inflation.

Overinvestment

In corporate finance, this refers to managers not acting in the best interests of the shareholders and investing too much (potentially in negative net present value projects).

Overissue

An excess of issued shares over authorized shares.

Overlap the market

Used in the context of general equities. Create a crossed market by expressing a willingness to sell on the bid side of the market and buy on the offer side.

Overlapping debt

The portion of debt of political subdivisions or neighboring special districts that a municipality is responsible for.

Overlay strategy

A strategy of using futures for asset allocation by pension sponsors to avoid disrupting the activities of money managers.

Overnight delivery risk

A risk brought about because differences in time zones between settlement centers require that payment or delivery on one side of a transaction be made without knowing until the next day whether the funds have been received in an account on the other side. Particularly apparent when delivery takes place in Europe for payment in dollars in New York.

Overnight position

A broker-dealer's position in a security at the end of a trading day.

Overnight repo

A repurchase agreement with a term of one day.

Overperform

To appreciate at a rate faster than appreciation of the overall market.

Overreaching

Used in the context of general equities. Creating artificial volume in astock through activity not generated by normal/natural buyers and sellers in the market.

Overreaction hypothesis

The supposition that investors overreact to unanticipated news, resulting in exaggerated movements in stock prices followed by corrections.

Overseas Business Reports

These are marketing studies of America's major trading partners which provide updated export and economic outlooks, industrial trends, trade regulations, distribution and sales channels, transportation, and credit situation in individual countries.

Overseas Economic Cooperation Fund

The OECF, a Japanese government development financial institution, provides developing countries and areas with grants and long-term, low-interest loans. As a result of difficulty in distinguishing between the Fund and the Export-Import Bank of Japan, a 1975 reorganization put OECF in charge of all direct loans to be made as official development assistance (ODA) with the grant element of 25 percent of more. The Fund was created in 1961; headquarters are in Tokyo, Japan. See: Export-Import Bank of Japan; Japan International Cooperation Agency.

Overseas investment

(Also one of the means of implementing Offsets - see under Offsets). Investment arising from the offset agreement, taking the form of capital invested to establish or expand a subsidiary or joint venture in tho foreign country.

Overseas Private Investment Corporation

OPIC is a government corporation which assists U.S. private investments in less developed nations by providing direct loans and loan guarantees, insuring against a broad range of political risks, and providing a variety of investor services. The overseas investments may include distributorships owned by U.S. manufacturers which are consistent with the economic interests of both the United States and the developing country involved. OPIC was formed as a part of the Agency for International Development in 1961 and became an independent agency 10 years later. Telephone: 800-424-6742.

Overshooting

The tendency of a pool of MBS to reflect an especially high rate of prepayments the first time it crosses the threshold for refinancing, specially if two or more years have passed since the date of issue without the weighted average coupon of the pool crossing the refinancing threshold.

Oversold

Used in the context of general equities. Technically too low in price, and hence a technical correction is expected. Antithesis of overbought.

Oversubscribed issue

Investors are not able to buy all the shares or bonds they want, so underwriters must allocate the shares or bonds among investors. This occurs when a new issue is underpriced or in great demand because of growth prospects.

Oversubscription privilege

In a rights issue, arrangement by which shareholders are given the right to apply for any shares that are not taken up.

over-the-counter (OTC)

A decentralized market (as opposed to an exchange market) where geographically dispersed dealers are linked by telephones and computer screens. The market is for securities not listed on a stock or bond exchange. The NASDAQ market is an OTC market for US stocks. Antithesis of listed.

Over-the-Counter Option

An option traded off-exchange, as opposed to a listed stock option. The OTC option has a direct link between buyer and seller, has no secondary market, and has no standardization of striking prices and expiration dates. See also Secondary Market.

Overtrading

Excessive broker trading in a discretionary account. Underwriters persuade brokerage clients to purchase some part of a new issue in return for the purchase by the underwriter of other securities from the clients at a premium. This premium is offset by the underwriting spread.

Overvalued

A stock price that is seen as too high according to the company's price-earnings ratio, expected earnings, or financial condition.

Overweight

Usually refers to recommendation that leads an investor to increase their investment in a particular security or asset class. The increase is usually with respect to a benchmark. Suppose that U.S. equities compose 40% of the benchmark portfolio. If one thinks the U.S. will outperform, the investor may increase the exposure to U.S. equity to more than 40%.

Overwithholding

Deducting and paying too much tax that may be refunded to the taxpayer or applied against the next period's obligation.

Overwriting

A speculative options trategy that involves selling call or put options on stocks that are believed to be overpriced or underpriced; the options are expected not to be exercised.

Own foreign offices

US reporting institutions' parent organizations, branches, and/or majority owned subsidiaries located outside the United States.

Owner's equity

Paid-in capital plus donated capital plus retained earnings less liabilities.

Ownership-specific advantages

Property rights or intangible assets, including patents, trademarks, organizational and marketing expertise, production technology, and management and general organizational abilities, that form the basis for a company's advantage over other firms.

P

P

Fifth letter of Nasdaq stock symbol specifying issue is the company's first class of preferred shares.

P2P

Business slang, usually used in reference to startups or internet startup,refers to "path to profitability".

PA

The two-character ISO 3166 country Code for PANAMA.

PAB

The ISO 4217 currency code for the Panama Balboa.

PAC

(1) See: Planned amortization class. (2) See: Preauthorized checks.

PAC Bond

Stands for Planned Amortization Class bond. A tranche class offered by some CMOs that has a sinking fund schedule and an ability to make principal payments that are not subordinated to other classes.

Pacific Basin Economic Council

The PBEC is a private sector group organized in 1967 to promote regional trade and investment. PBEC currently includes about 1,000 corporations and 14 national membership committees.

Pacific Economic Cooperation Council

The PECC is a nongovernmental organization founded in 1980 and aimed at promoting cooperation in the Asia-Pacific region. Members are drawn from 20 countries and territories: Australia, Brunei, Canada, Chile, China, Hong Kong, Indonesia, Japan, Korea, Malaysia, Mexico, New Zealand, the Pacific Islands, Peru, the Philippines, Russia, Singapore, Taiwan, Thailand, and the United States.

Pacific Rim

The Pacific Rim, referring to countries and economies bordering the Pacific ocean, is an informal, flexible term which generally has been regarded as a reference to East Asia, Canada, and the United States. At a minimum, the Pacific Rim includes Canada, Japan, the People's Republic of China, Taiwan, and the United States. It may also include Australia, Brunei, Cambodia, Hong Kong/Macau, Indonesia, Laos, North Korea, South Korea, Malaysia, New Zealand, the Pacific Islands, the Philippines, Russia (or the Commonwealth of Independent States), Singapore, Thailand, and Vietnam. As an evolutionary term, usage sometimes includes Mexico, the countries of Central America, and the Pacific coast countries of South America.

Pacific Stock Exchange

Used for listed equity securities. Regional exchange located in Los Angeles and San Francisco; only U.S. exchange open between 4:00 and 4:30.

Packing List

A list which shows number and kinds of packages being shipped, totals of gross, legal, and net weights of the packages, and marks and numbers on the packages. The list may be requested by an importer or may be required by an importing country to facilitate the clearance of goods through customs.

Pac-Man strategy

Takeover defense strategy in which the prospective acquiree retaliates against the acquirer's tender offer by launching its own tender offer for the other firm.

Package mortgage

A mortgage on a house and property in the house.

PAD

See: Preauthorized electronic debits.

Paid-in capital

Capital received from investors in exchange for stock, but not stock from capital generated from earnings or donated. This account includes capital stock and contributions of stockholders credited to accounts other than capital stock. It would also include surplus resulting from recapitalization.

Paid in surplus

See: Paid-in capital.

Paid up

When all payments that are due have been made.

Paid-up policy

A life insurance policy in which all premiums that are due have been paid.

Painting the tape

Illegal practice by traders who manipulate the market by buying and selling a security to create the illusion of high trading activity and to attract other traders who may push up the price.

Paired off

Used for listed equity securities. Matched buy and sell market orders, usually pertaining to the pre-opening market picture in a stock, or MOC orders (especially relating to futures/options expirations).

Paired shares

Stock of two companies under the same management that are sold as one unit with one certificate.

Pairoff

A buyback to offset and effectively liquidate a prior sale of securities.

Pallet

A low portable platform, usually wooden, on which cargo is stacked for storage or transportation; a skid.

Pan American Standards Commission

See: Comision Panaamericana de Normas Tecnicas.

Pan American Union

See: Organization of American States.

Panic buying or selling

Rapid trading of stocks or bonds in high volume in anticipation of sharply rising or falling prices, usually after unexpected news is released.

Paper

Money market instruments, commercial paper, and other.

Paper dealer

A brokerage firm that buys and sells commercial paper to make a profit.

Paper gain (loss)

Unrealized capital gain (loss) on securities held in a portfolio based on a comparison of current market price to original cost.

Par

Equal to the nominal or face value of a security. A bond selling at par is worth an amount equivalent to its original issue value or its value upon redemption at maturity-typically $1000/bond. See: Discount, premium.

Par bond

A bond trading at its face value.

Par value

Also called the maturity value or face value; the amount that an issuer agrees to pay at the maturity date.

Par value of currency

The official exchange rate between two countries' currencies.

Parallel bonds

Fixed income instruments denominated in the respective currencies of the countries where they are placed.

Parallel loan

A process whereby two companies in different countries borrow each other's currency for a specific period of time, and repay the other's currency at an agreed maturity for the purpose of reducing foreign exchange risk. Also referred to as back-to-back loans.

Parallel shift in the yield curve

A shift in economic conditions in which the change in the interest rate on all maturities is the same number of basis points. In other words, if the three month T-bill increases 100 basis points (one %), then the 6-month, 1-year, 5-year, 10-year, 20-year, and 30-year rates all increase by 100 basis points as well. Related: Non-parallel shift in the yield curve.

Parameter

A model is a combination of variables, such as GDP growth, and coefficients which multiply these variables. The coefficients are often estimated from the data. The coefficients are called parameters.

Parent company

A company that controls subsidiaries through its ownership of voting stock, as well as runs its own business.

Paris Bourse

National stock market of France.

Paris Interbank Offer Rate (PIBOR)

The deposit rate on interbank transactions in the Eurocurrency market quoted in Paris.

Parity

For convertibles, level at which a convertible security's market price equals the aggregate value of the underlying common stock; value/worth of the convertible bond considered only as an equity instrument (Conversion ratio times common price). See: Conversion value. For international parity, US$ price of a foreign stock's last sale in an overseas market (Local currency stock price times forex rate times ADR ratio). For listed parity, condition whereby no party has floor priority, and matching thus occurs. For options parity, dollar amount by which an option is in the money. See: Intrinsic value.

Parity value

Related: Conversion value.

Parcel Post Receipt

The postal authorities' signed acknowledgment of delivery to receiver of a shipment made by parcel post.

Parking

Putting money into safe investments such as money market investments while deciding where to invest the money.

Parking violation

Often used in risk arbitrage. Illegal holding of stock by a third party, or the financing of such a stock, in which the third party's sole reason for holding the stock is to conceal ownership or control of a raider, thus sidestepping the Williams Act requirements of 5% holding limits. See: Rule 13d.

Paris Club

The Paris Club has become a popular designation for meetings between representatives of a developing country that wishes to renegotiate its "official" debt (normally excluding debts owed by and to the private sector without official guarantees) and representatives of the relevant creditor governments and international institutions. These meetings usually occur at the request of a debtor country that wishes to consolidate all or part of its debt service payments falling due over a specified period. Meetings are traditionally chaired by a senior official of the French Treasury Department. Comparable meetings occasionally take place in London and in New York for countries that wish to renegotiate repayment terms for their debts to private banks. These meetings are sometimes called "creditor clubs." See: London Club.

Paris Convention

The Paris Convention for the Protection of Industrial Property, first adopted in 1883, is the major international agreement providing basic rights for protecting industrial property. It covers patents, industrial designs, service marks, trade names, indications of source, and unfair competition. The U.S. ratified this treaty in May of 1887. The treaty provides two fundamental rights:

— The principle of national treatment provides that nationals of any signatory nation shall enjoy in all other countries of the union the advantages that each nation's laws grant to its own nationals.

— The right of priority enables any resident or national of a member country to, first, file a patent application in any member country and, thereafter, to file a patent application for the same invention in any of the other member countries within 12 months of the original filing and receive benefit of the original filing date. The resident or national of a member country also can claim the filing date of a trademark application or industrial design filed in another member country within six months of the filing date in his or her own country or country of residence.

Part B prospectus

See: Statement of Additional Information.

Partial

Used in the context of general equities. Trade whose size is only part of the total customer indication/order, usually made to avoid a compromise in price and also to get some business instead of losing the customers inquiry/order to a competitor.

Partial compensation

Incomplete payment for the delivery of goods to one party by buying back a certain amount of product from the same party.

Partial Vote

When only a portion of the total shares in an account is voted. For example, a broker has 1,000 shares and sends out a card to each of four shareholder clients. If only three of the four client cards are returned to the broker, the broker will submit only 3/4ths(750 shares) of the total 1,000 shares to vote. If the fourth card arrives later, an additional vote can be counted.

"Participate but do not initiate"

Used for listed equity securities. "Participate in the side of the market indicated by the order, but do not initiate the interest that causes the trade to take place." This kind of order can cause one to "miss stock" because the broker of investor is at the mercy of the player who does initiate the trade. See: Market order go along, percentage order.

Participating buyer/seller

Used for listed equity securities. (1) Customer willing to buy/sell in line with market. (2) Buyer/seller who goes along with another buyer/seller in a percentage order.

Participating convertible preferred stock

Preferred stock that can be converted into common stock at the option of the holder. In contrast, to the usual preferred stock, the value of the preferred stock is refunded to the holder. That is, one gets conversion plus the value of the stock.

Participating dividend

Dividend received from ownership of participating preferred stock.

Participating fees

The portion of total fees in a syndicated credit that go to the participating banks.

Participating GIC

A guaranteed investment contract whose policyholder is not guaranteed a crediting rate, but instead receives a return based on the actual experience of the portfolio managed by the life insurance company.

Participating life insurance policies

Life insurance that pays dividends to policyholders depending on the company's success as provided by few claims and profitable underwritings and investments.

Participating preferred stock

Preferred stock that provides the holder with a specified dividend plus the right to additional earnings under specified conditions.

Participation certificates (PC)

Used in the context of general equities. Investments representing an interest in a pool of funds or in other instruments, such as foreign securities, that allow participation in the rise or fall of a security or group of securities.

Participation loan

A large loan made by a group of lenders, that enables a borrower to obtain financing above the legal lending limit of an individual lender.

Partner

Business associate who shares equity in a firm.

Partnership

Shared ownership among two or more individuals, some of whom may, but do not necessarily, have limited liability with respect to obligations of the group. See: General partnership, limited partnership, and master limited partnership.

Partnership agreement

A written agreement among partners detailing the terms and conditions of participation in a business ownership arrangement.

Party in interest

An ERISA-specified individual—such as an administrator, officer, fiduciary, trustee, custodian, or counsel—who is prohibited from making certain transactions involving a retirement plan. A trustee, for example, would be prohibited from using an IRA as collateral for a loan.

Passive

Income or loss from business activities in which a person does not materially participate, such as a limited partnership.

Passive Activity Loss (PAL)

A loss incurred in participating in passive investing.

Passive bond

A bond without any interest yield.

Passive income

Income (such as investment income) that does not come from active participation in a business. Specified by the U.S. tax code.

Passive Income Generator (PIG)

An investment that favors passive income, such as an income-oriented real estate limited partnership.

Passive investing

Putting money into a profitable business opportunity that is deemed passive by the IRS and thus benefits from tax deductions.

Passive investment management

Buying a well diversified portfolio to represent a broad-based market index without attempting to search out mispriced securities.

Passive investment strategy

See: Passive investment management.

Passive management

See: Indexing.

Passive portfolio

A market index portfolio.

Passive portfolio strategy

A strategy that involves minimal expectational input, and instead relies on diversification to match the performance of some market index. A passive strategy assumes that the marketplace will reflect all available information in the price paid for securities, and therefore, does not attempt to find mispriced securities. Related: Active portfolio strategy.

Pass the book

The process of transferring responsibility for a brokerage firm's trading account from one office to another around the world in order to benefit from trading 24 hours a day.

Pass-Through

Pass-through operations (also called transshipments) involve a foreign country's use of one country in a trade bloc as a means of gaining preferential treatment from other countries in the bloc. See: Transshipment.

Pass-through coupon rate

The interest rate paid on a securitized pool of assets, which is less than the rate paid on the underlying loans by an amount equal to the servicing and guaranteeing fees.

Pass-through rate

The net interest rate passed through to investors after deducting servicing, management, and guarantee fees from the gross mortgage coupon.

Pass-through securities

A pool of fixed income securities backed by a package of assets (i.e., mortgages) where the holder receives the principal and interest payments. Related: Mortgage pass-through security

Patent

The exclusive right to use documented intellectual property in producing or selling a particular product or using a process for a designated period of time.

Patent Cooperation Treaty

The Patent Cooperation Treaty, PCT, is a worldwide convention, open to any Paris Convention country. The PCT entered into force in 1978. Unlike the Paris Convention, which addresses substantive intellectual property rights, the PCT addresses procedural requirements, aiming to simplify the filing, searching, and publication of international patent applications.

Path-dependent option

An option whose value depends on the sequence of prices of the underlying asset rather than just the final price of the asset.

Pattern

A technical chart formation used to make market predictions by following the price movements of securities.

Pay-as-you-go basis

A method of paying income tax in which the employer deducts a portion of an employee's monthly salary to remit to the IRS.

Pay-to-play

Attempts by municipal bond underwriting businesses to gain influence with political officials who decide which underwriters are awarded the municipality's business.

Pay-up

The loss of cash resulting from a swap into higher-priced bonds or the need/willingness of a bank or other borrower to pay a higher rate of interest to get funds. Used in the context of general equities. (1) When an investor who wants to buy a stock at a particular price hesitates and the stock begins to rise; instead of letting the stock go, he "pays up" to buy the shares at the higher prevailing price. (2) Buy shares in a high-quality company at what is felt to be a high, but supportable, price due to its quality.

Payable through drafts

A method of making payment that is used to maintain control over payments made on behalf of the firm by personnel in noncentral locations. The payer's bank delivers the payable through draft to the payer, which must approve it and return it to the bank before payment can be received.

Payable date

The date when dividends or capital gains are paid to shareholders or reinvested in additional shares.

Payables

Related: Accounts payable.

Payback

The length of time it takes to recover the initial cost of a project, without regard to the time value of money.

Pay-down

In a Treasury refunding, the amount by which the par value of the securities maturing exceeds that of those sold. In the context of general equities, paying a lower price in an accumulation of stock. Antithesis of pay-up.

Payee

A person receiving payment through any form of money transfer method.

Payer

The person making a payment to a payee.

Paying agent

An agent who makes principal and interest payments to bondholders on behalf of the issuer.

Payment date

The date on which shareholders of record will be sent a check for the declared dividend.

Payment float

Company-written checks that have not yet cleared.

Payment-in-kind (PIK) bond

A bond that gives the issuer an option (during an initial period) either to make coupon payments in cash or in the form of additional bonds.

Payments netting

Reducing fund transfers between affiliates to only a netted amount. Netting can occur on a bilateral basis (between pairs of affiliates), or on a multi-lateral basis (taking all affiliates together).

Payments pattern

Describes the collection pattern of receivables. The pattern might describe the probability that a 72-day-old account will still be unpaid when it is 73 days-old.

Payments System

Collective term for mechanisms (both paper-backed and electronic) for moving funds, payments and money among financial institutions throughout the nation. The Federal Reserve plays a major role in the nation's payments system through distribution of currency and coin, processing of checks, electronic transfer of funds and the operation of automated clearinghouses that transfer funds electronically among depository intitutions; various private organizations also perform payments system functions.

Payoff diagram

In option pricing, a graph of the value of the option position at expiration as a function of the underlying asset price.

Payoff profile

The slope of a line graphed according to the value of an underlying asset on the x-axis and the value of a position taken to hedge against risk exposure on the y-axis. Also used with changes in value. See: Risk profile.

Payout period

The time period during which withdrawals from a retirement account or annuity are paid.

Payout ratio

Generally, the proportion of earnings paid out to the common stockholders as cash dividends. Morespecifically, the firm's cash dividend divided by the firm's earnings in the same reporting period.

PBGC

See: Pension Benefit Guaranty Corporation.

PC

See: Participation certificates.

P-coast

Refers to west coast listed equity securities. See: Pacific Stock Exchange.

PE

The two-character ISO 3166 country code for PERU.

P/E

See: Price/earnings ratio.

Peak

The high point at the end of an economic expansion until the start of a contraction.

Pecking-order view (of capital structure)

The argument that external financing transactions costs, especially those associated with the problem of adverse selection, create a dynamic environment in which firms have a preference, or pecking-order of preferred sources of financing, when all else is equal. Internally generated funds are the most preferred, followed by new debt, and debt-equity hybrids. Finally, new equity is at the least preferred source.

P/E effect

That portfolios with low P/E stocks exhibit higher average risk-adjusted returns than those with high P/E stocks. Related: Value manager.

PEFCO

Private Export Funding Corporation. A corporation that lends to foreign buyers to finance exports from the United States

Pegged exchange rate

Exchange rate whose value is pegged to another currency's value or to a unit of account.

Pegging

Making transactions in a security, currency, or commodity in order to stabilize or target its value through market intervention.

PEG Ratio

See: Prospective earnings growth ratio.

PEN

The ISO 4217 currency code for the Peruvian Nuevo Sol.

Penalty Clause

Clause in a countertrade contract that specifies sanctions against one or both signatories of the contract in the event of nonperformance on contractual obligations.

Penalty tax

A federal tax that can be applied if a plan holder does not meet certain requirements when making withdrawals from a tax-advantaged retirement plan (for instance, if the plan holder has not reached age 59-1/2). This penalty tax is owed in addition to any income taxes due.

Pennant

A chart pattern resembling a pointed flag, with the point facing to the right, which shows a diminishing variance of price.

Penny stock

Used in the context of general equities. Stock that typically sells for less than $1 a share, although it may rise to as much as $10/share after the initial public offering, usually because of heavy promotion. All are traded OTC, many of them in the local markets of Denver, Vancouver, or Salt Lake City.

Pension Benefit Guaranty Corporation (PBGC)

A federal agency that insures the vested benefits of pension plan participants (established in 1974 by the ERISA legislation).

Pension fund

A fund set up to pay the pension benefits of a company's workers after retirement.

Pension liabilities

Future liabilities resulting from pension commitments made by a corporation. Accounting for pension liabilities varies widely by country.

Pension parachute

A form of poison pill providing that in the event of a hostile takeover attempt, any excess pension plan assets can be used to benefit pension plan participants. This prevents the raiding firm from using the pension assets to finance the takeover. In the context of corporate governance, these provisions prevent an acquirer from using surplus cash in the pension fund of the target in order to finance an acquisition. Surplus funds are required to remain the property of the pension fund and to be used for plan participants' benefits.

Pension plan

A fund that is established for the payment of retirement benefits.

Pension reversion

Termination of an overfunded defined benefit pension plan and replacement of it with a life insurance company-sponsored fixed annuity plan.

Pension sponsors

Organizations that have established a pension plan.

Penultimate profit prospect (PPP)

The second-lowest-priced of the ten highest-yielding stocks in the Dow Jones Industrial Average that is said (by authors O'Higgins and Downes) to be the Dow stock with the best possibility of outperforming the average as a whole.

People pill

A form of poison pill providing that the entire management threatens to resign in the event of a takeover.

P/E ratio

Current stock price divided by trailing annual earnings per share *or* expected annual earnings per share. Assume XYZ Co. sells for $25.50 per share and has earned \$2.55 per share this year; \$25.50 = 10 times \$2.55. XYZ stock sells for ten times earnings.

PERC

See: Preferred equity redemption stock

Per capita debt

The total bonded debt of a municipality divided by the population of the municipality.

Per stirpes

A method for distributing the assets of an individual who dies without a valid will. The Latin means for each descendant.

Percent to double

Percentage that the stock price has to rise (fall) to double the price of the call (put).

Percentage financial statement

Balance sheet and income statement represented as percentages.

Percentage order

Used for listed equity securities. Market limited price order to buy/sell a specified percentage (usually 50%) of shares traded (sometimes after a fixed number of shares of the stock have already traded). See: participating buyer/seller, "Participate but do not initiate."

Percentage premium

Applies mainly to convertible securities. Premium over parity of a convertible bond divided by parity.

Perfect capital market

A market in which there are never any arbitrage opportunities.

Perfect competition

An idealized market environment in which every market participant is too small to affect the market price by acting on its own.

Perfect forecast line

Graph of a slope that matches the forecast of an exchange rate with the actual exchange rate.

Perfect hedge

A situation in which the profit and loss from the underlying asset and the hedge position are equal.

Perfect market assumptions

Conditions under which the law of one price holds. The assumptions include frictionless markets, rational investors, and equal access to market prices and information.

Perfect market view (of capital structure)

Analysis of a firm's capital structure decision, which shows the irrelevance of capital structure in a perfect capital market.

Perfect market view (of dividend policy)

Analysis of a decision on dividend policy, in a perfect capital market environment, that shows the irrelevance of dividend policy.

Perfected first lien

A first attachment on an asset that is duly recorded with the relevant government body so that the lender will be able to act on it should the borrower default.

Perfectly competitive financial markets

Markets in which no trader has the power to change the price of goods or services. Perfect capital markets are characterized by certain conditions: (1) Trading is costless, and access to the financial markets is free; (2)information about borrowing and lending opportunities is freely available; and (3) there are many traders, and no single trader can have a significant impact on market prices.

Performance Accelerated Restricted Stock Award Plans ("PARSAPs")

Also known as performance-accelerated restricted stock ("PARS") and time-accelerated restricted stock award plans ("TARSAPs"). Grants of restricted stock or restricted stock units which may vest early upon attainment of specified performance objectives. Otherwise, a time-vesting schedule would remain in effect.

Performance attribution analysis

The decomposition of a money manager's performance results to explain the reasons why those results were achieved. This analysis seeks to answer questions such as: (1) What were the major sources of added value? (2) Was short-term factor timing statistically significant? (3) Was market timing statistically significant? and (4), was security selection statistically significant?

Performance Bond

Security deposit, such as a bank guarantee or a letter of credit opened by the supplier, that guarantees compliance on the part of the supplier with the terms of the sale contract. The deposit, typically 10 percent of the contract amount, is payable to the buyer as liquidated damages in case the supplier defaults on performance.

Performance evaluation

The assessment of a manager's results, which involves, first, determining whether the money manager added value by outperforming the established benchmark (performance measurement) and, second, determining how the money manager achieved the calculated return (performance attribution analysis).

Performance fund

A growth-oriented mutual fund investing in growth stock and performance stock with low dividends and high risk.

Performance index

A risk-adjusted measure of how well a portfolio has performed.

Performance measurement

Calculation of the return a money manager realizes over some time interval.

Performance Requirements

"Performance requirements" refers to government-mandated or -approved activities that investors must undertake, usually as a condition of establishment or operation in a particular country.

Performance shares

Shares of stock given to managers on the basis of performance as measured by earnings per share and similar criteria. A control device shareholders sometimes use to tie management to the self-interest of shareholders.

Performance stock

High-growth stock in a company that retains earnings for further growth and therefore pays no dividends, but that an investor feels has significant future potential.

Perils of the Sea

Fortuitous accidents or casualties, peculiar to transportation on a navigable water, such as stranding, sinking, collision of the vessel, striking a submerged object, or encountering heavy weather or other unusual forces of nature.

Period-certain annuity

An annuity that provides guaranteed payments to an annuitant for a specified period of time.

Periodic call auction

Selling stocks by bid at intervals throughout the day.

Periodic payment plan

Accumulation of capital in a mutual fund by making regular payments on a monthly or quarterly basis.

Periodic payments

A series of payments from an annuity, qualified retirement plan, or 403(b)(7) account made over a certain term of years. A payment from an IRA, even if over a period of years, is not considered a periodic payment for tax purposes.

Periodic purchase deferred contract

A fixed or variable annuity contract for which fixed-amount premiums are paid either monthly or quarterly, and that does not begin paying out until a time elected by the annuitant.

Periodic rate

The monthly effective interest rate. For example, the periodic rate on a credit card with an 18% annual percentage rate is 1.5% per month.

Period of digestion

The time period of often high volatility after a new issue is released when the trading price of the security is established by the market.

Period of Investigation

The period, usually 6 months, beginning at least 150 days before and continuing 30 days after the first day of the month when an antidumping petition is filed, during which an exporter's home market (or third country) and United States prices and other appropriate facts are investigated to determine whether sales to the United States have been at less than fair value. See: Tariff Act of 1930.

PERLS

Principal Exchange-Rated-Linked Securities.

Permanent Assets

Fixed assets (plant and equipment) and permanent current assets.

Permanent Current Assets

The minimum level of current assets that a firm needs to continue operation. Because some level is always maintained, they are called permanent current assets.

Permanent financing

Long-term financing using either debt or equity.

Permanent Interstate Committee for Drought Control in the Sahel, The Committee

(French: *Comité Permanente Interétats de Lutte contre la Sécheresse dans le Sahel*, CILSS) provides drought protection assistance to the eight countries of the Sahel region (Burkina Faso, Cape Verde, Chad, the Gambia, Guinea-Bissau, Mali, Mauritania, Niger, and Senegal) through such forms as food silo construction, agricultural development, improving roads, and preventing desertification. The Committee, founded in 1976, works in cooperation with the United Nations, the World Bank, the European Economic Community, and the Organization for Economic Cooperation and Development.

Permanent spontaneous current Liabilities

The minimum level of spontaneous liabilities that is always maintained by a firm.

Permissiable nonbank activities

Financial activities closely related to banking that may be engaged in by bank holding companies (BHCs), either directly or through nonbank subsidiaries. For example, a BHC might own finance companies or engage in mortgage banking. The Federal Reserve Board determines which activities are closely related to banking. Before making such activities permissible, the Board must determine that performance of the activities by bank holding companies is in the public interest.

Perpendicular spread

Option strategy involving the purchase of options with similar expiration dates and different exercise prices.

Perpetual bond

Nonredeemable bond with no maturity date that pays regular interest rates indefinitely.

Perpetual inventory

Recordkeeping system in which book inventory is updated daily.

Perpetual warrants

Warrants that have no expiration date.

Perpetuity

A constant stream of identical cash flows without end, such as a British consol.

Perquisites

Personal benefits, including direct benefits, such as the use of a firm car or expense account for personal business, and indirect benefits, such as up-to-date office decoration.

Persona Grata

A diplomatic representative who is acceptable to the government of the country where he or she is assigned.

Personal article floater

Insurance policy attachment designed to cover specified personal valuables.

Personal exemption

Amount of money a taxpayer can exclude from personal income for each member of the household in calculation of a tax obligation.

Personal income

Total income received from all sources, including wages, salaries, or rents, and the like.

Personal inflation rate

The inflation rate as it affects a specific individual.

Personal property

Any assets other than real estate.

Personal tax view (of capital structure)

The argument that the difference in personal tax rates between income from debt and income from equity eliminates the disadvantage of the double taxation (corporate and personal) of income from equity.

Personal trust

An interest in an asset held by a trustee for the benefit of another person.

Persona Non Grata

A diplomatic representative who is no longer acceptable to the government of the country where he or she is assigned.

Petrodollars

This term refers to oil earnings of petroleum-exporting countries in excess of their domestic needs and deposited in dollars in Western banks. However, a large part of the revenues that OPEC countries were unable to spend has been recycled to oil-importing countries in an attempt to balance international accounts.

PF

The two-character ISO 3166 country code for FRENCH POLYNESIA.

PG

The two-character ISO 3166 country code for PAPUA NEW GUINEA.

PGK

The ISO 4217 currency code for the Papua New Guinea Kina.

PH

The two-character ISO 3166 country code for PHILIPPINES.

Phantom income

Income from a limited partnership that creates taxability without generating cash flow.

Phantom Stock Award

A type of incentive grant in which the recipient is not issued actual shares of stock on the grant date but receives an account credited with a certain number of hypothetical shares. The value of the account increases over time based on the appreciation of the stock price and the crediting of phantom dividends. Payout may be settled in cash or stock.

Phantom stock plan

An incentive scheme that awards management bonuses based on increases in the market price of the company's stock.

Phase space

A graph which shows all possible states of a system. In phase space we plot the value of a variable against possible values of the other variables at the same time. If a system had three descriptive variables, we plot the phase space in three dimensions, with each variable taking one dimension.

Philadelphia Board of Trade (PBOT)

A subsidiary of the Philadelphia Stock Exchange that trades currency futures.

Philadelphia Stock Exchange (PHLX)

A securities exchange trading American and European foreign currency options on spot exchange rates.

Philippine Stock Exchange

Established in 1992 through the merger of the Manila Stock Exchange and the Makati Stock Exchange, the Philippines'only securities market.

Phillips Curve

A graph that supposedly shows the relationship between inflation and unemployment. It is conjectured that there is a simple trade-off between inflation and unemployment (high inflation and low unemployment, and low inflation and high unemployment). Named after A.W. Phillips. Obviously, the relation between these important macroeconomic variables is more complicated than this simple graph would suggest. For a modern treatment, see work of Robert Lucas.

PHLX

See: Philadelphia Stock Exchange.

Phone switching

Transferring money between funds in the same mutual fund family by telephone request. There may be a charge associated with these transfers. Phone switching is also possible among different fund families if the funds are held in street name by a participating broker/dealer.

PHP

The ISO 4217 currency code for the Philippines Peso.

Physical asset

Actual property such as precious metals or real estate. Also called real or tangible assets.

Physical commodity

See: Commodity.

Physical option

An option whose underlying security is a physical commodity that is not stock or futures. The physical commodity itself (a currency, treasury debt issue, commodity) - underlies that option contract. See also index option.

Physical verification

A procedure auditors use to ensure that inventory recorded in the book is correct by actually checking out the physical inventory.

Phytosanitary Inspection Certificate

A certificate, issued by the US Department of Agriculture to satisfy import regulations for foreign countries, indicating that a US shipment has been inspected and is free from harmful pests and plant diseases.

P & I

Stands for principal and interest on bonds or mortgage-backed securities.

PIBOR

See: Paris Interbank Offer Rate.

Pickup

The gain in yield that occurs when a block of bonds is swapped for another block of higher-coupon bonds.

Pickup bond

A bond with a relatively high coupon that is close to the date at which it is callable, meaning that a fall in interest rates will most likely cause early redemption of the bond at a premium.

Picture

Describes bid and asked prices a broker quotes for a given security. Used for listed equity securities. Bid and ask prices and quantity information from a specialist or from a dealer regarding a particular security (i.e., "IBM's 1/4 to 1/2, 5m by 10m").

Piece

Apply mainly to convertible securities. Increment of bonds that trade in portions of $1000 minimum. Not all bonds can be traded in "pieces," and the increments can vary.

Pie model of capital structure

A model of the debt-equity ratio of the firms, graphically depicted in slices of a pie that represent the value of the firm in the capital markets.

Pier

A man made structure extending from the shore against which vessels may lie to load or unload cargo.

Piggybacking

The assigning of export marketing and distribution functions by one manufacturer to another.

Piggyback registration

When a securities underwriter allows existing holdings of shares in a corporation to be sold in combination with an offering of new public shares.

Piggybacking

A broker who trading stocks, bonds or commodities in a personal account following a trade just made for a customer. The broker assumes that the customer is making the trade on valuable inside information.

PIK (Payment-in-kind) securities

Highly speculative bonds or preferred stock that pay interest or dividends through additional bonds or preferred stock.

Pilferage

The theft of part of the contents of a shipping package.

Pink sheets

Refers to over-the-counter trading. Daily publication of the national quotation bureau that reports the bid and ask prices of thousands of OTC stocks, as well as the market makers who trade each stock.

Pip

Used for listed equity securities. Smallest unit of a currency (i.e., cents for US dollars).

Pipeline

The underwriting process that must be completed with the SEC before a security can be offered for sale to the public.

Pipeline Protection

Pipeline protection broadly refers to the protection accorded by a country for inventions, usually for pharmaceutical and agrichemical products, which already exist prior to that country's making patent protection available for such inventions.

Pit

A specific area of the trading floor that is designed for the trading of commodities, individual futures, or option contracts.

Pit committee

A committee of the exchange that determines the daily settlement price of futures contracts.

PITI

Stands for principal, interest, taxes, and insurance, the four main parts of monthly mortgage obligations.

Pivot

Price level established as being significant by market's failure to penetrate or as being significant when a sudden increase in volume accompanies the move through the price level.

PK

The two-character ISO 3166 country code for PAKISTAN.

PKR

The ISO 4217 currency code for the Pakistani Rupee.

PL

The two-character ISO 3166 country code for POLAND.

P&L

Profit and loss statement for a trader.

Place

The marketing of new securities, usually through sales to institutional investors. See: Float.

Placement

A bank depositing Eurodollars with (selling Eurodollars to) another bank is often said to be making a placement.

Placement ratio

The percentages of last week's new municipal bond offerings that have been bought from the underwriters, according to the Bond Buyer newspaper.

Plain vanilla

A term that refers to a relatively simple derivative financial instrument, usually a swap or other derivative that is issued with standard features.

Plain vanilla swap

See: Fixed for floating swap.

Plan agreement

A document detailing the terms and conditions of a rotirement plan such as an IRA.

Plan participants

Employees or other beneficiaries who are eligible to

receive benefits from a company's employee benefit plan.

Plan for reorganization

A plan for reorganizing a firm during the Chapter 11 bankruptcy process.

Plan sponsors

The entities that establish pension plans, including private business entities acting for their employees; state and local entities operating on behalf of their employees; unions acting on behalf of their members; and individuals representing themselves.

Planned amortization class (PAC)

(1) The class of CMO that has the most stable cash flows and the lowest prepayment risk of any class of CMO Because of a stable cash flow, it is considered the least risky CMO (2) A CMO bond class that stipulates cash flow contributions to a sinking fund. A PAC directs principal payments to the sinking fund on a priority basis in accordance with a predetermined payment schedule, with prior claim to the cash flows before other CMO classes. Similarly, cash flows received by the trust in excess of the sinking fund requirement are also allocated to other bond classes. The prepayment experience of the PAC is therefore very stable over a wide range of prepayment experience.

Planned capital expenditure program

Budgeted or projected outlays for major expenditures on permanent or fixed assets as outlined in the corporate financial plan.

Planned financing program

Budgeted or projected ways need for reasons or to obtain short-term and long-term financing as outlined in the corporate financial plan.

Planning horizon

The length of time a model or investor or plan projects into the future.

Plant

The assets of a business including land, buildings, machinery, and all equipment permanently employed.

Plata Basin Financial Development Fund

See: Fondo Financiero Para el Desarrollo de la Cuenca del Plata.

Plaza Accord

In a September 1985 meeting at the Plaza Hotel in New York, G-5 officials ratified an initiative to use exchange rates and other macropolicy adjustments as the preferred and necessary means to bring about an orderly decline in the value of the dollar. The agreement, intended to curb increasing U.S. trade imbalances and protectionist action, supported orderly appreciation of the main non-dollar currences against the dollar. See: Louvre Accord.

Player

Used in the context of general equities. Customer or trader who is actively involved in a particular stock or the market in general.

Playing the market

Trading in high, uncalculated risk usually refers to actions of amateur investors.

Plaza Accord

Agreement among country representatives in 1985 to implement a coordinated program to weaken the dollar.

PLC

See: Project loan certificate.

Pledging

See: Hypothecation.

PLN

The ISO 4217 currency code for the Polish Zloty.

Plow back

To reinvest earnings in a business rather than pay out them out as dividends. Common practice in high-growth companies.

Plowback rate

Related: Retention rate.

Plug

A variable that handles financial slack in the financial plan.

Plus

Used to quote a price in 64ths. Dealers in government bonds normally give price quotes in 32nds. To quote a bid or offer in 64ths, they use pluses; a dealer who bids 4+ is bidding the handle plus 4/32 + 1/64, which equals the handle plus 9/64.

Plus a match

Used for listed equity securities. Floor indication that someone is on the floor with equal priority standing who wants to buy/sell at least the same number of shares at the same price as one's own order. Outside. See: Matched orders. Compare to ahead.

Plus tick

Used in the context of general equities. Trade occurring at a price higher than the previous sale. Uptick. Antithesis of minus tick. See: Short sale.

Plus tick seller

Used for listed equity securities. A short seller (referring to the regulation requiring a plus tick to short).

PM

The two-character ISO 3166 country code for SAINT PIERRE AND MIQUELON.

PN

(1) The two-character ISO 3166 country code for PITCAIRN. (2) See: Project notes

PO

See: (1) Principal only. (2) Purchase Order.

POA

Purchase Order Adjustment.

Point

The smallest unit of price change quoted, or one one-hundredth of a percent. Related: Minimum price fluctuation and tick.

Point and figure chart

A price-only chart that takes into account only whole integer changes in price, i.e., a 2-point change. Point and figure charting disregards the element of time and is used solely to record changes in price.

Point Attractor

In non-linear dynamics, an attractor where all orbits in phase space are drawn to one point, or value. Essentially, any system which tends to a stable, single valued equilibrium will have a point attractor. A pendulum which is damped by friction will always stop, so its phase space will always be drawn to the point where velocity and position are equal to zero. See: Attractor, Phase Space.

Points quote

An abbreviated form of the outright quote used by traders in the interbank market.

Poison pill

Anti-takeover device that gives a prospective acquiree's shareholders the right to buy shares of the firm or shares of anyone who acquires the firm at a deep discount to their fair market value. Named after the cyanide pill that secret government agents are said to be instructed to swallow if capture is imminent.

Poison put

A covenant allowing the bondholder to demand repayment in the event of a hostile takeover.

Policy asset allocation

Way in which an investor seeks to assess an appropriate long-term "normal" mix of assets that represents an ideal blend of controlled risk and enhanced return.

Policy Framework Paper

The PFP lays out the steps a country will take while receiving structural adjustment assistance from the International Monetary Fund (IMF). It describes the origins of the country's difficulties, corresponding improvement efforts, and requisite financing as well as probable impacts on environment and society. The paper, updated annually, is developed by the recipient government in collaboration with IMF and the World Bank. By design, it also serves as a vehicle for attracting orderly assistance from other donors. See: Enhanced Structural Adjustment Facility.

Policy limit

The maximum dollar amount of coverage provided by an insurance company for a certain policy.

Policy loan

A loan often made at a below-market interest rate from an insurance company to a policyholder that is secured by the cash surrender value of a life insurance policy.

Policyholder

An individual who owns an insurance policy.

Policyholder loan bonds

Packaged loans acquired by policyholders that are secured by the cash surrender value of the policies, and are offered by a broker/dealer as bonds.

Political Risk

With regard to Eximbank and Overseas Private Investment Corporation programs, political risk coverage normally includes defaults or losses due to action of inaction by governments, including war and civil unrest, expropriations, and inconvertibility of local currency to dollars. Losses due to currency devaluation are not considered a political risk. See: Commercial Risk.

Pool

In capital budgeting, the concept that investment projects are financed out of a pool of bonds, preferred stock, and common stock, and a weighted-average cost of capital must be used to calculate investment returns. In insurance, a group of insurers who share premiums and losses in order to spread risk. In investments, the combination of funds for the benefit of a common project, or a group of investors who use their combined influence to manipulate prices.

Pool factor

The outstanding principal balance divided by the original principal balance with the result expressed as a decimal. Pool factors are published monthly by the

Bond Buyer newspaper for Ginnie Mae, Fannie Mae, and Freddie Mac (Federal Home Loan Mortgage Corporation) MBSs.

Pooling of interests

An accounting method for reporting acquisitions accomplished through the use of equity. The combined assets of the merged entity are consolidated using book value, as opposed to the purchase method, which uses market value. The merging entities' financial results are combined as though the two entities have always been a single entity.

Porcupine provision

Often used in risk arbitrage. See: Shark repellent.

Portability

The character of benefits that may be carried from a previous job to the next.

Portfolio

A collection of investments, real and/or financial.

Portfolio allocation by region

The distribution, by geographic region, of a portfolio's holdings.

Portfolio asset allocation

The distribution, by type of asset, of a portfolio's holdings.

Portfolio beta

Used in the context of general equities. The beta of a portfolio is the weighted sum of the individual asset betas, According to the proportions of the investments in the portfolio. E.g., if 50% of the money is in stock A with a beta of 2.00, and 50% of the money is in stock B with a beta of 1.00,the portfolio beta is 1.50. Portfolio beta describes relative volatilityof an individual securities portfolio, taken as a whole, as measured by the individual stock betas of the securities making it up. A beta of 1.05 relative to the S&P 500 implies that if the S&P's excess return increases by 10% the portfolio is expected to increase by 10.5%.

Portfolio diversification

Investing in different asset classes and in securities of many issuers in an attempt to reduce overall investment risk and to avoid damaging a portfolio's performance by the poor performance of a single security, industry, (or country).

Portfolio expected return

A weighted average of individual assets' expected returns.

Portfolio insurance

A strategy using a leveraged portfolio in the underlying stock to create a synthetic put option. The strategy's goal is to ensure that the value of the portfolio does not fall below a certain level.

Portfolio internal rate of return

The rate of return computed by first determining the cash flows for all the bonds in the portfolio and then finding the interest rate that will make the present value of the cash flows equal to the market value of the portfolio.

Portfolio Investment

In general, any foreign investment that is not direct investment is considered portfolio investment. Foreign portfolio investment includes the purchase of voting securities (stocks) at less than a 10 percent level, bonds, trade finance, and government lending or borrowing, excluding transactions in official reserves.

Portfolio management

Related: Investment management.

Portfolio manager

Used in the context of general equities. Professional responsible for the securities portfolio of an individual or institutional investor, such as a mutual fund, pension fund, profit-sharing plan, bank trust department, or insurance company. In return for a fee, the manager has the fiduciary responsibility to manage the assets prudently and choose which asset types are most appropriate over time. Related: Investment manager.

Portfolio opportunity set

The expected return/standard deviation pairs of all portfolios that can be constructed from a given set of assets.

Portfolio R2

Used in the context of general equities. Number between 0 and 1 that measures the strength of correlation of movement between the portfolio/stock and the index. Indeed, the R^2 is the square of the correlation. For hedging purposes, the higher the R^2, the better.

Portfolio restructuring

Applies to derivative products. Recomposition of a portfolio's asset mix by selling off undesired asset types (equities, debt, or cash) or specific securities within that class, while simultaneously buying desired types or securities. Often a firm is asked to bid on an old portfolio and give an offering of the desired portfolio. See: Program trading.

Portfolio separation theorem

Theory that an investor's choice of a risky investment portfolio is separate from his attitude towards risk. Related: Fisher's separation theorem.

Portfolio theory

See: Modern portfolio theory.

Portfolio transaction costs

The expenses associated with buying and selling securities, including commissions, purchase and redemption fees, exchange fees, and other miscellaneous costs. In a mutual fund prospectus, these expenses are listed separately from the fund's expense ratio.

Portfolio turnover rate

For an investment company, an annualized rate found by dividing the lesser of purchases and sales by the average of portfolio assets.

Portfolio variance

Weighted sum of the covariance and variances of the assets in a portfolio.

Port Shopping

Port shopping is the practice of exporters and importers choosing a particular port on the basis of their assessment of Customs' treatment, rather than on the quality of physical facilities and efficiency.

Position

A market commitment; the number of contracts bought or sold for which no offsetting transaction has been entered into. The buyer of a commodity is said to have a long position, and the seller of a commodity is said to have a short position. Related: Open contracts.

Position building

Buying shares to build up a long position or selling shares to create a short position in a particular security or group of securities.

Position diagram

Diagram showing the possible payoffs from a derivative investment.

Position limits

Applies to derivative products. Maximum position available in any one future or option contract for a given institution. For "bona fide" futures hedgers, there are no position limits.

Position self

Used in the context of general equities. Going long or short in anticipation of a stock's movement.

Position sheet

Used in the context of general equities. List of long and short positions for an individual trader or desk, at times accompanied by the trades from the previous trading session that brought these closing positions.

Position trader

A commodities trader who takes a long-term approach in maintaining positions in the market and does not close out of these positions until close to the delivery date.

Positive carry

Related: Net financing cost.

Positive convexity

A property of option-free bonds that the price appreciation for a large downward change in interest rates will be greater (in absolute terms) than the price depreciation for the same downward change in interest rates.

Positive covenant (of a bond)

A bond covenant that specifies certain actions the firm must take. Also called an affirmative covenant.

Positive float

See: Float

Positive yield curve

When long-term debt interest rates are higher than short-term debt rates (because of the increased risk involved with long-term debt security).

Possessions corporation

A type of corporation permitted under the US tax code whose branch operation in a US possession can obtain tax benefits as though it were operating as a foreign subsidiary.

Post

Particular place on the floor of an exchange where transactions in stocks listed on the exchange occur.

Post-audit

A set of procedures for evaluating a capital budgeting decision after the fact.

Post-dated check

A check that becomes payable and negotiable on a future date specified.

Post-Initiated Promotion

This is a scheduled low budget trade promotion totally within resources at post, such as BIO, BFC, or BSP.

Postponement option

The option of deferring a project without eliminating the possibility of undertaking it.

Postponing income

Purposely delaying receipt of income to a later year in order to reduce current tax liability.

Post-Shipment Verifications

PSVs are conducted to determine that a commodity is being used for the purposes for which its export was licensed. Firms or individuals representing the end user, intermediate consignees, or the purchaser may be subject to inquiries pertaining to the post-shipment verification. As part of the PSV process, BXA forwards a cable to the U.S. embassy or consulate in the respective geographical location to conduct an on-site inspection to ensure that the commodity is physically present and used as stated in the application. Post-shipment verifications are usually conducted six-to-eight months subsequent to export of the commodity. PSVs are also conducted by BXA agents.

Post-trade benchmarks

Prices after the decision to trade.

Pot

The portion of stock or bond issue that is returned to the managing underwriter by the participating investment bankers for sale to institutional investors.

Pot is clean

Phrase used when managing underwriter has sold the entire pot.

Power of attorney

A written authorization allowing a person to perform certain acts on behalf of another, such as moving of assets between accounts or trading for a person's benefit.

POW WOW

The POW WOW is a trade show (held annually in the United States and annually in Europe) which brings together U.S. sellers and foreign buyers of travel-related services pertaining to travel to the United States.

Pow Wow Selection Committee

A committee of private industry representatives in foreign countries which is responsible for selecting invitees to the International POW WOW.

PR

The two-character ISO 3166 country code for PUERTO RICO.

Prearranged trading

Possibly fraudulent practice whereby commodities dealers carry out risk-free trades at predetermined prices to acquire tax advantages.

Preauthorized checks (PAC)

Checks that are authorized by a payer in advance, and written either by the payee or by the payee's bank and then deposited in the payee's bank account.

Preauthorized electronic debits (PAD)

Debits to a bank account in advance by the payer. The payer's bank sends payment to the payee's bank through the Automated Clearing House (ACH) system.

Preauthorized payment

Accelerating cash inflows by directly charging a customer's bank account with permission.

Pre Carriage

Usually freight charges for port or airport delivery arising before the principal international carriage.

Precautionary demand (for money)

The need to meet unexpected or extraordinary contingencies with a buffer stock of cash.

Precautionary motive

A desire to hold cash in order to be able to deal effectively with unexpected events that require cash outlay.

Precedence

The established system of priorities of trades in an exchange. For example, the highest bid and lowest offer have highest precedence; the first bid or first offer at a price has highest priority, and large orders have priority over smaller orders.

Precious metals

Gold, silver, platinum, and palladium, which are used for their intrinsic value or for their value in production. These may be traded either in their physical state or by way of futures and options contracts, mining company stocks, bonds, mutual funds, or other instrument.

Precompute

Method of charging interest in which the annual interest is either deducted from the face amount of the loan when the funds are distributed or is added to the total amount and divided into the regular payments.

Preemptive right

Common stockholders' right to anything of value distributed by the company.

Preference

Refers to over-the-counter trading. Selection of a dealer to handle a trade despite the dealer's market not being the best available. Often the "preferenced dealer" will then move his market in line.

Preference share

Preferred shares of a corporation that have first claim to preferred dividends.

Preference stock

A security that ranks junior to preferred stock but senior to common stock in the right to receive payments from the firm; essentially junior preferred stock.

Preferential Trade Area for Eastern and Southern African States

PTA, established in 1981, supports economic development and cooperation (agriculture, communications, customs, industry, monetary affairs, natural resources, and trade). Membership includes: Burundi, Comoros, Djibouti, Ethiopia, Kenya, Lesotho, Malawi, Mauritius, Rwanda, Somalia, Swaziland, Tanzania, Uganda, Zambia, and Zimbabwe. PTA's headquarters are in Lusaka, Zambia.

Preferred dividend coverage

Net income after interest and taxes (before common stock dividends) divided by preferred stock dividends.

Preferred equity redemption stock (PERC)

Preferred stock that converts automatically into equity at a stated date. A limit is placed on the value of the shares the investor receives.

Preferred habitat theory

A biased expectations theory that believes the term structure reflects the expectation of the future path of interest rates as well as risk premium. The theory rejects the assertion that the risk premium must rise uniformly with maturity, but instead profits that to the extent that the demand for and supply of funds do not match for a given maturity range, some participants will shift to maturities showing the opposite imbalances, as long as they are compensated by an appropriate risk premium whose magnitude will reflect the extent of aversion to either price or reinvestment risk.

Preferred shares

Preferred shares give investors a fixed dividend from the company's earnings and entitle them to be paid before common shareholders. See: Preferred stock.

Preferred stock

A security that shows ownership in a corporation and gives the holder a claim, prior to the claim of common stockholders, on earnings and also generally on assets in the event of liquidation. Most preferred stock pays a fixed dividend that is paid prior to the common stock dividend, stated in a dollar amount or as a percentage of par value. This stock does not usually carry voting rights. Preferred stock has characteristics of both common stock and debt.

Preferred stock agreement

A contract for preferred stock.

Preferred stock ratio

Preferred stock at par value divided by total capitalization, which gives the portion of capitalization that consists of preferred stock.

PREG

Financial ratio defined as stock price divided by sales over earnings growth. Often used in the valuation of Internet stocks. Related: PSSG.

Pre-License Checks

PLCs are conducted to determine that dual-use items on an export license application are destined for a legitimate end-use by a reliable end-user. Firms or individuals representing the licensee (the applicant), the consignee, the purchaser, the intermediate consignee, or the end user may be subject to inquiries pertaining to the pre-license check. As part of the process, BXA forwards a cable to the U.S. embassy or consulate in the respective geographical location to conduct an inspection or meet with company representatives to conduct inquiries on BXA's behalf.

Preliminary Determination

The dumping determination by the International Trade Administration announcing the results of the investigation conducted within 160 days (or, in extraordinarily complicated cases, 210 days) after a petition is filed or an investigation is self-initiated by the International Trade Administration. If the International Trade Administration determines that there is a reasonable basis to believe or suspect that the merchandise under consideration is being sold or is likely to be sold at less than fair value, liquidation of all affected entries is suspended, and the matter is referred to the International Trade Commission. "Preliminary determination" also refers to the decision by the ITC where there is a reasonable indication that an industry in the United States is materially injured, or threatened with material injury, or the establishment of an industry in the United States is materially retarded by reason of the imports of the merchandise which is the subject of the petition. The ITC must make its decision within 45 days after the date on which the petition is filed or an investigation is self-initiated by the International Trade Administration. If this determination is negative, the investigation is terminated. See: Tariff Act of 1930.

Preliminary estimate

The second estimate of GDP released about two months after the measurement period.

Preliminary prospectus

An initial or tentative version of a prospectus.

Premature distribution

A distribution from an IRA before the owner reaches age 59-1/2. Generally, a 10% penalty tax is owed on such a distribution. Also known as an early distribution or an early withdrawal.

Premium

(1) A bond sold above its par value. (2) The price of an option contract; also, in futures trading, the amount by which the futures price exceeds the price of the spot commodity. (3) For convertibles, amount by which the price of a convertible exceeds parity, and is usually expressed as a percentage. Suppose a stock is trading at $45, and the bond is convertible at a $50 stock price and the convertible bond trading at 105. A similar bond without the conversion feature trades at $90. In this case, the premium is $15, or 16.66%=(105-90)/90. If the premium is high, the bond trades like any fixed income bond; if low, like a stock. See: Gross parity, net parity. (4) For futures, excess of fair value of future over the spot index, which in theory will equal the Treasury bill yield for the period to expiration minus the expected dividend yield until the future's expiration. (5) For options, price of an option in the open market (sometimes refers to the portion of the price that exceeds parity). (6) For straight equity, price higher than that of the last sale or inside market. Related: Inverted market premium payback period. Also called break-even time; the time it takes to recover the premium per share of a convertible security.

Premium bond

A bond that is selling for more than its par value.

Premium income

The income received by an investor who sells an option.

Premium raid

An attempt to acquire a large portion of a company's stock to gain control by offering stockholders a premium over the market value for their shares.

Prepackaged bankruptcy

A bankruptcy in which a debtor and its creditors pre-negotiate a plan of reorganization and then file it along with the bankruptcy petition.

Prepaid

A term used to signify that transportation charges will be paid by seller at point of shipment.

Prepaid interest

An asset account showing interest that has been paid in advance, which is expensed and charged to the borrower's P & L statement.

Prepayment penalty

A fee a borrower pays a lender when the borrower repays a loan before its scheduled time of maturity.

Prepayment speed

Also called speed, the estimated rate at which mortgagors pay off their loans ahead of schedule, critical in assessing the value of mortgage pass-through securities.

Prepayments

Payments made in excess of scheduled mortgage principal repayments.

Prerefunded bond

Refunded bond.

Prerefunding

Procedure of floating a second bond at a lower interest rate in order to pay off the first bond at the first call date and to reduce overall borrowing costs.

Presale order

An order to purchase part of a new municipal bond issue that is accepted by an underwriting syndicate before an official public offering.

Present value

The amount of cash today that is equivalent in value to a payment, or to a stream of payments, to be received in the future. To determine the present value, each future cash flow is multiplied by a present value factor. For example, if the opportunity cost of funds is 10%, the present value of $100 to be received in one year is $100 x [1/(1 + 0.10)] = $91.

Present Value Components Analysis

An analytical tool that establishes a base NPV for a project that can then be adjusted for the incremental NPV effect of separate elements of the project's overall potential sales.

Present value factor

Factor used to calculate an estimate of the present value of an amount to be received in a future period. If the opportunity cost of funds is 10% over next year, the factor is [1/(1 + 0.10)].

Present value of growth opportunities

Net present value (NPV) of investments the firm is expected to make in the future.

Present Value Index (PVI)

The ratio of the NPV of a project to the initial outlay required for it. The index is an efficiency measure for investment decisions under capital rationing.

Pre shipment Finance

Short term funding for inventory and production costs associated with manufacturing goods being exported.

President

Highest-ranking officer in a corporation after the chief executive officer.

Presidential election cycle theory

A theory that stock market trends can be predicted and explained by the four-year presidential election cycle.

President's Export Council

The President's Export Council (PEC) advises the President on government policies and programs that affect U.S. trade performance; promote export expansion; and provide a forum for discussing and resolving trade-related problems among the business, industrial, agricultural, labor, and government sectors. The Council was established by Executive Order of the President in 1973 and was originally composed only of business executives. The Council was reconstituted in 1979 to include leaders of the labor and agricultural communities, Congress, and the Executive branch.

Twenty-eight private sector members serve "at the pleasure of the President" with no set term of office. Other members include five U.S. Senators and five Members of the House, the Secretaries of Agriculture, Commerce, Labor, State, and Treasury, the Chairman of the Export-Import Bank, and the U.S. Trade Representative. The Council reports to the President through the Secretary of Commerce.

The President's Export Council, Subcommittee on Export Administration (PECSEA), formed in June 1976, advises the PEC, the White House, and Commerce on all export control matters, including those which affect Commerce, State, Defense and Energy. The PECSEA membership comprises 25 industry representatives, selected by the Secretary of Commerce.

Pre-sold issue

An issue that is sold out before the coupon announcement.

Pre-tax contribution

Payment to an account made with funds from a worker's paycheck before federal income taxes are deducted.

Pretax earnings or profits

Net income before federal income taxes are subtracted.

Pretax rate of return

Gain on a security before taxes.

Pre-trade benchmarks

Prices occurring before or at the decision to trade.

Previous balance method

Method of calculating finance charges based on the account balance at the end of the previous month.

Price of admission

Used in the context of general equities. Cost to become a player in a stock in an inordinately aggressive market (i.e.,locking on one side, size or price concessions); trader becomes aggressive in order to break the domination of customer activity by another dealer.

Price-book ratio

Compares a stock's market value to the value of total assets less total liabilities (book value). Determined by dividing current stock price by common stockholder equity per share (book value), adjusted for stock splits. Also called Market-to-Book.

Price change

Increase or decrease in the closing price of a security compared to the previous day's closing price.

Price compression

The limitation of the price appreciation potential for a callable bond in a declining interest rate environment, based on the expectation that the bond will be redeemed at the call price.

Price continuity

Minimal price changes due to transactions.

Price discovery process

The process of determining the prices of assets in the marketplace through the interactions of buyers and sellers.

Price-earnings ratio

Shows the multiple of earnings at which a stock sells. Determined by dividing current stock price by current earnings per share (adjusted for stock splits). Earnings per share for the P/E ratio are determined by dividing earnings for past 12 months by the number of common shares outstanding. Higher multiple means investors have higher expectations for future growth, and have bid up the stock's price.

Price effect

Impact of a change in interest rates on bond prices.

Price elasticities

The percentage change in quantity divided by a percentage change in the price. Answers the question: How much will the demand for my product decrease if I raise prices by 10%?

Price gap

A term used when the price of a stock rockets or dives in a direction away from its last price range, such as a stock with a trading range of $10-$12 that closes at $12 and climbs to $14 the next day.

Price give

Used in the context of general equities. Willingness of a buyer or seller to negotiate on price, within reason, from the price at the last sale or the indicated level. See: Takes price.

Price immunization

Portfolio protection strategy that focuses on the current market value of assets and liabilities.

Price impact costs

Related: Market impact costs.

Price indexes

See: Consumer price index and producer price index

Price leadership

A price charged by the dominant producer that becomes the price adopted by all the other producers.

Price momentum

Related: Relative strength.

Price persistence

Related: Relative strength.

Price range

The interval between the high and low prices over which a stock has traded over a particular period of time.

Price risk

The risk that the value of a security (or a portfolio) will decline in the future. Or, a type of mortgage pipeline risk created in the production segment when loan terms are set for the borrower in advance of setting terms for secondary market sale. If the general level of rates rises during the production cycle, the lender may have to sell the originated loans at a discount.

Price-sales ratio

Determined by dividing current stock price by revenue per share (adjusted for stock splits). Revenue per share for the P/S ratio is determined by dividing revenue for past 12 months by number of shares outstanding.

Price-specie flow mechanism

Adjustment mechanism under the classic gold standard allowing disturbances in the price level in one country to be wholly or partly offset by a countervailing flow of specie (gold coins) that would act to equalize prices across countries and automatically bring international payments into balance.

Price spread

An options strategy that involves buying and selling two options on the same security with the same expiration month, but with different exercise prices.

Price support

Government intervention to set an artificially high price through the use of a price floor designed to aid producers.

Price takers

Individuals who respond to rates and prices by acting as though prices have no influence on them.

Price uncertainty

Chance that the future price of an asset will change.

Price value of a basis point (PVBP)

Also called the dollar value of a basis point; a measure of the change in the price of a bond if the required yield changes by one basis point.

Price-volume relationship

A relationship espoused by some technical analysts that signals continuing rises or falls in security prices that are related to changes in volume traded.

Price-weighted index

An index giving a greater influence to higher-valued stocks by weighting all component stocks by their price.

Prices (of equity)

Price of a share of common stock on the date shown. Highs and lows are based on the highest and lowest intraday trading price.

Priced out

The market has already incorporated information, such as a low dividend, into the price of a stock.

Pricey

Term used for an unrealistically low bid price or unrealistically high offer price.

Pricing efficiency

Also called external efficiency; a market characteristic that prices at all times fully reflect all available information that is relevant to the valuation of securities.

Primary dealer

Usually refers to the select list of securities firms that

are authorized to deal in new issues of government bonds.

Primary distribution

Sale of a new issue of stock or bonds, as distinguished from a secondary distribution.

Primary earnings per (common) share

Earnings available for the payment of dividends to common stockholders divided by the number of common shares outstanding.

Primary market

Where a newly issued security is first offered. All subsequent trading of this security occurs is done in the secondary market.

Primary offering

Direct/Sale of a firm's newly issued shares by the firm to investors.

Primary trend

General movement in price data that lasts 4 to 4 1/2 years.

PRIME

Stands for prescribed right to income and maximum equity, a certificate that entitles the owner to the dividend/income from an underlying security, but not to the capital appreciation of that security.

Prime paper

The highest-quality, investment-grade debt of corporations as decided by rating agencies such as Moody's.

Prime rate

The interest rate at which banks lend to their best (prime) customers. More often than not, a bank's most creditworthy customers borrow at rates below the prime rate.

Prime rate fund

A mutual fund that buys portions of corporate loans from banks and pays the interest to shareholders.

Primitive security

An instrument such as a stock or bond for which payments depend only on the financial status of the issuer.

Principal

(1) The total amount of money being borrowed or lent. (2) The party affected by agent decisions in a principal-agent relationship.

Principal-agent relationship

Occurs when one person, an agent, acts on the behalf of another person, the principal.

Principal amount

The face amount of debt; the amount borrowed or lent. Often called principal.

Principal Exchange-Rated-Linked Securities (PERLS)

A debt instrument with its principal and interest denominated in U.S. dollars, but with principal repayment depending on the exchange rate of the U.S. dollar against a foreign currency.

Principal-only (PO)

A mortgage-backed security (MBS) whose holder receives only principal cash flows on the underlying mortgage pool. All the principal distribution due from the underlying collateral pool is paid to the registered holder of the stripped MBS on the basis of the current face value of the underlying collateral pool.

Principal stockholder

A stockholder who owns 10% or more of the voting stock of a company. Such stockholders must report all trading in the stock to the SEC pursuant insider trading rules.

Principle of diversification

That portfolios of different sorts of assets differently correlated with one another will have negligible unsystematic risk. In other words, unsystematic risks disappear in diversified portfolios, and only systematic risks persist, those related to particular assets.

Print

Used in the context of general equities. As a verb execute a trade, evidenced by its printing on the ticker tape. As a noun, a trade.

Prior-lien bond

A bond usually arising from reorganization with precedence over another bond of the same issuing company that is equally secured.

Prior-preferred stock

Preferred stock that has a higher claim on all dividends and assets in liquidation than claims of other preferred stock.

Priority

Used for listed equity securities. System used in an auction market, in which the first bid or offer price is executed before other bid and offer prices, even if subsequent orders are larger. NYSE rules stipulate that the bid made first should be executed first, or if two bids came in at once, the bid for the large number of shares receives "priority." The bid not executed is then turned to the broker, who informs the customer that the trade was not completed because there was stock ahead. See: Standing.

Private Export Funding Corporation

PEFCO is a private company, accessed through its member banks and a few exporters, that works with Eximbank in using private capital to finance U.S. exports. The corporation acts as a supplemental lender to traditional commercial banking sources by making loans to public and private borrowers located outside of the United States who require medium and/or longer-term financing of their purchases of U.S. goods and services.

Private-label pass-throughs

Related: Conventional pass-throughs.

Private letter ruling

A ruling by the IRS in response to a request for interpretation of a tax law.

Private limited partnership

A limited partnership with no more than 35 participants that is not registered with the SEC.

Private market value (PMV)

The break-up market value of all divisions of a company if divisions were each independent and established their own market stock prices.

Private Mortgage Insurance (PMI)

Policy protecting the holder against loss resulting from default on a mortgage loan.

Private placement

The sale of a bond or other security directly to a limited number of investors. For example, sale of stocks, bonds, or other investments directly to an institutional investor like an insurance company, avoiding the need for SEC registration if the securities are purchased for investment as opposed to resale. Antithesis of public offering.

Private-purpose bond

A municipal bond allowing more than 10% of the proceeds go to private activities.

Private unrequited transfers

Resident immigrant workers' remittances to their country of origin as well as, e.g., gifts, dowries, inheritances, prizes, charitable contributions.

Private Voluntary Organizations

PVOs are non-profit, tax-exempt and nongovernmental organizations governed by a group of private /citizens whose purpose is to engage in voluntary, charitable and development operations overseas. The U.S. Agency for International Development has registered over 150 PVOs which are eligible to receive USAID funding.

Privatization

Government procedure to pursue a free-market economy for certain state-owned assets such as companies, operating monopolies, natural resources, etc., and make them available for new investments by invited private businesses which assume part or all of their ownership and management.

Probability

The relative likelihood of a particular outcome among all possible outcomes.

Probability density function

The function that describes the change of certain realizations for a continuous random variable.

Probability distribution

A function that describes all the values a random variable can take and the probability associated with each. Also called a probability function.

Probability function

A measure that assigns a likelihood of occurrence to each and every possible outcome.

Proceeds

Money received by the seller of an asset.

Proceeds sale

OTC securities sale whose revenue is used to buy another security.

Processing Delay

Time a selling firm takes to record receipt of a payment and deposit it.

Producer Price Index (PPI)

Index measuring changes in wholesale prices, published by the US Bureau of Labor Statistics every month.

Product cycle

The time it takes to bring new and/or improved products to market.

Product cycle theory

Theory suggesting that a firm initially establish itself locally and expand into foreign markets in response to foreign demand for its product; over time, the MNC will grow in foreign markets; after some point, its foreign business may decline unless it can differentiate its product from competitors.

Product Differentiation

A source of competitive advantage that depends on producing some item that is regarded to have unique and valuable characteristics.

Product Groups

Commodity groupings used for export control purposes. See: Export Control Classification Number.

Production Cost Advantage

A source of competitive advantage that depends on producing some product or service at the lowest cost.

Production-flow commitment

An agreement by the loan purchaser to allow a monthly loan quota to be delivered in batches.

Production payment financing

A method of nonrecourse asset-based financing in which a specified percentage of revenue realized from the sale of the project's output is used to pay debt service.

Production possibilities schedule

The maximum amount of goods (i.e., food and clothing) that a country is able to produce given its labor supply.

Production rate

The coupon rate at which a pass-through security guaranteed by Ginnie Mae is issued.

Productivity

The amount of output per unit of input, such as the quantity of a product produced per hour of capital employed.

Product risk

A type of mortgage pipeline risk that occurs when a lender has an unusual loan in production or inventory but does not have a sale commitment at a prearranged price.

Profile buyer/seller

Trader trying to get involved in a stock who presents self as a buyer/seller to draw a call from a customer. That is the trader has nothing real, or natural.

Profit

For the purposes of constructed value in an antidumping duty investigation or review, the profit used is the profit normally earned by a producer, from the country of export, of the same or similar product as that under investigation.

By statute, the amount of profit shall not be less than 8 percent of the sum of general expenses and cost.

Profit center

A division of an organization held responsible for producing its own profits.

Profit forecast

A prediction of future profits of a company, which may affect investment decisions.

Profit Graph

A graphical representation of the potential outcomes of a strategy. Dollars of profit or loss are graphed on the vertical axis, and various stock prices are graphed on the horizontal axis. Results may be depicted at any point in time, although the graph usually depicts the results at expiration of the options involved in the strategy.

Profit margin

Indicator of profitability. The ratio of earnings available to stockholders to net sales. Determined by dividing net income by revenue for the same 12-month period. Result is shown as a percentage. Also known as net profit margin.

Profit Range

The range within which a particular position makes a profit. Generally used in refernce to strategies that have two break-even points - an upside break-even and a downside break-even. The price range between the two break-even points would be the profit range.

Profit-sharing plan

An incentive system providing that employees share in company profits through a cash fund or a deferred plan used to buy stock or bonds.

Profit Table

A table of results of a particular strategy at some point in time. This is usually a tabular compilation of the data drawn on a profit graph. See also Profit Graph.

Profit taking

Action by short-term securities traders to cash in on gains created by a sharp market rise, which pushes prices down temporarily but implies an upward market trend. See: Ring the [cash] register.

Profitability index

The present value of the future cash flows divided by the initial investment. Also called the benefit-cost ratio.

Profitability ratios

Ratios that focus on how well a firm is performing. Profit margins measure performance with relation to sales. Rate of return ratios measure performance relative to some measure of size of the investment.

Pro forma capital structure analysis

A method of analyzing the impact of alternative possible capital structure choices on a firm's credit statistics and reported financial results, especially to determine whether the firm will be able to use projected tax shield benefits fully.

Pro forma financial statements

A firm's financial statements as adjusted to reflect a projected or planned transaction. "What-if" analysis.

Pro Forma Invoice

An invoice provided by a supplier prior to the shipment of merchandise, informing the buyer of the kinds and quantities of goods to be sent, their value, and important specifications (weight, size, etc.)

Pro forma statement

A financial statement showing the forecast or projected operating results and balance sheet, as in pro forma income statements, balance sheets, and statements of cash flows.

Program trades

Orders requiring the execution of trades in a large number of different stocks at as near the same time as possible. Also called basket trades. Related: Block trade

Program trading

Trades based on signals from computer programs, usually entered directly from the trader's computer in to the market's computer system and executed automatically. Applies to derivative products. A process of electronic execution of trading of a basket of stocks simultaneously, for index arbitrage, portfolio restructuring, or outright buy/sell interests. See: super dot.

Progress payments

Periodic payments to a supplier, contractor, or subcontractor for work as it is completed as desired, in order to reduce working capital requirements.

Progress review

A periodic review of a capital investment project to evaluate its continued economic viability.

Progressive tax system

A tax system that taxes the wealthy at a higher percentage rate than the less wealthy.

Progressive taxation

Characterizes a convex tax schedule that results in a higher effective tax rate on higher income levels. Increases for some increases in income, but never decreases with an increase in income.

Project Finance Loan Program

Program under which banks, the Ex-Im Bank, or a combination of both may extend long-term financing for capital equipment and related services for major projects.

Project Financing

Financing by a bank or consortium of a major project with long-term revenue generating potential in which the lender's security is based on the expectation that revenues generated by the project will be sufficient to service debt incurred for the project, and/or a mortgage on the project's assets. Project financing is often referred to as "limited recourse financing" because it does not rely for security on recourse to the assets and revenues of the borrowers.

Project License

The Bureau of Export Administration uses the project license to authorize large-scale exports of a wide variety of commodities and technical data for specified activities. Those activities are restricted to capital expansion, maintenance, repair or operating supplies, or the supply of materials to be used in the production of other commodities for sale. Items intended for resale in the form received are not permitted and must be effected under a Distribution License.

Project link

An econometric model forecasting and describing the effects of changes in different economies on other economies.

Project loan certificate (PLC)

A primary program of Ginnie Mae for securitizing FHA-insured and coinsured multifamily, hospital, and nursing home loans.

Project loans

Usually FHA-insured and HUD-guaranteed mortgages on multiple-family housing complexes, nursing homes, hospitals, and other special development.

Project loan securities

Securities backed by a variety of FHA-insured loans-primarily multifamily apartment buildings, hospitals, and nursing homes.

Project notes (PN)

Notes issued by municipalities to finance federally sponsored programs in urban renewal and housing and guaranteed by the U.S. Department of Housing and Urban Development.

Projected benefit obligation (PBO)

A measure of a pension plan's liability at the calculation date assuming that the plan is ongoing and will not terminate in the foreseeable future. Related: Accumulated benefit obligation.

Projected maturity date

With CMOs, the date at the end of the estimated cash flow window where final payment is made.

Projection

The use of econometric models to forecast the future performance of a company, country, or other financial entity using historical and current information.

Promissory Note

Short-term credit instrument consisting of a written promise by the buyer (importer) to pay a specified amount of money to the seller (exporter) on demand or on a given future date. Promissory notes are often negotiable.

Property inventory

A list of personal property with corresponding values and initial costs often used to substantiate insurance claim and tax losses.

Property rights

Rights of individuals and companies to own and use property as they see fit and to receive the stream of income that their property generates.

Property tax

A tax levied on real property based on its use and its assessed value.

Proportional representation

A method of stockholder voting that allows minority shareholders and groups of small shareholders to have a better chance of getting representation on a board of directors than under statutory voting.

Proprietary trading

Principal trading in which firm seeks direct gain rather than commission dollars.

Proprietorship

An unincorporated business that is owned and operated by only one person who has complete liability for all assets, and complete rights to all profits.

Prospective Earnings Growth (PEG Ratio)

Based on forecasts from proprietary sources such as Institutional Brokers' Estimate System (IBES), First Call, or Zach's. Growth is forecast of earnings minus current earnings divided by current earnings. Forward-looking measure rather than typical earnings growth measures, which look back in time (historical).

Prospectus

Formal written document to sell securities that describes the plan for a proposed business enterprise, or the facts concerning an existing one, that an investor needs to make an informed decision. Prospectuses are used by mutual funds to describe fund objectives, risks, and other essential information.

Protect

Assure the salesperson or trader that interest, buy or sell, will be attended to, given any change in the trading circumstances, as follows: At a price: If the stock trades at a certain price or price range, the trader will show this market to the salesperson and thus allow participation under these favorable circumstances. Floor protection: Representation of a client on the floor of the exchange-so that if size were to trade at his price or a better price, salesperson would participate. Volume (OTC): If a certain amount of volume trades (that parallels the protectee's interest), trader assures salesperson of reasonable participation in the trading activity. The extent of this protection depends on liquidity, number of market makers, and other aspects of the stock.

Protected Strategy

A position that has limited risk. A protected short sale (short stock, long call) has limited risk, as does a protected straddle write (short straddle, long out-of-the-money combination). See also Combination and Straddle.

Protectionism

Notion that governments should protect domestic industry from import competition by means of tariffs, quotas, and other trade barriers.

Protective covenant

A part of an indenture or loan agreement that limits certain actions a company may take during the term of the loan to protect the lender's interests.

Protective put buying strategy

A strategy that involves buying a put option on the underlying security that is held in a portfolio. Related: Hedge option strategies.

Protest

Instructions given to a collecting bank that drafts falling due for payment are to be formally presented to the drawee by a notary, who is to formally record any default.

Protest System

The Protest System, a part of Customs' Automated Commercial System, tracks protests from the date they are received through final action. A protest is the legal means by which an importer, consignee, or other designated part may challenge decisions made by a District Director of Customs.

Protective Order

With regard to antidumping cases, a term for the order under which most business proprietary information is made available to an attorney or other representative of a party to the proceeding. See: Tariff Act of 1930.

Protocol

See Link Contract. The term is also used to specify government-to-government agreements that govern reciprocal trade between two countries. Bilateral government protocols may prescribe how the governments treat each other's suppliers and the general framework for the development of bilateral relations. The protocols also may set out the terms governing reciprocal trade turnovers of specified products such as commodities for industrial goods or industrial plants. Unlike bilateral clearing agreements, each trade transaction is settled through extension of government credits and guarantees. See: International Agreements

Protocol of Provisional Application

A legal device that enabled the original contracting parties to accept general GATT obligations and benefits, despite the fact that some of their existing domestic legislation at that time discriminated against imports in a manner that was inconsistent with certain GATT provisions. Although meant to be "temporary," the Protocol has remained in effect; and countries that signed the PPA in 1947 continue to invoke it to defend certain practices that are otherwise inconsistent with their GATT obligations. Countries that acceded to the GATT after 1947 have also done so under the terms of the Protocol.

Prototype plan

A qualified retirement plan sponsored by a financial institution. It may be adopted by executing a written agreement. A prototype is generally more flexible than the IRS Form 5305 or 5305-A and may have additional special features. Also called a master pension plan.

Provision for income taxes

An amount on the P & I statement that estimates a company's total income tax liability for the year.

Provisional call feature

A stipulation in a convertible issue that allows the issuer to call the issue during the noncall period if the price of the stock reaches a certain level. In the case of convertible securities, right of an issuer to accelerate the first redemption date if the underlying common should trade at or above a certain level for a sustained period. Most typical terms are 150% of conversion price for 20 consecutive days. Note that under these circumstances the security has appreciated, at a minimum, 50% since being issued.

Proxy

Authorization, whether written or electronic, that shareholders' votes may be cast by others. Shareholders can and often do give management their proxies, delegating the right and responsibility to vote their shares as specified.

Proxy Committee

A group of individuals appointed by the board of directors of the company to formally represent the share holders who send in proxy cards, to vote the represented shares in accordance with the shareholders' instructions.

Proxy Committee Ballot

The ballot signed and submitted at the meeting by the Proxy Committee. It is the legal voting of shares represented by proxies assigned to the Proxy Committee and should always be completed.

Proxy contest

A battle for the control of a firm in which a dissident group seeks, from the firm's other shareholders, the right to vote those shareholders' shares in favor of the dissident group's slate of directors. Also called proxy fights.

Proxy fight

Often used in risk arbitrage. Technique used by an acquiring company to attempt to gain control of a takeover target. The acquirer tries to persuade the shareholders of the target company that the present management of the firm should be ousted n favor of a slate of directors favorable to the acquirer, thus enabling the acquiring company to gain control of the company without paying a premium price.

Proxy Fight

Competition of outside group with management for stockholders' proxies in order to accumulate votes to elect a new board of directors.

Proxy Solicitor

A specialist (firm) hired to gather proxy votes.

Proxy statement

Document intended to provide shareholders with information necessary to vote in an informed manner on matters to be brought up at a stockholders' meeting. Includes information on closely held shares. Information required by the SEC that must be provided to shareholders who wish to vote for directors and on other company decisions by proxy.

Proxy vote

Vote cast by one person or entity on behalf of another.

Prudent-man rule

A common law standard against which those investing the money of others fiduciaries) are judged.

PS

The two-character ISO 3166 country code for PALESTINIAN TERRITORY, OCCUPIED.

P&S

Purchase and sale statement. A statement provided by the broker showing change in the customer's net ledger balance after the offset of any previously established positions.

PSA Prepayment Rate

The Bond Market Trade Association's Mortgaged Asset-Backed Securities Division's prepayment model based on an assumed rate of prepayment each month of the then unpaid principal balance of a pool of mortgages. PSA is used primarily to derive an implied prepayment speed of new production loans. 00% PSA assumes a prepayment rate of 2% per month in the first month following the date of issue, increasing at 2% percentage points per month thereafter until the 30th month. Thereafter, 100% PSA is the same as 6% CPR (Constant prepayment rate).

PSSG

Financial ratio defined as stock price divided by sales over sales growth. Often used in the valuation of Internet stocks. Related: PREG.

PT

The two-character ISO 3166 country code for PORTUGAL.

PTE

The ISO 4217 currency code for the Portugese Escudo.

Public Book (of order)

The orders to buy or sell, entered by the public, that are generally away from the current market. The order book official or specialist keeps the public book. Market-Makers on the CBOE can see the highest bid and lowest offer at any time. The specialist's book is closed (only he knows at what price and in what quantity the nearest public orders are). See also Market-Maker and Specialist.

Public Company

A company that has held an initial public offering and whose shares are traded on a stock exchange or in the over-the-counter market. Public companies are subject to periodic filing and other obligations under the federal securities laws.

Public debt

Issues of debt by governments to compensate for a lack of tax revenues.

Public housing authority bond

Bonds of local public housing agencies that are secured by the federal government and whose proceeds are used to provide low-rent housing.

Public limited partnership

A limited partnership with an unlimited number of partners that is registered with the SEC and is available for public trading by broker/dealers.

Public offering

Used in the context of general equities. Offering to the investment public, after compliance with registration requirements of the SEC, usually by an investment banker or a syndicate made up of several investment bankers, at a price agreed upon between the issuer and the investment bankers. Antithesis of private placement. See: Primary distribution and secondary distribution.

Public offering price

The price of a new issue of securities at the time that the issue is offered to the public.

Public ownership

The portion of a company's stock that is held by the public.

Public-purpose bond

A specific type of municipal bond used to finance public projects such as roads or government buildings. Interest on municipal bonds is federal income tax-free.

Public Securities Administration (PSA)

The trade association for primary dealers in US government securities, including MBSs.

Public securities offering

A securities issue placed with the public through an investment or commercial bank.

Thc Public

Individual investors who trade single securities independently or invest in intermediaries such as mutual funds, as opposed to professional investors.

Public Utility Holding Company Act of 1935

Legislation intended to eliminate many holding company abuses by reorganizing the financial structures of holding companies in the gas and electric utility industries and regulating their debt and dividend policies.

Public warehouse

Storage facility operated by an independent warehouse company on its own premises.

Publicly held

Describes a company whose stock is held by the public, whether individuals or business entities.

Publicly traded assets

Assets that can be traded in a public market, such as the stock market.

Puke

Slang for a trader selling aposition, usually a losing position, as in, "When in doubt, puke it out."

Pull

Used in the context of general equities. See: Cancel.

Pullback

The downward reversal of a prolonged upward price trend.

Pulling in their horns

Investors selling off positions after a stock or bond market has increased sharply or setting up hedging positions to guard against a negative turn of the market.

Purchase

Buy; be long; have an ownership position.

Purchase accounting

Method of accounting for a merger that treats the acquirer as having purchased the assets and assumed the liabilities of the acquiree, which are then written up or down to their respective fair market values. The difference between the purchase price and the net assets acquired is attributed to goodwill.

Purchase agreement

Used in connection with project financing; an agreement to purchase a specific amount of project output per period.

Purchase and sale

A method of securities distribution in which a firm purchases securities from the issuer for its own account at a stated price and then resells them, as contrasted with a best-efforts sale.

Purchase fee

A charge assessed by an intermediary, such as a broker-dealer or a bank, for assisting in the sale or purchase of a security.

Purchase fund

Resembles a sinking fund, except that money is used to purchase bonds only if they are selling below their par value.

Purchase group

See: Underwriting syndicate.

Purchase loan

A consumer loan taken to finance a purchase.

Purchase method

Accounting for an acquisition using market value for the consolidation of the two entities' net assets on the balance sheet. Generally, depreciation/amortization will increase for this method (due to the creation of goodwill) compared to the pooling method resulting in lower net income.

Purchase-money mortgage

A mortgage given by a buyer in lieu of cash when the buyer is unable to borrow commercially for the purchase of property.

Purchase Order

A document used to formalize a purchase transaction with a supplier. A purchase order, when given to supplier, should contain statements as to the quantity, description and price of the goods or services ordered; agreed terms as to payments, discounts, dates of performance, transportation terns, F.O.B. point and all other agreements pertinent to the purchase of its execution by the vendor.

Purchase Price

A statutory term used in dumping investigations to refer to the United States sales price of merchandise which is sold or likely to be sold prior to the date of importation, by the producer or reseller of the merchandise for exportation to the United States. Certain statutory adjustments (e.g., import duties, commissions, freight) are made, if appropriate, to permit a meaningful comparison with the foreign market value of such or similar merchandise. See: Tariff Act of 1930.

Purchase Requisition

The form used by departments to request the Purchasing Department to procure goods or services from vendors.

Purchaser

Within the context of export controls, the purchaser is that person abroad who has entered into the export transaction with the applicant to purchase the commodities or technical data for delivery to the ultimate consignee.

Purchasing Agent

An agent who purchases goods in his/her own country on behalf of large foreign buyers such as government agencies and large private corporations.

Purchasing power

The amount of credit available for securities trading in a margin account, after taking margin requirements into consideration.

Purchasing power of the dollar

The amount of goods and services that can be exchanged for a dollar as compared with amount of a previous time period.

Purchasing Power Parity

Purchasing power parity is a theory which states that exchange rates between currencies are in equilibrium when their purchasing power is the same in each of the two countries.

Purchasing power risk

Related: Inflation risk.

Pure discount bond

A bond that will make only one payment of principal and interest. Also called a zero-coupon bond or a single-payment bond.

Pure expectations theory

A theory that asserts that forward rates exclusively represent the expected future rates. In other words, the entire term structure reflects the market's expectations of future short-term rates. For example, an increasing slope to the term structure implies increasing short-term interest rates. Related: Biased expectations heories.

Pure index fund

A portfolio that is managed so as to perfectly replicate the performance of the market portfolio.

Pure monopoly

A market in which only one firm has total control over the entire market for a product due to some sort of barrier to entry for other firms, often a patent held by the controlling firm.

Pure play

A company involved in only one line of business.

Pure yield pickup swap

Moving to higher yield-bonds.

Purpose credit

Credit used for the purpose of buying, carrying or trading in securities.

Purpose loan

A loan that is backed by securities and that is used to buy other securities under certain government regulations.

Purpose statement

A form filed by a borrower that describes the use of a loan backed by securities, and guarantees that the funds lent will not be used illegally to buy securities against Federal Reserve regulations.

Put

An option granting the right to sell the underlying futures contract. Opposite of a call.

Put bond

A bond that the holder may choose either to exchange for par value at some date or to extend for a given number of years. If the price is above par, the put is a "premium put."

Put-call parity

Applies to derivative products. Option pricing principle that says, given a stock's price, a put and call of the same class must have a static price relationship because arbitrage opportunities or activities will always reestablish such a relationship.

Put-call parity relationship

The relationship between the price of a put and the price of a call on the same underlying security with the same expiration date, which prevents arbitrage opportunities. Holding the underlying stock and buying a put will deliver the exact payoff as buying one call and investing the present value (PV) of the exercise price. The call value equals C = S + P - PV(k).

Put-call ratio

The ratio of the volume of put options traded to the volume of call options traded, which is used as an indicator of investor sentiment (bullish or bearish).

Put guarantee letter

A bank's letter certifying that the person writing a put option has sufficient funds in an account to cover the exercise price if required.

Put on

Used for listed equity securities. Trade, or cross, a block of stock at the designated price and quantity. See: Print.

"Put it on "

Used for listed equity securities. "Go to the floor to transact." See: Print.

Put option

This security gives investors the right to sell (or put) a fixed number of shares at a fixed price within a given period. An investor, for example, might wish to have the right to sell shares of a stock at a certain price by a certain time in order to protect, or hedge, an existing investment.

Put an option

To exercise a put option.

"Put pants on it "

Used in the context of general equities. "Elaborate on your intentions or your inquiry," especially with respect to size, side, and price. See: Open up.

Put price

The price at which an asset will be sold if a put option is exercised. Also called the strike or exercise price of a put option.

Put provision

Gives the holder of a floating-rate bond the right to redeem the note at par on the coupon payment date.

Put ratio backspread

A complex options strategy adopted when one believes a stock price will decline but wants to protect against it rising.

Put to seller

Exercise a put option; require that the option writer to purchase the stock at the strike price.

Put swaption

A financial instrument giving the buyer the right, or option, to enter into a swap as a floating-rate payer.

The writer of the swaption therefore becomes the floating-rate receiver/fixed-rate payer.

PVBP

See: Price value of a basis point.

PW

The two-character ISO 3166 country code for PALAU.

PY

The two-character ISO 3166 country code for PARAGUAY.

PYG

The ISO 4217 currency code for the Paraguay Guarani.

Pyramid scheme

An illegal, fraudulent scheme in which a con artist convinces victims to invest by promising an extraordinary return but instead simply uses newly invested funds to pay off any investors who insist on terminating their investment.

Pyramiding

A type of stock swap option exercise in which a small number of previously-owned shares is surrendered to the company to pay a portion of the exercise price, for which a slightly larger number of option shares may be purchased, which are then immediately surrendered back to the company to pay additional amounts of the exercise price, and so on until the full option price has been paid and the optionee is left with just the number of shares equal to the option spread. With the advent of broker-assisted "Cashless Exercise/Same Day Sale" programs (see above), pyramiding has fallen out of favor.

q

Q

Fifth letter of a Nasdaq stock symbol specifying that it is in bankruptcy proceedings.

QA

The two-character ISO 3166 country code for QATAR.

QAR

The ISO 4217 currency code for the Qatar Rial.

Q ratio or Tobin's Q ratio

Market value of a firm's assets divided by replacement value of the firm's assets. Named after James Tobin of Yale University.

Quadratic programming

Variant of linear programming in which the objective function is quadratic rather than linear. In portfolio selection, we often minimize the variance of the portfolio (which is a quadratic function) subject to constraints on the mean return of the portfolio.

Quadrilateral Meetings

These are meetings involving trade ministers from the U.S., the European Community, Canada, and Japan to discuss trade policy matters.

Qualification period

A period of time during the first few months or weeks of a new policy when an insurance company will not reimburse a policyholder for a claim in order to allow the insurance company time to find any fraudulent information in the application.

Qualified Domestic Relations Order (QDRO)

A judgment, decree, or order that gives a pension plan participant access to retirement assets that must be used to pay an ex-spouse or dependent children.

Qualified endorsement

A signature on the back of a negotiable instrument transferring the amount to some other party but that includes wording that limits the endorser's liability.

Qualified opinion

An auditor's opinion expressing certain limitations of an audit.

Qualified plan or trust

A tax-deferred plan allowing employer and employee contributions that build up savings, which are paid out at retirement or on termination of employment. Tax is paid only when amounts are drawn from the trust.

Qualified retirement plan

A retirement plan established by employers for their employees that meets the requirements of Internal Revenue Code Section 401(a) or 403(a) and is eligible for special tax considerations. The plan may provide for employer contributions, as in a pension or profit-sharing plan, as well as employee contributions. Employers can deduct plan contributions made on behalf of eligible employees on the business's tax return as business expenses. Plan earnings are not taxed to the employee until withdrawn.

Qualified Terminable Interest Property Trust (Q-TIP)

A trust that allows a surviving spouse to receive income generated from the trust, while the actual distribution of the trust's assets is made to other beneficiaries such as the grantor's children.

Qualified total distribution

A payment representing an employee's interest in a qualified retirement plan. The payment must be prompted by retirement (or other separation from service), death, disability, or attainment of age 59-1/2. Payment can be in installments as long as the complete distribution is made within a single tax year.

Qualifying annuity

An annuity allowable as investment for a qualified plan or trust.

Qualifying share

Shares of common stock that a person must hold in order to qualify as a director of the issuing corporation.

Qualifying stock option

A benefit granted by a corporation that allows employees to purchase shares at a discount price.

Qualitative analysis

An analysis of the qualities of a company that cannot be measured concretely, such as management quality or employee morale.

Qualitative research

Traditional analysis of firm-specific prospects for future earnings. It may be based on data collected by the analysts, there is no formal quantitative framework used to generate projections.

Quality of earnings

Increased earnings due to increased sales and cost controls, as compared to artificial profits created by inflation of inventory or other asset prices.

Quality option

Gives the seller choice of deliverables in Treasury bond and Treasury note futures contracts. Also called the swap option. Related: Cheapest to deliver issue.

Quantitative analysis

An assessment of specific measurable securities or investment factors, such as cost of capital, value of assets; and projections of sales, costs, earnings, and profits. Combined with more subjective or qualitative considerations (such as management effectiveness), quantitative analysis can enhance investment decisions and portfolios.

Quantitative Restrictions

Explicit limits, usually by volume, on the amount of a specified commodity that may be imported into a country, sometimes also indicating the amounts that may be imported from each supplying country. Compared to tariffs, the protection afforded by QR's tends to be more predictable, being less affected by changes in competitive factors. Quotas have been used at times to favor preferred sources of supply. The GATT generally prohibits the use of quantitative restrictions, except in special cases, such as those cited in Articles XX (which permits exceptions to protect public health, national gold stocks, goods of archeological or historic interest, and a few other special categories of goods), or Article XXI (which permits exceptions in the interest of "national security"), or for safeguard purposes, when the appropriate procedures in Article XIX have been followed.

Quantity risk

Occurs when the quantity of an asset to be hedged is uncertain.

Quality spread

Difference between Treasury securities and non-Treasury securities that are identical in all respects except for quality rating. For instance, the difference between yields on Treasuries and those on single A-rated industrial bonds. Also called credit spread.

Quant

A person with numerical and computer skills who carries out quantitative analyses of companies.

Quantize

To convert an asset or liability into a currency other than the regular trading currency.

Quantitative analysis

An analysis of the mathematically measurable figures of a company, such as the value of assets or projected sales.

Quantitative research

Use of advanced econometric and mathematical valuation models to identify the firms with the best possible prospectives. Antithesis of qualitative research.

Quanto swap

See: Differential swap.

Quantos

Currency options with a guaranteed exchange rate that enable buyers who like an asset, German bonds for example, but not the asset's pricing currency, to arrange payment in a different currency for a fee.

Quarter stock

Stock with a par value of $25 per share.

Quarterly

Occurring every three months.

Quarterly financing

February 15, May 15, August 15 and November 15, or next working day offerings of several "coupon" security issues. Quarterly issues currently consist of a 3-year note, a 10-year note, and a 30-year bond. The Treasury sometimes offers additional amounts of outstanding long-term notes or bonds, rather than selling new security issues. See: Reopening.

Quasi-public corporation

A corporation that is operated privately, but is supported by the government in its operations and that often traded publicly.

Quay

A landing place or pier, usually of solid construction, where vessels berth to load or unload cargo.

Quick assets

Current assets minus inventories.

Quick ratio

Indicator of a company's financial strength (or weakness). Calculated by taking current assets less inventories, divided by current liabilities. This ratio provides information regarding the firm's liquidity and ability to meet its obligations. Also called the Acid test ratio.

Quid pro quo

An arrangement allowing a firm to use research from another firm at no cost in exchange for executing all of its trades with the firm that provides the research.

Quiet period

Time period an issuer is "in registration" with the SEC and may not promote its forthcoming issue.

Quorum

The minimum number of people who must be present or must provide a proxy to vote at a meeting in order to make a valid decision.

Quota

See Import Quota.

Quotas and Quota System

Absolute quotas permit a limited number of units of specified merchandise to be entered or withdrawn for consumption during specified periods. Tariff-rate quotas permit a specified quantity of merchandise to be entered or withdrawn at a reduced rate during a specified period. Quotas are established by Presidential Proclamations, Executive Orders, or other legislation.

The Quota System, a part of Customs' Automated Commercial System, controls quota levels (quantities authorized) and quantities entered against those levels. Visas control exports from the country of origin. Visa authorizations are received from other countries and quantities entered against those visas are transmitted back to them. Control of visas and quotas simplify reconciliation of other countries' exports and U.S. imports.

Quotation

An offer to sell goods at a stated price and under specified conditions.
a authorizations are received from other countries and quantities entered against those visas are transmitted back to them. Control of visas and quotas simplify reconciliation of other countries' exports and U.S. imports. See: International Monetary Fund.

Quotation board

The electronic board at a brokerage firm displaying prices other financial data.

Quote rule

Rule requiring market makers to publish quotations for any listed security when a quotation represents more than 1% of the aggregate trading volume for that security.

Quoted price

The price at which the last trade of a particular security or commodity took place.